THOSE CASTLES OF WOOD

THE STORY OF THE EARLY LODGES

OF

ROCKY MOUNTAIN NATIONAL PARK

AND

PIONEER DAYS OF ESTES PARK, COLORADO

✳✳✳✳✳✳✳✳✳✳✳✳✳✳

By

Henry F. Pedersen, Jr.
(Copyright 1993)

First Printing

Printed in the United States of America

Front Cover Picture: Fall River Lodge
(Sanborn Souvenir Co.)
Back Cover Picture: Sprague's Lodge
(Flatiron Post Card Co.)

TABLE OF CONTENTS

PROLOGUE: Page 1

CHAPTER I
THEY FIND THE MOUNTAINS
The Explorers: Page 5

CHAPTER II
THE ROADS OF HAPPY ADVENTURE
The Navigators: Page 23

CHAPTER III
OPEN FOR BUSINESS
MacGregor Ranch, Hupp, Rowe,
Ferguson And Estes Park Hotel: Page 38

CHAPTER IV
WE ARE AT YOUR SERVICE
Elkhorn Lodge, Lamb's Ranch
And Long's Peak Inn: Page 62

CHAPTER V
EARLY IN SERVICE FIRST TO GLORY
Horseshoe Inn, Moraine Lodge
And Cascade Lodge: Page 85

CHAPTER VI
THREE LITTLE TRAIL COMPANIONS
Fern Lodge, Forest Inn
And Bear Lake Lodge: Page 110

CHAPTER VII
FRIENDSHIP, FUN AND GOOD FOOD
Brinwood, Fall River Lodge
And Deer Ridge Chalet: Page 138

CHAPTER VIII
ROCKY MOUNTAIN NATIONAL PARK
A Synopsis of History
And Policies to 1962: Page 171

CHAPTER IX
THOSE OFF STAGE PLAYED A PART
Stanley Hotel, H-G Ranch, Hewes-Kirkwood,
Lewiston Hotel And Crags Lodge: Page 198

CHAPTER X
THE FIRST SHALL BE LAST
Sprague's Ranch, Sprague's Lodge
And Stead's Ranch: Page 253

CREDITS

I am very grateful for all of the support that I have received from many citizens and organizations in my community and the State of Colorado that have enabled me to write this brief account of a phase of our history that has physically disappeared from Rocky Mountain National Park. I am printing many photos from my personal collection and others that have been loaned me for inclusion in this book. Under each photo I wish to acknowledge the source of that picture. Those provided me by Rocky Mountain National Park are designated (RMNP); those given access to me from collections provided to the Estes Park Public Library are designated (EPPL); those from the MacDonald Collection are designated (McDC); those from the Colorado Historical Society are designated (CHS); those from the Estes Park *Trail Gazette* publications are designated (EPTG); those from the Joe Mills Collection are designated (Mills); those from The Bill Robinson Family are designated (Robinson); and finally those from the Estes Park Area Historical Museum are designated (EPHM). Other individuals, collections, photographers and publishers will be given recognition. I wish to publicly thank all of those with whom I have visited about the history of the lodges and activities of Estes Park whose names I have referred to in this book. I wish to give particular acknowledgment to Bill and Fannye Robinson and Otis and Opal Whiteside who gave me a greater insight into early lodge and livery activity of the Estes Valley. A special thank you goes to Mr. James Mack, the Chief Interpreter of Rocky Mountain National Park, for allowing me the privilege of examining records and photos at Rocky Mountain National Park's Library, and to Paula Steige of the wonderful MacDonald Book Shop in Estes Park who loaned me some of her family photos and who gave me the encouragement to start this project in the first place. I extend my gratitude to Lennie Bemmis and Judy Hoxsey of the superb Estes Park Public Library who provided me access to copies of many historical photos including those from the collection of the Estes Park Area Historical Museum, and to Lynn Swain and Betty Kilsdonk of the Estes Park Area Historical Museum for providing me the opportunity to examine the records of their excellent facility. I extend grateful appreciation to my friend Walter Richards of Estes Park who has given so much of his time, talent and professional expertise in providing me with invaluable assistance in processing the negatives and prints of those pictures that you see in this book. Without him, my task would have been made much more difficult. Finally, I say thank you over and over again to my wife Sara who offered constructive and professional suggestions to improve this manuscript, who critiqued and corrected my woefully awkward grammar, and more importantly provided me the time and opportunity to forgo more pressing earthly duties so that I might research and complete this book. I hope that you enjoy this story and will be challenged by it to further uncover other aspects of nearly forgotten history that are deserving of remembrance.

THOSE CASTLES OF WOOD

THE STORY OF THE EARLY LODGES

OF

ROCKY MOUNTAIN NATIONAL PARK

AND

PIONEER DAYS OF ESTES PARK, COLORADO

By

Henry F. Pedersen, Jr.
(Copyright 1993)

PROLOGUE

There Is Nothing More Comforting
In Towns Or Cities, Anywhere, That
Can Compare To The Light Of A Cabin.
Ranger Jack Moomaw, 1973

I have said many times that I was born too late and that I wished to have lived a hundred years ago. "I'm too late," --I tell my practical wife, busy with her own joy at living in these mountains despite the 'user friendly' yet distracting amenities constructed due to the local government and chamber of commerce officials' desire to cater to the caprice, comforts and complaints of the tourists who crowd into this alpine valley. I long to experience the *real* America that caught the gaze of those early visionaries who wended their way along dusty trails in search of their dream, content with an amble at the end of a tiring day up a flower draped trail to a sequestered destination shared with the wild creatures. All stood mesmerized by glorious mountains and sparkling brooks that alone brought respite from the challenge to survive in a world that was soon to change, not necessarily for the best. Back then there was no need for go-carts, miniature golf, giant slides or the golden arches of the fast food epoch to find pleasure in a mountain valley that demanded to be appreciated for its natural beauty bereft of the movers and shakers for profit who cloyed at simple delights such as a warm red sunset unimpaired by power lines, interstate bands of concrete and highrise condominiums.

Now there are people filling in all the little creases of the wide plains through which those covered wagons slowly turned their wheels behind the benign bulk of a team of six huge oxen, whose drivers arched high their

1

necks to see what lay just beyond the next rise of tall, ochre yellow ripening grass. I try to close out from my mind the competing sounds of stereos, emergency fire and police sirens screaming at fever pitch. I hear the metallic roar that vibrates the motor bike whose young rider seeks a thrill at the expense of all those around who prefer a quieter horizon, absent of cacophonously clangorous crowds that have moved out into those few hidden places left in America where sanity receives reassurance. I feel the need to trek, alone, into my special place of retreat, distant from the changed vistas of high-tech conveniences that have caused my personal horizon to be clouded.

Today, on a pristine pure August afternoon found me miles above Estes Park, Colorado, in Rocky Mountain National Park, sitting on a huge, multi-hued rock next to a turquoise blue torrent of snow fed water. I watched the dipper bird dive into his frosty pool of 36 degree water in quest for hard earned sustenance causing the trout, a collateral object of my voluntary exile from human companionship, to take cover from a feathered intruder probing into his watery larder. Colored flowers of Columbine blue, Arnica yellow and Paint Brush crimson, begging for my admiration, were my companions together with the bright eyed, curiously bold chipmunk and its distant relative the Pine Marten keeping me under close scrutiny from the shadows. I catch a glimpse of those gentle reclusive creatures, new antlers held high, surveying their world of Ponderosa Pine and Douglas Fir from a rock out-cropping, somewhat aloof and wary of the homo sapiens species intent on capturing them on film or between the cross hairs of a powerful thunder stick mounted with space age scopes that made the so called *sport* of hunting unfair. This was my time, brief as it was, all alone from fellow humans and on my own. Find a new trail, climb that rock face over there, bait my hook, outwit a couple of fish for dinner and try to stay warm and dry as the air became electrically charged by a rapidly approaching storm on a collision course with me just below Black Lake.

Love comes in different packages, eros, agape, or whatever the philosopher may deign to call it, and this day was a day of love for me, loving what I was doing, where I was and challenging myself to find happiness without the artificial props we call progress. But I knew it would not, could not, last for at the end of the day I knew I must find my way back to the full parking lot where my small red four-wheel friend dutifully stood waiting my return. My creel held two fish, one Rainbow and another a German Brown, both being 'at least 10 inches in length and no more than one of each species' according to the regulations that shrieked out at me from the book of bureaucratic behests tucked in my old worn army jacket. Oh for the times when one could pull them out by the bucket full. The antique bamboo pole was broken down to carrying capability and my boots were flecked with dried mud and grass stained, obviously causing my appearance to look professional. As I emerged from the fire trail, used only by us modern pioneers, and of course the rangers who sought with more celerity access to problems radioed to them by their fellows clad in green, I was asked the usual question by those just starting up the regular trail. "Did you have any luck?" the young couple brightly inquired of me as I found increasing traffic on the trail that hours earlier had been my own personal fief. Slacking my pace for an instant, I thought about the simple but incisive question. "Yes, I guess so," I responded still in my reverie, followed by "but I wish it could last." They gave me a puzzled look as I moved on with quickened step to find myself back in a world that could be so beautiful if humans would not try and change every darn thing they set their hands and eyes upon. Just be, --well, be pioneers, who passed through a land, taking little yet giving much while marveling at the wondrous world of dangerously vibrant beauty that compelled them to be at their very best.

Looking about as my little friend conducted me home with little guidance, a task this 20 year old antique had competently performed without more than a gentle turn of the wheel or a change of gears, I discussed matters of importance with myself taking both sides of the debate. The topic was that I could have been a pioneer if I had lived a century earlier. I was sincere in my soliloquy. If I had found myself back in the 1800s, who would I have wanted to emulate, to have had as a friend? Who would have been my hero? No, not Buffalo Bill. He took too much out of the environment with all of his buffalo slaughter not necessarily to feed others but more especially to feed his own ego. Anyway, he only was interested in sensationalism with questionable accuracy on his version of past glories before goggle eyed audiences who were willing to pay the price for a ticket. No, it wouldn't be a soldier of General Custer's demeanor who hacked his way through highly practical civilizations of native peoples as he and others with the sword and gun pushed forward the industrial reign of manifest destiny, inspired by political vanity, through unbroken stands of virgin timber and grass as far as the eye could see. I could have been a friend of Bill Gollings, known as Paint Bill. This nearly untutored yet artistically accurate painter from Sheridan, Wyoming, who sat upon his horse recording with brush and pencil his cowboy life of excitement fraught with sadness, yet triumphant in reflecting beauty for others. It would have been a real joy to have chummed around with Charlie Russell, the multi-talented artist who sculpted and philosophized unabashed about life about him. He lived to escape the pedestrian future forecast for him in St. Louis to find his life intertwined with the vanishing cowboy and Indian world of Montana, that to him was excitingly decent compared to what was lured west by tales of the Great Northern Railway. Russell was not the least interested in the future complications of an onrushing *modern world*, whatever that meant, but yearned to remain firmly intrenched in the past with *his bunch* of ordinary folk, the worst of whom he conceived to be better than the best of the important people who crowded in to profit from their desire to change everything.

The personages of the Estes Valley whom I would have so enjoyed knowing and to have shared a hike up Windy Gulch west of Moraine Park, would have been those men and women who named and lived with these mountains, trails, lakes, glaciers, and lovingly built with their own hands those wonderful lodges I choose to call Those Castles Of Wood. Yes I could have built a lodge tucked in some reclusive dell, taken the greenhorns on expeditions into Ponderosa groves in the back country, taught them to fish, to recognize beauty in the profusion of flowers that sprang up alive to greet the dawning of each new day. I would have been a friend of W. E. James on Fall River, climbed a steep mountain with Dr. Workman on the way to Fern Lake, sat enraptured to a new story told in front of a blazing fireplace by Joe Mills, or the best of all delights gone fishing with Horace Ferguson who possessed the technique to pull them out of the lazy waters of Horseshoe Park. But my

3

first choice of a companion, who could teach me the way to enjoy life amply adorned with a myriad of his own experiences of living as a pioneer sufficient for two lifetimes, would have been Abner E. Sprague. There would be no question about that. When I first came to the Estes Park area as a teenager on holiday, I remember visiting Sprague's Lodge and hoping to get an opportunity to fish in the two Sprague's lakes that he had constructed as a fish hatchery. My map reported a Sprague Mountain, a Sprague Glacier and so much more. I presumed that these might have been named for some politician, soldier, government surveyor, or, like Long's Peak, the 14,255 foot sentinel of this region, named for someone who only saw the white maned masterpiece from a distance but who never climbed it. I was wrong. The Sprague name that appeared so prominently on my Rocky Mountain National Park maps originated with a real person, who lived, breathed and loved these mountains and personified the true spirit of a pioneer. He was a lodge man who had so much to do with the beginnings of Estes Park and Rocky Mountain National Park and who lived long into this present century to become known as Estes Park's unofficial historian.

Perhaps you, also, might feel that pull back to an earlier century as I, and will join me on revisiting a time that has been dimmed in our memories but should not ever be forgotten. This is a brief recollection, not an exhaustive survey, of a more gentle and uncrowded time in our history when one would come to this land in the clouds, filled with fish, fun and friendship, and sleep close to the stars in log structures that now exist only in our rich, nostalgicly preserved memories.

Meeker, Long's Peak, Lady Washington, 1920 (F. J. Francis)

4

CHAPTER I: THEY FIND THE MOUNTAINS

The Explorers

Go Ye, And Look Upon That Land,
That Far Vast Land That Few Behold,
And None, Beholding, Understand;
That Old, Old Land, Which Men Call Now,
That Land As Old As Time Is Old.
Go Journey With The Seasons Through,
Its Wastes, And Learn How Limitless,
How Shoreless Lie The Distances,
Before You Come To Question This,
Or Dare To Dream What Grandeur Is.
Joachim Miller, 1879

Over the centuries of time before 1800 many feet trod the primitive trails, wandering tribes of nomadic peoples as well as great herds of animals, crisscrossing the vast sea of waving grass of the great plains of Nebraska and Kansas. They kept in focus, with squinting eyes defying a glowing sunset, the distant pinnacles of white and blue that as ghostly apparitions were visible just beyond that fiery orb that closed one day for some while simultaneously opening another far away. Those mountain monarchs, homes for swirling clouds that battle the resident winds, served as trail guides and early day triangulation points for the travois burdened dogs and horses as well as the infrequent pioneer who sought a better chance to sustain life or perhaps make a new beginning. They moved on endlessly, not concerned with time or direction, over grass hummocked paths and deep depressions that made them wary with trepidation and fear for the unknown danger that lay around the next muddy bend. Worry was a constant companion, yet kept subjugated to the infinite resolution to keep moving to a better hunting ground, perhaps a green meadow near a clear creek playing free, untrammeled, ready to offer a drink to the weary. To others those same snowy magnets served to repel them, mental boundaries beyond which they dared not venture. They were content only to claim a portion of the blue sky and sandy soil as theirs for *settling in*, assigning to the more courageous of spirit those high realms in which to find their Shangri-la.

Few white men had gone into those sublime locations that beckoned some, frightened others, but always were on the minds of all as they watched a new weather change come rushing down their glacial faceted ramparts. Spanish conquistadores had threaded their way into the southern part of those mountains, later to be called the Rockies, in search of Quivera, their city of gold proven only to be conceived and constructed in their fanciful minds and greedy hearts. Of course there were the natives peoples who sought rest and refreshment in those cool environs without claiming their places of rendezvous as permanent territory. It was quiet in this primeval sphere, left to the flora and fauna to relish the warm sunshine dancing in undulating patterns on the life sustaining crystal waters. To balance the equation in their chancy paradise was always the need for shelter from Father Winter's ice and beguilingly beautiful snow that to the careless brought suffocating white death. This was an environment to test the best of their blood line, genes that had predestined their will and ability for survival. But all that was to end as the Louisiana Purchase of 1803 dictated that a survey be undertaken in order to assess the potential of this vast new horizon the young nation had purchased. Twenty-seven year old Lieutenant Zebulon Montgomery Pike from Lamberton, New Jersey in 1806, with his party of twenty-three men, traversed a fragment of these millions of acres while upon a military mission and ascertained that his new nation's land acquisition was a veritable unfathomed ocean replete with waves of tall grass sheltering masses of curious creatures. Although his biographers documented his glimpsing on November 15th a high point on the skyline in the range of distant mountains that he referred to as *the highest peak*, he ventured no closer to it continuing his march southwesterly locating another grand alpine sentinel closer to his trail, now still glowering down in hulking white elegance over the extant city of Colorado Springs. It also never was scaled by him, that being left to another many years later, although it bears his name, --Pike's Peak.

Major Stephen Harriman Long, of Hopkinton, New Hampshire, was sent out by President James Madison on the first official expedition to ferret out in more detail what lay in this unmapped portion of a young nation emerging into the dawn of new accomplishments with which an old world soon must come to terms. On June 30, 1820 at 8 A. M. the Rocky Mountains were observed glittering in the reflected rays of the sun by his small party of twenty who first surmised that what was seen were banks of cumulus clouds. Because of the ambient air temperature of the early morning associated with the vapor in the atmosphere, it appeared that reflecting pools of water were scattered in the great valley that lay in front of this curious phenomenon. Following the notes of the Pike expedition, giving loose rein to his mount and directed only by his own eager nature to discover, Long saw that *highest peak* on July 3, 1820 from a distance of forty miles east, near to where the St. Vrain, Poudre and Thompson rivers emptied their snow melted treasures into an ever widening South Platte River headed to more lazy terrain. As with Lieutenant Pike, Major Long was not diverted from his southerly march to conquer that mass of granite in the distance as he recognized his mission to be more of observation than detailed exploration. However, his men in honor of their thirty-five year old commander, bestowed upon this wondrous, compellingly beautiful stair step to the citadel of the Almighty, the name Long's Peak. That peak would not be climbed by white men or women until more than four decades later, but Major Long's botanist, Dr. Edwin James in 1820 -- a young man himself from Weybridge, Vermont and then only twenty-three years of age --with two soldiers recorded the first ascent of Pike's Peak while the rest of the troop camped below. That mountain was first called James Peak, but by 1843 traders generally referred to it by its present name, Pike's Peak. Long's party rode on past the great peak to return to the area of Saint Louis on October 13th by way of the Arkansas River. Dr. James was a fine botanist, but as a geographer or topographer he and others of the party misjudged the height of Pike's Peak when he recorded its elevation at 11,500 feet, almost three thousands of feet lower than the true summit. To be perfectly fair to the young doctor, it was not in his estimate of the peak's height that was in error but in a misinterpretation by others of the true elevation of the valley floor.

Others now followed, moving up watercourses in search of beaver as did the legendary *little big man* Christopher (Kit) Carson. That was in the years of 1840 and 1841, a time when eyes were upon the Mexican army as it sought dominance in the southwest, its unofficial boundary just over those shining mountains and hidden from view. John C. Fremont, the military explorer, saw Long's Peak at a distance on his expedition through the Rockies in July of 1842 as he led his men westward. Unnamed hunters and assorted numbers of Indians -- Utes, Sioux, Arapaho, Shoshone, Cheyenne and it was reported even the legendary Apache -- at one time or another valued the peace and tranquility of the exalted valleys packed with game. These mountains and all of their resources were to remain essentially unspoiled and at peace for a few more precious years. Solo white adventurers began drifting through, curious to find their way up and over the seemingly impenetrable wall fluted of limestone and granite, as was the intent in 1843 of Rufus B. Sage. In his diary published in 1857, and tantalizingly titled *Rocky Mountain Life, Or Startling Scenes And Perilous Adventures In The Far West*, it was obvious that this man from the East had become a prisoner to the majesty of all that he beheld. That addiction I hasten to point out has been the beneficent malady afflicting so many of us who followed his trail later in more modern contrivances with memories drifting back to swings on porches on pine scented cabins, now long gone, when we breathed in all that was good, clean and uncomplicatingly energizing. Mr. Sage briefly stopped at old Fort Lancaster, then located on the South Platte River in the flat lands that lay before the sublime peaks to the west of Lyons, Colorado and later recorded his experiences. "Having purchased a horse for the purpose, I proceeded to the mountains on a hunting excursion, where, unattended by any one, I had a further opportunity of testing the varied sweets of solitude. What a charming retreat for some one of the world-hating literati. In surveying, from a commanding summit the vast prairie skirting the mountain range upon the east, the mind is perfectly astounded at the immense expanse thus brought within the scope of vision. Here the beholder may scale beyond the clouds far heavenward, and gaze upon a world at his feet."

It could be presumed that his delight for what he beheld focused upon the valley of present day Allenspark near the south slope of Long's Peak, and its more diminutive but no less impressive sister, Ezra Meeker's Mount Meeker. This presumption is partially founded on the fact that the valley of the Big Thompson further north had not as yet been discovered nor had any claim to its pristine depths been documented. But it surely must be presumed that there would have been occasional footprints belonging to a wandering red or white warrior in assorted dress of buckskin mufti who had moved silently through this wide meadow at an altitude of 7,500 feet we now call Estes Park that is the venue of my narrative. However, it is not really important to this story as to who first breathed in this rarified elixir as theories can go either way to prove the existence or nonexistence of human presence in this lofty basin that was defiant of adequate description. The most important fact is that no one came to stay, to take up their permanent dwelling place in the valley so hospitable in the warm summer sun yet so intimidating and brutal in

7

the frozen silence of winter. High winds, some approximating a velocity of 100 mph with sub-freezing temperatures and incapacitating snows, drove out before them all but the most steadfastly determined to remain. This secluded valley was located in the head waters of the Fall and Big Thompson Rivers, tributaries of the great, flat river in the grasslands twenty-five hundred feet below whose energy would be depleted by farmers and those engaged in nation building as the Platte meandered north then east on its 600 mile journey to meet the Missouri River. The Thompson River bears the name of an early member of the Northwest Fur Company, David Thompson, who had frequented this area in several capacities including a surveyor and trapper, and whose name was bestowed upon this landmark by other members of that firm to his memory. It was not for long before the hoofed denizens of that twenty-five square mile expanse of wilderness would find company with man who would change those creatures' lives, as well as their own, dramatically as we shall learn.

Joel Estes was the son of Peter and Esther Hiatt Estes, his father of German and Scottish parentage. Joel, a large, raw boned man of the country, was born in Kentucky territory in 1806, then moved to Missouri where he was to meet Martha Ann Stollings, a girl of his same age recently arrived with her parents Jacob and Sarah Stollings from West Virginia. After a suitable period of courtship as deemed proper to the times, Joel and Patsy, as she was called, were married in 1826 and were to live in Andrews County, Missouri for more than thirty years farming and raising stock. They also raised thirteen children, all of whom grew into productive adults, a feat uncommon in pioneer days when so many children were lost to disease. In 1849 new Mormon emigrants primarily from England, Sweden and Denmark were pushing their handcarts through Nebraska and Wyoming Territories to Utah, their *New Zion*, following a near disease free north bank of the Platte River. They pressed on with military precision, wooed by Brigham Young's promises of employment and an assurance of eternal life ringing in their ears. The Forty-Niners also were trooping in more disorderly battalions to California in quest for their share of a golden paradise of different dimensions. Joel Estes was caught up with the gold fever, seeking his fortune in those distant regions near the great Pacific from whence stories of success had trickled back to the hills of Missouri. The tales were amply embellished in direct proportion to the distance between the raconteur and the sweat of the miners' toil that better could reveal the truth. Joel, with his oldest son Hardin Woodson Estes, rode their horses west leaving the rest of his large family in a land turning red with blood, now caught up in preliminary skirmishes of racial strife that soon would divide the advocates of slavery from those who sought universal freedom. He returned home, months, possibly a year later after selling his mining claims located in Grass Valley, California for $30,000. To illustrate how quickly fortunes were made, or lost as may be the case, those working his former claims struck pure gold and sold out in thirty days for $500,000.

Joel Estes was a product of his environment and times, and locality. The future state of Missouri in the 1840s was divided with parochial attitudes on class distinction and power. It was shaped by circumstance and forceful personalities of its leaders depending upon how far south your home was located. He lived in an area that countenanced slavery, the possession of that root product valued by many to the extent others of earlier ages were im-

8

pressed with the quantity and size of precious gems found in their mitered hats. Joel owned five slaves, all of whom he brought with him to Colorado to assist in the cattle drive. It is interesting to note that one of his companions on that long, enervating trip was his friend, Dave Lincoln, a cousin of the soon to become President Abraham Lincoln. In what was claimed to be the first cattle drive across the plains, albeit of more modest size compared to the torrent of beef to flood to railheads years later, he drove his herd across the prairie. The land pulsated with resurgent life forms released from winters' unforgiving embrace, as his wagons pointed west to Colorado, then generally referred to as Pikes Peak County. Patsy shared in this task as well as shepherding the six unmarried portion of their brood of children, Milton, Wesley Jasper, Joel Jr., Francis Marion, Sarah and Mary Jane. Their destination was the community of Auraria, in 1860 to be reconstituted and renamed Denver in a political move aimed at territorial status. James W. Denver was then Governor of Kansas and for him the city was named in a blatant appeal, laced with prudently political kudos, for his influence in Colorado territory's campaign for statehood. Later the family pressed on to Golden Gate, now known as Golden, the former name given by Joel as being the gateway to the Central City Mining District. They concluded their odyssey by filing upon a tract of land twenty-two miles north of Denver, near Fort Lupton, and settled down to raise cattle.

But gold was still very much in Joel's craw of tasted fantasy, especially after the major strike by John Greggory in 1859 at his *diggings* on Clear Creek was reported to be the richest square mile in the world at that time. One bright day on the 15th of October, 1859 while following game trails on a combined hunting and prospecting excursion with son Milton, his life was to take an unexpected turn. His name was destined to live on beyond his phantasms of expectations. He would no longer be remembered as a farmer, nor as a cattle man, --not even a prospector. His name would forever be linked with words like *resort, vacation retreat* and *mountain paradise.* Of course he was not aware of his protracted fame as he looked down from that last ridge we now know as Park Hill, overlooking the river valley of the Thompson, and beheld what had before been only a dwelling place for wild creatures, wind and rainbows. His son, then nineteen years of age, expressed in words his feelings about that exciting day, remembered forty years later as if it were yesterday. "We stood looking down at the head waters of the Little Thompson Creek, where the Park spread out before us. No words can describe our surprise, wonder and joy at beholding such an unexpected sight. It looked like a low valley with a silver streak, or thread, winding its way through the tall grass, down through the valley and disappearing around a hill among the pine trees. This silver thread was the Big Thompson Creek. It was a grand sight and a great surprise. We did not know what we had found. Father thought it was North Park for that was the only Park we had ever heard of in this part of the Rockies. He soon gave up that idea when we looked round the Park for a few days and saw no signs that white men had ever been there before us. There were signs that Indians had been there before at some time however er for we found lodge poles in two different places. There was absolutely nothing to dispute our sway, and we were monarchs of mountains, valleys and streams. The streams were filled with mountain trout, speckled beauties and the Park was a paradise for the hunter. Father was carried away with the find for he was a great lover of hunting and fishing." What a grand sight it must have been after a difficult trip up steep and nearly non-existent trails, now to be experienced in comfort by millions each year who would follow up the modern Highway 36 of the North St. Vrain Canyon. Joel had his own words about his impressions as later reported by members of his family. "This is the very place I have been seeking. Here we will make our home." He constructed two rough cabins and a corral in 1860, used the area for hunting and fishing, but did not move his family to this bountiful valley until 1863, their closest neighbor living more than twenty-five miles below. His son Francis Marion Estes revealed the reason for not moving up earlier, saying that his father had returned to Missouri to free his slaves as well as joining up for several years to fight in the Confederate Army. He was a product of his time and locality and in his precinct of the near South the color gray was more popular than blue.

When the Estes family settled in their valley, the population of the immense Colorado Territory numbered little more than 25,000 inhabitants. But in less than twenty years, as word of gold strikes and free land reached the ears of those who had survived the strife of an unholy war that left much of the United States in mental tatters, the crop of pioneer seed now supplemented by souls blown in on the eastern wind, had ripened in the new state of Colorado to more than 194,000. In 1861 a new generation of the Estes family was soon to be established even though females of the marrying persuasion were scarce in those mountain recesses. Undeterred, Milton, then twenty-one returned to Fort Lupton to marry his 19 year old sweetheart, Mary L. Fleming, who had arrived with her parents in 1859. His return several years later, in company with his parents, his other younger sisters and brothers, his wife and their two young sons, brought much joy as well as further parental responsibilities. Their third child, Charles F. Estes, was born on February 10, 1865 becoming the first white child to be born in the Park. In later years Mary Fleming Estes, having produced several more children after vacating her mountain home, recalled with fondness their years living in a cabin with a sod roof near the banks of Willow Creek, now renamed Fish Creek. "We kept well, enjoyed the climate, had plenty of fun, were monarchs of all we surveyed, had no taxes to pay and were contented as long as we remained. But I wish I had pictures of ourselves in those old days. ---And clothes! How we must have looked." Their clothing consisted mainly of animal skins sewn together and, when they became worn or dirty since the cleaning of leather garments was not then in vogue nor practical, they simply went out hunting for a new suit of clothes, dress or warm coat. The family lived off the land that knew no limits of plenty, a veritable Nimrod's paradise, with fish, game and berries providing food and fiber for their wants, especially the berries that grew as thick as weeds. The women of the family worked hard to provide for their families and it was said that the hot biscuits, berry pies and baked wild game that came out of the dutch ovens, and iron kettles suspended over an open fire, could not be surpassed anywhere.

Religion was not forgotten in their new home with the first sermon by Reverend Richardson of Denver being preached in the summer of 1865. There were seventeen in this first congregation, of course ten of whom were members of the Estes family, the other seven made up of the Reverend. Richardson, his wife and their five children. The Estes family raised cattle and sheep but at no time was there a need to live off the domestic stock because of the abundant supply of elk, deer and mountain sheep that browsed near their front door. One winter Milton recalled killing more than 100 elk as well as deer, sheep and antelope, all by using his muzzle loading gun. His weapon, and that of his father, were the first guns used in the Park. Milton called his weapon *Knock 'Em Stiff*, and because of the ponderous proportions and his aim was true, "when it went off something usually dropped." It is significant to note that his weapon is now owned by the State of Colorado and still may be hanging in its capitol building. With a bi-monthly trip to Denver to pick up their mail, they purchased supplies and traded dressed game and skins for what Joel had sought so eagerly, gold dust. In the beginning 1860s mail from Missouri took thirty days to arrive in Denver and, since they managed to pick up their mail every two months, news from home became old even before their trail stained letters were read. Letters then were not as important as facing the continuing saga of existing, evidenced by Milton Estes' opinion on that subject. "As a rule frontiersmen did not bother much about mail for they had become accustomed to doing without."

Supplies were packed in until 1861 when Estes and his sons improvised a road up the St. Vrain River canyon that allowed for his use of a two wheeled cart to bear the loads previously assigned to beasts of burden as well as their own strong backs. Indians never were observed by the family in the valley the Arapahoes referred to as *The Circle*, Long's Peak and Mount Meeker also receiving their pseudonym of *Two Guides*, and consequently they never were bothered. Even if they had been seen in the Park, Joel was known to Indian tribes while living in Fort Lupton. His fairness to them had earned him the title of *Big White Chief*. Later we would learn that Indian peoples frequently traveled across the high mountain range to the west of Estes Park, especially on three trails that led to Grand Lake, their Spirit Lake, nearly fifty miles distant. One was known as *Big Trail*, following near the present day Flattop Mountain route; the second, *Dog Trail,* ascended the Fall River; and the third, known as the *Child's Trail* proceeded along a more gentle track, partially in view of the beautiful heights of Tombstone Ridge, later called Trail Ridge Road. The Arapahoes referred to it as Child's Trail for the reason that although it may have been smooth it was so steep that the children had to dismount from the horses and walk to the top.

Traveling up Joel Estes' trail in 1868 was the subject of a chapter in a book of remembrances by the legendary Abner Sprague. "I wish I could describe that trail up Muggins Gulch as I saw it on that trip. All was untouched by the axe of man. Flowers everywhere. One must go where the needs of man despoiled the beauties of nature, to enjoy as we enjoyed this, our explorations for things new. The cart trail leading in our direction we did not hesitate to follow it. We did not know why there should be a cart track, or what anyone would want so far from the settled plains. If it was wood, we had passed through enough to supply the world. It had us guessing and we were bound to follow until we found out. We came to the open treeless ground near the head of the gulch, and around a turn in the trail, beheld the snow peaks we were looking for, right there in front of us and so near that we imagined we could feel the breath from their fields of snow. We pushed our ponies to the divide and there, ---but what is the use, I can see it as I saw it then but cannot describe my feelings when I looked down on that tree dotted flat, with the stream winding through the unfenced meadows. The dark forest of Black Canyon at the farther side and the snow-capped peaks topping all, cutting a clear silhouette in the deep blue of the sky. The surprise of it made us speechless." The Muggins Gulch referred to by Sprague was named by Joel Estes after George *Muggins* Hearst who herded for two men pasturing their cattle in the Park. Hearst had a small cabin in this narrow valley on the Estes Road, strategically located to prevent the cattle from drifting back to the meadows below to the east. Joel named many of the geographical features of his new discovery after his arrival, and though most have been given other names, Muggins Gulch survives.

Now and then in those early years curious visitors found their way up to this place and were graciously received by the Estes family. One of the most noteworthy tourists was Mr. William N. Byers who founded in 1859 the *Rocky Mountain News* after his arrival from Omaha, Nebraska. He enjoyed climbing mountains and was determined to master the lordly bulwark, Long's Peak, seen from his Denver City more than 60 miles southeast. As a point of information, Denver in 1858 was laid out by William Larimer using the peak as a northwest-southeast reference point thus accounting for the unusual alignment of its downtown streets. The mountain had a pronounced effect upon this man who had written reams of copy on more auspicious subjects, yet none could compare to this magisterial symbol right in his own *backyard*, as evidenced by his words written in 1864 after returning from his first trip to the Park. "A very gem of beauty. The landscape struck us at first sight as one of the most lovely we have ever beheld!" Although he and his party were unsuccessful in their struggling siege of its eastern ramparts, attaining only the formation we now call The Keyhole, he and George Nichols did succeed in making the first ascent of Mount Meeker. Mr. Byers was greatly impressed by the warm hospitality of Joel and Patsy Estes, as well as their entire family, who shared their simple home and food with him and his entourage. Joel Estes, Jr., the youngest son, known as the fisherman of the family, had learned of the Byers' party in the Park and guided them to the foot of the mountain. After their lack of success to gain its topmost crest, their stay at the small ranch while resting for a return to Denver was made more pleasant by this young man's constant supply of fish, one of which was reported to be of gigantic proportions. From small streams then it was not uncommon for this young fisherman to garner fish of great avoirdupois, up to 3 1/2 pounds, specimens that older fishermen of modern times would pay dearly just for the bragging rights if not its possession. In appreciation for their friendship, he returned to Denver and named this region *Estes Park*, a name that still brings acclamations of appreciation from contemporary visitors for the reception proffered them by people of the Estes Valley. This effort to share their mountains with others, *the newcomers*, was clearly evident in the attitude of those who operated the tent camps and delightful lodges that began appearing in the late 1870s. A story in the newspaper of the times, *The Mountaineer*, the edition dated June 21, 1913, announced the local doctrine on this issue. "The controlling sentiment of the Park is that the comfort, health and pleasure of our guests shall be our first consideration."

The winters of 1864 and 1865 were long, unsympathetic to mortal man and woman. November of 1865 brought thirty inches of snow, drifting into impassable ridges whereby many of Estes' cattle died in the icy horror with the survivors being herded with great strife for beast and man to the lower foothills. The short days and long nights were plagued by severely cold temperatures. Oil lamps brought little solace to this hardy band who often found their food supplies in March somewhat meager. The family in those slim months was not adverse to extracting, by a process of boiling, the marrow-like substance from bull elk antlers strewn about after the creature's masculinity no longer required their bulk. The Estes family were members of the Primitive Baptist Church and as such never labored on Sunday, except once when their calendar in a near empty valley became confused as one day's hard work melded into another. The combination of weather and isolation proved too long and arduous for Joel and Patsy. The years of solitary subsistence without neighbors with whom to share their experiences and kismet, had charged a heavy price. They were nearing the age of 60 years and their bodies no longer possessed the resilience nor ruggedness required for pioneering pressures. They sold their holdings to Michael Hollenbeck and Hank Farrar for a little cash, a yoke of oxen, maybe a yearling steer and perhaps a horse thrown in for good measure to seal the bargain. Joel and Patsy moved away on April 15, 1866 to New Mexico, some say traveling first to Texas, for warmer winters never to return again. Few of their children journeyed back for a curious glimpse into the Park that now forever was to be associated with their family. Joel died December 31, 1875 near Farmington, New Mexico and was buried at Vermejo, Colfax County, New Mexico. Patsy joined him in a new paradise upon her death in Fremont County, Iowa on August 6, 1882 while living with her daughter, Mrs. Sarah Hiatt. Milton's son, Ed, was the first of the family to return for a brief visit years later. Milton said that the family elected to move to warmer climates with better grass so that they could continue their cattle raising, in larger mode, with less stress and dangers. The Milton Estes family, after sojourns further south including New Mexico, established their residence at 1273 Evans Street in Denver, Colorado surrendering to the blandishments of a more gentle domain in which to spend their retirement years. Still, Long's Peak in distant view, aloof to those few who had assaulted her ice shrouded nobility, never allowed them to forget those trailblazing days. Their early days were difficult times yet they perceived real happiness shared with untamed herds, blue skies hemmed in on all sides by phalanxes of craggy peaks and with their God who blessed their quiet tranquility with strength. Mary Fleming Estes died in 1905, Milton following along eight years later allocating to his second wife Emma Armstrong Estes the task of publishing his memoirs.

William Byers would return again in 1868 in the company of a party of six including the one-armed Major John Wesley Powell, conqueror of the Colorado River of the Grand Canyon. They recorded their names on August 23, 1868 in a register they placed on the flat topped five acre summit, thus becoming the first known white persons to ascend Longs Peak's 14,255 foot promontory. On the ascent, L. W. Kepplinger gave his name to a small lake of poetic quality he discovered while out in the lead scouting by way of a southwesterly approach. Following their triumph the mountain was to become an objective worthy of others including members of Professor Hayden's Survey team in August of 1871 whose guest Miss Anna E. Dickinson met the challenge by recording her name as the first woman to stand proudly upon this preeminent temple to the ages. There could have been others who claimed a share in Estes' unpatented claim, yet it was difficult to follow the paper trail. You must understand that a nearly unknown Big Thompson valley was a long way from any court house. Also, record keeping back then was not an exact science, but complicated, labor intensive and more probably nearly non-existent. A granite marker was erected in remembrance of the Joel Estes family, on whom most all of the residents in 1927 could reasonably agree probably was the first permanent family in the valley. The local residents abjured any personal opinions of primacy of their valley that could have run the gamut of an assortment of famous and infamous personalities. Together they stood, on a hillside east of town on July 1, 1927, to pay well earned homage to all those who forged their community out of raw, unrefined elements into products of enduring determination, especially to their namesake family now long absent from view.

Joe Mills, the popular lodge owner and local writer, that warm summer day, summed up their opinion as the marker was unveiled, and where it remains today for all to admire. "We are assembled here today to commemorate the first white settlement in this region, to honor the memory of Joel Estes and his contemporaries, the early pioneers. Let us, for a brief moment, forget the hurly-burly of our modern, complex civilization, and turn back to those far-off, those epoch making days. This region now teeming with tourists and automobiles, was then an unexplored land of fearsome mystery, as primitive as it had come from the hand of its Creator. No settler's cheery, lamp-lighted window beckoned the traveler onward. It was strange, hostile, beyond the frontier. And yet, that same brave, adventurous spirit which drove Columbus .....drove the pioneers westward too, ...that same courage beat in the high heart of Joel Estes when in 1859 he discovered this mountain paradise. His name will live as long as the immortal peaks, and with it will live the names of other settlers, his neighbors. Swift years have passed since these hardy spirits first blazed trails into these mountain valleys, swift years bringing many changes. But we trust that the hospitality which so markedly characterized pioneer life, still remains; that we who live here, unworthy descendants of that glorious company, may have inherited some of their hospitable spirit. Our pioneer fathers handed down to us this rich legacy of magnificent mountain wilds. We cannot do less, as a sign of our appreciation, than to make it possible for others, less favored and removed from them, to enjoy them with us. What more fitting memorial to those first daring settlers than that we preserve this primitive area, unspoiled, for posterity." To that sincere peroration, that beseeches us in the environmentally chaotic 1990s to take heed, I say, Amen and Amen.

Estes Park was to become as the authors Foscue and Quam correctly titled their manuscript, *The Resort In The Rockies*. Milton Estes wrote, years after his exodus, about this vast change in the Park's appearance from that long ago time when his father's home alone cast its shadow across the tall grass. The new system of roads, multistory structures, gobs of fresh new faces scurrying about and more especially the lack of game grazing in the fields now populated with schools, businesses and moving autos impressed him with much effect as when we reflect upon a time in our own lives when we stood on a mountain top and caught our breath at the changes wrought by modernity. "In looking at Estes now," Milton meditated with a tinge of remorse for an unretrievable past, "it does not look natural to me, for I well remember the game, hunting and fishing as it was in early days when we had everything our own way." Others would try to have their own way, after the departure of Milton, yet the clock was moving too quickly for the treasure that was Estes Park to be in the pockets of a few. The power of the press would tell all, coupled with the resoluteness of the people, so that Estes Park would not be denied its eventual position as a premier destination for those yet unborn.

In 1867 a man, who would be involved in the first fatal gun fight of classic frontier proportions in the Park, arrived and purchased the former Estes claims from whomever maintained some degree of ownership at that particular moment. He was to remain on the property for between 12 and 20 years depending upon those historical memoirs you examine, or believe. He was Captain Griffith J. Evans, affectionately known as Griff. Griff Evans, with his first roots in Llanberis, Wales, arrived in Denver, Colorado in 1863 from Michigan and soon thereafter acquired enough money that he could call himself well fixed. Then his partner caused their business to founder leaving many unpaid creditors. Griff, being a man of honor, sold nearly everything he had to pay off the debts and keep his reputation for honesty unblemished. He learned of Estes Park and thought it might provide him the opportunity to recoup his resources and to this high valley in 1867, at an age estimated to be thirty-seven, he journeyed with his wife Jane and two children. They lived in the weathered buildings erected by Joel Estes, paying for the same with a small amount of money he had subsequently earned. He was so poor that he borrowed pack animals for the transport of their meagre possessions, releasing the animals at trails end to find their programed way back down to the home grasslands. His gun provided for their sustenance as it had for the Estes family, whereby selling meat and hides enabled him to acquire a team of horses and tools with which to construct additional cabins. He had an idea that others might need a bed and food in this near empty land and would be willing to pay for such a treasure trove. It is therefore fitting that we confer upon this bewhiskered Welshman, Griff Evans, the title of Estes Park's First Inn Keeper. He built several rough pine cabins out behind his sod roofed log ranch house and was always willing to take in the travelers who ventured up the trail from whatever direction.

Griff's hospitality in September and October of 1873 was chronicled by the English trekker Isabella Lucy Bird in a picturesque diary of her trip to western United States entitled *A Lady's Life In The Rocky Mountains*. She eloquently described Griff Evans' home and gave her impression of the region that held her emotionally hostage for that brief moment in history when she shared a peace with new friends in the highlands she could never forget. "From the ridge on which this gulch terminates, at a height of 9,000 feet, we saw at last Estes Park, lying 1,500 feet below, in the glory of the setting sun, an irregular basin, lighted up by the bright waters of the rushing Thompson, guarded by sentinel mountains of fantastic shape and monstrous size. Long's Peak rising above them all in unapproachable grandeur, while the Snowy Range, with its outlying spurs heavily timbered, comes down upon the Park slashed by stupendous canyons lying deep in purple gloom. Never, --no-where, have I seen anything to equal the view into Estes Park. The mountains 'of the land which is very far off' are very near now, but the near is more glorious than the far, and reality than dreamland. So in this glorious upper world, with the mountain pines behind and the clear lake in front, in the 'blue hollow at the foot of Long's Peak', at a height of 7,500 feet, where the hoarfrost crisps the grass every night of the year, I have found far more than I ever dared to hope for. We came suddenly upon a small lake, close to which was a very trim looking log cabin, with a flat mud roof, and with four smaller ones. Picturesquely dotted about it were two corrals, a long shed in front of which a steer was being killed, a log dairy with a water wheel, some hay piles and various evidences of comfort. There has been fresh meat each day since I came, delicious bread baked daily, excellent potatoes, tea and coffee, and an abundant supply of milk like cream. I have a clean hay bed with six blankets, and there are neither bugs nor fleas." As a point of information --having little to do with this narrative, the sod on Griff's roofs was replaced in 1877 when a man named Hill erected a saw mill up in the Mill Creek basin and provided wood shingles to adorn the apexes of previously constructed buildings. Although the use of such a new innovation provided a drier interior, no longer to see grass, shrubs and small trees waving from the tops of log cabins simulating prayer flags in Nepal was less whimsical.

Then making his entrance from center stage in this broad landscape was an unlikely person who by his own controversial land schemes unwittingly advertised the existence of Estes Park and its incomparable resources to the world outside. This fulsome bravado eventually led to his voluntary expulsion homeward fifteen years later. A peer of the British aristocracy of the western regions of Ireland, he was a graduate of the bluest of blood schools, Christ College, Oxford University and a devout adventurer obsessed with an overbearing appetite for possession and control of space and all that dwelled therein. The Right Honorable Windham Thomas Wyndham-Quinn, 4th Earl of Dunraven, was born in Ireland in 1841, lived at his Adare Manor in County Limerick, and finally died in London in 1926 after involving himself in as many adventures that would have occupied the lifetimes of ten men. He was described as a courageous man of broad brow, hollow cheeks, balding, strong chinned, with full mustache and handsome in his aristocratic, straight backed posture. During his lifetime he was a member of the Senate of the Irish Free State, Queen Victoria's Undersecretary of the Colonies, a battalion commander in the Boer War and a sportsman who twice sent his 90 foot racing yacht to America seeking a victory for the British Empire in what is known today as the America's Cup Race. Very early in his post university days he was sent as a war correspondent for the London *Daily Telegraph* to cover the fast evolving events that later were to be identified as The Abyssinian War, followed by an assignment to report the horrors of the Franco-Prussian War from its front lines. After perceiving vast and sundry vistas of the eastern world by the time he had reached the age of twenty-eight, he determined to gain a more expansive view of 'the former colonial fiefs' of America to which he had previously turned a blind eye in ennui. His words expressed his change of heart toward America. "I was young, and my boyish brain cells were stored to bursting with the tales of Red Indians and grizzly b'ars; caballeros and haciendas, prairies and buffaloes; Texans and Mexicans, cowboys and voyageurs." Seeking satisfaction to his contrived notion of America, he arranged his honeymoon trip in 1869 with his new bride, for the first of his sixteen trips to America, in search of *sport and adventure* as he termed it. After a long day on the beaches and water while on the east coast, this first visit came to an abrupt end resulting in an immediate return to his home with a severe case of sunburn.

In 1871, while passing through Chicago, pursuing goals for an adventurous spirit no longer satisfied in quiet hills of Irish green covered peat bogs, he had a chance meeting with General Phillip Sheridan, Union hero of the recently concluded and euphemistically called War Between The States. The General handed to Lord Dunraven, a title to which he was most smitten and referenced by his Castle Dunraven at Glamorgan, a letter of introduction to other military commanders of his Plains Command of Kansas and Nebraska with directions to extend the services of army scouts to his lordship in quest of a taste of the real out-of-doors. These wards had been heralded abroad with increasingly bombastic reports of promethean proportions to be filled with game for easy conquest. Two of the scouts assigned to him were John 'Texas Jack' Omohondro and William 'Buffalo Bill' Cody, the later as referred to in my Prologue became famous for his slaughter of wild creatures to satiate the appetites of railroad construction workers, the military and foreign notables to whom many of our governmental officials still stood in awe. Long after the Earl's discovery of Estes Park these three mountain musketeers made subsequent hunting trips including the year 1875 when they threaded their way through the rugged untamed territory known as the Upper Yellowstone River precincts of Wyoming. This near primordial, geyser cloaked woodland possessed with goblin-like beauty of remarkable uniqueness, had then only recently been selected for special designation by President Grant and our nation's Congress leading to it's honor as our first National Park in 1872. Later Dunraven, who would live long enough to write seven books one of which concerned his sojourns through the Yellowstone wilderness, would have his name attributed to one of the passes now to be located on maps of that Park.

Sometime after our nation was first linked together in 1869 with bands of steel at Promontory Point, Utah as two engines of the Central Pacific and Union Pacific Railroads deftly touched their cow catchers in symbolic victory salute, and before 1873 when financial troubles beset the financial empires of America, Lord Dunraven first saw Denver. It was reported that he traveled by train from Kansas City, others say it was by way of Cheyenne, Wyoming. He was not flattering in his comments about this dusty citadel upon the plains. Perhaps it recalled his days as a correspondent on the battle fields now appearing analogous with gunfire confrontations evident in rough streets of a community seeking rapid respectability. "Denver was a quaint place in those days, little more than a comparatively lawless frontier town, as depicted by Bret Harte," wrote Dunraven in 1922 in his book of memories. Upon the death of his father in the fall of 1871, he inherited 40,000 acres of land with huge manor houses, and thus with an abundance of time and the wealth of Croesus spent his days traveling, hunting, sailing and choosing from an ample menu of adventure. His penchants, it was divulged, were women, his pipe, good liquor and sports, the priorities of which depended upon to whom one made inquiry. But it was obvious, in the rare appearance of his wife on his travels, that he indeed cut a fine figure with the ladies who were flattered to be in his company. It was Christmas Eve in Denver, 1872, while bending the elbow with foreigners in exile at a social gathering, that his interest became diverted to a place of which he had no knowledge, --Estes Park. While in the closest imitation of an English pub with the devious name of Corkscrew Club, its

17

name quite possibly suggestive of the objectives or mentality of this convivial fraternity, he met a young Irish mining engineer by the name of Theodore Whyte. Whyte relished hunting and filled the Earl with visions of hunting beyond unbridled dreams to be found with no measure of impedimenta in Estes Park. Those beasts were there for the taking he most likely assured the Earl, and thereafter nothing would deter his lordship after such a full blooded testimonial by a kinsman. "My western experiences were not confined to hunting and exploring. I and a friend from Sligo (Ireland) packed some necessaries on a mule, bought a couple of horses, and proceeded to pay a visit to Estes Park," the Earl explained, somewhat cavalierly if not accurately many years later. Actually there were two of his peers with him, Sir William Cummings and the Earl of Fitzpatrick, and Dunraven's male attendant, or gillie of Scottish parentage, identified simply as Sandie. After their purchase of supplies, they dined at the Frenchman Frederic Charpiot's Restaurant at 1540 Larimer Street. It was known as the *Delmonicos of the West* to the many Europeans on tour as its reputation as a celebrated establishment had been widely spread throughout the West as well as abroad since 1860. They traveled north by train to Longmont, Colorado, then known as Burlington, and acquired a wagon with mules to convey them west as the Earl described "through the strange shaped masses of bright red sandstone, ...to follow along the bank of the St. Vrain River teeming with trout ....to twist up through the foothills, along grassy slopes, through pine forests and past fantastic masses of rock ....to a long valley rejoicing in the euphonious title of Muggin's Gulch."

Upon his entrance into the Park, after assisting the mules with their shoulders and holding back on a chain to slow the ascent down the snowy, ice hazardous rut of a road, they drew up their cortege before the humble establishment of Griff Evans on a sunny December 27th day. Dunraven's intent was to shoot a few of the local four legged inhabitants, but then as he examined the splendorous scene spread out on all sides, he had other thoughts. He surveyed the verdant valley of grass, protected by great white mountains adorned by necklaces of green no artist nor poet can fully compose on paper, and his first idea of animal conquest was forgotten. Why, this was even far more spectacular than what Whyte in his most grandiloquent of metaphors had pictured! Long after he vacated the Park would he continue to remember that experience. Although nostalgic in tenor, he wrote with no remorse for the denouement of his great plans envisioned for the Estes Valley. His vivid description gives clear insight into a realm that he alone expected, yea demanded to rule. "Estes Park was, and still must be, a glorious place. A great plain, or rather park, for a huge well-timbered park best describes it, intersected by numerous streams, branches of the Great Thompson, opening into great, glorious, heavily timbered valleys and canon, the whole dominated by snow clad Long's Peak. There was no track in those days, and it was a paradise for hunter and trapper. Mountain sheep, blacktail and whitetail deer in abundance, and an occasional mountain lion or bear. Bears were numerous at times. Just under the snowline, clouds of locusts flying over perished, --I suppose by the cold, and were collected in heaps in the gullies and bears were very fond of them. Beavers and otters were plentiful, and the streams were full of trout. The air is scented with the sweet smelling sap of the pines whose branches welcome many feathered visitors from southern claims, an occasional hummingbird whirrs among the shrubs, trout leap in the creeks, insects buzz in the air. Estes Park was inhabited by a little Welshman, Evans, who made a living I don't know how, and by Mountain Jim who trapped. He (Jim) is an extraordinary character, civil enough when sober but when drunk, which was as often as he could manage, violent and abusive and given to declamation in Greek and Latin. In those parts and in those days everybody rode, and if you had to go a few hundred yards you ran about for half an hour to catch a pony for the journey, and, once on it, a deliberate pace was impossible. You felt a wild desire to gallop about and shout! It was, and doubtless is a grand climate."

Dunraven remained for a period of time longer than he had originally contrived for a brief hunting trip, occupying one of Griff's cabins, sleeping on the mattress spread out on the floor before a crackling fire. Although his accommodations could not be compared to Adare Manor, there was something about this beautifully isolated hollow that grasped firmly the thoughts and aspirations of a thirty-one year old bon vivant. He describes a day when idling about his cabin. "After a time people began to wander in. The first I well remember. I was sitting smoking at the door of a little one-room shanty when to me appeared a queer little old chap on a pack horse, and says he, 'Say, stranger, --is this a good place to drink whiskey in?' I said it was if only there was whiskey. He looked disappointed and wandered off." The following summer of 1873 he returned with his 45 year old personal physician, George Henry Kingsley, as was often the rule with the wealthy who preferred not to be adrift in the seas of 'colonial savagery' without medical preparedness. Accompanying the duo was Theodore Whyte who was there under the pretext of hunting but who suspicioned a quest for a larger prize. The next Spring of 1874 again found Dunraven again at Griff's ranch. By this time he was not content just to appreciate the refreshment that one could derive from being in the pure air, unbounded, unfettered and free from the boisterous material symbols of success that lathered up the populaces of cities and towns of America as well as the world about into competitive frenzies. He fancied owning a piece of that pie in the sky. On second thought, he craved ownership of the whole pastry shop, and to this agenda he hired Theodore Whyte to put a plan for 'preservation of the natural features of this region in their primeval state' into practice. Willing to pay handsomely for all the crumbs he could sweep up from the loafers, unemployed miners and ranch hands on Larimer Street in Denver, Whyte made open invitation to all who would do his employer's bidding. As money was no barrier to this young blade of privilege, Dunraven discoursed to his English friends gathered about him one day the resolution to own all land from where they stood on Griff's front porch to the distant snowy boundary. Those wealthy sycophants, such as Fitzpatrick and Cummings, urged him on recognizing an opportunity to better sponge off this young aristocrat's benevolence that clearly appeared to be on the way to urbane enhancement.

Dunraven had inaugurated his plan the previous year, 1873, by purchasing Griff's holdings for $900, a princely sum to a near pauper who was content to earn but a few quid a day in hard toil. By the time Griff left the Park he had four more children, and $18,000, not in a pair of rough textured work clothes, but in the deep pockets of his dark business suit that went well with his *proper* wool felt hat. In Denver, Dunraven learned the ropes about a 'quaint way Americans had of acquiring land' not practiced in the British

Isles, homesteading, and Theodore Whyte managed the campaign of 'quasi-legal acquisition.' Lawyers told him that the government, including the local District Attorney, was not too particular about the process about which a homestead was claimed, and would not look too closely at the paper work. Settlers were greedily sought in a territory whose political pundits gave obeisances to those who might hasten statehood, a status soon to be achieved in 1876. *The Englishman*, to which generic country classification he was identified by settlers more often than not with derision in tone, threatened the struggling, honest homesteader in the Park with his cavalier manners steeped in condescension and overt avarice. His success with 'street people' his agents encountered in Denver, Boulder and Longmont, who were not adverse to a few dollars placed in their pockets in exchange for signatures on governmental documents, was evident. Each cooperating party could expect to receive from $10 to $50 and a payment for the government of $1.25 per acre. It meant nothing to them to surrender their homestead rights to an allotted 160 acres when they never intended to endure the strife and decent hard work required to shape the land into productivity. They were out of work and money was their god, or gold a reasonable substitute. Dummy entry claims suddenly sprouted throughout the Park, clearly identifiable as Dunraven claims by the four logs laid in a square to constitute the required *improvements* of a homesteader, and for good measure a brush fence hastily fabricated to enclose the little lady's *herb garden*.

By May of 1874 his sphere of influence had increased to 4,000 acres and by 1875 reportedly it had grown to 14,000, and by some estimates the apogee of his factotums's successes had reached 30,000 acres. How accurate these estimates were is anyone's guess and pure conjecture, and gossip. What is clear, is that his sub rosa stints to circumnavigate the law had an enormous impact upon honest residents in the Park and elsewhere. When he realized that the Park was being populated by others and no longer could it be his absolute domain filled with herds of deer and elk, he imported pure blooded horses and at least 1,400 head of white faced Hereford cattle to roam about aimlessly. Fishermen were required to keep a wary eye out for the Englishman's crown branded bulls that sent them running to the trees for being in their pasture, --a true Dunravian trait adapted to the bovine chutzpah. As confrontations in 1875 and 1876 between settlers and his surrogates Whyte and C. Golding Dwyer became heated, many began to dispute Dunraven's claimed right to fence off roads and drive cattle across their property. One basic question was at the root of all Dunravian assertions, the correct answer to which was essential to any progress for Estes Park. Was this to become a real community of kindred souls, left to work out their own destinies with honest toil and shared friendship, or would it be fenced in as a playground for the landed gentry, --foreigners as well? A resolution of the issue was soon made evident as it was difficult to keep this giant land grab under wraps and quiet. One, who was camping in the Park, suspicioned that all was not right and that a fraud of extensive and malodorous proportions was in progress. In other words, something reeked to high heavens and he was going to ring the bell. His name was Thorn, a name that found its way under the handsome saddle of Dunraven who sought to fend off the attacks by local citizens, and more importantly the news media. Mr. Thorn, after being shunted away by incredulous editors or perhaps those newspaper scions who had established a venal relationship with the narcissistic Earl, finally was able to tip off an honest reporter who smelled a good story drifting down from the haunts of a privileged pasture. The cat, --or more appropriately the monarchial lion, was out of the bag. The intrepid reporter of *The Denver Tribune* broke the story with a flair in his introductory headline. The effect upon the public was electric. **"What!!, an Englishman 'Milord' to lay claim to all the most valuable land of Estes Park that he and a few of his foreign bobs and nabobs, counts and no accounts might have convenient place to hunt and fish!!"**

All the Earl's horses and all the Earl's men couldn't put the spilled contents back in the bag again. It thereby provided new tales for the newspaper's readers to ponder, some of which provided a new surge of the curious to sally forth up the Estes trail, this time however to take up the scores of claims that Dunraven would agree to surrender. When it was all over, after contests, lawsuits and allegations of shameless land stealing by one who spuriously manipulated the legal system to his own advantage, the 30,000 acres of refuted claims had shrunk to approximately 6,600. He no longer would be an absolute despot, undisputed, and learned to his dismay that the dark clouds arising was a whirlwind of public outrage that could devastate his harvest long before it was in the barn. The dearth of wins over those he encountered in the Park portended folly for his continuous provocation of those who looked upon his titled presence with pioneer disdain. They were not inclined to intimidation just because he attempted to look down from his lofty position of power, wealth and past vestiges of prestige. They were here to stay! Then to compound the issue of land reform was the incident between Griff Evans and Mountain Jim Nugent that had brought the long arm of the criminal courts to reach up to the drama played out upon Dunraven's own stage.

Jim Nugent was a one-eyed, athletically handsome man who was refined and courteous when sober. His disfigurement was the result of an encounter in July of 1869 near Grand Lake when a sow bear with cubs viciously attacked him. When he was discovered in a pool of blood and after a cursory examination of his head wounds, the citizenry raised the cry of "Indian attack!" His past was discernably destitute of authentication yet his general appearance in tattered buckskin while his conversation was peppered with the lore of literature, gave credence to a life lived as a reclusive yet well educated nomad. The straight aquiline nose and long hair hanging in ringlets classed him as a true prince of paupers and from his one room cabin, miles to the south of Griff's ranch, he closely observed those passing by on the trail who kept their distance. Although rarely in an attitude of sobriety, it was said than when he was besotted with drink that he could prove irrational as well as dangerous in defense of his own questionable position in the Park's pecking order. His closest friend was an old yellow dog who like himself was of doubtful parentage yet of unquestioned loyalty to persons and causes he deemed worthy. His brief interlude of tenderness associated with chivalry and genuine affection for an English lady, Isabella Bird about whom I have previously discussed, has been cause for chapters written by those who knew him as an honorable person of strong and abiding principles. His troubles, as well as those of many of the other residents in the Park, were orchestrated by the tactics of the Earl and his well financed constituency. Griff Evans, himself of British Isles lineage, gave his loyalty to this personage of grand circumstance who had prompted a source of revenue to flow his way. It was to his identification with the minions of Dunraven, such as one Lord Hague, that any vestige of earlier friendship for Jim was stripped away. As the result of events that could have been scripted years later, --set to the tinkling accompaniment of a player piano with layers of melodramas involving a woman, greed, land grabbing, drunkenness and deceit, Griff shot Jim to death. Some say it was accidental, in a drunken stupor as Griff himself was not averse to occasional bibulous conduct. Others thought it was not Griff's intent, the death only the result of a ricocheting bullet off a wagon wheel in an attempt to frighten Jim off the premises. Jim lingered long enough to bestow upon the shaken Welshman a curse of future accountability somewhere, perhaps now having been settled up. Griff was found not guilty in this flawed world, the effect of absented witnesses who chose to follow a distant trail south rather than accept civil responsibility.

After taking a trial balance of his questionable credits under attack, as well as of his ever increasing debits compounding from overcharged conduct, Dunraven came to this conclusion. "It was evident that we were not to be left monarchs of all we surveyed. Folks were drifting in, prospecting, and making claims. So we prepared for civilization. We made a better road, bought a sawmill in San Francisco, hauled in machinery, felled trees, and built a hotel." He determined to become respectable in the eyes of the community, although to him that status should have been recognizable by even a cursory examination of his royally bestowed credentials that he flung about himself in arabesque display. He vowed to make something out of an obviously difficult situation and recoup some of his vast expense by tapping into the stranger now venturing past his ranch. The old ranch acquired from Griff still was under the management of that affable, country-eloquent and outward charming Captain Griffith Evans. Dunraven conjured up the idea that the stranger now appearing had money to spend but no respectable place to lay his head, and that such folk would pay handsomely for good facilities and appropriate treatment. Where else would they go, he reasoned. The first hostelry for the Estes Valley was on the drawing boards in 1876 as tourists were flocking into experience the ecstasy previously extolled by Isabella Bird. "The scenery is the most glorious I have ever seen, and it is above us, around us, at the very door." How very true.

Dr. Frederick V. Hayden, chief of survey team, 1873 (RMNP)

W.H. Jackson, Photographer, U.S. Government Survey, 1873 (RMNP)

Lake Irene Near Milner Pass, circa 1890 (RMNP)

Settlers Cabin, circa 1880 (Mills)

Joel Estes Family, 1859 (EPHM)

Estes-Evans-Dunraven Ranch Before Lake Estes, 1910 (Mills)

Thompson River Valley East of Estes Park,
1910 (EPHM)

Griff Evans With Murphy,
circa 1900 (EPPL)

Griff Evans Home and Ranch, circa 1873 (EPHM)

John Cleave At His Post Office, 1902 (EPPL)

John Cleave Home And Stage, 1905 (EPPL)

Estes Park, circa 1902 (Mills)

The Navigators

Long ago at the end of the route,
The stage pulled up and the folks stepped out,
They have all passed under the tavern door,
The youth and his bride and the gray three-score;
Weary with dust and gleam,
For the day had passed like an empty dream,
Soft may they slumber and trouble no more,
For the weary journey its jolt and its roar,
In the old stages over the mountain.
Sally Ferguson Reed, 1916

A lodge owner remembered by this verse the stages and wagons of earlier days. They shook, bumped and rattled along those hacked out, yet marvelously engineered roads, around rocks, trees and crevices to pack in, as much comfort as possible, the thousands who sought Eden in the Estes Valley whose lives would be forever changed at the end of their trail. The gates were open and people moved in, some to spend a brief period of time, others to make the Park their home. It had always been a strenuous effort to reach this high valley and it was due to the efforts of foresighted men and women that the journey of future passengers would be made considerably easier. Before 1872 the only means of transportation up to the Park and beyond was by a team of horses or mules, or the contentious yet adjustable pack burro that had much to do with opening the resources of an expanding western United States. Joel Estes and his sons cut one of the first trails that led others into their own personal discoveries using two-wheeled carts. But for passengers such transport was dangerous to the extreme with these light vehicles tumbling over on the steep ascents and descents that lead to the high country requiring only those of resolute spirit, and agility of limb, to make this journey. However over time the rough places were worn smooth by the ceaseless movement of stock, horse riders and increasing numbers of draught animals including some oxen whose hoofs cut deeply into the soft sandstone. They made permanent grooves in granite outcroppings as they bore their burden of timber, meat and occasional packets of mail destined for the expanding threads of civilization that wove a calico pattern across the Great American Desert. By 1872 teams of horses could pull four wheeled supply wagons along the improving trail as gun powder was increasingly applied to blow off rock cornices and protruding trees, thus allowing wider vehicles safer passage. There were three trails that one could use, all with varying degrees of danger and difficulty, to access the Park. One shorter but extremely steep route up canyons and around mountains, originated west of Loveland, Colorado. Another clawed its way west from Berthoud traversing a rudimentary tortuous terrain satisfactory for supplies and only the most determined wanderers up the Little Thompson creek to intersect the present Highway 36 near Meadowdale Ranch.

The third trail had its inception at Jamestown, Colorado, northwest of Boulder, tracing a route closely approximating the present Highway 7 through Allenspark, Colorado, along the foot of Long's Peak and later to descend into the Estes Valley.

In the summer of 1874 Alexander Q. MacGregor, while living with his family in the Charles Dennison home east of the Estes-Evans ranch, secured a charter from the territorial government of Colorado to build a toll road primarily for wagons bringing up equipment and basic supplies from a point in the foothills west of Lyons, Colorado. It began at Glen Evans, close to a geological formation called Steamboat Rock that early passengers described as having "its lower strata buried beneath the ground like a monster vessel parting the waves with its bow and rushing forward at tremendous speed." He and a small number of helpers laboriously constructed it in the late summer and early fall of 1874, its completion occurring in 1875. The road was open and he conducted business under the name The Estes Park Wagon Company with toll for the enterprise first collected at noon on July 28, 1875. The first keeper of the toll gate was Alonzo Parsons and the charge was one dollar per team, each way. However, as an encouragement for local travel, a discount was given of up to fifty percent "for regular users," with the receipts for the first three and one-half days amounting to $31.95. Later MacGregor amended his charter to enable him to change the location of the road to the extent that the majority of the present highway as we now see it emerging from Lyons is about on the same bearing and alignment as when he built it. However the early roads required the use of land closer to the streams inasmuch as contractors of that time had no equipment sufficient to tunnel through or around the rock barriers that we now hurriedly drive by without a thought to their original obstacles for the pioneer. One 1878 commuter recalls crossing the creek twenty-nine times before surmounting the heights that led down to the new hotel in the Estes Valley. If you look carefully you can still see these first efforts that afforded transport to the high country tucked away down by the streams. The toll road meandered up from Lyons, through Little Elk Park where toll was later paid at Minings' Toll House on the east side of the road and just north of Pinewood Springs. Then it wove a serpentine track up, down and what some passengers suspicioned sideways on the west flank of the Little Thompson Creek. It followed along a cleft in the hill, around Meadowdale Ranch and finally after a steep descent crossed the Big Thompson as the narrowing river effervescently departed the Estes Park valley with a final watery roar. The road terminated at the MacGregor Ranch recently established near the Black Canyon creek two miles north of the Estes Valley.

Mr. MacGregor sold his road franchise to Longmont interests around 1884 who recognized an enterprise of great potential. MacGregor intended to devote more of his time to ranching as tourists, even then, had a tendency to divert residents from their daily schedules. He was to become involved in many business ventures centered on his ranch commencing with the assembling of a saw mill powered by a water driven turbine plummeting down a 30 feet free fall on Black Canyon Creek. Now construction lumber became available to partially replace logs as the prime ingredient of the builder's trade. He served as a weather observer for the government, to record temperature variations and depth of snow and kept a small store, the first such commercial establishment in the Park, in one of his ranch buildings to provide tent campers with basic supplies. The dancing flames from those campfires dotting the plateau west of his grand meadow, a favorite subject for painters, could be seen miles away to conjure up visions of a distant Indian camp in the imaginations of eager visitors descending Park Hill. There was an improvement in the trail out of Loveland in 1875 or 1876 to reach the Estes Valley by means of a *new free road* as it was termed, absent of any toll charges, and it was situated about three miles south of the present day Big Thompson Canyon Highway 34. This roadway, constructed by some leading citizens of Loveland who did not desire their community to be bypassed by the increasing numbers of travelers journeying up the MacGregor Road, was financed by money raising efforts and donated labor. It took its name, Bald Mountain Road, from the geologic feature over which the road must find itself, passing through Rattlesnake Park to ascend Pole Hill to Diamond Spring, then twist its way precipitously around the mountain side into Mulligan Gulch. The Bald Mountain road was ballyhooed by its promoting troubadours as the answer to about anything that was ailing you. It soothed your nerves they said 'by a brisk jaunt through pine scent groves.' It allayed your back pains it advised by its 'lounge crafted padded seats that would lull you to a state of near bliss,' and getting to Estes Park was advertised as poetically as did Lord Byron speak of the way to Marathon in ancient Greece. "The mountains looks on the sea, not of mad waters, but of grand and glorious landscapes of plain, foothill, crag, mountain and rivulet. It is a wonderland, a little enchanted wilderness, fair as Calypso's Isle, yet weird and fantastic in some of its features," was printed in a promotional tract by those collaborators whose job was to move dollars up the trail by whatever words they must use to do it. Their entreats described in inaccurately free verse accounts of the stage rides on those putative paragons of craftsmanship but never referring to the true facts of the escapade upon this road. Who could not surrender to the scrivener's flowery digest of the trip that was dangerously misleading. "The stage over *Baldy* Mountain is but a few hours of brisk but comfortable ride in an easy, well-balanced, stage drawn by four spirited horses. It is a smooth, romantic ride in approved stages pulled by horses that are always in good condition." This was far from the truth. The road had always been inadequate for passenger traffic, only suitable for the cartage of goods. The mail by a postal contract over this road in the 1890s continued under the competent command of the Sprague Brothers, Abner and Fred, until Bald Mountain road no longer proved out as a main artery but a clogged vein into the Park. The brothers then moved their stage line to the Lyons road where they contracted with the Postal Service to pack the mail up to Moraine Park where a post office had been established for the many now residing in cabins and lodges expanding in the western regions of the Park.

The Bald Mountain Road was steep, with three very long and daunting drags up horrific grades that reached magnitudes approximating fifteen and twenty percent degrees of angle, unheard of for roads of our times that now strive for numbers in the range of three to seven percent, if that. In fact these sierra safaris proved so wearisome that the stage regularly halted only eight miles out from Loveland to fortify the flock, now somewhat more pusilanimous and clinging in demeanor, with a relief and refreshment pit stop at Cliff Cottages. The journey was not yet completed for the wagons must endure one more hair raising gulch. It was aptly called Solitude, no doubt reflecting the lonely feeling experienced by passengers who knew that there was no turning back on this one track *boulevard for the damned.* I'm certain the passengers likened old Solitude to Sir John Mandeville's *Valley Perilous.* Although the trip was not replete with 'dashing brooks and great calm canyons embowered with pine and spruce' vaunted by the stage owner's pamphlet clutched tightly by the ladies of the chariot as an icon of security, it was all worth while when they arrived at the highpoint overlooking the Estes Valley. The passengers gratefully were allowed time to get out of the wagon and what they beheld, Estes Park laying 1500 feet below them, brought exclamations that wiped away their previous fright. They all agreed that "we have never looked on grander scene!" as the sun was setting before them over a new world of rivers, streams, "a lovely garden of flowers surrounded by a belt of snowy peaks." From this climax point the wagonmaster in a grand crescendo, yet with some degree of trepidation not revealed to those seated behind him, worked his way down Emmons Gulch to more level terrain south of Estes Park. The problems in making the descent were difficult but surmountable, if one were careful, but it was the return trip that brought into play all the native abilities, strength and ingenuity of the driver. He urged his team of frothing beasts up that tortuous road, rife with unchartered hazards in arroyos, over ridges and around slippery sided mountains, with shouts that could compete with the lusty lungs of an army in full charge. The driver often followed behind the wagon and team in order to be ready to block the wheels when the team paused for a rest, not to do so might cause the whole kit and caboodle to career in tragic-comic display heavenward over rocks and precipices, shrieks and groans echoing down the canyon walls. Later a better pitch was located at Park View, avoiding Emmons Gulch and other places of hazardous lineage that had made true believers in God of driver and passengers. Old timers, themselves once passengers, remembered hanging on for dear life to the wagon -- wide eyed and with shouted prayers generously offered -- that plunged down the water courses substituting as roadbeds. That rite of passage then led through the present day Crocker Ranch to emerge upon the grasslands near the Thompson River.

Finally in 1878 a stage line was established by Longmont, Colorado banker Walter Buckingham, whose large Longmont Transfer Company had its home base in a large livery stable. His wagons made good time on this road as four-horse drawn Concord freight and passenger stages covered the distance of 30 miles to Estes Park in one day's travel on a very dusty road. The stage's prime destination was of course, Lord Dunraven's opulent new Estes Park Hotel recently opened to the public in 1877. As so often was the case with manor owners in Europe erecting small chapels for their own family's place of worship or for the guests, so did Dunraven build a chapel in the same style and color as his hotel. It was said that the chapel was regularly frequented by travelers giving thanks for safe deliverance from those chancy means of conveyance. The chapel was later intentionally burned down by the LeCoste Brothers, later lessees of the property, for a reason not disclosed. Now Estes Park was establishing itself as a destination of some substance rather than as a casual hunting and fishing camp as advertisements began appearing in the Denver newspapers that a visitor from Denver could make the trip up to the Estes Valley and back "with even one day for fishing, and in as little time as four days!" Another news item of 1881 from Estes Park stressed the fact that your every need could be met in this new mountain community. "To those who wish to camp out and want to buy their groceries, provisions and all things needed in camp life, they can be furnished them at the Estes Park Store which is conducted by Mr. M. H. Lammis, one of Longmont's young merchants, who has come among us to spend the season and to remain as long as business will justify. Judging from the amount of goods he is shipping in, he must intend to remain a while, at least, and from the amount of goods he is selling to railroad camps, ranchmen, camps, boarding-houses and others of the Park, we should decide that so far he had no reason to regret his venture. In short, any one coming here need not think but what all their wants can be supplied, for if what they need is not in stock at the Park store, it can be on hand by return stage, --from a toothpick to a pair of overalls." The west was shrinking to more manageable proportions as the world definitely was becoming lilliputian.

However this winding artery, now throbbing with reoxygenated carriage life, could hardly be classified as a road at all, more properly in the rating book as a widened trail. Yet as this was the primary entrance to the Estes Valley, passengers had to content themselves to a white knuckle experience hoping that their reward would be an earthbound paradise and not one of more celestial proportions. Messrs. Gilbert and Hubbell later took over the line with a modicum of improvements, yet the journey for early stage passengers resulted in unassigned and unexpected duties along the way. Willing or not, the male passengers were asked to assist the driver in removing rocks from the path of the stage and at times putting a stout shoulder to the wheels to extricate the coach from a deep hole or over sharp protrusion of obstacles recently revealed by wayfaring freshets of rain water. A change to fresh horses was made at a point twenty-three miles from Longmont so that the long haul could be made to the village of Estes Park by late afternoon. Sometimes these relay horses were found to have wandered down the side of a canyon in search of a tasty repast while waiting their assignment and travelers would have to spend a chilly night in the stagecoach as the driver and whomever he could commandeer wandered in search of these four footed truants. In the fall of 1883 a road was built from Lyons, Colorado, over Race Hill to connect with the Little Thompson River at a location artfully, if not accurately called Little Moose Park just east of present day Pinewood Springs, but its use was of short duration. A stage line owned by Messers Phetherbridge, Henry and Metcalf, that ran from Boulder to Lyons, was discontinued when the Burlington Railroad that same year extended its line from Denver to Lyons in hopes of capturing a new source of traffic. A fine hotel in Lyons, The St. Vrain and hosted by Mr. J. E. Godding, served the railroad trade, and others, who awaited the stage ride the next morning up to the Park. They could stay at the Burlington Hotel as well if they had been satisfied with the railroad service up to that point of time. The next spring Hubbell bought Gilbert's interest in what was then known as the Longmont-Estes Park Stage Line. Seeing the possibility for greater volume of travel with the advent of the railroad, he shifted his main facilities to Lyons and modified the name to the Lyons-Estes Park Stage Line. The twenty-five mile trip to Estes Park, although shortened in miles, still took a long half day and the road was steep, narrow and dangerous.

The subsequent owners of MacGregor's road, by devious means and a name change to Estes Park Toll Road Company, sought to extend that charter by tacking on another 20 years to the end of the original franchise term. Abner Sprague, then one of the primary lodge owners, together with other Park inhabitants angered over soaring toll charges that made no allowances for the poor traveler who had to pass this way, filed a lawsuit in 1899 challenging this effort. However, prior to the decision of the courts to which symbol of civilization many held in contempt, activists including Abner Sprague and J. E. Blair, banded together and pulled down the toll gates. The settlers had had enough of this shabby treatment by the new owners, --*flatlanders*, whose prime motivation was alleged to be pure greed. The matter was finally put to rest when the Supreme Court of Colorado affirmed the settlers' right of free passage over the road, the court's reasoning as presented by Sprague was that this new toll company had not constructed a toll road under a government franchise but merely utilized for profit a toll road constructed by others without expenditure of their sweat or dollars. A new owner for the stage line, W. F. Cantwell, came on the scene and replaced the equipment with eight-horse, steel spring coaches in 1900. These better constructed coaches clipped off almost an hour from the driving time, but the driving of those rigs, as well as occupying a passenger seat on such a cantankerous contraption, was no job for sissies. Those old days of the horse drawn stages were remembered by the old timers who at the very thought of a ride up to Estes brought a tingle along the spine. They could remember the extravagant stories of *creeping* Indians and all sorts of imagined dangers that lurked just behind the next tree or rock recounted by the driver who hid a demoniac grin behind his black bushy mustache. He urged on his steeds with a flourish of his long leather whip that caused the leaders to lunge toward the edge of the road as though they were going to tumble into the foaming water of a raging stream, perchance to roll the whole shebang of passengers and their portmanteaus down a precipice.

Other early road voyagers recalled roaring down the steep hills and around tight bends, lead horses on full gallop, the heavier wheel horses on a frantic trot. Passengers hugged each other in newly acquired friendships, hanging onto anything to keep them from proving correct the law of physics that moving bodies do not follow a curve but rather project themselves into space on a straight tangent to arrive at a point of no return, in this case onto rocks far below the road. It was a real thrill to come into the valley of Estes Park. In fact just getting there was enough of an exhilaration to last the whole vacation, some opined. Mr. Sprague had another remembrance of the trip up to the Park having little to do with the scenery that rushed by. "Mostly it will bring back the taste and smell of dust; dust in your eyes; dust in your mouth; dust in your lungs; up your nose, and all through your baggage, besides your body gritty with it from head to heels. The traveler reached his hotel too worn out and tired to take a bath in a wash basin (those days were before the freighting in of even the old tin bath tub), but to supper and bed, sometimes too tired to eat, after only trying to get the taste of dust out of your mouth and the smell from your nose, declaring before going to sleep that too much of such fun was plenty, that if ever civilization was reached again they would never leave a railroad when traveling." The stage trip was often beset with cold rain and hail storms with the result that all became wet and nearly frozen for lack of heavy wraps. Few thought it would be cold and climatically inhospitable in the mountains during the summer when only a few

28

thousand feet lower the toilers in the fields stood in the shade of a cotton-wood tree for cool relief. The kindly nurturing of the passengers was not a first priority of the stage owners nor did they expend great sums of money for creature comforts. It was their job to get their charges to their destinations in one piece, wet, bruised or frozen it mattered not. Often when the stage would slither around the curves on the wet, soggy roads, the frozen, gnome-like passengers didn't much care if it did upset. They surmised such incidents would start the blood circulating again to rewarm their torpid flesh. But despite all that they endured in reaching Estes Park, it was all worthwhile judging from the fact that after a month's stay in the Park most came back the next year having forgotten the discomforts of the trip, the bruises now soothed by fond memories.

Despite many changes of ownership coupled with promises of 'superior service' by hustlers for the numerous stage lines emanating from Longmont, Boulder and Lyons, service was inferior and equipment third rate. The typical stage coach in use by The Estes Park Stage Company as it subsequently called itself is not to be compared to the movie version romanticized in a John Wayne motion picture. Those deployed to reach Estes Park around the turn of the century were little more than large wagons containing three rows of seats, canvas covered, and as those criticizing the service said, were "propelled by overaged and undernourished quadrupeds." The canvas rolled down so far on the sides so as to obscure much of the heralded view. Many on board were heard singing as they raced by, words from religious songs such as 'We are on the road to Zion', or 'Going to the promised land', perhaps evincing an anticipation of a wonderful vacation ahead or only vocalized hope for divine reception if the driver was to prove inattentive to the dangers of the road. The Burlington Railroad proclaimed, in graphic stentorian headlines of 1900, outrage at its decreased revenue traced directly to the poor stage line service, vowing to handle its own stages. Cheers reverberated up and down the St Vrain Canyon to this welcome news for accidents had been so frequent that the newspapers strongly suggested that "the wretched equipment and management deserved of a new name, The Broken Leg Hill Line." Past and future visitors to the Park said they would boycott Estes unless a change were made to "insure decent treatment and safety to life and limb," with some people already in the Park and knowing of their own recent trip on unsafe vehicles, chartering their own stage service to take them to the valley by way of the Bald Mountain Road. The indignation expressed by the railroad soon proved illusory for by 1902 its own stage line proved no better in quality, especially lacking in comfort expected from those advertisements that had wooed them to the end of the line in Lyons.

Crowded conditions and poor springing of the heavy frames made this harsh, discomforting and inelastic twenty-four mile ride to the Park sufficient cause for anger, absent of accolades, for those stage owners whose promises of good service had proven false. It was not unheard of for the stage owners to require 'a little extra fee to get a private surrey' to make the identical trip for which payment had already been made for trumpeted nonexistent 'first class conditions.' In spite of all the bad press, the Burlington Railroad, then known as the Chicago, Burlington and Quincy Railroad, maintained a steady stream of activity conveying tourists to its terminus at Lyons where they put up with whatever horse drawn stage systems were available or shifted for themselves.

The disquietude in the traveling public sparked one small plutocrat to distant himself from the railroad as he advertised "We are not the company that has the contract with the Burlington Railroad, and we can provide comfortable surreys at a lesser cost!" Others arrived in increasing numbers on another railroad known by different names as the stages met these passengers in Loveland on a daily basis and in Longmont three times a week. Some newspapers referred to prominent passengers arriving in Loveland on the Colorado Standard Division of the Denver and Gulf Railroad, others naming it the Colorado Central, while those who said they were more accurate in such matters referred to it as the Colorado & Southern Railroad. Whatever was the correct name, the fact remains that thousands ventured up the St. Vrain and later the Big Thompson Canyons, first upon those horse stages, later in more comfort in a Stanley Steamer and its successor large White Motor Company manufactured buses to settle in for a summer's residency in wooden lodges that were emerging amongst the pines and aspens. Within a few years horses for the tourists' transportation to the Park would be looked upon as an unpopular alternative. The chugging, popping, soft seated Stanley Steamers floating on white puffs of hot air, would within a span of a bare few years occupy an improved road that reached the category of *highway* despite the dirt and mud that were no longer major handicaps to safe movement over these holiday byways now reaching greater significance.

A new road in 1901, the Big Thompson Canyon approach, was under discussion and a survey was strongly recommended to ascertain its feasibility. The main proponent of this road was Mr. Cornelius H. Bond, the Sheriff of Larimer County, Colorado, very much involved in the political apparatus of the county but completely honest and respected. The survey revealed a grade that would average 3 percent and never exceed 7 percent in any one place, traversing a distance of thirty miles on but a single track. The County Commissioners asked for bids, all to be rejected as too high except for one very low offer of W. A. Riley, a Loveland contractor. W. A. Riley had confidence in his engineering abilities but his financial judgment to complete the project for $24,000 would prove faulty as a later assessment of the true costs would reveal. The county was slow in paying him more than the first $9,200 of the contract after it was revealed that it would be nearly impossible to complete the road at such a low bid. The contractor and county were at an impasse, and after Riley's consultation with a Denver lawyer revealed that he owned the road until paid, he came up with a 'grand vision' for a new means of transportation into the Park. He would lay tracks on the rough road right of way and establish an electric railway, right up the nearly impassable Big Thompson Canyon. This certainly captured the county officials' attention with veiled alarm. Riley hired Abner Sprague, a self taught yet highly experienced engineer, at the time residing in Loveland, whose knowledge and experience had in part been gained by his association with railroads in Nebraska. He was to be the chief engineer of a company known as the Loveland and Estes Park Electric Railway. Because of lack of funding, and poor plans by the organizers, not the fault of Mr. Sprague, only a part of the road bed was passable to Estes Park in spite of promises of assistance from the Colorado & Southern Railroad that perhaps might have benefited the most by its completion. The commissioners, fearing that they would never get any kind of a road completed, and being somewhat over the barrel with a legal opinion concerning the road's ownership that would have to be adjudicated, Larimer County settled with Mr. Riley and took over the project promising 'excellent results.' That magnanimous gesture of support came up somewhat hollow as the county only staked the effort to $27,000 in tax revenues. Their reasoning for moving the road along to some form of culmination, it was rumored by contending parties, was to provide a better and quicker way for residents of Estes Park to reach the county seat in Fort Collins where they could serve on juries and pay their taxes. Politicians never change. A basic, one lane road opened to some degree in 1902 with better passage gained in the next few years. Within a few years the Union Pacific Railroad was bringing in passengers to its station in Fort Collins for transfer to three, nine passenger, steamers that met the train each day. After the excited tourists boarded their steaming carriages, the forty-five miles whizzed by in three hours as all eyes were on the lookout for the highly touted wildlife in the foothills and during the spectacular river portion of their route up the new Big Thompson road. When the new thoroughfare proved satisfactory for the new steam powered carriages, old Bald Mountain Road was abandoned, taking its proper place with nature to dwell alone with the now distant shrieks of former passengers still to be recognized in the winds whistling down those 'gentle hills.'

In 1905, those traveling north from Denver on the trains would depart Denver at 8 A. M and arrive in Estes Park about 5 P. M., with a change at Loveland to get on the horse drawn stage that stood waiting. The cost for this round trip available between May 15th and October 31st, including your rail and stage costs, was $6.50. A passenger was allowed one free piece of hand baggage, with other luggage charged out at the rate of 75 cents per hundred pounds. Freight was carted up for a flat rate of 50 cents per hundred weight. Mr. F. O. Stanley of Newton, Massachusetts, who was soon to carry on a pilot program with his flotilla of steamers up this new road, offered to complete the road to wider and smoother specifications in 1907 and take over the whole operations if he could secure an exclusive franchise from the county to carry passengers to and from the Park. His proposal was turned down as no monopoly was intended by country officials in their previous soliciting of solutions to a road left uncompleted. Eventually by push and pull, citizen's meetings and all of the finagling lobbying efforts for which American pressure groups are famous, the road was completed in 1920 to its present width by the use of impressed convict labor from the county pokey as well as through the efforts of local entrepreneurs. Now it was only a matter of time before Estes Park would feel the need to develop more lodging as private vehicles and small buses began using the roads from Lyons and Loveland up to the Park with more frequency. In fact at times there was so much traffic on this basic thoroughfare that often, when vehicles would meet going in opposite directions, one had to back into a wide turnaround area to allow passage. Heavy vehicles were said to come up the more steep inclines in reverse unable to pull their loads in forward moving gears. Bridges, some painted bright red, often were damaged by runaway loads of goods and passengers, and others were washed out in heavy rain storms, the water cascading down in frightful torrents that often leapt the roadway in The Narrows. The road was further improved in 1925 by a county appropriation of an additional $25,000 paid to a contractor who hired twenty Mexican workers to give the road base a better surface, and further widening and raising it to a higher level above the de-

31

fiant river as the agencies bringing up cargo increased in size.

When Mr. Stanley first arrived in the Park in 1903 he saw the potential for greatly expanding the use for the new Stanley Steamer previously developed by his brother F. E. and himself. The roads were adequate and horse drawn passenger contrivances were not what he envisioned for this struggling new community that had no functioning electrical system and only a poor excuse to call a water transmission utility. In this Twentieth Century community its required use of candles and kerosine lamps held it prisoner to a prior century. His many summers in this community would bring about many positive changes for which all agree shall forever redound to the eternal credit of this man from Maine, Mr. Stanley. In 1907 the first automobile stage service from either approach to the Park was commenced from Loveland and its scheduled time through the Big Thompson Canyon was completed in an incredibly rapid time of two and one half hours. Mr. D. O. Osborn and his two sons that year formed the Estes Park Auto Company with three, 5-passenger, touring Stanley Steamers in its small fleet that conveyed passengers and freight up the rough narrow road. Riding on Mr. Cantwell's stage line from Lyons to the Park in his sturdier coaches that claimed a shorter running time, even then was no picnic promenade. Stanley saw his opportunity when the stage line became available for purchase. The Stanley brothers, together with Oscar Peter Low of Estes Park, established the Estes Park Transportation Company in 1908, and they planned to use the highly popular Steamer eventually to convey new visitors to their hotel under construction on a high and scenic tract of land. The Estes Park Transportation Company literally got into gear in 1909 through the St. Vrain canyon from Longmont and Lyons using portions of the original MacGregor road as modified. Later this company would join in the competition on the road up from Loveland and commanded a respectable share of commercial traffic including meeting the railroading public at Loveland's train depot, a town then populated by 300 citizens. The roads were the prime responsibility of the two companies for there was little revenue from government or otherwise to maintain them in passable condition. These two vanguard transportation lines remained a popular alternative for the thousands of Estes Park visitors. Other efforts were inaugurated by two or three recently initiated automobile stage lines to the Park, including one from Fort Collins and others from Greeley and Boulder. There even was an attempt to convey the tourists to the Park from a round about way. A terrible road penetrated through the mountains from the south by way of the high altitude coal mining community of Ward, as its owners preferred to follow the high ridges rather than the lower crowded valleys.

The first Stanley Steamers used in the tourist trade in 1907 were small, five passenger affairs that gradually were lengthened to hold eight. With the advent of its grandest genus of models, twelve passengers could climb on board. The engine for the small variety of coaches, aroused to action by steam, generated 30 horsepower while for the larger model known as *the mountain wagon*, newer engines of 60 horsepower were designed for this *Type A Steamer*. As the engine was improved and the vehicle's capacity for passengers increased, so was the steamer able to lengthen its distance before requiring water supplementation. The first mountain wagons carried 30 gallons of water enabling it to propel the passengers, and assorted cargo hanging along the sides and rear of the odd looking contrivances, a distance of ten miles as it huffed its way up toward its acme of destinations in the Park. Then better efficiency was achieved requiring only one gallon of water for each mile traveled before necessitating a refill. With a mechanical refinement by the addition of a new Mayo radiator condenser, a tank of only 25 gallons of water would allow uninterrupted journeys of up to 150 miles. The steamer dyspepticly belched steam and smoke while dripping assorted liquids and it could be heard coming miles away, chugging away under a full head of steam to the accompaniment of whistling air that blew through the safety valves. For years after these behemoths ceased to be used, one could still find the old tanks and cisterns for the water adjacent to the modern highways that now serve this resort community. To show the acceptance of the Stanley and Osborn efforts, this published article appeared on July 19, 1913, a flashback to a freeze frame of previously uncomfortable passengers, struggling to remain on board a swaying omnibus pulled by tired horses from which they had no view other than of canvas curtains. "From being one of the most difficult resorts of access to the average tourist, which was the case only a matter of 6 or 7 years ago, Estes Park has rapidly grown to be one of the easiest to reach of all beauty spots in Colorado. It is in fact the most enjoyable of the one-day trips from Denver, although no one should attempt to see it in a day if there is the possibility of spending a longer time viewing its inexhaustible variety of scenery. The best part of it and the larger part of the journey, --the scenic part, is not made in a stuffy train, but must, perforce, be enjoyed by automobile. On the hottest days, the trip through the canyons is made without discomfort, the motion of the machines insuring a cooling breeze throughout the entire ride, while there are no obstructing car windows to shut off half of the wonderful scenery through which the road leads."

People often did not know what to expect as they emerged from the dusty train ride from further East, into a bright sunlight that shone down on a milling group of horses, wagons, boxes of goods, --and strange appearing, talking, motor cars that were arranged in military precision chugging and wheezing in a contented attitude. One young lady, it was reported in 1912, meant to hold the railroad ticket sellers to the exact letter of what they had assured her, and upon her arrival in Loveland, surrounded by suitcases, stood waiting for the appearance of her means of transport to the Park. "ALL ABOARD! FOR ESTES PARK!" went out the cry of the conductor of those giant Stanley Steamers, standing in shining array while ingesting their final gallons of aqua pura. She didn't move although it was obvious her next destination was the Park. The increasingly agitated bearded fellow, standing by the driver seated behind the wheel of his huffing partner, tried once again. "ALL ABOARD! This is the LAST auto to the Park!" He paused, hesitating as to what should be his next move. He sidled over to the young lady who appeared increasingly anxious as she looked about observing her fellow passengers dutifully seated upon the padded rows of seats. "Aren't you going to the Park?" he questioned with marked irritability the well dressed young woman who was confident of the plans made for her. "Oh yes, but I'm going by boat," she matter of fact-like explained. "But there **IS** no boat line that runs to the Park!" the conductor haughtily intoned. "There must be!" pulling out the railroad brochure attached to her ticket that trumpeted out in bold relief, and placing a well manicured index finger on the appropriate line that read *a line of steamers operates between Loveland and Estes Park*. The conductor grabbed the evidential brochure, examined it closely, then pointed his own less tended finger toward the waiting puffing leviathans and shouted, "THAT'S RIGHT MA'AM!, AND THEM'S THE BOYS! THEM'S THE STEAMERS!, STEAMER AUTOS!" She meekly folded the travel article and moved quickly to her place amidst competing giggles and mumbled advice from her fellow passengers.

Several other transportation companies used these roads in addition to the Stanley fleet. Private jitneys, as they were called, rubbed fenders with other ornate specimens of vehicles best suited for a traipse through a flat city park instead of a trip to a new mountain mecca that lacked sufficient oxygen for respectable internal combustion. In 1916 Osborn's company was absorbed into Roe Emery's Rocky Mountain Parks Transportation Company at which time the Osborns were running eighteen Steamers of various sizes in the Loveland to Estes Park shuttle including a freighting operation out of their building at the northwest end of Elkhorn Avenue. The transportation of tourists later became much more sophisticated and schedule oriented especially after Mr. Emery acquired the Estes Park Transportation Company from the Stanley family and his associates at that time, Clayton Newel *Casey* Rockwell and Charles Byron Hall, in 1916 or 1917. Roe Emery was born in Lake City, Minnesota in 1875, entered the trucking business and raised and trucked cattle from Wyoming down to Denver. While serving as the distribution manager for a large freight company that serviced James Hill's Great Northern Railway, he convinced the imaginative leader of the need for motorized transportation of the railroad's visitors to the new Glacier National Park established in 1910. Emery was very successful in this endeavor to open that National Park's gates to the eager tourists and, as a collateral consequence, the Burlington Railroad, now fetching passengers from Denver to Lyons, solicited Emery to achieve a similar commercial result for its tour enterprise in the brand new Rocky Mountain National Park.

From 1916 until 1952 Roe Emery acquired, owned or formed a number of transportation systems in Denver, Estes Park and throughout Colorado while at the same time constructing or acquiring a number of hotels to serve his burgeoning tour business. His first wife had been a sister of the owner of the White Motor Company, ironically his name being Black, and hence he converted his acquired fleet of Stanley Steamers and Coleman motor buses to a fleet of larger and more comfortable White Buses. In Glacier Park his big red, open-topped buses, were emblazoned with that Park's symbol, the Mountain Goat, while the new buses for Rocky Mountain National Park reflected the face of the Mountain Sheep, curly horns and all. Additional lines were purchased, leading to the Park from Greeley, Longmont and Loveland, by his Rocky Mountain Parks Transportation Company as well as other bus lines throughout Colorado including the Colorado Motor Way and the Yellow Cab Company of Denver. All of his companies were consolidated into one organization in May of 1927 under the name of Rocky Mountain Motor Company. Two of its directors were Charles Boettcher of a now nationally known Denver brokerage house, and the father of his second wife, Professor of Engineering at Colorado State University, Dr. L. G. Carpenter. Whether his first marriage ended by divorce or death is not clear, but in 1917 he married Dr. Carpenter's daughter, Estes Park school teacher and seventeen years his junior, Jeannette Carpenter. Their happy marriage was to end on a bloody highway

near Wahoo, Nebraska on January 14, 1943. Roe, and several of his managerial staff, were leading a fleet of new vehicles in procession from Des Moines,
Iowa to Denver's National Western Stock Show, with Jeannette in a vehicle
further behind. Whether one of the towed vehicles veered out of control or it
broke loose is not entirely clear, but her life came to an end at the age of 51
years. One of their daughters became the wife of former Congressman Morris
Udall of Arizona.

Rocky Mountain Motor Company's Estes Park headquarters, known as
the Transportation Center, was in the building on Elkhorn Avenue that is now
a warren-like den of tourist shops identified as the Park Theater Mall. In that
terminal was an office, storage facility, garage and dormitory for the young
men who piloted the buses and trucks of the system during the summer season
when most were in demand. Arthur K. Holmes, who at the time of his death
in 1954 was an officer of the company, followed by Byron Hall, Casey Rockwell from North Dakota who was previously involved with horse and wagon
transportation, and Roy McKnight were Mr. Emery's passenger and freight
transportation company managers in the village. They were very careful
whom they hired as drivers as a 1920s' form letter evidenced. Sent out for
references to applicants' solicitations, these questions always were asked. No-
tice what qualifications were most important in priority of inquiry. "Will you
please advise us as to his character, honesty, and personality. Also, we will
appreciate any information you can give us as to his experience and ability in
driving a White automobile." Roy McKnight's wife, Cleone, and he lived at
the company's hotel, the Estes Park Chalet south of Marys Lake in the winter
and in a company log house at the southwest end of Elkhorn Avenue. Cleone
had as one of her duties for the company making beds and seeing to the creature comforts of her group of young men who served as drivers and whose
alumni now successfully populate many of this country's leading companies,
offices and medical complexes.

The company's first buses had no self-starters so it was imperative that
once they were started they kept going. They also found their way along the
winding roads as the evening approached with gas powered lights, --if they
were working. After the company replaced the Stanley Steamers with its first
fleet of fourteen, eleven-passenger, gasoline powered White Motor Company
buses, they caused heads to turn as the shiny red buses whizzed by at the unheard speed of 20 miles per hour with neither windscreens nor top covers.
One of the rules of the road was impressed upon the new drivers. "Always
remember that the car going up hill has the right of way, and horses AL-
WAYS have the right of way." Old timers remembered 10 or 12 busloads of
excited tourists being loaded at one time at the Loveland station for the trip
up the dusty Big Thompson Canyon road, baggage tied on the rear outside
compartment. Upon their arrival at the hotels it was near impossible to identify what baggage belonged to whom because of the accumulation of acquired
dirt. Margaret Houston of Estes Park enjoyed a chuckle as she recalled an incident where the patience of a driver was strained beyond measure yet remained intact. One of his peevish passengers on a sightseeing trip up the old
Fall River Road was constantly complaining. "I don't like my seat! I can't see
any animals! This bus goes too fast! Why can't you stop longer for some
good pictures?" The young driver's courtesy to this passenger took a devilish
turn at this last assault and he requested his nemesis to take a seat in the back

of the bus, --way back by the windows adjacent to the luggage rack that extended out from the rear of the vehicle. "That's the best place to get pictures!" he shouted down the aisle. Then, as was the usual procedure in order to negotiate the hairpin turns up the steep road, he backed the bus to get a better angle by which to make one especially tight turn. At this precipitous point the mountain drops away from the road in breathtaking plunges of many hundreds of feet to the next level of road surface below. When he had backed the bus so that the rear end hung suspended in the air over this abyss, he set his brake. "Take all the pictures you want. I'm in no hurry," he told the crank. He heard no further complaints from the sweating, red faced man, and western justice was achieved with no loss of life.

Upon the opening of the transcontinental road over Fall River Pass in 1920, through the efforts of local politicians, the Chamber of Commerce and the back breaking toil of convict labor, Estes Park and the newly opened National Park now were really on the maps of America in bold type and receiving attention from travel agencies and tour representatives throughout this country and abroad by the use of the 'world renowned skyway' from Estes Park through Rocky Mountain National Park. A regular schedule for excursions up Fall River Pass was established by the transportation company, and shortly thereafter the company secured the exclusive franchise from Captain L. C. Way, then the Superintendent of the new National Park, for the rights to convey tourists through the Park. This action was to secure the enmity of one who labored long for creation of the National Park, Enos A. Mills, as we shall later observe. By 1930 the Big Thompson road, now the primary approach to the Estes Valley, was selected to receive federal appropriations and as the result the Forest Service contributed $100,000 from its budget to improve the road up to the boundary of the new National Park. The next year a bill in Congress to appropriate an additional three million dollars for significant and meaningful upgrading of the road, already outdated when the first chugging buses loaded zealous patrons demanding what they had been promised by the ticketing selling railroads, failed to receive approval. The country was in a state of depression and struggling to pay its bills. The local chamber of commerce looked to its own state government with palms outstretched and uplifted in solicitude. Finally state aid was secured in a sum adequate so that by August of 1937 the new Big Thompson highway was completed to federal standards and shortly thereafter took its place on the national road network as U. S. Highway 34, later to intersect to the west with U.S. Highway 40 at Granby, named for Granby Hillyer of Lamar, Colorado, lawyer friend of tunnel builder David Moffat.

With the opening of the summer season of 1938 the appreciative citizens of Estes Park celebrated one entire weekend, flags flying on light posts and faces alight in gala festivity, to commemorate the official opening of the Big Thompson Highway. An elaborate parade briskly moved down Elkhorn Avenue with two of Estes Park's oldest and most respected citizens, Abner Sprague and F. O. Stanley, as the grand marshals of the event. Mr. Sprague, then 88 and Mr. Stanley who was nearing 89, had planned on driving in one of Mr. Stanley's famed Steamers in which parade would be exhibited all forms of transportation used in evolving the open meadow of the Upper Thompson River valley from a place where elk grazed to a tourist mecca. But at the last moment this respected relic had another idea by which this day, and its cast iron heart, would be remembered. After previously negotiating thousands of miles of nearly nonexistent mountainous road beds while portaging untold numbers to happy memories, it wouldn't start. It seems ironic that now, after all it had gone through, it was unable to make the short trip down a modern paved street. One of its valves had sprung a leak. There was not the needed thirty minutes to regain its lost steam pressure before the parade band started down the street to frenzied *hoorays* and *huzzahs* from the crowd. So Mr. Stanley and Mr. Sprague led the gathering by riding in a modern automobile which had driven into the Park ostensibly by way of a highway their pioneering spirits and foresight had brought to fulfillment.

Estes Park had traveled many difficult roads in its drive to respectable maturation. The journey started with the tired feet of the solitary trapper, the small cart that brought in simple fare, that rough trip in neck wrenching wagons, the improved stages with padded seats and ultimately to the unforgettable red buses with a schedule to keep that brooked no interference from man nor beast. Correction! The beast did have the right of way on the road in the Estes Valley. Finally in droves the private autos that now compete for diminished parking space arrived essentially to replace the monopolistic public conveyances of a bygone time, and the lodges and local citizenry even more duly prospered. As a point of historical perspective, at the time the Estes Valley was making movements to locate itself on some map as strangers straggled into a vast new horizon mostly populated with wild animals and widely scattered homesteading visionaries, Alexander Graham Bell was placing the first call in 1876 over his new invention, the telephone, to an assistant in another room. "Mr. Watson, come here. I want you." The first telephone line connected Estes Park to Lyons and other parts of America in 1900. Similar words, now with the arrival of such civic advocates such as F. O. Stanley, would come to be repeated by the growing numbers of cottage and lodge owners, commencing with Griff Evans standing in front of his little cabins 'out back' to the manager in his grand foyer of the most elaborate of the hotel men's trade, The Stanley Hotel. "Come and stay with us, - -we want you!" echoed from the lodges built for tourists, - -and they came. But from 1932 onward, the roads for those favorite hideaways for hot and dusty travelers in the National Park led downhill as we shall see.

A. Q. MacGregor And His Road,
1876 (EPPL)

Four-Horse Team On Lyons Road, 1890 (Mills)

Coming To Estes In Style, circa 1890s (EPTG)

Toll Gate At Minings Ranch On Lyons Road, 1892 (EPPL)

Park Hill At Top Of Lyons Road, circa 1900 (Mills)

Mules On Lyons Road Haul Lumber Late 1890s (Mills)

A Welcome Drink On Lyons Road, Late 1890s (Mills)

Big Thompson Canyon Road, circa 1903
by Purcell (McDC)

Steamers on B. T. Canyon Road,
circa 1908 (Private)

Mountain Steamers Leaving Loveland Depot, 1912 (RMNP)

Transportation Center In Estes Park, circa 1920s (Mills)

Bus Tour On High Drive, 1928 (Mills)

End Of The Road On Fall River Road, 1922 (F. J. Francis)

Breaking Through Near Fall River Pass, 6-13-23 (Mills)

Digging Out Fall River Road, 6-13-23 (Mills)

Rangers Guide Bus Tour On Fall River Road, 1928 (Mills)

Tillman Carter, 1934, First Commercial Cargo Over Trail Ridge Road,
Who Fifty Years Earlier Had Guided A Pack Train Over This Pass (Mills)

Buses Await Snow Removal, Fall River Road 1925 (Francis)

Rangers Escort Bus Through Big Drift, June 1928 (Mills)

Bus Tour On Fall River Road, 1926 (EPHM)

Horseshoe Park And Trail Ridge Road, circa 1935 (EPHM)

Horse has Right-Of-Way on Fall River Road, circa 1920s (Mills)

"Cooling Off" With a View Near Summit, circa 1920 (Mills)

Tour In White Motor Bus At Rock Cut, circa 1935 (EPHM)

Bear Lake Road, circa 1940 (EPHM)

Freelan O. Stanley And Abner E. Sprague, 1938 (EPTG)

CHAPTER III - OPEN FOR BUSINESS

MacGregor Ranch, Hupp, Rowe, Ferguson, And Estes Park Hotel

*Climb The Mountains And Get Their Good
Tidings, Nature's Peace Will Flow Into
You As Sunshine Flows Into Trees. The
Winds Will Blow Their Own Freshness Into
You, And The Storms Their Energy, While
Care Will Drop Off Like Autumn Leaves.*
John Muir, 1901

What were the reasons these first tourists hazarded their bodies and property to be pummeled about in the maelstroms churned up by the plunging Concord stages and their successors? What could possibly be the allure for them to leave their prim and proper residences with all of the built in comforts, trading those even temporarily for a little room, heated for the most part with a pot bellied stove, and the hand fashioned wooden bedstead piled high with blankets when the heating source was banked for the night? And what about the biffy out in the shadows of a grove of Ponderosa pine, often three steps too far. More especially, why would any sane person sojourn to an area where the breathing was more labored, human assisting amenities few and submit oneself to listening in the enveloping darkness to the howl of the coyote that demanded an explanation for your presence in this discovered aerie of eagles? The answers to these somewhat whimsical questions that border on the subjective perhaps were more relevant in the pre-1900s times. However I might suggest those answers may be similar for these more sophisticated days. Imagine you are in Rocky Mountain National Park now and allow your mind to drift with the flow of that bright, chuckling little stream near where you sit relaxing. You clutch a sandwich, and a cold soft drink refrigerated in a can wedged behind a rock in the brook, and share your solemnity with no other human being. The sun warming your back filters through aspen trees framing in artistic composition the face of Hallett's Peak leaning out to perceive the happenings below in Bear Lake.

You may arrive at a rationale for your own choice of sanctuary, but I direct you to a travel report dated 1880 wherein its reasoning might approximate your own more than one hundred years later. In re-examining my own feelings when I first visited this Estes Valley to share the attic room of the old McGraw Guest Ranch out Devils Gulch Road, I find agreement with this early day assessment. I was glad I had come then, and doubly happy to have been fortunate enough to have seen some of those old lodges before they were gone. In that 1880 account it heralded valid reasons to forgo some of those past comforts, for a too brief period of time in God's own country, comforts that even now can destine our lives to surrendered complacency.

Water: "The absolute purity of the water fed by mountain springs! A man has little desire to drink anything else while here." **Proximity to services**

yet removed to tranquility: "Only 25 miles from the rails, yet secluded and with daily mail the sojourner may be near and yet far from the active world." **Excellent weather**: "Climate is wonderful with a pine bracing atmosphere whose nights are cool and pleasant and the days always have a cool breeze blowing." **Few mosquitoes and no poisonous snakes**: "You can sleep out of doors with impunity for the ground is usually dry, and free of insects and reptiles." And finally, granted more true for the quantity then than now because of revised National Park Service policy yet available if one is willing to expend a few more calories in that most noble of quests, **Fishing**: "The supply is inexhaustible and nowhere can there be found better opportunity for catching them."

Where did they go for rest, refreshment and to acquire a reverence for this multidimentioned retreat of nature? They first pitched their tent at the camp sites provided by the ranchers, squeezed into the few cabins sprouting up on the rocks and rills, or if you had the money you asked your driver to please deliver you to the new hotel near the river. Later you adopted a little cabin as your own that pioneer families were erecting, guided by their evolving philosophy attributed to practicality --"If you are going to be pestered by strangers who come and want this or that, --then ask for a meal, some fishin' worms and all that sort of stuff, you might as well have them stay a while and make a little money for your efforts." The clusters of 'neat little cottages' observed by that 1880 reporter, that rose up all over flowered glades and forest embraced moraines of the Park, were to mature into the lodges located in dells, as one wrote home "appearing like happy valleys that peep up fresh and winning as a pansy face." Those havens of realized dreams, whose old box camera photos, capturing odd looking, wooden sided, flower potted, elk horn mounted, kerosene lamped, warm and welcoming guest lodges, were hung as prized portraits on a kitchen wall at home or took up privileged places on hallowed pages in well worn albums evincing once happy times. It is impossible to describe all the hostelries, lodges and quaint resorts that meant so much to thousands of former guests, such as the couple who silently renewed wedding vows while seated on a porch rail glorifying in the last glow of a sunset behind a distant ridge, --or the young couple who boosted cowboy booted children into oversized saddles atop a paint pony, --or perhaps the shy single girl who found her future mate while in his arms as they pranced about in square dancing togs. To say I will discuss all of those cherished destinations of the vacationing public does disservice to those large or small lodges that perhaps were short lived or were not privy to an incisive evaluation that survived to find itself edified in an historical record. If I am presumptuous in my facts, opinions or grasp of history, chalk it up to poor memory, lack of substantive data leading to accuracy, or an effort to make a complicated story enjoyable.

My profound intent is to instill within you a sense of affinity to, and an awareness of, generations of honest service gratefully extended to tourists who came expecting a room and a meal but who received from whose pioneering lodge owners so much more. They may have purchased the use of a room or a horse, but they received probably more than they deserved, certainly more than was expected, --for no extra charge. Call it respect and decency, friendship and knowledge, roaring fireplaces and great food, millions of stars shared with those who knew the great stories of this land. What would I term that which a guest received from those long gone lodge owners that came with the price of the room?   Some define it commitment, I prefer to call it love.

THE MACGREGOR RANCH

The first addresses in the Park from where a traveler could mail a vacation post card was the MacGregor Ranch as mail arrived from Longmont each Wednesday on the stage and returned to the valley on Thursday.   The view from the ranch, and the Estes Park Hotel of which I will write about in more detail, was exceptional to which fact an early day guest allegorically attested as a true Republican.   "On looking up to Long's Peak, notches in solid rock look like stair steps at a distance of 12 miles away although they are five to six hundred feet in height.   Even a Democratic Presidential nominee would feel his insignificance in the presence of such a magnificent guardian."   Alexander Quinter MacGregor to whom I have made reference, first came to Denver, Colorado in 1869 as a lawyer from Milwaukee, Wisconsin to try his hand at the practice of law where it was first necessary to obtain credentials for admission to the bar in the Territory of Colorado.   Maria Clara Heeney, of Black Earth, Wisconsin, met her future husband in Colorado in 1872 and that same year returned to Wisconsin to be married.   Mr. MacGregor appears to be a tolerant man for when the young couple returned to Colorado, then moved up to the Estes Valley, his wife brought along her mother.   Mrs. Georgianna Heeney, a woman of independent means and temperament, filed on her own homestead adjacent to her daughter and son-in-law, perhaps to keep an eye on her daughter who was eleven years younger than her husband.   The MacGregors as a married couple arrived in the Park around 1874, although the original homestead claim of 160 acres was filed upon in 1873.   While laboring to erect a *proper* home after vacating their temporary tent housing on the ranch, they briefly resided in the Charles W. Denison home while Alex at the same time labored on his toll road.   The remaining twenty-two years of his life were devoted to many trades useful to the fifteen or twenty families who in 1875 and 1876 shared in the establishment of homes in the Park.

When he came to Estes Park, MacGregor intended to ranch and raise livestock, not practice law, and to that end completed his home around February of 1875 with the help of a face now familiar to many newcomers, the mountain man of the valley, hunter, guide and fisherman, Hank Farrar. Alex's successful effort in road building was his reasoned response to a recognition that neither he, his neighbors, nor those who would follow would fare very well without better ingress and egress for their wagon loads of needed supplies and their own products destined for the masses now circling up their permanent wagons in the lower valley towns.   To the MacGregors were born three sons.   The first, bearing a name appreciated by Georgianna Heeney, was George, born in 1875 followed by Donald in 1878, and finally Halbert ten years later in 1888.   For a short time the family catered to the ever increasing number of travelers who found their way up his new road from Lyons.   Initially the MacGregors provided a hillside for many of the tents and covered wagons that fanned out through the Park.   One camper's diary exemplifies the joy experienced by so many who were privy to a long ago campfire, ashes

40

that have long since grown cold yet the memory of which still sparks the flames to life in retrospection. "The greatest rivalry amongst campers seems to have been in the matter of camp fires, each party striving to create the largest blaze. The white tents and wide awnings gleamed through the dark pines and the blaze of the crackling camp fires threw into bold relief the picturesque groups of men, women and children. Never was a more contented, jolly set of mortals that ever sniffed mountain air than were we."

In those early years of the MacGregor Ranch, in order to make ends meet, the family like other small ranchers who raised varying crops of wheat, oats, rye and barley, began taking in paying guests from seven to nine dollars per week including room and board, and their washing thrown in with the family wash if there were time and space at no charge. But an extra fifty cents per day was added on for your horse, but you fed your own critter. Around 1876 a post office was established at the ranch, the first post office in the Park. His wife, known by her middle name Clara and an accomplished painter with several of her pictures hanging in art museums and the library of the City of Denver, became its post mistress. It was said that "In Mrs. Mac-Gregor's home, culture and refinement are not far from strangers for the hum of the sewing machine and the silvery notes of the piano are heard here." A store was added to the ranch that provided supplies for those camping about as well as other ranchers who rode out to pick up their mail. The store had a reputation for a good selection of fishing tackle, and by a contract with Mr. Hildreth their guests were provided with ponies to ride the inspiring trails that originated from the ranch, seeking out new discoveries in those lofty provinces that were to them, and us, sublimely endowed with special qualities. On one such ride his guests discovered and allegedly named a lake, "--whose appearance of a natural lawn blooming in mid-summer, surrounded by rock and ice amidst such frigidity and desolation," dubbing it Lawn Lake. Its ice blue waters more recently were defamed by man's poor stewardship, the result leading to horror when a dam tacked onto it in 1911 by Hugh Ramsey burst on July 15, 1982.

Mr. MacGregor, known to his friends as Alex or Mac, built a small saw mill that I previously reported that could produce between three and four thousand board feet of lumber a day. By 1880 the ranch was 1200 acres in size, and through additions of subsequent homestead claims by his sons and Mrs. Heeney and prudent purchases, it grew to well over 1,700 acres. Their home was enlarged, a second home erected, and cabins were added so its lodging capacity was sufficient for thirty guests. Alex then set to work sawing large amounts of timber for lumber he required for a new barn and other ranch structures. Chickens stepped warily about, alert for brighteyed weasels hunkered down by a rock in readiness, as well as did the pampered dairy cattle on guard for coyotes. This domestic stock was counted upon by the guests, as well as to provision the store with milk, butter and eggs as was the garden that added garnishment of fresh vegetables to the tables of meat and fish. Wild raspberries, strawberries, currents and gooseberries, that grew in abundance amongst at least forty varieties of identifiable perennial flowers, frequently graced the dining tables, as was the case with so many of the ranchers' homes throughout the Park. What did those guests think of this bucolic, backwoods, end-of-the-road address by the waters of the Black Canyon Creek? "Wonderful!" One wrote home that "Soft breezes sigh through the

41

pines in sweet cadence that keep everyone cool and happy. This is far preferable to the city hotel life with its intense heat."

Alex had studied law in Wisconsin and when he arrived in Denver worked himself into the position of Clerk of Arapahoe County Court and within ten years of his arrival in the Park served one term as a County Judge. *Judge* MacGregor, as he often respectfully was recognized, worked hard for his community. These MacGregors were business people and it soon was becoming clear that crops and livestock raising was less trouble and more profitable than what could be derived from the vagaries of a traveling public. Of course cattle can prove contentious subjects for discussion with the neighbors as MacGregor's black Angus herds often drifted about the Park, especially over to the ranch resort of W. E. James. Friends and visitors were always welcome, as they are even today long after the last MacGregor was laid to rest. It was a sad day in the Park in 1896 when the report came of Alex MacGregor's death, while on a mountaineering and prospecting trip with his son George northwest of the Park, when it was his misfortune to be in the wrong place when an errant bolt of lightning sought to ground itself. At the time, George was enrolled in the mining school at Golden, and young Halbert was only eight years old. Thus it fell to Donald to leave his employment in Denver with the hardware and machinery company of Hendrie & Bolthoff to take over the management of the ranch with his mother. Grandma Heeney continued living with the family until her death in 1901. Donald purchased the interests of his brothers in 1909 and in 1910 and moved his wife, Minnie Maude Koontz MacGregor, and six year old daughter Muriel to the ranch to make Estes Park their permanent home. By this time the ranch was almost exclusively devoted to raising cattle and crops.

Donald met Minnie Maude, the daughter of a prosperous family who had struck gold in Georgetown, Colorado, in Denver where the Alex MacGregor family lived during the winter months of the late 1880s. Their family homes were not far apart, and after a period of courtship they were married in 1903. As an interesting side reference, Donald's father and his future father-in-law both were to die in 1896. Their only child, Muriel Lurilla MacGregor, born in 1904, graduated from Denver University Law School in 1936 to became a lawyer although her practice at the ranch was devoted more to office work, wills and bill collection. She buried her parents, who both died in 1950, in the family mausoleum located on the ranch, and in which she too was interred after her death in February of 1973. Muriel never married, preferring to devote her time and best efforts to the management of the ranch and the care of her beloved cattle and pets. Her later years were plagued with ill health, limited income from a ranch she refused to sell, and she was conscious of the fact that her neighbors and town folk looked askance at her independent and solitary lifestyle. They particularly exhibited irritation at her inability to restrict her black Angus cattle to the ranch. Donald MacGregor, his wife and Muriel lived long enough to establish a successful mountain stock ranch, and through Muriel's Last Will and Testament the present day MacGregor Ranch Trust was established to preserve important vestiges of a venerable working ranch. She now lies close to her parents on her ranch and perhaps watches with pride all the school children who enjoy the MacGregors' homestead, and her beloved cattle that in life gave her joy and some small measure of melancholy. To see the ranch, the second and enlarged home having been reworked into a museum illustrating the lives and times of the MacGregors including their books, pictures, furniture and Nineteenth Century ranch ambience, turn north from the majors roadway that avoids downtown Estes Park on to MacGregor Lane and continue on for one-half mile. The ranch entrance beckons you in for an educational experience that is well worth the time shared with personable people who enjoy their work.

Let me pause for a moment from my discussion of the early lodging facilities associated with the Estes Valley to refer to three families who were in the Park at the same time as the MacGregors and are worthy of remembrance. I wish to commend them to you as pioneers who assisted in establishing the Park for what it truly is today. Their names are frequently mentioned in historical documents and who are examples of those who came to challenge a wide open land for a chance at success in a castellated country shared with soaring spirits.

JOHN HUPP

Born in 1820, he and his wife Eliza, ten years his junior, were living in Otterville, Missouri with their seven children in 1875. Learning of the possibility of acquiring free land in a territory ripe for statehood, he gathered the family together and rode the boards of their wagon into the Estes Valley in the early summer of 1875. It was a long trip west for John Hupp, arriving at a time in his life when most men having reached 55 years of age were content to engage in less stressful activity. However, he was as determined as any of the younger men he met on the trail to own land, and to this purpose staked out several claims on Beaver Flats, an area a few miles west of the small cluster of humble abodes that later would assume more prominent proportions as the Town of Estes Park. John was a peaceful man and, after being informed by Dunraven's emissaries that he was on *their property* and lacking knowledge to offer up much of an articulate rebuttal, he moved higher up the draw to a small hollow then locally referred to as Beaver Park. In this area, ascertained to be about as far away as possible from Dunraven's roving herds of crown branded cattle, he was determined to resist any further threats to remove him as an intruder from this property. His move proved fortuitous, as he was left alone and water in ample supply for farming and cattle raising was found at his new homesite in a basin we now know as Upper Beaver Meadows. The Hupps had four daughters and three sons, all of whom joined in the construction of their half log and half frame, two story, home close to an abundant spring that still flows free in cold refreshing profusion. Unfortunately, John was to live but two years after their home was completed, expiring in the cold month of December in 1877. Eliza nearly singlehandedly maintained the home and worked the land for nearly twenty-two years longer and always had a spare room for someone who rode up to admire the flowing creek in their meadow filled with beaver ponds and loads of fish. Francis, or Fannie as she was nicknamed, remained at home to assist her mother after the other children had departed. Eliza joined her husband at their new abode eternally positioned, in 1900, and strangely the young woman also died quite suddenly the following year.

These three members of the family vowed never to depart from their land, and their wishes were granted. They lay buried nearby on a gentle slope where the crisp wind blows the curing grass about their heads, out where their cattle had roamed but now claimed by stately elk who contest for territory every fall with the high pitched squeal of their bugles. A grave marker was erected, possibly the only one in Rocky Mountain National Park, through the efforts of a grandson and the compassion of former Park Superintendent Allyn Hanks who deemed it appropriate to have the family's selected red granite marker erected to the lasting memory of those enduring pioneers. It reflects their names with the first rays of the morning sun that still shines upon the land on which they loved, laughed and survived the storms of an ever changing landscape in pursuit of a happiness that often proved elusive. I believe this marker is emblematic of all the hardships and achievements of those who came before us to the Estes Valley. One of their sons, Charles, who was a valued associate in many business endeavors in the village, also was employed at the Horseshoe Inn where he served as the winter caretaker. He would have been pleased to know that, like his parents and sister, he would remain to the very end near to the land that had meant so much to his family as he was found dead in bed at the Inn by Ranger Jack Moomaw on April 4, 1926 of an apparent heart attack. The name Hupp also is still emblazoned on a hotel sign on Elkhorn Avenue, the efforts of one of their sons, Henry, of whom I will write more in a later chapter. Other pioneers preferred to remain forever in their mountains. including children of lodge owners who lie sequestered near giant old trees that were once small and young as these children would ever remain. There are others, whose names and crumbled monuments are known only to God, who lie buried near to where they were considerate of the needs of strangers, their guests, and where they now listen to the soft tread of a doe and her fawn slowing passing by in silent respect. There was one early resort owner's ashes that were ceremoniously scattered to the scudding wayward winds high atop Trail Ridge Road as recent as 1965, and it is interesting to read that the ashes of a former Superintendent of this National Park also were scattered in the Park in 1973 at one of his favorite spots for meditation. Whether we have lived here for most of our lives or only glimpsed briefly into the ethos of the Estes Valley, we all leave something of ourselves behind when we depart briefly, or forever. I suggest that we leave our own hearts and souls in these mountains where many of us initially discovered them. They seem more at home here with kindred spirits.

The Hupp property was sold to Pieter Hondius, Sr. after Fannie died at which time he erected a fine set of ranch structures west of the Hupp's homesite. He subsequently leased the land to Walter Jones who raised hay for the horses of the Elkhorn Lodge of which Hondius's wife was one of its owners. The land and all improvements were purchased by the National Park Service in March of 1932 for $140,720 and all structures of the Hupp and Hondius families were destroyed in 1933. When you turn west, off of the lower reaches of Trail Ridge Road, drive or better yet hike in about a quarter of a mile to a small parking lot on your left. Cross the dirt road, mosey up the gentle south facing grassy slope and walk directly north a short distance to where you can see a large juniper tree. The still beautiful stone and marked graves come into view. Then continue to the end of the dirt road into Upper Beaver Meadows. From the parking lot, cross over the little bridge under which a garrulous silver stream in rapid descent from the Ute Trail seeks to flee from the vanilla scented giant Ponderosa grove. It has much to tell you of its life shared in this alpental with those dear friends now resting in the sunlight upon the hill not so far away. A little further down the trail to the south you may see an old spring that offered up its life giving cold waters to nourish man, beast and emerging crops of the past. This is the approximate location of some of the Hondius buildings and if your feet are adventurous they might carry you further to the west, up a rocky precipice, where in distant times a battle for turf was played out between the Utes and Arapahos. On your way back to the busy highway to continue exploring the Park, perhaps you might share a quiet moment or offer up a silent prayer at the little memorial to those who first loved this broad valley that you now more fully appreciate because of their sacrifices. John, Eliza and Fannie would like that, --still to be remembered.

ISRAEL ROWE

This dynamic personage also joined in the growing rush of settlers for land and opportunity in the Estes Valley as word spread East. He arrived in 1875, together with his wife and two small children, and contracted to work for Alex MacGregor on the new toll road. While acting as assistant foreman of the road gang, for whom Mrs. Rowe cooked all of the meals over an open fire, he located land that now comprises much of the existing Crocker and Meadowdale Ranches adjacent to Highway 36, --the Lyons road. The land claimed was at least 2,000 acres in size, though not all went to deed, on which he constructed a nine room home and a number of out buildings at the base of Mount Olympus. It was near to that homestead that the old Bald Mountain Road made its debut as a point of entrance into the Estes Valley, and quite probably his children, Charles Judson, age five, and Dora, age two, at play on their porch waved to the driver and excited passengers who clung to whatever was available while straining their eyes for a hopeful end of a long, dusty trip. The Rowes would willingly find a place at their table for strangers who needed a friend, advice and a meal. Mr. Rowe was an excellent hunter and guide and confronted these mountains with knowledge and experience that few others could claim. On one of his investigative trips in the Lumpy Ridge area north of Estes Park, he came upon a lovely pool of water in a cleft of rock. It compared in quality of color, cut and clarity to a gem setting, to which he bestowed the name, Gem Lake.

Mr. Rowe on another trek in pursuit of additional trails and destinations of beauty to which he could escort others, stumbled upon a vast area of ice and snow, the location of which he revealed to William L. Hallett. Hallett, a summer resident, also had a fervent curiosity to discover all the hidden secrets tucked away in the front range of the Rockies. Mr. Hallett, while examining this unusual formation of ice and snow recessed between two mountain masses, a veritable frozen grotto, fell into a crevasse from which he succeeded in extricating himself only by an act of providence and his strong will to survive. Ascertaining that this ice mass was unique, pushing to the back of his mind his near fatal association within its grasp of prismatic glistening ice, he applied himself to gain for it scientific recognition. Through his efforts, and the technical assistance of such men as Professor George H.

Stone of Colorado College for whom the Arapahoe region known to them as Bear Paws was renamed to Stones Peak, the formation met the clinical scrutiny of scientists thereby taking its place in the list of North American glaciers. For years thereafter it intrigued glacierists who came from near and far to observe this frozen formation thought impossible so far south in the Rockies. The glacier from 1886 until 1932 bore the name of Hallett's Glacier. Later it was renamed following authenticating research in recognition of its true discoverer. Hence this glacier remnant, from a time distanced ice age, remains for contemplation on the north end of the Park by its rightful name, Rowe Glacier.

Rowe sold his property to John Stuyvesant, a descendent of peg-leg Governor Peter Stuyvesant of New Amsterdam, now New York City, and moved to a small cabin near his former employer on the MacGregor Ranch. Later he shifted again to another home, no longer extant, on the present site of The Stanley Hotel. He guided for the rich dudes who inhabited the suites of Dunraven's Estes Park Hotel as well as hundreds of more modest means who sought fulfillment by identifying with nature's macrocosm removed from all claims of man's evanescent achievements. He continued to be an influence in the community for many years, and those who located in this valley sought him out for his wisdom of these mountains in his *outdoor university* to arts and sciences from which he graduated with a doctorate degree in humaneness. His children were tutored together with the children of W. E. James, on whom I will dwell in the next chapter, but later he moved his family to Longmont in 1882 so that the children's educational needs could best be met. He, like many who dwelt long in partnership with nature on her terms with no complaints, learned that a life lived in close proximity to other human beings in a valley town was not living. He needed space, wide open vistas and a trail that led to new discoveries. Thus he returned to serve as a guide in the Estes Valley and in southern Wyoming until 1884, and while upon a late fall hunting and guiding expedition he contracted pneumonia and died in Medicine Bow, Wyoming. Israel Rowe was a true mountain man and proud of his abilities as a guide for others. He pointed a way to a new trail but always in the footsteps of ethical conduct and concern for his fellow man, the animals that shared his mountain tops and his Estes Valley that had made his life of dedicated service to the tourist and his wide spread of neighbors all possible. So to him I say, wherever you may be, Lead on, O Israel, we shall follow when our trails meet beyond your glacier.

HORACE W. FERGUSON

A man of Kentucky and considered by his peers a true, courteous southern gentleman, he was making his home east of Sedalia, Missouri in 1870. Mrs. Horace Ferguson, like so many of her time, had severe asthma, and when Horace learned in 1870 of a group of people who were to travel west to Colorado the next spring, he sold his flour mill, joined up with the Saint Louis Colony migration, and with their six children boarded the brand new Kansas & Pacific Railroad passenger train. Their destination, Evans, Colorado, a small community four miles south of newly organized Union Colony now called Greeley, was reached in April of 1871 after he had postponed an

46

earlier trip because of the deteriorating health of his wife. In examining notes and accounts of many of the early settlers in the Estes Valley, as well as those of others who traced the rutted trails years later, it was evident that a search for returning health in high and dry air of the mountains was a significant reason for their migration to new homes amongst the peaks. Upon their arrival Mr. Ferguson only was able to locate a haggard hotel structure in which to temporarily settle his family. Even that edifice required pitching a tent inside because the severely impaired roof leaked constantly. The price of the ticket through the Saint Louis organization included five acres of land west of Evans. He subsequently purchased more land, built a two story brick house, bought cattle and started a garden, --a good start but fraught with a series of disasters that lurked ahead. His wife's health did not improve and she was chronically bedfast except for sojourns up the Poudre Canyon on holiday or while engaged in berry picking in the foothills and mountains 25 to 30 miles west of Evans. When Mrs. Ferguson responded in the higher atmosphere her husband remarked enthusiastically, "She picked up again in the same wonderful way!"

They remained in Evans for several years, then rented a farm west of Loveland where the land was higher and his wife's breathing was less labored. Cattle were *punched,* but with the advent of snow one year commencing on November 15, 1871 to reach extreme depths until the late Spring of 1872, the wet, blanketing whiteness prevented the herd from reaching natural or man provided nourishment. Despite the loss of over half of the herd, the family stuck it out to struggle on, refusing to admit failure. For the better part of four years he valiantly tilled the soil for his garden crops that paid some of their bills. What was his most memorable reason for leaving the flat country of the eastern plains of Colorado? It certainly was not the weather for the Estes Valley that would be his next home was not a warm Pacific island removed from the cold. His justification for making a change clearly was his constant losing battle with swarms of grasshoppers that came in thick black clouds to devour most of his garden crops and corn fields. Horace explained his dilemma after his final corn crop was decimated. "I never saw a finer crop of corn. Apparently the grasshoppers thought so also as they came down upon it and devoured everything in sight!" By the fall of 1875 everything was mortgaged with only a few cattle and some chickens left of his investments. His wife Sally Thompson Ferguson, a Virginian by birth, was still ailing and one of their sons, twelve year old Horace, Jr. called Holly, had recently succumbed in death from pneumonia. He was at his wits end! By a chance perusal of a Denver newspaper he came upon the article that proclaimed Lord Dunraven's assertions that **he** had purchased Estes Park and that only **his** guests would be welcomed. Horace had heard reports that the *Englishman* was boasting too much to scare off others when the facts were becoming manifest for him to question "whether this foreign claim jumper's title might be on shaky ground." In any event, it was cause enough to go up to Estes Park and look around. Why not! He had nothing more to lose. As he was from Missouri, he had to see this place for himself.

That fall he met our earlier acquaintance, Hank Farrar the guide, prospector, and a true survivor of the elements that came down heavily upon those who sought to live year around in the high country. Hank was an excellent hunter and fisherman and with whom Mr. Ferguson struck up a loose

47

confederation of shared effort. The effort was mostly on Horace's part with the sharing part of the bargain the strength of Hank. They agreed to hunt and fish and Horace's eldest son, Hunter, had the job of carting their harvest to the Denver markets for sale. The fish alone would bring fifty cents a pound and the meat whatever was the going price when the load arrived as there were more commercial hunters than fishermen. Horace started fishing that same day he met up with Farrar, in a beaver pond in Horseshoe Park. He had no fishing tackle other than two hooks but, through improvisation of a pole and line, before the day was over he had brought out 320 speckled plump trout, all from one mammoth beaver pond! Right then he concluded that in this high valley he just might have that chance for success that had eluded him before. Inasmuch as his wife's health was always better in the mountains, this was the enforcing logic that led to his vow to make his new home in the Estes Valley.

The Ferguson family first brought their wagons up the Bald Mountain trail in 1876, pushing the wagons with as much effort as the horses exerted energy to pull them. The roads were nearly non-existent on the way to their homestead near Marys Lake, three miles west of present day Estes Park. Horace said he picked out this tract of land "on account of the spring, --always being monstrous fond of a good drink of water." On the day of their arrival, April 21st, after three difficult days of travel through the eight inches of newly fallen snow, their tiring ordeal was not in character to a welcoming *Springtime In The Rockies* refrain. One of the family recalled a near tragic incident, requiring an immediate response on the last day of the trip, when a wagon decided to roll over. "The wagon had our chickens in it, and when it turned over they were killed. We had to stop right there and pluck and dress all of those chickens before we could move on." Threats from Lord Dunraven veiled in *advice* from his agents Theodore Whyte and C. Golding Dwyer suggested that "it would be very difficult to make a living on only forty acres," when Ferguson's claim was clearly one hundred sixty acres. Horace looked straight into the patronizing and contemptuous eyes of the agents and said, "I've come to stay and I reckon I can stick it out somehow!" Ferguson was of Scottish descent, from the Highlands, and he was intent on routing the English gents in his own version of Bannockburn as did his kinsmen so long ago across the vast Atlantic Ocean. He later explained his plan of opposition. "I have made up my mind, that if I was on land claimed by the English Company, I'd fight them and enjoy nothing better than showing them up in the courts. I wasn't going to let them bluff me out of the Park the way I'd seen them do to other men." He did stay after it was determined by an examination of the records that for some reason the English group had not previously filed upon Ferguson's property as they had contended. After moving onto the land the family constructed a two room log home one half mile north of, as Frederick H. Chapin described, "a small sheet of alkaline water, formerly a great resort for big-horn, elk, and deer, which came in great numbers to the lake, as they would to a salt lick." It is hard to believe that he was describing Mary's Lake, but then in 1887 it was not benefited by western slope water that began flowing through the Alva Adams Tunnel on its dedicatory day in June of 1947. Also in his time at the ranch, the steep, isolated, promontories we still catch sight of east of Mary's Lake were gathering places for the Big Horn sheep, often finding themselves trapped and easy targets for hunters who thought it great sport to shoot them from their perches.

I want to break into this narrative of the Ferguson's Ranch to identify the two origins of the name Mary's Lake to which geographical feature I have often referred. In an earlier chapter I introduced Griff Evans but I did not mention the fact that a young lady, Mary Jane Roberts who was his niece and also from Wales, was a visitor to his ranch at the time Isabella Bird was in residence. At her uncle's ranch she was the regular partner of Lord Dunraven in the English card game of Whist that he taught her on one of his first excursions into the valley. She said the reason for Dunraven's confidence in her abilities was that "I never forgot what was the trump. The Earl really got mad when any one asked him what was trump." Jim Nugent, of whom I have previously written, was a friend of the young woman as well as her future husband John Buchanan. On May 22, 1874 as she was returning with Buchanan from a horseback ride, they chanced to see Jim at uncle Griff's ranch. In learning that their ride over to see the shallow and flower filled pond was a special treat as this was her birthday, Jim informed them that the little body of water had no name and then said, "We will name it Lake Mary in honor of Mary's birthday." After her marriage, John and Mary Buchanan built a home, called the Buchanan Ranch, on a quarter section and one half mile south of her lake, now more personally recognized as Mary's Lake. To this quaint little home in the late 1870s the famous painter Albert Bierstadt came to call and where he painted a now famous oil depiction of Sheep Rock east of the lake. All enjoyed the beauty and tranquility of Mary's Lake, and its qualities and secluded setting prompted the Fergusons to settle nearby. After John Buchanan died, Mary later remarried and moved to Los Angeles as Mary B. Holcomb. Others claim the lake's signature arose out of the fact that Milton Estes' wife was Mary Fleming and as a present to his bride named the pool after her. I would more accept the first account for no one knew more about the area, nor traveled as widely the region than Jim Nugent. To complicate the issue, Lord Dunraven always referred to the shallow, alkaline depression as Saint Mary's Lake, a name of religious significance in Ireland.

Horace, after establishing himself in the mountains, was plagued -- as was the case with the James family and later the Spragues -- with swarms of, not grasshoppers, but of a higher order of animal life with the same insatiable appetite to feed off the local resources. These were humans who came up *for a visit*. This bane still afflicts more recent inhabitants who tactfully seek to recommend a nice motel for that variety of visitor claiming an old, often difficult to recall, affinity for friendship in days of yore. So to protect himself, Horace decided to take in those pesky visitors and make them paying guests. His oldest daughter, Anna, then twenty-three years old, described what happened when their wagon wheels came to rest on their own land that April of 1876 and in subsequent years. "We built two rooms on the house before we moved in, added two more having a dining room, kitchen and bed rooms. We also built a cabin or two. This place was known as The Highlands Hotel, and our first boarders were campers. We only served meals, but we built more cottages and could seat 85 people in the dining room. We had many people from Longmont, Denver and the East." That uplifting name, *The Highlands*, was bestowed upon their unpretentious new lodge by one of Horace's daughters because its flower bedecked hillside deserved something more appropriate than the generic map designation of Ferguson's Ranch. Their land reminded this family of Scotland, a land of soft heathery fells from whence the Fergusons derived their character and courage that all their neighbors and guests respected. In 1878 quarters for guests were somewhat primitive, four rooms connected to the original two room, sod roofed, cabin. By 1880 the home had increased in size to take in more guests; also they began adding a number of tent houses. Thereafter, five 3 room log cabins were observed about the premises for what the family called, --*boarders*. The lodge was now able to accommodate from thirty to forty guests with even non-guests taking their meals in the dining room while camped elsewhere. To The Highlands sojourned many guests over the years to enjoy the good fishing and hospitality of the Ferguson family, especially Horace and Hunter who served as the proprietors. Then later, James Ferguson took over the operation to further develop and enlarge the resort.

Frederick H. Chapin, born in Lafayette, Indiana in 1852 and later a resident and businessman of Hartford, Connecticut, was a member of the Appalachian Mountain Club. In his report of observations while walking in the Estes Valley of 1887, written for the club in 1889 and entitled *Mountaineering In Colorado*, he described the view from the Highlands. "His ranch is delightfully situated, and, though a mile from the river, is supplied with cold clear water from a never-failing spring. From the cabins around Ferguson's ranch a magnificent view is obtained of the great Mummy Range; and the sunset lights on the cliffs of Lily (i.e. Twin Sisters) Mountain to the east are indescribably beautiful. The mornings during this season are clear and beautiful; but in the early afternoon the great peak of the Mummy will perhaps throw off its cloud streamer, and in an hour or two thunder will rattle among the crags of Sheep (i.e. Rams Horn) Mountain and the rain pours down upon the dry pastures. In a few hours the sun almost gains the mastery once more; and though the pine-belts and valleys may be covered with ascending vapors, the peak of Lily will glow with gorgeous hues. It is probably some such spectacle as this that makes one of the early writers about this valley claim for it the finest scenery in the world." The name Lily Mountain had been attributed to several mountains back in the 1870s, although it is thought to be a misspelling of an early settler's family name, Lillie, hence Lillie's Mountain. The Colorado Geographic Board, after much debate by its members and residents of the valley, dodged the issues of orthography and origin to settle on the name Twin Sisters in 1907.

Sally Ferguson's cooking was a drawing card for the young resort. Her dairy herd produced rich butter, and if the milk were served now it would drive health conscious, cholesterol avoiding, modern calorie counters into a state of panic. That heady brew was described as "rich milk with the cream floating upon it." The visitors loved the lodge especially because of the effort expended by all of the Fergusons, including the children Hunter, Anna, Sally, Fanny and the youngest, James. That was the beginning of the lodge where travelers came from all parts of the nation on the stages from Lyons, to The Highlands or through Moraine Park with a stop at Sprague's Ranch that could always find a room for a traveler. The Fergusons' guests didn't complain even when their accommodations consisted of a tent, with meals served in the Ferguson kitchen, when the rooms and cabins were occupied. In fact back then it was not uncommon for the visitors to bring their own tents for the reason that in the 1870s and 1880s there were insufficient rooms to accommodate a public now awakening to the fact that the music of nature in the Estes Valley was an affordable rhapsody. Horace was straight as an arrow both in personal character and while he sat the saddle of his favorite horse. Visitors long remembered his early evening ritual when he rode his horse right into the Big Thompson River for some fishing. "Boy, did he catch them!", one guest recalled in an old news item, as he often returned with a wash tub full of fish. He also was an excellent shot with the old blunderbuss and is alleged to have bagged a large bear on the shores of what is now a prime tourist attraction that gives remembrance to his adventure by its name, Bear Lake. To illustrate the fact that the Ferguson family had come to stay, their daughter Anna in the summer of 1876 when returning from Denver, was persuaded to help a friend in Longmont with her sewing. In that home she met Richard Montgomery Hubbell, her friend's brother, and it was love at first sight. They were married October 26, 1876 at the resort by Reverend Collman of the Methodist Church of Longmont, their union to be recorded as the first wedding in the Park. There were only a few in attendance, perhaps the Spragues and Hupps, for as the bride remembers, "there weren't more than 25 persons in all the Estes Park district, and my wedding was small." Anna repeated her vows clad in a long sleeved, high necked, gray-blue poplin bridal dress while Richard pledged his love clad in a black suit suitable to his position as a general manager of a Longmont store.

This brief journalizing of The Highlands cannot be separated from another famous person whose name is found upon one of our most beautiful mountains. Horace Ferguson made a friend of William L. Hallett, as did Israel Rowe, who in 1877 arrived with his mother by Pullman on the Union Pacific and Colorado Central Railroads to the Denver area after graduating from Massachusetts Institute of Technology. Inasmuch as his trip west was not by wagon, horse or on foot, he always considered himself not worthy of being classified as an Estes Park pioneer. However, by his respect for what he saw, his writings, the love of these mountains and the esteem that all local residents had for him, I firmly believe he filled all of the requirements for this category of special folk. He returned the following year with his bride, Vena Sessions, on their honeymoon and contracted with Abner Sprague to take them on a 30 day camping trip from Estes Park to Hot Sulpher Springs and back. The story of this honeymooning pack trip, in which Abner shared the 10 x 10 foot tent with the young couple --he claiming one side of the center pole, they the other -- is a tale well worth reading in the memoirs of Mr. Sprague. Hallett's former summer home, still standing on three acres of ground given him by Horace Ferguson, he christened Edgemont. To this day, and notwithstanding the interval of successive owners over more than one hundred years, it is still identified historically as the Hallett House. His abilities as a guide were superb for friends and strangers alike, sharing with them many of the significant natural monuments we now find marked on National Park maps. One of which he must be the most proud gazing down with dominant bearing, its sharp promontory hovering over Bear Lake, was named for him as Hallett's Peak in 1887 by Professor Frederick Chapin and his hiking companion Dr. Edward Otis, themselves later to receive equivalent honors as peaks would bear their names. Of Mr. Hallett's abilities, Chapin had this evaluation. "Hallett knows thoroughly every trail and stream for many miles around." That's not a bad feat for an Eastern boy, raised in the big cities, who capitulated to a land that held him in willing bondage. After his death in 1947 at the home of his son in Brooklyn, New York, his wishes to be buried in his beloved Colorado were carried out, where his body and soul can dwell in peace.

The Highlands also is long gone after living for a few brief years into this century, to be replaced by summer residences. Horace remained in the Park until his death in 1912 at the Brinwood Ranch and Hotel where his progeny were its proprietors in Moraine Park. The article that appeared in the local newspaper following his death spoke kindly and truthfully of this man. "He was positive in character, firm in convictions, kind and generous by nature and a friend worth having. He was an ardent lover of nature's wonderful creations surrounding his home. Many will remember him as an interesting, accomplished companion in land and stream sports, or sitting with his guests before an open fire in the evening in earnest discussion of current topics or recounting the experiences of early days in the Park. He was the life, the animating spirit of every company of which he was a member." He exemplified the character that it took for himself, and his contemporaries, to risk everything in a diligent yet morally correct fight for what was right and who provided a wonderful retreat for those tired holiday seekers who survived the arduous roads that led to Estes Park. The Highlands is the small beginning to the lodging industry that from its seed was to flower in profusion as surely as the wild flowers returned to the meadows, rocks and rills of the high Rockies. To this beginning, Fergusons' Ranch resort, The Highlands, must be appreciated for what it was to early travelers, not for what it lacked in modern amenities. It was a friendly door that was always open to those who arrived by foot, horse, buggy or stage from the valley towns for friendship, refreshment and a story told in front of a blazing fireplace about bears, Indian trails, mountain climbs and pioneer codes of conduct. As you drive south on Marys Lake Road, at the top of the hill just west of Prospect Mountain, you will see the Hallett House, and 300 yards to its west The Highlands used to welcome you with the smells of good food that wafted out of Sally Ferguson's kitchen. The small lodge mostly is forgotten now, but it was a wonderful place for friendship, and *go'un fishin* with Horace.

What is the definition of a *pioneer*? One lexicon defines the word as 'one who goes before and opens and leads, or prepares the way for others coming after.' I'm certain the MacGregors, Hupps, Rowes and Fergusons, and Mr. Hallett, met that specificity of terms.

THE ESTES PARK-ENGLISH-DUNRAVEN HOTEL

Lord Dunvaven's grandiose plans for his property were studied with considerable interest by those reading their copy of the *Rocky Mountain News* dated July 29, 1874. The agenda was announced as if nothing of an untoward nature had befallen his first assault upon the Park. After successful challenges to many of his claims brought about a spirit of reformation to his heart, influenced by a shrinking or perhaps a more penurious purse, a new corporation was formed to conduct his affairs. "A New company, of which the Earl of Dunraven is the principal stockholder, has purchased all available lands in Estes Park, embracing some 6,000 acres. The company proposes making extensive and costly improvements. Among these will be a large hotel, a sawmill, new roads through the park, a hotel at Longmont, and a half-way house on the road between that place and the park." Although the hotel was not yet under construction, the newspaper could not contain its ardor and had a further scoop for its competing journalists on July 8, 1876. I suspect it was more of a pre-arranged advertisement veiled in the language of a news item, now termed *managed journalism.* "The large hotel contemplated for the accommodation of summer visitors will be built next year, the lumber being cut this season. The warm weather has already brought into the Park many visitors, more than usual for so early in the summer. The streams are yet high, too high for the best fishing but will soon be down. There is so much snow on Long's Peak that climbing to the summit will hardly be practicable before August. The Park is very beautiful now, the grasses most luxuriant, and enjoyed by the twelve hundred head of cattle besides many horses and a few sheep."

In the 1870s, German born Albert Bierstadt was one of the nation's most prominent landscape painters, and the Earl became familiar with his work from his New York City visits. He invited the artist to visit him in the Park to make some sketches of mountains and of potential locations for his hotel that would be aesthetically pleasing to the tastes of the class of clientele he sought to attract. Bierstadt was most ebullient about the scenery of the Park and upon his return to his home immediately commenced a large oil rendering of Long's Peak as would appear through the windows of the new hotel. It has been theorized, with ample reasons for this contention, that this famous painter with brush in hand selected the actual location for the Earl's hotel as he was present as a guest at its grand opening. The Bierstadt Lake in the National Park was so named for him by Theodore Whyte as it was a favorite site for the artist for contemplative composition and thought. Whyte, in an act of reconciliation to the locals, sent out printed invitations to them all to attend a grand ball to kick off the gala opening in July of 1877. Whether they came can be questioned, for it might have proven awkward then to toast the good health of its owner and the success of his business venture after having been bullied for years. Forgiveness was not of the first priority to a settler's struggle for survival in a harsh society. Stamina and stubbornness more were counted upon, and as necessary as how to ride a horse or shoot a rifle. But time would heal some of the wounds.

Of course the most prestigious mountain mansion for the well endowed tourist became the Estes Park Hotel, --Dunraven's, the *proper* place to bunk up in 1877. It was described in a travel reviewer's column. "One of the finest, neatest little hotels in the mountains. It can accommodate from 50 to 75 guests and is filled. It is built of substantial stone, finely appointed and furnishes its guests with an abundance of trout." The hotel was constructed at a cost of $15,000 not including furnishings, a sum that to us more than a century later seems paltry, but back then was considerable. The general foreman was John T. Cleave, born in Cornwall, England in 1839 and a ship builder by trade, who had previously erected a small home in 1874 on his homestead just southeast of the location for the new hotel. The Earl observed in a walk about one day that Cleave's property had an excellent spring capable of supplementing his hotel's limited water supply. In 1877 he traded Cleave out of his land for another 160 acre tract the Earl owned further west. After the hotel was erected the post office was moved, over the objections of local families, from MacGregors to a Dunraven building adjacent to the hotel where Cleave would serve as the Postmaster. He and his wife Margret May Cleave, the aunt of Shep Husted who himself would live to become one of the most famous and knowledgeable guides as well as a lodge owner in the Park, lived in the ranch house that formerly was the home of Griff Evans. When he left the employ of Dunraven, the post office moved with him to be centered amongst the gathering of odd looking, log and slab-like structures that would metamorphose as the preface to a true village. The new location on which he built his second home and general store, and later the post office, is now the intersection of Moraine and Elkhorn Avenue, a gold mine in disguise that in later years he was to discover. Two children were born to them, Paul, and Virginia who later became the wife of local timberman John N. Griffith. John Cleave remained the Postmaster for twenty-nine years and his store in the little village was managed for a period of time by Charles E. Lester, a name that later I will speak of in more detail.

Cornelius H. Bond was born in Guernsey County, Iowa in 1854, attended college in Concord, Ohio and by 1879 arrived in Loveland, Colorado on Saint Patrick's Day bent on seeing the West and to be a part of it. That summer was to find him camping out in Willow Park near the Spragues but his youthful fantasy to live within the splendor of the mountains was diverted into politics and business as the necessity of earning a living and establishing needed credentials became apparent. He returned to Iowa for another four years, then the draw of Colorado proved irresistible. He became a resident of Loveland, engaged in a number of businesses, and served as Sheriff of Larimer County from 1896 to 1904. Sheriff Bond recommended to the County Commissioners in 1902 the route for the new road through the Big Thompson Canyon. His numerous trips to the broad valley of the upper Thompson gave him the insight to visualize the collection of buildings, dusty streets and scattered peoples shaped into a town where folks could live, grow and prosper in a more orderly system. In 1905 John Cleave sold his 160 acres, home, store and post office to Cornelius Bond for $8,000 who with others incorporated the Estes Park Townsite Company. By 1906 the company had laid a water line down to the center of their new town from Black Canyon Creek and which water conduit remained in use until the Town of Estes Park, incorporated in 1917, assumed full responsibility for it in 1929. A plat was drawn up and twenty-five foot wide town lots were sold to the public in 1906 for $50 each. At first no city park appeared on the first plat, but in a re-plat lot lines for an entire block were erased and in the blank space was penned in the word, *Park*. For some forgotten reason the park was not officially dedicated, but finally during the lifetime of Cornelius' son, Mayor Frank Bond, Bond Park was appropriately named in 1944. Cornelius Bond in his new town appropriately entered the real estate and insurance businesses. He served three terms in the Colorado Legislature wherein he was instrumental in creating the State Highway Commission that in turn influenced the construction of Fall River Road. After a lifetime of service, he died in 1931.

John Cleave after selling his property, now obviously for much too low a price, moved away to Fort Collins and later on to farm near the present Mesa Verde National Park in southwestern Colorado. After another few years he and Margret were drawn back to their real home in the Estes Valley when vivid memories would not allow them a longer period of absence. They lived their final years with John and Virginia Griffith out on the future Bear Lake Road until Margret died in 1921 at age 76 and he followed in 1925 after attaining his 86th year. They all are buried -- John and Margret Cleave, John and Virginia Griffith -- under four Colorado grey granite stones in a family cemetery outside of the National Park, and their headstones bear these tributes to four early settlers who deserve more recognition for their achievements to this community than what they have received. Virginia's proudly refers to her origins, "Born in Estes Park" while her husband's reads and it is my hope it speaks the truth, "Gone but not forgotten." Margret's poeticly speaks to the Cleave's past efforts for this community at it reads "When autumn's sunset colors fade away, to rest with work well done." John Cleave's is the shortest, most simple in its eloquence, yet its bears witness to one man's achievements after more than a century has flown by in one word. Who was John Cleave? His stone says it positively, "Pioneer - 1874." The only reference remaining to them in a community that essentially nearly was all theirs, appears upon a street sign identifying the small byway as Cleave Street.

The Estes Park Hotel was crafted architecturally out of wood, brick and stone, although it appeared to the observer as a three story, large white frame building. The front porch initially was uncovered, then it became a covered front veranda extending the full length of the hotel. When first erected the second story had a porch that wrapped around three sides of the hotel. Later this feature was removed as the roof line for the first floor required it to slope downward for drainage. I think the real reason for this change lies in the fact that this overhang was deemed unsafe for revelling guests with induced judgmental impairment who should not have access to such heights. Bricks were incorporated into the structure for added strength, the large front fireplace and other architectural enhancements. Griff Smith, the wagon driver who brought up the loads of brick from Denver in 1877, recalled that as a consequence of the tremendous pounding and jarring sustained by his wagon on that rough, twisting toll road, his loads of brick were reduced in size and weight by one-third thus making every course of brick laid up to appear more narrow that was usual. Many tall narrow windows, with dormer openings projecting out of the third floor within the roof line in a look of arched prudishness, faced out upon a well landscaped lawn. The front veranda, with appropriately placed rocking chairs for those less inclined to strenuous activities beyond the conquest of a croquet wicket, overlooked a small, artificial lake. Over cleverly placed rocks, water cascaded down through this diminutively lovely loch in stair steps, its source a diversion from Willow Creek, now known as Fish Creek, that had its own fountainhead in an overgrown lily pond, Lily Lake. The Earl later, though some say it was before the completion of the hotel, lavishly built his own version of an English hunting lodge for his summer home that is still used as a summer residence.

The resort had its own dairy, butcher and blacksmith shops that were made available to local residents. Tennis courts and a large billiard room close to the dance hall added to the completeness of the facilities. Nine holes of golf were available on the course that began and ended at the hotel, after a break in action at Dunraven's Club House adjacent to the fairway. The present 18 hole golf course is an augmentation of much of the original recreational grounds including the original club house, now enlarged. A large stable to the north of the hotel, connected by a telephone device to the hotel's front desk, provided the guests carriages for six dollars a day and riding ponies for a dollar. Guide services were provided by Israel Rowe, and by another whom the hotel manager C. H. Hinman said "knew the country like a book." He was referring to the legendary Hank Farrar who lived in a cabin on the Big Thompson River and would guide Dunraven's guests using the Earl' horses or those that he would contract to provide. The hotel was situated on high ground behind a large gate, about one and a half miles from the Big Thompson River, through which the entrance road brought in many stage coach loads of guests willing to pay the price of fifteen to seventeen dollars per week for a booking. The view from the veranda was extremely expansive, especially of Long's Peak that scrutinized this new found activity with timeless durability, possessed with the knowledge that it would outlast this new incursion of man into its spacial sphere.

The original thirty furnished apartments, later increased to fifty with a wing added on the north end of the edifice, were accessed over colorful Navajo rugs spread about the floor in an impressive, white pillared sitting room and lobby called The Rotunda. There were some cabin accommodations on the premises, one referred to as *Waldorf*, as well as what the hotel brochure described as *tent houses*, a common method to less expensively increase the number of guest spaces during those periods of unexpected high demand. The quality of service was consistent regardless of the type of accommodations available, and all the furniture was fashioned out of black walnut wood. The room embellishments, although not lavish, were certainly in good taste and opulent compared to the simple design offered by the little cottages and canvassed tent frames that were elsewhere available to travelers possessed of smaller purses. One newspaper, in commenting upon the sophisticated class of registrants of the hotel wrote, "It was patronized by those skeptics of the camping out quarter." The self proclaimed image of the hotel appealed to snobbishness, particularly the well heeled Englishman and his lady who felt comfortable with those of their own class. "Our accommodations are appealing to the fastidious." The large dining room was adorned with long white curtains, crystal lights suspended on long gold chains and polished wooden floors embracing the profusion of white tableclothed tables. This room served three distinct purposes. It was first a fine dining facility featuring everything such as fresh trout entrees and the richest of French cuisine served to famous people as his old friends Buffalo Bill and General Phil Sheridan. Also on Sunday it served as a church before the chapel was added, and at other times the chairs and tables were arranged so that local organizations would have a meeting house. Per chance to a flashback the Earl had of his early encounter with the old man who wondered about the adaptability of the Park for drinking whisky, Dunraven brought to his hotel wagon loads of good Irish whiskey for the guests, and of course his own pleasure, in sufficient quantities to last the entire season. What was not consumed he buried in a secret location on the hotel grounds quite forgetting where he had stashed it upon returning the next summer. He was tempted to violence when his searching proved unproductive, suspicioning his winter caretaker's possible discovery as a source of body warmth over the long cold months of solitude. For years thereafter it would prove an interesting pastime both for guests and locals to meander through the grounds in a ruse suggesting casual contemplation of nature but in reality, as one admitted, "searching for that damned liquor!" No one knows if it was discovered. But even if it had been, those lips -- that would quaff the product of the distiller's best effort blended with a small measure of the Park's praiseworthy waters -- would remain forever sealed.

The Earl enjoyed his parties, with many initiated at the Estes Park Hotel from 1877 to 1886. It was true that more than a few attained riotous proportions to say the least with the Earl himself right in the forefront of the melee. It was difficult if not impossible for general managers to have a long term employment at the hotel as many of the guests were personal friends, business associates or relatives of *His Lordship* and they did not tolerate any interference with their extracurricular activities. Managers came and were discharged as fast as an old revolving door could be spun, and hence many of them did not recognize the Earl himself on holiday from the *auld sod* where tradition and social status required gallant, courtly deportment. His wife never accompanied him, although there were others of the fairer sex who joined in at his popular parties at the hotel, or wherever his tiller was turned. Theodore George William Whyte married, for the second time, Maude Josepha who was the daughter of the 7th Earl of Airlie of Scotland. Airlie was a companion of Dunraven on his trip from England in 1874 as was Maude who first made the acquaintance of Whyte in Estes Park. Lady Maude, as she was known to the locals, was a far different personality from her husband. She was gracious, well respected, a game and democratic sportswoman as well as a perfect hostess at hotel festivities. Margret Cleave served her as a personal maid and, as some said, her *confident*. On one auspicious occasion Dunraven arrived at the hotel, with great pomp and questionable circumstance, on the arm of the English actress Mrs. Alice Monroe. In the group were some of his cronies who continued the enjoyment of Irish whiskey of the highest quality they had previously imbibed to the rhythm of the swaying carriage from Lyons. This party was exceptional, but not for its breadth of raucous amplitude that was routinely expected. Noise could not be avoided as the warmth of the large pitch burning fireplace, in partnership with generous portions of food and grog, wrought an atmosphere of revelry. What made this night of frolics for registered guests noteworthy was the fact that leading the noisy singing and pounding of the walnut furniture -- general Hell raising -- was Dunraven and Mrs. Monroe. This evening revealed the presence of a new manager on duty who had been carefully instructed by Lord and Lady Whyte to protect the furnishings and preserve a modicum of pastoral peace for the guests. The manager took his duties quite seriously and, not having been previously introduced to the Earl who to him was a perfect stranger, commenced to eject the two biggest trouble makers, the Earl himself and his *femme fatal,* from the premises. Quite possibly there appeared in the Denver papers the next day an add for another general manager. Some previously discharged managers would later reappear after the Earl had sailed away to Ireland, restored to duty by a sympathetic Lady Maude.

The hotel had a splendid reputation for quality service and many reports of its expertise in catering to the needs of is guests would have earned it a four star rating in the periodicals of today. Here is but one example of a travel editor's sweeping hyperbole of June 17, 1881. "Now that the warm days of summer have come again it is but natural for one to begin to inquire, --where shall I go that I may enjoy life in all of its fullness? Where can I

57

find the free mountain air, the purest of water, the finest scenery, in short, the grandest spot in Colorado? Unto those who are undecided where to go, and unto some of those who have decided, reconsider your decision, to all such we would say, come to Estes Park and spend a few days, weeks or the season. The Estes Park Hotel is again under the management of the popular hotel man, Alexander McC. Stetson, formerly of the Astor House, New York, and late of the Glenarm, of Denver. This hotel is now opened for the reception of guests. Its merited reputation as the best kept hotel in the State has been fully established in the past and will be maintained, and the proprietor promises that no expense shall be spared to insure the comfort of the guests, or to add to the pleasure. His popularity while here two years ago has not been forgotten by the hundreds that ate at his table during that season when tents had to be put up all around the hotel for the accommodation of guests."

Mr. Charles E. Lester, himself later to own his own lodge, was the last general manager of the hotel before its demise, with his stewardship commencing in 1898. Mr. Lester in his memoirs states that despite the fact that he managed the Earl's hotel for many years, and operated a store on the ranch property with Theodore Whyte in 1887, he never met his employer nor was the Earl of Dunraven ever at the hotel after 1887. It seems Dunraven had tired of Estes Park with its increase of taxes and soaring costs associated with increased competition from a plethora of cottages and lodges providing the public with a variety of less pricey accommodations. He leased his property, land, hotel, horses, --the works, to others. In short he was getting bored. He needed new challenges to a restless soul, and as his memoirs reflect he witnessed and joined in the excitement of a world that was rapidly charging into a truculent, less genteel, Twentieth Century demanding of men of his vigor. Around 1907, after several unsuccessful leases to others such as LeCoste, Bartholf and even to his own associate Whyte, he sold his "neat little hotel." His land empire, including 6,400 acres of uncontested land and another 600 still in litigation, was deeded for the sum of $80,000 to a partnership made up of our now familiar Freelan O. Stanley, and B. D. Sanborn of Greeley, Colorado. Despite a successful hotel venture with reasonable profits from his cattle, it is estimated that his overall losses from his privateering in the Park amounted to $300,000. Dunraven, true to his restless past deportment, remained an active participant in government, an officer in the Boer War, and allocated the use of his yacht as a hospital ship in World War I. He was present in France in 1919 to witness the signing of the document that proved illusory for the protection of the world, The Treaty of Versailles. He died in 1926 at the age of 85 years in Ireland, a land of great beauty yet not sufficiently adventurous for containment of his restive nature that sought its cosmos in a widening universe. As an interesting side note, the Bierstadt painting that Dunraven purchased for $15,000, a tremendous sum for its day, was later sold by his heirs to some Colorado residents for $5,000. They in turn donated it for permanent display in the Denver Public Library. Its beautiful proportions, alive with bold strokes of color, can be examined there today as an accurate portrayal of a view from Dunraven's Estes Park Hotel that forever will be known as The English Hotel.

The hotel opened in 1898 to a season with bright expectations and auspicious intentions under the management of Mr. Lester, and with a new name of which the Earl would be pleased although to me it always flew that pennant. It was called The Dunraven Hotel. Its brochure of 1908 proclaimed in exaggerated self esteem the treatment guests could expect as their Stanley Steamers moved smartly up the attractive flower bordered driveway to the front door, that is if one had money and was in good health. "The Dunraven Hotel, formerly the Estes Park Hotel owned by Lord Dunraven, has been entirely rebuilt and greatly enlarged. It now offers facilities for luxury and general comfort unsurpassed by any hostelry in Colorado. The house has been thoroughly modernized in every respect, and now has a number of rooms with private baths, and also several handsomely appointed suites. Positively no tuberculosis patients will be taken at the hotel. By an arrangement just completed with all of the other resorts in the Park, persons suffering from tuberculosis will be strictly barred. One great advantage enjoyed by the Dunraven Hotel over every other hotel in the Park, is its central location, and the much shorter stage ride required to reach it, barely 23 miles from the railroad, and the shortest route, the one from Lyons, is but 18 miles, while the nearest of the other hotels is eight miles farther. (Ed. Note: This was before the Stanley Hotel opened in 1909.) All of the old coaches operated on the stage line in previous seasons have been replaced with modern, comfortable vehicles, similar to the world-famous stages used in the Yellowstone National Park. Where formerly vehicles operated from Lyons were the only ones entering the park, the Colorado & Southern is now running a splendid coaching service from Loveland direct to the Dunraven Hotel. The hotel is open from June 15 to October 1st. The Dunraven Club (i.e. Dunraven's summer home) is a feature of the resort that has just been opened this season. The club house is a handsome new structure close to the Dunraven Hotel, and commanding one of the finest views in Estes Park. It is designed after the splendid home of Lord Dunraven. There are excellent billiard rooms connected with the Club, and private grill rooms for parties. An orchestra is provided furnishing music afternoon and evening. No coaching party in the Park is complete without a stop at the Dunraven Club. The capacity of the Dunraven Livery has been more than doubled this season. Many excellent riding and driving horses have been added to the stable, and a number of new rigs of the latest pattern have been purchased. The livery is operated in connection with the hotel. Drivers or guides are furnished for individuals upon request. Cottagers or campers in the Park may also be furnished with rigs or saddle horses at any time. The barn is connected by telephone with all parts of the Park, and orders are promptly delivered and called for anywhere."

On this hotel I have dwelt longer than I expected. Perhaps it is for the reason that Earl of Dunraven's boasting, haughty threats, copious columns of publicity, lawsuits and eventual construction of a quality hostelry gained for the Estes Valley enormous reams of newsprint that no advertising executive could ever provide. A public, recovering from the ache of a civil war and the sting of financial woes that followed, took solace in a high valley which ballyhoo tempted them out of lethargy to seek hope and laughter. The Earl truly appreciated the beauty of this Park although somewhat vengeful of others who felt the same way. Regardless of what we may think of him, --whether he be damned as an avaricious, pompous, playboy or honored as another breed of pioneer to the tourist trade, only time will set the record straight. Preferring a coach to a pony, and a drink of good Irish whiskey over high country *spring water,* can never undermine the fact that he built a grand place in which to find lodging in a valley that to him was possessed of a "simply grand view." In one of those views that meant much to him now is found upon our regional map Mount Dunraven, 12,271 feet tall. He opened up the Estes Valley to the world from which fact we can never retreat into the shadow of Long's Peak, as now our Park had really been discovered. Some of his words uttered before his death caught me up in some deep emotion as I realized that he was offering up to us a challenge to the future for sensitive and responsible progression of our Park. "I would love to see again the place I knew so well in its primeval state. No work of man could destroy the grandeur and the beauty of Estes Park." Sail on Commodore Dunraven to new adventures. We shall remember you by your acts and your words, particularly the last that were your finest.

I am certain that those 173 voters who cast their ballots in the Presidential election of 1908 in the Estes Valley were duly impressed with the knowledge that a former source of suspicion and suppressed envy was now in the capable hands of Messrs. Stanley and Sanborn. True to their word, the hotel was maintained to a high standard with frequent redecoration and tasteful upholstering to the plush furniture. Alas, this would all come to the same end accorded so many other historic structures in the mountain towns of Colorado. Residents arose to begin another lovely summer day the morning of August 4, 1911, but instead rushed to witness the fiery destruction of the Dunraven, their English Hotel, that was gone from their view in a large explosion and twenty minutes duration of flame. It was alleged to be an act of arson by a disgruntled employee, a bell hop or chef from the kitchen staff, who had been removed from his employment the previous day by Mr. Lester. The hotel was never rebuilt for by that time Mr. Stanley was heavily involved in his new endeavor on the hill adjacent to the village. If you take the first turn to the left, on Fish Creek Road, as you approach Estes Park from the east on Highway 36, drive about three quarters of a mile where you can see the Earl's personal residence in which he dreamed mighty thoughts and accomplished many dreams that, willingly or otherwise, provoked others into following his lead as owners of the new resources of the Park, tourist lodges. Some say his home was not actually located on this spot. Years after the fire destroyed the hotel and before Lake Estes inundated most of the Estes-Evans-Dunraven Ranch, some reports indicate that the home then positioned at the foot of Fish Creek near the present Highway 36 was moved to the south to rest upon its present foundation. Others say that the home has always remained in its present location and that another large home on the Dunraven Ranch was the structure removed from its original site with the impressive view across the broad Big Thompson River valley. A quarter of a mile further along Fish Creek Road on the left and opposite the golf course clubhouse, if you look closely back up the hill about a hundred yards, you still see remnants of the hotel's foundation. The little pond has been removed for the blacktopped roadway traversing what had been those stair stepped water cascades, but that splendorous view still commands the attention of present generations of visitors.

Travelers enjoyed the Estes Valley and especially the pioneers of different shades of development who greeted them while climbing off a horse or down the steps of a dusty stage. Let us remember what it must have been so long ago to stand in the quiet of an evening on a tree lined trail, the wind blowing through one's hair, and know that He created this for us all. These lines, written in 1920 by the author and lodge owner Clem Yore who greatly loved this Estes Valley, give poetic verse to the spirit of the trail as timeless as the earth itself.

A Little Lane Through Aspen Trees,
Little Breath Of Bracing Breeze,
Shadowy Shapes Of Sunshine There,
Wild Flowers, Bird Calls Everywhere.
Along The Trail The Shadows Please,
Heaven Born These Images,
We See The Sunlight Streaking Through,
And Shadows Tell Us --Oh! So True,
That God's Along The Trail.

MacGregor Family At Home, 1893 (EPTG)

Hallett House, circa 1880s (CHS)

Author At Hupp Graves, 1993 (W. L. McNichols)

Horace Ferguson, circa 1910 (EPTG)

Ferguson's Ranch, 1888 (RMNP)

The Highlands, 1895, by F. E. Baker (EPPL)

Beaver Pond In Horseshoe Park, circa 1930 (Mills)

A Good Catch of Trout, circa 1920s (F. P. Clatworthy)

Highlands Wagon Awaits Mail, 1888 (EPTG)

Lord Dunraven, circa 1893 (EPHM)

Adare Manor, Limerick, Ireland Home Of Lord Dunraven 1841-1926 (EPHM)

Estes Park Hotel, circa 1878 (RMNP)

Guests Of Hotel, circa 1878 (RMNP)

Dunraven Dairy, circa 1880s (Mills)

Dunraven Ranch, Cleave with son, circa 1877 (EPHM)

Living Room Of Estes Park Hotel, circa 1880s (RMNP)

Dining Room Of Estes Park Hotel, circa 1880s (RMNP)

Hotel Accommodations, circa 1880s (RMNP)

Estes Park Hotel With Veranda Removed, circa 1880s (RMNP)

Miss Lytie Hart Arrives By Stage, circa 1895 (EPPL)

Hotel With Final Additions, circa 1900 (Private)

Hotel, Cabins And Grounds, circa 1905 (RMNP)

Hotel With View Of Long's Peak, 1910 (W. T. Parke)

Fire Destroys Estes Park Hotel, August-1911 (RMNP)

Elkhorn Lodge, Lamb's Ranch, Long's Peak Inn

In My Dreams Of Joy's Delight,
I View The Land Of Mountain Heights,
Where Skies Are Clear And Stars Are Bright.
Where Parks And Vales, Are Nestling Low,
By Mountains Rimmed With Eternal Snow.
With Pine And Spruce, And Balsam Fir,
Emit Their Fragrance, On The Air.
With Landscapes Fair, Where Lakes And Streams,
Enhance The Beauty Of The Scene.
Elkanah J. Lamb, 1906

It was becoming increasingly popular for families to take their vacations in the Estes Valley. Fishing was excellent, weather far better in the summer and fall than in Denver and its smaller sister cities, and above all there were loads of opportunities to pitch a tent and relax. But there were an increasing number who preferred to sleep under a roof and clean sheets yet the price of The Estes Park Hotel was excessive for the average Colorado family. There were others who shied away from dressing up, *fancy-like*, for dinner as was expected at Dunraven's diggings, and not enough rooms were available at MacGregors and The Highlands. Three homesteads transmuted themselves like a life cycle of nature commencing with the egg, then the larvae, the pupa and finally an emergent winged insect. The little cabins on Fall River, in the Moraine basin and in the Tahosa Valley, began changing form and certainly size in 1877, to evolve into ranches compatible for cattle, chickens, crops and children and added a few rooms out back, temporarily stemming the march of civilization drawn to these high plateaus behind frothing spans of scheduled steeds. The rancher withdrew as a caterpillar into his chrysalis of a long winter to evaluate his predestined future at a time when wind and snow made access to these Parks less hospitable to the stranger. When he emerged the following spring of 1878 the final form of development was at hand. What emerged into an incredibly blue sky of Colorado, from a rapscattled huddle of weathered wood with the pump out behind, was the mountain refined creation we called the tourist lodge, --with plumbing fixtures made more relevant to human comfort and conformation. These family autographed inns inveighed against stuffy aloofness with painted on smiles and reflected the friendliness of the owners, abhorring a contrived polished personality that they were not and would never be. Their modus operandi always would be in touch with their humble origins and to welcome those yearning for a more comfortable wilderness experience at an affordable price. But analogous to the life of our friend the butterfly, the longevity of life of the lodges was all too brief, evanescent, as they fell back to an earthly world of desuetude, discard and destruction, the result of attitudinal superiority and administrative tinkering with mountain Americana. The lodge epoch, of decent folks caring for others on holiday, was an ephemerally happy interlude in the history of the Estes Valley and especially in Rocky Mountain National Park. Although one of these early lodges was Sprague's Ranch, I will discuss that resort at the same time I present the story of Stead's Ranch as they must be discussed together for their correct historical identification.

THE ELKHORN LODGE

Mr. William Edwin James, born in Camden, New York, spent much of his youth deriving a living from forestry products. Marrying Ella McCabe on Christmas Day, 1865 in upstate New York, he settled down to commence a grocery business he deemed more suitable for a married man rather than sequestered with his axe in the hardwood forests. However that venture was decimated, caught up in the national financial fiasco termed the Panic of 1873 and, in search of a fresh start in order to provide for his wife and family, boarded a train from Syracuse, New York for Denver in the fall of 1874. While taking time off from more serious pursuits of looking for new employment, he and several new friends zigzaged their way up to the Estes Valley on a hunting trip. He was immediately infatuated with the mountains, especially with the fishing where it took no effort to garner a gunny sack full in a short time. Without getting approval from his wife -- a macho stance not dared by modern man cognizant of the consequences -- he located immediately a tract of land not already grabbed by the *English bunch* and set to work to hew enough virgin timber to fashion a sixteen foot square, sod roofed cabin. This land he claimed by a liberal application of the pre-emption process currently in vogue, and in 1875 moved the family to their new home in a near empty land where hardly more than two dozen human beings breathed in the rarified pine scented air. That cabin still stands, framed by ancient pines and entwining aspen boughs, north of Estes Park and a short distance from the present Devils Gulch Road. Later known as McCreery Springs, it was so named for the Reverend William McCreery, a Presbyterian Church circuit rider recently arrived from Pennsylvania, who later went on to become a prominent preacher and builder of schools and churches. Mr. James then located a more preferred site for his permanent residence amply blessed with grass and good water from Black Canyon Creek for cattle and his future crops. It certainly suited his wife who did not take to living in a cabin back in a little canyon, where at every sound heard in the night she imagined 'Indians creeping up to scalp us.' The sod roof also leaked frequently requiring much indoor planning when heavy snows wicked in frosty droplets the result of warm Chinook winds shrieking down adjacent Lumpy Ridge.

The new claim of eighty acres on the upper end of Black Canyon, on which through hard work Mr. James erected another cabin -- with wood shingles -- faced towards the first rays of sunshine emerging from the foothills of an eastern horizon. It was located on the site of the present MacGregor ranch, but at that time was presumed open for homesteading. However the Judge's mother-in-law considered the James' assertion of ownership preposterous as she said it was hers by her prior location. Springing to the defense of Georgianna in harkened family allegiance as well as to keep peace in the family, the Judge defended her claim in court. After a bruising legal bout

63

in which the Jameses were the losers, members of the James family thereafter considered Mrs. Heeney a *jumper* and the Judge a *petty fogging lawyer* with hard feelings to remain for many years. Mr. James quickly adjusted to the situation, assisted by the infusion of a bequest from his wife's father who had recently died. Being an enterprising merchant in goods, and to him land was similar to a commodity for trade, he swapped his first claim further out Devils Gulch Road for land on the Fall River previously filed upon by the Reverend McCreery. James sought land at a lower level for his ranching operations and the Reverend, opting for a less riparian location to aid in the relief of virulent asthma attacks, preferred one where he could gain mental refreshment from a vocation of raising souls not crops. It was an acceptable solution to both men and their friendship remained steadfast for the rest of their lives. Reverend William McCreery passed to his spiritual reward in 1926 the same year Lord Dunraven 'shuffled off this mortal coil.' The descendents of the McCreery family still reside near to, and care for, the old sod cabin with fond affection and a strong sense of historical belonging. While Reverend McCreery devoted his days to practicing what was good and ethically enduring, his companion in death, The Earl, was content to be remembered for his aristocratic penchant for position, property and power. To each of us is given the same chance for our days of tomorrow in the book of history, the final chapters of which should be under close personal scrutiny.

The James family relocated to the Fall River property in 1877 where they built their third home in less than four years, this time a frame structure consisting of two small bedrooms, a living room, dining room and a kitchen. When they were unpacking their furniture brought from their vacated cabin, they could not locate their large black cat, Tommy. Building the first fire in the stove, the old Majestic cast iron friend with the fire source on one side and the oven on the other, who should make his appearance from the oven when the bread was to be baked? It was Tommy, not the worst for wear but hot, sooty, hungry and most chagrined at his inappropriate choice of hiding places. This family member would live long enough to become the pal, playmate and baby doll to the youngest child. The James' children consisted of Eleanor, Charles, Howard and Homer. Eleanor Estes James was the youngest and was born in 1880 in Longmont where her family lived during a portion of the long winters. A self proclaimed tomboy, she could be seen with bangs flying riding her pony everywhere with devilish gusto. Her middle name was bestowed upon this dynamically determined young person in recognition of the family who had discovered this beautiful land in which they found a new opportunity for joyful expression. The eldest child, Homer, became a medical doctor, practicing his profession briefly away from Estes Park, then to return to become occupied with real estate investments including the lumber yard but no longer practicing medicine on any active scale of endeavor. He championed the construction of the 18 hole golf course on which he was still seen playing at the age of ninety-two. Middle brother Charlie, who like his brothers was an excellent fisherman, unfortunately died at the age of twenty. Howard P. James, of whom Ella James considered 'a born hotel man,' proved the truth of that maternal instinct when he assisted her in the Elkhorn's management upon the death of his father and later when he became the sole operator of the Elkhorn. Eleanor forecast her future at Black Canyon if the court case had brought in a different verdict. She recorded, "I've always been grateful to

Mrs. Heeney for jumping Father's claim. Otherwise, I'd still be picking cho-kecheeries at the upper end of Black Canyon."

The ranch on Fall River grew to nearly two hundred acres on which Father James ran his cattle operation, then a more profitable means of employment of resources in the Park than it was to be in succeeding years. In 1878 a sideline developed, Ella James' personal endeavor as a contributing partner to the production of income as long winters and a short growing season proved harsh and persistently burdensome to the agricultural industry of the high mountains. She took in summer boarders and discovered such an affinity toward this project that she hesitated to consider *it work*. It was work none the less, but the kind that was to her liking as she gained the friendship of so many who grew to appreciate her concern for them. Hence the family added a few rooms and constructed a cabin or two as the herd was reduced to an economically manageable size. Father James at first was diffident to the tourist trade, unsure of any enduring quality to a business made up of feeding and housing strangers. However, the ranch became increasingly impacted by his wife's paying guests and a decision had to be declared to Mr. James' reasoned challenge, "It's either the cows or the cabins." A settlement of the issue was made for them as more tourists came to the ranch "begging to stay." Then of course there were the supplications of old friends wanting a base of operation from which they might probe the hinterlands recently opened up by the new toll road. Both persuasions wormed their way into the James home and generosity, and to them Father James surrendered as each succeeding summer found him, and all his family hard at work on yet another cabin. It was time to give their growing enterprise a name. The wandering elk roamed freely their pastures albeit their number was shrinking at the hands of man intent on slaughter for profit for the Denver market that had acquired a voracious appetite for wild game. The James' boarders were fascinated by these antlered, camel-like, bearded beasts that wandered about the property. It was only natural that they christened their ranch with the appellation, the Elkhorn Lodge. The Jameses like the Fergusons learned that it was less labor intensive and certainly more pleasurable to earn a living from succoring the appetites of travelers than cattle, and though both of the species had similar needs for care, comfort and shelter, only one of them was willing to pay for this attention. Mr. and Mrs. James, and later their sons Homer, Howard and daughter Eleanor, began totally, in mind, heart and soul, offering their ranch to visitors as a first class tourist facility that would increase in size to become one of the largest and best in the Park.

By the summer of 1880 more than fifteen tourist rooms were in use, sufficient to house between thirty-five and forty guests. Mr. James still had some cattle but they were being grazed on another tract of land he owned together with a partner, a man named Ewart from Chicago, in Cascade Park, an area we now call Horseshoe Park. Most of the thirty-three little cabins that were eventually built on the Elkhorn property, as business needs and available funds found justification, began life as tent cabins, similar to ones on the outer precincts of The Dunraven Hotel but certainly less auspiciously appointed. The Elkhorn tent cabins came with canvass ceilings that extended down the walls to meet wood at the level of the window sills. Later the buildings were completely enclosed, sliding windows added, and simple furnishing such as beds, casual chairs and of course a table with an ornate bowl with matching white china pitcher adorned with painted flowers. The Twentieth Century at the Elkhorn was ushered in first with cold water taps, and anon each cabin was fitted out with a hot water faucet. When those first hot and cold water taps were introduced into each cabin, squeals of joy were emitted from the feminine side of a traveling duo. To be perfectly fair, the exhortations of glee often were male gendered as one former guest exclaimed just thinking back on that bit of *luxury*. "Boy Oh Boy! Now you could shave, with no more trips out to the bathhouse every time we wanted a drink of water!" Later, some of the cabins were cut in two and attached to the back of others to serve as what they called *private johnnies*, thus eliminating lonely perambulations in the cold darkness clutching the trusty lamp and also a rock for defense to the imagined dangers lurking in every shadow movement.

A brief recap of the roots of the Estes Park school system is worthy of a pause as The Elkhorn Lodge owners had much to do with its birth. For the first years on Fall River the James children were taught by a teacher W. E. James employed and who roomed at the ranch. Later Mr. James deemed it appropriate to seek the creation of a regular school district where children of all the families in the Park could receive a proper education. To this end, on November 19, 1883 a petition requesting a new school district was sent to Loveland, then the county seat of government, for the attention of the same W. H. McCreery in his capacity as County Superintendent of Schools. Others signing the petition included familiar names such as Fred Sprague, Horace Ferguson, John T. Cleave and the widow Eliza Hupp, and an election was held at the post office on the 26th of November resulting in all eleven votes being cast in the affirmative. James was elected President of the Board who hired a teacher, Dr. Judson Ellis, at a stipend of $40.00 per month with an additional sum of $15.00 for food. The school opened in a three room cottage at The Elkhorn Lodge with fifteen students in attendance ranging in age from six to eighteen years, the children of the families of James, Hupp, Ferguson, Pierson and Spaulding. Classes were held in this little building for three years, and after more than 110 years the lovely stick frame school --now in retirement mode -- still gazes out curiously towards the Town of Estes Park. She is hopeful that her years of recess might come to an end, longing to hear again the footsteps and laughter from the descendents of her former pupils who might yet tramp up her slightly askew steps. A new school was erected near the northwest corner of Moraine and Elkhorn Avenue in 1886, constructed primarily by William James, his sons Homer and Charlie, and John Cleave. It is interesting to read of an incident that clearly revealed the insincerity of Lord Dunraven's local proxy and hotel manager, Theodore Whyte, as reported in 1915 by Louise Reed Hayden. "At the annual district meeting in May, 1885, Mr. Theodore Whyte of the old English company offered to deed a piece of land to the school board as a site for a school house and to furnish the lumber for putting up the frame. He suggested that the building might be used for church services and all public meetings. He assured the people that he'd have no doubt summer guests in the Park would be sufficiently interested to give entertainments for the purpose of raising a fund for the school building. His proposition was unanimously accepted as were some plans for the school house. As far as I have been able to find out Mr. Whytes's offered land was never deeded to the school district and his offered lumber never received." In addition to serving as the school house, this little building, as with so many other public buildings of the West then and now, served as a meeting house, church and polling place. Mr. Cleave, living across the street who was the Secretary of the Board, was in charge of opening up the school house on election days. In an election in the late 1880s one person reported Mr. Cleave's official actions. "He opened the polls at 7 A. M. by standing outside the poll and shouting, 'Hear Ye, Hear Ye! The Polling Place of the United States is now open. Come Ye and vote!' He then rang the school bell twice." The votes cast that year were, around seventy-five, were cast for Republicans except one who declared himself firmly as a Democrat and two saying they were associated with the Mugwump political persuasion.

During the long winters with visitors long gone home and rereading for the upteenth time their vacation diary, the James family found time for togetherness and quiet reflection over a season with new found friends as they sat before the roaring fire in the living room roasting apples and cracking nuts. There were always crocks of cider to wash down the hazelnuts and butternuts, and barrels of apples Mr. James had shipped in from New York State, --"the only place that could grow proper apples," he advised. Father smoked his cigar and mother read romance stories to the children until 9 P. M at which time with lamps lit they headed to bed to the cacophonous song of moaning winds that sought access to the gathering. Sleep was important to a full day commencing at 6 A. M. with the relighting of the fireplace, their source of room heat together with the stove. One of the early guests was Pieter Hondius, Sr., a citizen of Holland, who was a direct descendent of a long line of Fifteenth and Sixteenth Century cartographers. Two examples of the Hondius' specialty are now on display in the prestigious Huntington Library of California. In 1895 he was advised by his doctor to seek a higher and drier climate for his asthma, such as Switzerland or a new place called Colorado. Mr. Hondius chose Colorado and, armed with a letter of introduction to Mr. S. Newhouse in the Boston Building of Denver, arrived in July of 1895 where he found directions to Estes Park. In Europe, similarly in the more urbane venues of eastern United States, Colorado and the West conjured up pictures of Indians battles, violent outlaws and wide open places where decent people must continuously be on guard. This vision of Colorado had a pervasive influence upon the twenty-seven year old Pieter, whereupon his arrival by train to the respectable City of Denver found him stepping upon the depot platform, rifle in hand, ready for any eventuality. That summer, he appeared at the front door of The Elkhorn Lodge requesting board and room for which he was prepared to pay for as long as it took to regain his health. After meeting young Eleanor, then beautiful at fifteen, his stay at the lodge and on his own subsequently acquired property in the Park would be extended to a lifetime. They were married a number of years afterwards and to them in 1923 was born one son, Pieter, Jr., who remains a valued citizen of this community.

Mr. Hondius, Sr. purchased over the years 2,000 acres of land including the John Hupp holdings in Upper Beaver Meadows, known to the Arapaho Indians as *The Place Where The Woman Died*. As an interesting fact of history, on which I shall write in a later chapter, after the commencement of the Twentieth Century nearly all of the elk that had numbered into the thousands had disappeared from these broad meadows. Some wild sheep and deer still managed to hang on despite overwhelming odds, but the large elk, who lacked much of the agility for survival as their smaller cousins, had been served up to be masticated with potatoes and gravy. When the Elkhorn Lodge was enlarged to the proportions we see it today, photos revealed elk horns on walls with a huge tangle of them in a near monument attitude upon the front lawn. Those trophies for the most part were acquired in Wyoming, particularly Yellowstone National Park, where great herds still wandered about, unpursued and regal. Mr. Hondius participated in the elk herds' reintroduction to the ranges of the Park in the spring of 1913. He permitted the Forest Service free access of his ranch properties as a new home for the first small herd of twenty-five elk. He encouraged the State of Colorado's tourist commission, then formally known as the State Board Of Immigration, to promulgate widely facts and photos of the beauty of Colorado and especially the Estes Valley. He labored long in the trenches of public debate for the establishment of a new National Park thus preventing the Department of Agriculture from selling off great tracts to the private sector or by grants to the states.

William James is remembered as 'a perfect host with his round, cheerful face and his happy manner at making every one feel at home.' His was a personality that gathered a crowd about him at the lodge, to share with guests tales of bear hunts, and of his many activities in his greatly loved Park. His daughter wrote affectionately of her parents. "Father stood for strength, courage and usefulness in the community, while Mother looked after the comforts of the guests and provided good things for the inner man." For all of his 18 years at the Elkhorn Lodge, William James appreciated children and was ever mindful of their happiness. When mothers of the children staying at the lodge were not looking, he pressed a piece of candy into their little hands while smiling in sly beneficence. One summer day Mrs. F. W. Crocker of Denver, later an owner of a local ranch bearing the Crocker name, arrived with her friend Miss Hyde of the family of the Mentholatum Company fortune. Mrs. Crocker's infant son, Sherwood, was the reason for her move to Elkhorn for the summer as doctors had advised a cool dry climate if the child were to live. Ella James was not certain if this sickly child should stay at their ranch, but when Mr. James learned of the child's circumstance, he took charge of the youngster and within a few weeks the boy's health had so improved that Eleanor reported "Sherwood was in father's lap eating griddle cakes." The Crockers and the Jameses remained fast friends and Miss Hyde stayed at the ranch to give supplementary school lessons to the four children.

After the death of William James in 1895, Homer, two years out of medical school and practicing in the mining town of Alma, Colorado, returned to share with his mother the prime responsibility of operating the Elkhorn Lodge. They had the valued assistance of the youngest son Howard and of course young Eleanor who was content to dress, and some say, act like a boy, yet more aware of her feminine gender after first encountering the young man from Holland. It was evident early on that this young lady would prove a challenge as she herself explained in her charming little story about the guest who came to The Elkhorn to see 'baby Eleanor' and accepted an invitation to dinner. It appeared that the lady had once looked after her six years before and remembered her charge as "the *baby* with the bangs, a dirty face and looked like a boy." Tommy the cat was then eleven years old and was content to be dressed in dolls clothes and rolled about in the baby carriage, slowly chase chipmunks, or sit in a high chair at the dining table as he was this day.

Well the cat went too far on this occasion as the guest was seated next to the cat. Brother Charles had caught the dinner and a fine looking trout, brown with batter, was carefully placed on the guest's plate to the acclamations of the recipient. Tommy also was duly impressed, and quick as lightning, --and so completely out of character for a baby doll, reached out and pawed away the entree. The story was left unfinished, but it must be presumed that the feline friend was permanently excused from the table, doll baby or not, and old Tommy would remain just a cat on the floor, if that were possible.

The emergence of a greatly enlarged Elkhorn Lodge occurred in 1900, and further additions were made in 1907 and 1912 at which time the entire lodge property could comfortably accommodate 180 guests. A portion of the last addition in 1912 contained a complete candy kitchen and all the guests knew where an errant child could be found. In those years it was a popular recreational activity for children to have taffy pulling parties, and children were just as important to the James family as guests as were their parents. The lodge also added an attractive ballroom, a billiard room, a quiet parlor for the ladies and elegant new suites. The aim of the Elkhorn Lodge was not to be just the best lodge, but more especially the best home away from home for their guests. With the return of guests, their children and grandchildren over the years, this certainly reflected an appreciation of this philosophy. Ella James always monitored the activities of the lodge, keeping everything quite proper and *cultured* and to the lodge often were invited members of the newly inaugurated Literary Society of Estes Park whose regular meetings were conducted in the new school house. At such meetings, programs included music, poetry readings and a 'delightful duet' sung by Mrs. Abner (Alberta) Sprague and her sister-in-law, Mrs. Alson (Arreanna Sprague) Chapman. Many were single men and women who used this uplifting opportunity to do some courting as the girls brought dinner baskets that were auctioned off. Of course if a *young thing* wanted a certain handsome swain to bid the most for her basket, entitling the young man to escort her home, she would subliminally alert him by wearing a geranium flower that just so happened to match another pinned to her basket. If there were an absence of talent at the meetings or the program proved to be unduly short, the Society could always rely upon Warren Rutledge, the Irish guide on the Devils Gulch Road, to unsheathe his phonograph with the huge cornucopian horn. At any brief break in the activities or at the slightest degree of encouragement, he played popular tunes like *In The Shade Of The Old Apple Tree*, *Silver Threads Among The Gold*, or Warren's favorite selection, *Casey Would Dance With The Strawberry Blond*. It was an unforgettable evening in the quiet village of Estes Park where friends gathered in decent pursuit of culture, accompanied by a fine dinner with a pretty girl. Mrs. James was a lovely lady with a distinct and persuasive personality, although her signals often were mixed when it came to Sunday recreational activities. As an example, she routinely hid the billiard balls, considering it a noisy and an inappropriate game for the Sabbath. But when it came to playing cards for money she had an explanation, although puzzling to others, that was absolutely logical to her. She refused to play cards for money, although the usual wager on a game was ten cents. When Mrs. James won and came away with a pocketful of dimes, she explained her actions. "Oh, I was not playing for money! This was only the prize!"

The season commenced around Memorial Day and continued to well

69

into September. It was said that the month of June was a slow one for tourists, "except for stenographers, brides and grooms." Howard James, Sr. and his mother greeted the guests as they arrived through the large gate on the eastern perimeter to proceed along a circular drive leading to a large tree trunk supported front porch. Mother and son made an affable pair, minted for treasured memories, to the extent that guests found it difficult to leave at the end of the summer, especially the ladies who hugged and kissed a beaming Howard. I can well remember as a boy a similar greeting by the owner of an old lodge in southern Wyoming when my Dad first rolled the old black Oldsmobile up to the front porch. The woman who owned this very rustic resort stood in front of the slightly slumping log structure that still oozed a warmth from fifty previous summers of dedicated service. Extending her freckled hands to me, a small boy clad in a worn cowboy hat and slightly scuffed high boots, she gave me a special bear hug. I just knew this was the place for me as I saw the other kids galloping down to see the horses get fed. And I can yet hear the tall, dignified, jean and flannel clad Mrs. Clara Craig of Brooklyn Lodge speak those words, that she really meant and I'm sure were equally voiced years before by the James family upon their guests' arrival. "We're **so** happy to have you with us. Welcome to our lodge!" Rarely in the 1990s does a traveler get that special greeting, or for that matter any at all at the check-in desk of a chain motel. And by the way, who is the owner of this place? Don't ask, just hand over your credit card for the computer to evaluate, that is if the system is not down.

Activities at Elkhorn were legion and varied to suit the age, gender, mood or tenor of the occasion. There were steak fries, with the children racing over the hill west of the lodge on their horses to where the dinner was to be served. The livery, stabling 110 horses, was looked over by employee Johnny Adams and why no one was killed or even injured in those Elkhorn derbies is anyone's guess. Two slot machines stood right by the front door, one for nickels and the other with the dime slot for big spenders, and guests lined up before supper for a chance in such a risque exploit. Bridge and bingo parties were common as were the staged cowboy and Indian encounters. Cabaret evenings, with dining room tables pushed to the side, were regular events as the floor was covered with corn meal to absorb the fruit punch and whatever cascaded about as small children chased about in their costumes. Charles Eagle Plume astounded all with his intellectual lectures about Indians and exhibits of their dances, as did the Indian performers from Cheyenne Frontier Days invited down each year for dinner and a show. And of course the very favorite for the young were the weekly informal *hops,* and for the energetic older folk the square dances whose leader and fiddler could be heard all the way down to Town Hall. There even was a swimming pool, probably the first for this mountain region, scooped out of the ground into which a streamlet from Fall River trickled. Boy was that water cold! The older guests, called the *rocking chair brigade,* enjoyed sitting on the front porch keeping tabs on the youngsters carousing out in the big front yard, or perhaps rocking away in the cool of an evening with one eye cocked for the teenagers who sought anonymity as they sneaked in long after the assigned hour. There was much camaraderie amongst the guests, young and old alike, to the extent that when people returned the following summer and one of last summer's crowd was absent, there was a sense of melancholy as the table previously assigned to that family had a new set of faces. Famous people were guests including Cornelius Otis Skinner, Miss Adams of Hull House, former Secretary of the Navy Paul Nitze and Will Hayes the campaign manager for President Taft who later became the movie czar and Postmaster General. The funniest person, who dressed up at parties in a caveman outfit, was Augustus Busch, the beer baron from Saint Louis. Tourists often spent a month or the whole summer, at the lodge, some going so far as renting a room for their maids. That boded well for warm relationships approaching near family status as Labor Day drew near with the conclusion of another successful season.

After the death of Ella James in 1917 at the age of 74, in which her epitaph loudly echoed the fact that "we were fortunate to have Mrs. James as our neighbor," Howard and his wife Edna assumed prime responsibility for this extremely popular lodge, assisted by Eleanor Hondius and the housekeeper for nearly three decades, Mrs. Kramer. Mr. Hondius took no part in hotel operations, contenting himself with his ranching business and the new Hondius Water System piped down from the ranch in Upper Beaver Meadows. However, he had not counted upon the effects of ragweed and Timothy grasses on which his animals fed as his asthma and hayfever were aggravated to the degree that he often spent the summers domiciled in Lawn Lake lodge that was owned and managed by the operators of Horseshoe Inn. Supplies periodically were brought to him by employees of the Elkhorn. Howard James was considered by all the most superb fisherman in the Park and, while he often conducted guests on fishing trips, he exceeded in 1920 his highly extolled reputation as an angler. On that bright summer day, a Friday that was regularly scheduled for the noon fish fry, he led the whole complement of guests, 140 in number, up to Horseshoe Park for a picnic. He proved his premier qualities by catching and supplying the whole assembled multitude with sufficient quantities to satisfy all of their appetites. I can only recall a more grand show stopper with fish, and that was recorded much earlier in Holy Writ. The cuisine at Elkhorn was memorable and in abundance to gourmand proportions. Have you ever had Elkhorn cream pie or Elkhorn Welsh rarebit? It was unforgettably and sinfully delicious as was the boiled salt mackerel that was an option on the breakfast menu. While I am on the subject of breakfast, although I am not certain of its date, I read of an amusing activity of which Mr. Frederick Chapin, the namesake of Mount Chapin and a frequent guest at the Elkhorn, was the direct beneficiary. Mr. Chapin occupied one of the ground floor rooms of the lodge close to the chicken coops, and he thoroughly enjoyed an egg for breakfast. A certain hen had the propensity for the bedding in Mr. Chapins' suite and timed her flight into the open window of his bed chamber when he left for his bracing walk before breakfast. In hopped the brood hen and nearly on command laid one egg on his bed announcing her effort with a triumphant cackle. Unable to cure this chicken of its disgraceful habit, management sought to bring something good out of disaster. Upon hearing the cackle, Mrs. Hondius scurried into the absented bedroom, shooed away the chicken, carefully picked up the egg and dashed to the kitchen. When Mr. Chapin entered the dining room, aglow with the crisp air and in the mood for his breakfast, there at his table sat the egg, cooked, and with toast and jelly if you please. He was never the wiser and it was a source of amusement to Eleanor Hondius.

When in Europe in the summer of 1928, the Hondiuses hastened back at the news of Howard's serious illness. After their return, he lingered for only a month and then, sadly, another of the James pioneers was gone. Eleanor set herself to the task of the lodge's management, duties that would last for another ten years. It was during their winter vacation to Palm Springs, California in 1934 that her husband's health declined and he too died, another severe blow to her past and future. On December 15, 1939 she sold all of her interest in the Elkhorn to Howard's widow Edna who remained in business with her son, Howard, Jr. Howard, Jr. took his lodging experience to new levels of achievement when he later became the chief executive officer of Sheraton International Hotels Corporation. At the close of every season during the James and Hondius family era at the Elkhorn there was a mixture of sadness as well as anticipation as the Harvest Moon Party, that concluded a summer of fulfilling pleasure, approached. The living room was decorated with aspen branches and tables were over laden with food. Oh what a selection of victuals! There were chafing dishes of lobster Newberg and creamed mushrooms, platters of chicken, ham, roast beef, tongue, salads of all description and so much more, all to be washed down with kegs of cider, the traditional drink at Elkhorn from its earliest days. In a dramatically ceremonious end to the banquet, the young kitchen workers and waitresses marched in carrying plates --held high --of pumpkin and mince meat pies, cream puffs and assorted cakes that defied description. Another season for the Elkhorn Lodge was at an end as was the name of James and Hondius in its ownership, for the first time in 84 years, when in 1961 Howard, Jr., known as Bud James who then was running the lodge with his wife Margaret, sold the lodge and its last remaining 20 acres to Robert Venner of Lincoln, Nebraska. From him possession passed through a series of owners whereby the lodge essentially reverted to a caretaker status. Eleanor Estes James Hondius after telling her last humorous story, said her final good bye to her family and friends in early 1969.

The Elkhorn Lodge, stands in quiet repose at the west end of Estes Park's main street like a revered, somewhat forgotten, historic landmark although its new owners I read in the newspapers have other ideas for its use. She has over the past few decades awaited the opportunity to once again display in refurbished attire that old vision and philosophy of the James family. May her day of past glories once again dawn as surely as a new sunrise bathes the Village of Estes Park with a renewed opportunity for service.

James, Later McCreery Homestead, Rev. McCreery In Center, 1890 (EPPL)

Early Elkhorn Lodge, circa 1878 (RMNP)

Elkhorn Lodge, circa 1880s (RMNP)

William E. James, circa 1893 (EPTG)

Road To Elkhorn Lodge, circa 1890s (RMNP)

Parlors In Elkhorn Lodge, 1884 (EPPL)

Guests At Elkhorn Lodge, 1895 (EPPL)

First Public School House And Cleave House, 1896 (EPPL)

First Structure Of New Elkhorn Lodge, circa 1900 (RMNP)

Guests Arrive At New Lodge, 1900 (EPPL)

Completed Lodge With Grounds, circa 1915 (McDC)

Enlarged Lodge And Elk Antlers, circa 1930 (CHS)

LAMB'S RANCH AND LONGS PEAK HOUSE

The Reverend Elkanah J. Lamb, born in 1832 in Wayne County, Indiana, became a preacher for the Church of the Brethren while living near Beatrice, Nebraska in the 1860s and later was assigned to the mission field of Colorado Territory. He first saw the Estes Valley in August of 1871 while traveling in company with twelve men and women who were surveying the religious needs of the vast area northwest of Denver. Reverend Lamb, a strong, vigorous man well over six feet tall, was intent on knowing as much as he could about this wondrous mountain valley, and recorded its first appearance to him. "The Park comprises about ten thousand acres, the Big Thompson River coursing through like a silver ribbon, meandering from the extreme west side, through canyons and gorges in its eastern course, til it reaches wheat fields and alfalfa meadows thirty and forty miles away. Just enough evergreens scattered in little clumps, sometimes in larger groves, to enhance the beauty of the landscape. A scene of beauty and joy forever." He appeared in demeanor and actions larger than life, determined to surmount any obstacle he confronted and relished a challenge of contest. As much an explorer as he was a dynamic preacher, he was in constant pursuit of knowledge of God's marvelous world in which he found himself blessed to be a part. From the snow, green trees and tumbling streams, to the frolicking deer that curiously watched his odd assembly of professional Christian itinerants in heavy leather thonged leggings and boots, he received profound inspiration. Elkanah was in charge of the troop although no vote had been taken. It was just the nature of one who assumed actions were an inspiration motivated by God's own hand. Inasmuch as his name, Elkanah, meant *possessed by God*, how could he act otherwise?

He led his flock up the game trail below Long's Peak into a subalpine kingdom contrasting remarkably with the wide expanses of rolling prairie that had been his, and their, preaching pulpit. For an assortment of reasons, none but their leader ventured any further than timberline, preferring to remain in their high camp to await Elkanah's return. Emblematic of his nature, he alone pressed on to the summit of Long's Peak whereupon he was emotionally overwhelmed with what he saw, no doubt poised excitedly with head bare, gazing about at the handiworks of his God to Whom he gave all the credit. He exclaimed, "I stand on this historic pile of granite and quartz, a huge monster nearly three miles above sea level and ten miles around its base. The sight is magnificent! To the north and south, and especially to the west, there is a wilderness of snow-capped mountains, lakes, streams, and waterfalls. Mingling with this promiscuous maze are immense, dense, dark forests of pine, spruce, and balsam firs, presenting to nature's lover a grand scenic display of beauty, compelling admiration and adoration of nature's God. Oh, what Almighty power to build revolving worlds, with stupendous mountain ranges, all moving with velocity through the immensities of eternal space!" His return to camp was accomplished in an unusual method, down the east face of this awesome peak, to become the first to accomplish such a feat, and with no climbing equipment. Presenting a breathtaking sight --grappling with rocks, digging holes in the ice with a broken pocket knife, tumbling like a person possessed of an aberrational fit as the tails of the long black overcoat flew around his bearded face -- he descended the twelve hundred feet to Chasm Lake. Equipped with little more than his strong faith in his Almighty God, his peril plagued experience would make a complete book in itself. This rock cleft route is now printed on maps of the east face of Long's Peak as Lamb's Trail or Lamb's Slide.

Times were hard as he received no more than forty or fifty dollars from offerings and gifts in a whole year of dedicated effort on the missionary circuit. Yet he doggedly persevered in dedicated service to those who needed his missionary zeal presented in a stentorian voice. However in the mid 1870s those pesky grasshopper of Horace Ferguson's torment continued to crowd out the sun on the plains of eastern Colorado. A collateral consequence of their voracity led to the disaster of many of his little churches as Elkanah wrote, "They impoverished the country to such an extent that it served to lessen a preacher's salary." Being a realist and accepting the fact that his God expected him to cope with this situation as he had with others devised by man or the environment, he declined the offer from his Church Conference in Denver to remain on the missionary circuit. As there was no guile in him and mindful of his earthly physical needs as well as those of the spirit, he resolved to settle his problems himself, not leaving everything to God. I commend that philosophy to those in our modern generation who sit about waiting for others, seen or unseen, to resolve their dilemmas often self inflicted. Elkanah explained his decision. "I concluded to locate for a season and go to the mountains for a refuge and financial interests. Say what we may about and against filthy lucre and unrighteous mammon, you cannot get clothing, bread, coffee, sugar, and other concomitants without sheckles or good credit, and good credit cannot be maintained without cash in the background." Therefore in 1875 he located a claim in front of Long's Peak on which he erected a rough, fourteen by twelve foot log cabin and began a collateral career that would bring him joy, a lot of hard work and further justification for his faith especially after his deliverance from his introduction to the perils of mountain climbing.

His new home was known as Lamb's Ranch in what was later referred to as the Elkanah Valley, nine miles south of Estes Park, in which he and his second wife, the widow Jane Spencer Morger, lived for many years with their own child Jennie born to them after their marriage in 1868. Also in residence was his son Carlyle Lamb, born in Guthrie Center, Iowa in 1862, and one of five children born to him and his first beloved who died in Nebraska. Another roadway therefore is of interest, establishing the shrewdness and tenacity of the early day clergy. Elkanah Lamb working in concert with his son, chopped for two weeks clearing the first road sufficiently wide enough for wagons to traverse a southerly route to his homestead property and beyond from the small village of Estes Park. The travel to Long's Peak and south at that time would of necessity originate in Estes Park, and it was reported that the toll gate of Lamb's road was near his home. Abner Sprague recalled that road. "To make it inviting, the gate was left open so that you could drive up to the house and not turn back on account of the closed road. When you had made your call, or received the information that you were at the end of the road, -- and started on the return trip, you would find the gate closed and would be asked to pay toll, both ways." Later this road, recognized as Lamb's Road, would link up with another years later to constitute a portion of the Peak To Peak Highway. The broad aspen tree covered valley for many years where Long's Peak House stood in full display would bear the name Elkanah Valley, this designation used for the return address of many later residents including the owner of Hewes-Kirkwood Lodge to the south. However this valley in the years ahead was tagged with another name by the U. S. Board on Geographic Names in 1916, one that to it was more appropriate to the mountainous region where many peaks soon would reflect Indian tribal identification. A name change came at the urging of Enos Mills -- for unknown reasons unwilling that his uncle's name be accorded broader significance -- as he preferred the name Glacier Valley. But in a pure play on politics, the imprimatur to the name Tahosa Valley now became its monogram, an Arapahoe word signifying *The Land of the Sky* while others with whom I could disagree said it was of Kiowa origin signifying *Dwellers of the Mountain Tops*.

In 1880 their home, with several adjacent structures, was renamed from Lamb's Ranch to Long's Peak House, perhaps a perception of its artistic positioning in symbiotic partnership with that towering white guidon around which fleecy clouds floated by in perfect formation. The Lambs conceived of Long's Peak House not just as their home but more especially to serve as the jumping off point for those desirous of climbing the peaks immediately to the west, and thus it took upon itself an aura of a small alpine lodge. As a part of any remote lodging facility, small vegetable gardens, cattle and other domestic stock were mandatory to fill the plates and vessels for increasing numbers of travelers when supply lines stretched long distances from the eastern plains. Thus this high valley in the shadow of mountains, shared its turf with man and an assortment of grazing and pecking creatures. Reverend Lamb was a practical, disaster defying, man who knew his survival was dependent upon his partnership of human talent and eternal intervention. Reverend Lamb and his son guided *flatlanders* to their *pile of granite* on its first trail that this team built in 1880, and that Carlyle exclusively maintained until 1902. Elkanah reported that they entertained parties ascending Long's Peak and guided *pilgrims* to the summit for the price of $5.00 a trip per person. When queried about his location in the mountains and of such a radical change from earlier life as a full time preacher of the Word, his quip would exhibit a recognition of humanity to the extent that his survival more depended upon his own abilities than the salubrious intentions of repentant sinners. "This location would seem to indicate more tangible and swifter strides towards Heaven than small salaries, partly paid in promises and hubbard squashes. If they would not pay for spiritual guidance, I compelled them to divide for material elevation." They continued in their mountaineering profession and as sole conservators of their trail to the top of Long's Peak until 1902. The location of their establishment at 9,000 feet would have appeared awesome, lonely and forbidding in 1875 to those of lesser constitutions. Thirty-five miles from any post-office or store, neither accessible to electricity or radio, certainly no telephone communication, and above all no neighbors to come to one's assistance. A settler would have to be up to his very best, fully dependent upon his inner strength and amenable to the acceptance of divine inspired resources. Elkanah was admirably suited to the task of creative pioneering.

Reverend Lamb was often seen preaching in the little village of Estes Park, many times without a formal invitation. His rule of thumb for ascending a pulpit of any description was, "As long as there are eight or ten gathered together in the name of the Lord, I will preach," and he did with great fervency. His sermons commenced after draping his white hankie on a table, counter or whatever was suitable for a pulpit, and then to deposit his cigar on the window sill. His sermons lasted well over an hour and, as they were remembered, were punctuated and peppered with protestations of "Hell, fire and damnation!" One member of the congregation recalled, "the longer they went on the louder he got." Midway through sermons he frequently picked up his hankie to trumpet a blast from his nose, then repositioning his slightly rumpled *prayer cloth* upon the table he continued without so much as skipping a participle. His blowing, shouting, pounding and elocution of electrically charged passages from scripture would have given the Angel Gabriel and his horn strong competition. John Cleave enjoyed the sermons and could be counted upon to be there every Sunday to take up the collection, and it was recalled that the collection plate was more heavily laden when the sermons were shorter. Reverend Lamb through the years continued his ministry, particularly preaching with unforgettable fervor in the mountains of Colorado and he was often observed, still an impressive looking man in his more elderly years, ambling along Estes Park's main street with a walking staff, pausing frequently to offer advice on God's gospel to a passing public. He was a colorful pioneer and valued exponent for the God endowed resources of the entire Estes Valley. He died on April 9, 1915 in Fort Collins, Colorado where his son then resided after selling the ranch, thereupon rightfully taking his place with the saints above. Carlyle Lamb, who made his first ascent of Long's Peak in 1879 and his last of 146 successive hikes to the summit in 1935 at the age of 73, lived well into his nineties before his death at his home in Fort Collins. Elkanah's friend and neighbor, Charles Edwin Hewes, who wrote delightful, often bequilingly arcane poetry with introspective thought provoking meaning, authored this titillating piece, dedicated to a man of many moods, like himself.

ELKANAH

Elkanah was a preacher of old,
A United Brethren, fearless and bold,
With strong persuasion, invective and scold,
He quipped his text with a powerful hold.

He ne'er in pulpit displayed the least doubt,
Struck from the shoulder, put the devil to rout,
His six feet of person shook in the breeze,
Like a gale roaring fierce among the trees.

Twas grand to see his venerable form,
Thrill with emotion and bend in the storm,
But when he reacted, had checked his pace,
Let down like an old horse after a race.

He was troubled with doubt which ran a pace,
Made him feel he'd overstated his case,
Then deep in despond with question, dispair,
He'd wrestle and battle and almost swear.

76

As a last resort he'd go to a friend,
Confide, confess, argue close to that end,
He strengthened and to again do his best,
But always he quit with his set protest.

'I have preached the Word for fifty years,
And stormed the gates of Hell,
But in that Old Book I must confess,
There's some strange things to tell'.

LONG'S PEAK INN

Enos Mills, Sr. was born of Quaker parents in 1834 near Richmond, Indiana and was raised until he was sixteen years old on the farm in Joseph County, Indiana. Seeing a better future for himself, he walked westward as there were no railroads in 1851 beyond Peru, Illinois. He freighted goods out of Keokuk, Iowa for five years, met Elkanah Lamb's sister, Anna Lamb, and married her on July 28, 1856. In 1858 they moved to Linn County, Kansas near to the Missouri line. Mr. Mills said their move was precipitated by the desire "to help make Kansas a free state." He said, "The ruffians came over the boarder to kill our neighbors, and for seven years we remained as a picket post." He, his wife, brother Enoch and Elkanah were caught up with the gold fever in Pikes Peak country like so many others, and in the summer of 1860 drove a mule team west as far as the diggings at Breckinridge, Territory of Colorado where they filed on a mining claim. Breckenridge -- today its name a tad distanced in spelling from the disgrace associated with an early day national leader for whom the village was named -- at that time consisted of a single building in which was located a huge barrel of whiskey whose free enterprising purveyor sold for twenty-five cents a sip. Grog and other comestibles were paid for in gold dust by the teeming hordes of boisterously muddy men intent upon disrupting the flow of the Blue River with their pans and dirt rockers. Anna was the first white woman to reach that far into the backcountry of Colorado but despite the efforts of her men to find yellow color in that chaos, they abandoned their unproductive claim and survived by selling meat to the other miners who were more persistent. Enos became ill and Anna drove back to Denver where they earlier had witnessed an Indian war dance right in the center of town. Finding their way back across the 600 miles of open grasslands without incident, they reclaimed their more mundane lives as farmers near Pleasanton, Linn Country, Kansas. They parented and raised six children, three girls and three boys one of whom was Enos Abijah Mills and another was Enoch Josiah Mills, the Joe Mills who would follow his brother to Estes Park later to build Crags Lodge. Enos, Sr. remained in Pleasanton until his death on February 17, 1910 while his wife, outliving her famous son Enos, Jr., completed her days in Fort Scott, Kansas.

The younger Enos A. Mills was born at Fort Scott in 1870 on April 22nd, a day years later proclaimed as a time to honor and plant trees, -- Arbor Day. He was bothered as a young man with allergies and his mother suggested that he take a look at Colorado. For her this was a repository of beautiful memories and healthful for uplifting pursuits of life even though her own journey twenty-four years before was flawed by her husband's illness and their unrequited search for hidden wealth. By the summer of 1884 young Enos in Kansas City had earned enough money as a baker's assistant to purchase a ticket west where he lived with his uncle Elkanah and cousin Carlyle, working for them in various capacities on the ranch and in Long's Peak House. Returning the following summer of 1885, he made his first ascent of the great peak at the age of fifteen. The out-of-doors thrilled him by its ordered complexity of diverse form and effect, and his decision to pursue a life as a scientific observer of nature was one from which he derived immense pleasure and fulfillment. Building his own small cabin at the base of Twin

Sisters Mountain, opposite to and possessed with a commanding view of Long's Peak from which he drew strength, he regained his health and at the same time found a purpose for life. From this little cabin he climbed all the mountains in his view, and many others hidden beyond the sunset which was his favorite time of the day. He vowed to become the finest of guides for seekers of nature's beauty with whom he might share the exhilaration of his widening world. His next thirteen years were a time of preparation as winter and spring months were devoted to mining the Anaconda holdings of Butte, Montana to earn enough to permit him to explore Colorado as well as the distant white vastness of the Alaskan ice age. Gaining confidence as a speaker, he initiated his newly found talent in a lecture in Kansas City in 1895 on the topic of woodlands.

In the winter of 1899 fires closed down the Montana mines and, electing to see what lay further west on the Pacific, met a man of international reputation who changed his direction for life into a clearer definition of purpose. His new friend, that he chanced to meet on a beach near San Francisco, was John Muir, the legendary naturalist from Dunbar, Scotland. The visionary Muir, considerably older yet as young in spirit and vitality as his new acquaintance, was impressed with Enos's eagerness to learn all there was about nature. Muir motivated Enos, not only to study forests and the creatures that dwelt therein, but to preserve them for future generations yet unborn, and thus the quintessence of life for him, its essence, verve and his only religion would now be nation-wide preservation of nature. He had been given a task, to him a holy mission, and in but sixteen years would prove his worth, often as a trenchant adversary, culminating in his most noble achievement. Now he was anxious to be about his business. John Muir and Enos Mills would remain in lifelong brotherhood in their toil to gain man's respect and appreciation of all of nature. While working at Lamb's ranch he was an habitual user of the Estes Park Library providing to him hundreds of books from which he would devour avariciously, in hungry mental mouthfuls, the knowledge he never received in limited formal education on the Kansas farm. He rationalized that it was imperative that he gain knowledge in many scholarly disciplines such as mathematics, scientific statistics and its vernacular, techniques of persuasion, philosophy and certainly government. In short, he required a speedy liberal education if he were to have any chance at intellectual persuasion of men and women whose influence for his cause was crucial.

Returning from Butte for the last time in the summer of 1902, he purchased the Long's Peak House and its 160 acres from Carlyle Lamb who actually held the title to the property. The name over the door now read Longs Peak Inn. Enlarging it into a center to house those who wanted to study, explore and appreciate nature at its best and on its own terms, he had no lack of fellow devotees. People came by the hundreds at first. Then the tide widened to thousands over the years requiring a staff to assist him when he found himself away guiding or giving lectures. Mountains were always special to Enos as a remedy, not just a palliative, for boredom, distress or worry. He once wrote, "A mountain is in a class by itself. This towering and historic landmark of granite, old as the earth, will knit up the raveled sleeve of care and enrich the imaginations of multitudes." This was to be the tone of all of his messages, nature allegorically fashioned with a personality -- whereby he clothed the trees, rocks, animals and flowers in an emotional context -- to move men and women into a new dimensions for action. Although he used his voice and pen to reflect his observations and express his opinions about happenings in nature, he never intended to be a philosopher. He observed and informed others of his findings, leaving them to form their own opinions, yet hopeful of a course of conduct that mirrored his own. His career traveled divergent roads that led to the same destination. He was made Colorado's official State Snow Observer requiring him to snowshoe all over the state in the winters equipped with little more than his long coat, a camera and his answer to all nutritional needs in the high altitudes, boxes of raisins. He began lecturing throughout the country, on bears, chipmunks, birds, trees and on whatever interested him, subjects he deemed important to nudge America onto his natural resource team that needed more energetic and dependable players.

The speed in which he climbed to the top rung of the ladder, as *America's First Professional Nature Guide,* was phenomenal. Propelled to such heights by the his fifteen books the first of which was published in 1898, they were read nationwide together with articles in national magazines from which paragraphs were frequently quoted. He had friends in lofty offices such as President Theodore Roosevelt and the Chief of the United States Forest Service, Gifford Pinchot, who created for Enos Mills in 1907 the position of Government Lecturer on Forestry. To this task he applied himself on the lecture circuit encouraging state and national forest preservation and National Forest Reservations, the vanguards of more National Parks. Rocky Mountain National Park was the most noteworthy product of this hard work and devotion to the purpose earlier inspired by Mr. Muir. It was when he was away from home lecturing in early June of 1906 that news reached him of the total destruction of Longs Peak Inn in a devastating fire. He returned immediately, obtained a foreman who knew how to work with logs and rocks, and set about with untiring rapidity coupled with environmental ingenuity the building of a new Longs Peak Inn on a much greater scale that to some architectural purists was "not *Early American* but rather *Extremely Rustic.*" Its building materials consisted of fire killed trees, granite rocks and stumps found about the property or carefully carried down from Battle Mountain, a name given to it by Mills because that was where the competing winds joined in combat for control of the storms. The only finished wood in the lodge was for the window casings and the front door. Table tops sat upon roots of trees and the huge lattice-like screen was an immense, twelve foot diametered, agglomeration of cobwebby tentacles of tree roots that diffused the sunlight into intricate patterns. In struggles of promethean proportions, not unlike to a Labors of Hercules, on July 4th, 1906 the first part of the lodge was sufficiently completed enabling his guests to be served dinner in the new dining room incapable of description.

A further description of the new lodge is warranted inasmuch as it no longer welcomes the morning sun into the shadows of the night at the eastern face of Long's Peak. The best known feature of the lodge was the staircase with split log steps, banisters of smooth poles and spindles of small pine and spruce trees. Two rough stone fireplaces warmed the guests who were seated about to listen to nature talks by the lodges's premier authority and the roof of the main living room was supported by rounded, fire colored trees. The theme throughout the lodge intended to give the guest an experience of dwelling within corridors of nature, with furniture fashioned out of dwarfed trees bent into grotesque but beautifully imbued shapes inherent in nature's own myriad of patents. Even the wastepaper baskets appeared as miniature log cabins without a roof. The use of upright trees seen penetrating the porch roofs into the sky above created the illusion of totem poles whose knobbiness appeared as queer faces gazing puckishly down at arriving guests. No paint was used nor stain other than clear oil applied to the wooden floor planking and clear shellac to add a shine and smooth surface for the table tops. In the lodge building, besides the large living room, dining room, small post office and book store, was the Nature Room for his informally oriented Trail School. This small chamber was filled with photos of flora, fauna, flower exhibits and artifacts to be observed in his outdoor laboratory. And of course one could, on the great front porch, engage in good conversation with a chattering chipmunk who shared a patch of sunlight with a guest extending out a token of appreciation, the ubiquitous peanut.

The Inn could accommodate more than 100 guests in the lodge and the dozen log cabins scattered about, some of which contained as many as ten rooms. Some were graced, as a vacation writer of 1913 expressed, "with city style baths and steam heat probably reserved for Boston people." Enos had his own quarters and office in a separate cabin adjacent to a grove of trees where a merry little stream tumbled about the grounds like a child engaged in play. He allowed neither card playing nor dancing in the lodge, and a piano was not present as such sounds, he advised, "drowned out the sound of nature." He encouraged lunching on raisins supplemented with a raspberry sandwich and Hershey bar for light, yet energy rich rations to achieve on the most formidable of trails. Possessed of very strong convictions on nature, as well as other matters of importance to an active spirit, his sentiments were forcefully exhibited to friends and enemies alike. He was very partial to wild flowers, and it was *death* or ostracism to anyone picking flowers as explained by the signs posted about his property. In fact on the dining room tables only one example of but three different species at a time was permitted and the guests were not encouraged to do the picking, -- he did. Unfortunately his ire was particularly fierce for two who were greatly loved by others, Charles E. Hewes and his own brother Joe Mills. I will explain this in a subsequent chapter. Two accounts, one from an employee and another from a guest might give you a sense of being present in the lodge, the ambience, the electricity in the atmosphere of Mill's natural laboratory.

Mr. Robert Gookins, who was employed at the Inn in 1913 and 1914 looked back on his days in the kitchen and dining room. "In 1913, after graduating from high school, I came with my brother and became the 3rd cook at the Inn. I peeled 150 pounds of potatoes regularly, prepared chickens for cooking and made the coffee. Mr. Mills wanted the coffee very strong, and guests were seen quite often diluting it with hot water. Mr. Mills was very strict with employees, dismissing summarily those who broke the rules, and would not allow any tips to be received, for he said 'this was a non-tip house.' Most of the seasonable employees were college students or teachers. I later became a waiter the next year and had to set up the table in accordance with the exact orders of Mr. Mills. They had no menus and the waiters had to remember as many as 6 tables of guests, that being 24 separate orders at one time. When I was there one of the other waiters even served the Clarence Darrow family. The help lived upstairs in the lodge and often sat at the head of the stairs to hear Mr. Mills telling the tales of the West. We were young and more or less inexperienced in the folk lore of the mountains and we really thought he was *taking in* the green Easterners with his tall tales and sometimes we had a hard time trying to keep from laughing out load. Looking back after 61 or 62 years I think he was giving some good talks and knew more than we thought. I enjoyed my two summers there, but did not get rich. The pay for the waiters and chamber maids, and some of the kitchen help, was only $105 for the summers work, plus room and board."

Mary Belle Totten, my friend now long deceased, was a distinct individual who traveled the world in her more than nine-two years. After her college days in Detroit she and her girl friend found themselves guests at the Inn in August of 1920. She wrote brief accounts of her experience on Inn stationery on which was prominently printed, **Long's Peak Inn**, *The Non-Tip House In The Rocky Mountain National Park With The Pines, Birds And Wild Flowers*. I think her letters are a real treasure and as complete an account of the activity around the lodge that I have ever found still available for reading. Here follow a few excerpts of her incisively humorous style.

"It is a beautiful place. A main building, built of logs, which is the dining hall, office, store and lobby. This Mr. Mills who runs this hotel is a writer and naturalist. There are wonderful collections of flowers and curios in his library and museum. In the main building here, there are two very large fireplaces built of stone; rustic seats and chairs all around. The lodging places are away from the main building. Some of them are large, others are small holding only one family. The log cabin we are in has three rooms, that means sleeping quarters for six people, separate doors for each, of course. The mountains tower up above the place. It is really beautifully situated. The clouds hang down around Long's Peak for an hour or so and then it rains. The showers come up in a hurry and only last a few minutes. There are mountains all around here and it looks just like I thought it would. The air up here is nice and cool, but the sun is very hot. There are just dozens of chipmunks around the place, very tame, and come right up and eat out of your hand, in fact they crawl all over you hunting for peanuts. We climbed halfway up a mountain side this morning and got a grand view. It made me puff to go up, but the coming down was easy. The furniture here is a good deal like 'Old Hickory' only more so and the fireplaces are extremely large stone ones where fires are always crackling in them. The stars around here, my goodness! There are millions of them! Everybody goes to bed early, 9 or 9:30 and they get up early, about 6:30 to 7 A. M.

"This Mr. Mills is quite a character. He won't let people pick more than one flower of each kind. He thinks it wasteful and destructive to carry off an armful of flowers. He believes the flowers are so much more beautiful growing out of doors than they are in the house, that people should leave them growing to beautify the fields and mountain sides. He gave a little talk last night about mountain horses that I enjoyed very much. His horses are his pets, and he makes friends of all the animals out here near his home. Lots of people ride horseback, and most all of the women wear breeches, no matter how old or young, thin or fat. We feel decidedly old-fashioned in a skirt, but I feel better than I would in pants. At a distance you can hardly tell the women from the men. We had an *Author's Night* last night, and several men of prominence spoke. The tone of this place is distinctly 'high brow.' The professors here are as thick as peas in a pod. There are poets, novelists and artists. There are only a few 'low brows' like myself, and darn the luck, most of them are teachers! (Miss Totten was a teacher) The meals here are good, and they are always willing to bring you a second helping of anything. That's more than you can say of lots of places. We walked all the way into Estes Park Village, about twelve miles on road and a trail, and enjoyed it especially that it was down hill. We had a wild ride back on a bus, a big truck-like affair with seats like a rubber-neck bus, and loaded with 12 people in all. They only charge $1.50 per head to bring you back on the road that is 9 miles. They certainly have you. Only one way to get back, or else you walk. Tomorrow we are planning on taking an all day trip, and leave at 7 in the morning and get back at supper time. We are going to Fern and Odessa Lakes, and there are 7 women and a guide, also a woman. This place out here looks like no man's land, --women, women, everywhere, and once in a while a man. Yesterday we climbed up to Chasm Lake, way up on Long's Peak, set in walls of granite, and is fed by melting snow, rain and hail and doesn't have any outlet. It is a terrible climb up there, about 7 miles from here, half of it is over big, loose rocks and boulders. Even on August 18th we crossed a field of snow. AND, we got caught in a very severe hail and rain storm. We were soaked to the skin. And our shoes! I never thought shoes could get so wet! We stopped at a cabin at timberline and got pretty well dried out. It rained yesterday but now has cleared off. Last night the moon was beautiful and it looked so very bright and near. It hung up above the range of mountains until about one in the morning then suddenly seemed to drop down behind the ridge. There is a brook which goes winding down through the grounds, rippling along over the stones and last night in the moonlight the ripples looked like silver. There is quite a lot of snow on the mountain tops. This has been a beautiful day with not a cloud in the sky, and the sky is the bluest thing you ever saw. I will have to tell you what we had for Sunday dinner at 1 P. M.: Tomato soup, fried chicken, mashed potatoes, gravy, green peas, apple fritters, green tea, lemon pie and chocolate ice cream. Supper is served at 6 P.M. I'll be there with bells on! I'm sorry to leave this place so soon!"

And many throughout the years shared these same convictions, some more famous but none more appreciative than Mary Belle. They included Charles Evans Hughes, Frank Lloyd Wright, Eugene V. Debs, Lowell Thomas and the lion of finance John D. Rockefeller. It was tough to leave behind such a unique experience, but then most took away part of it in their fond memories of a vacation well spent, intellectually stimulated by one owner whose mind, body and soaring spirit strove valiantly, perhaps litigiously, to enlist another warrior in the battle for nature's preservation. Late in life, in August of 1918 at the age of forty-eight, he married Esther A. Burnell who had come to Estes Park for the first time in 1916 from Des Moines, Iowa with her sister Elizabeth. She was a guest at the Inn and typed manuscripts for Enos, and later took up her own homestead on the Fall River close to the Fish Hatchery. Enos Mills died on September 21, 1922 at the Inn, the effects of an injury sustained months before in a New York City subway accident and blood poisoning that was related to a tooth infection. He was buried on September 25th, at sunset, near to his beloved Inn. The lodge, that by 1931 had in residence each day up to 125 guests at a rate between $5 and $10 per day, continued to be operated by Esther until it was sold by her in 1945. Within a few years the lodge sadly would come full circle again, mirroring the tragedy that befell its predecessor forty-three years before. I am grateful that Enos was not here to see his lodge go up in smoke in 1949 as Long's Peak Inn was destroyed once again by fire. Esther died in 1964, and their one child, a daughter Enda Mills Kiley, survives to care for her father's homestead cabin and preserve his memory through the sale of his books while continuing his good fight started so long ago. I feel a kinship with Enos Mills when I lean down to straighten up a small tree burdened with an errant rock, a heavy load of snow or an old grandfather tree that in death has flung out a branch to hold the youngster close to its side. Enos Mills wrote many fine stories that epitomized much of the splendor of nature. I believe one of his finest works is found within this short snippet of prose that moves me, and hopefully you as well, to show concern for even the most simplest of life's secondary dramas, as we ponder the struggle and end of a tree that could be a measure of our own life's work.

A LITTLE TREE

I never see a little tree bursting from the earth, peeping confidingly up among the withered leaves without wondering how long it will live and what trials and triumphs it will have. It will beautify the earth and love the blue sky and the white clouds passing by, and ever join merrily in the movement and the music of the elemental dance with winds. It will welcome the flower-opening days of Spring, be a home for the birds, and enjoy the summer rain. And when comes the golden peace of Autumn days I trust it will be ready with ripened fruit for the life to come. I never fail to hope that if this tree is cut down it may be used for a flag pole to keep our glorious banner in the breeze, or be built into a cottage where love will abide; or if it must be burnt, that it will blaze on the hearthstone in a home where children play in the firelight on the floor.

Parson Lamb's Ranch, circa 1880s (Mills)

Reverend Elkanah J. Lamb,
before 1890 (Private)

Enos Mills, Sr. And Anna Lamb Mills,
1867 (Mills)

Long's Peak House, 1880 (Mills)

Carlyle Lamb, At Long's Peak House, circa 1900 (Mills)

Enos Mills And Scotch At Long's Peak Inn, 1902 (Mills)

Joe Mills And Scotch, Long's Peak Inn, circa 1904 (Mills)

Guest Rides Sidesaddle At Inn, 1905 (Mills)

Free Enterprisers Sell Fish Worms At The Inn, 1905 (Mills)

Long's Peak Inn Before Fire Of 1906 (EPPL)

Long's Peak Inn Burns Down, 1906 (Mills)

Forest Cabin At Long's Peak Inn, 1905 (Mills)

Charles Hupp Brings Wood For New Furniture, 1906 (Mills)

Dining Room At Long's Peak Inn, 1907 (F.P. Clatworthy)

A Lounge At Long's Peak Inn, 1907 (F.P. Clatworthy)

Longs Peak Inn, circa 1910 (Private)

Guests Arrive By Horse To The New Inn, 1907 (Mills)

Guests Arrive By Auto, circa 1920 (EPPL)

Enos Mills, 1921 (EPPL)

Horseshoe Inn, Moraine Lodge, Cascade Lodge

The Water Comes Seeping In Brooklets,
From Snow On The Peaks That Soar;
The Brooklet Flows Onward And Ever,
To The River's Wide Tumble And Roar.
I Sit And Gaze At The Beauty,
Of This Wonderful World Where We Live;
And I Think Can Man Doubt God's Greatness,
He Alone Has This To Give.
Clara L. Warner, 1926

HORSESHOE INN

Not much is known of this lodge. It came early and departed just as quickly, the first casualty of the National Park's policy of removal of privately owned lodges. Willard H. Ashton had been living in Roxbury, Massachusetts with his wife Grace and their children, but reluctantly moved to Rockford, Illinois to work for his father in the Ashton Dry Goods Store of which he would eventually become the proprietor. While there a promoter for a land venture in the Estes Valley convinced the family to come out and see what it was like and thus in 1905 the family, Willard, Grace and their three children journeyed to Denver by train. Then, like others drawn by news of Estes Park's unusual beauty, rode on the Burlington Railroad to Lyons and continued up the North St. Vrain canyon in a four-horse drawn wagon to the little village. At Sam Service's Livery Stable, later to become the Rustic Theater then divided into a barber shop and gift store immediately behind his general store, they rented two burros as their means of transportation in and around the village. It was not Willard's intention to take up permanent residence but only to look for an investment in land for a summer home and to this resolve the quintet set out to see the territory with bed rolls and supplies purchased from Sam. The environs had an immediate and positive effect upon them as they remained for the entire summer. How the children loved those burros!

On one excursion out of the village, sun warming their backs as they enjoyed flower filled, nearly empty meadows, they rode up to Horseshoe Park on several rental horses required for longer trips. Continuing up the aspen shaded trail to visit a high lake recommended to them, they were much taken with the scenery around Lawn Lake. A small dam was in evidence, obviously laboriously raised up by men for irrigation water storage for dry land crops near Loveland, Colorado. The Ashtons, discovering a weathered cabin where the workers had lived was still tight and reasonably habitable, moved in their gear for two nights of perfect isolation. Willard and Grace, city born and bred and not expected to be attracted by the remoteness affording them no human conveniences to which they had been accustomed, discovered a con-

85

gruence to their new surroundings. Simply stated, they liked what they saw, absent of human amenities and all. No, it was more than that. Their Eastern friends' predictions of dire consequences such as "who knows what lurks back in those dark canyons," were proven entirely groundless as they expressed by their words of praise for the surroundings an immediate affinity for the lakes, snowcapped vistas, the rocks, flowers, and especially the people they had met in the village. Descending into Horseshoe Park for directions from the owners of an old ranch house they observed situated where the meadows left off and the tall red-brown Ponderosas thickly grew, they learned that this home and its 160 acres, called Horseshoe Ranch, was for sale. It met their criteria for a summer home, moreover it possessed investment possibilities for the small ranch house, outbuildings and tents scattered in the meadow that had obliged the basic needs of tourists in past years. They sought tranquility, dry air, cool temperatures and above all absolute unspoiled beauty. That same year they bought Horseshoe Ranch, settled in its broad park-like landscape where they discerned a total absence of other dwellers except the few deer and small wild creatures that gamboled through the high grass and willows. There were no elk as most all in the Estes Valley had previously been shot or frightened out by the greed of business minded hunters for profit. We in the Estes Valley can hardly imagine our community without large herds of elk, 'too many' town folks and wildlife management officers complain vocally even in 1993 as the numbers have grown into the thousands of animals. But it was not always that way. In a previous chapter I have touched on this subject. Let me explain in more depth one source of the problem.

Prior to 1900 game was abundant and early residents, such as the Joel Estes family, said they did not depend upon their own domestic herds for food because elk, deer and wild sheep were so plentiful. Because of the availability of game, hunters trooped in to supply the valley towns, railroad construction workers and burgeoning gold field camps with fresh meat. Between 1900 and 1910 most all of the antlered creatures had been shot. There were some deer hidden back in high canyons that escaped the bullet, but they were quite shy, unwilling to pose for a camera that could resemble a firearm, and thus were not observed in any great numbers. When emerging numbers of tourists questioned their whereabouts and village merchants realized the drawing power for visitors by these animals visibility, a community plan was set into motion. An effort to restock the mountain valleys commenced in 1912 by locals and continued by Park personnel when the National Park came on line in 1915. Small herds of 25 elk, after being shipped by rail from Gardiner, Montana from surplus numbers found within Yellowstone National Park, were transported by six wagons to Estes Park from the Lyons' rail head in 1912 and again in 1913. Groups of animals were released in Upper Beaver Meadow, others in Moraine Park, locations wherein the elk might have a natural proclivity to bond with the land and multiply. Other small elk populations were placed closer to the village but those efforts were marginally successful as with a Mr. Miller's struggle to establish his wild life ranch out Devils Gulch Road. The deer needed no such help and in time recovered under the protection of Park Rangers. If nature had been allowed full participation in this partnership effort to reverse man's previous rapacity, the final result of this unique plan might have been different. However, Park officials received and followed bad advice, formulating a misguided plan of priorities to protect the prey and slaughter the predator.

In the initial years of the 1920s, Park authorities ordained that in order to protect the animals reintroduced as well as deer and wild sheep, other species of wildlife possessed with a predatory nature for red meat must be *controlled*. That word, shed of its scientific aura of acceptability, revealed its real meaning, --killing. Superintendent Roger Toll, an educated and kindly man, for some reason fell for this plan in 1922 and professional hunters and trappers were brought in to shoot and poison the coyote, lynx, mountain lion, fox, wolf and bobcat. Packs of dogs were unleashed against those wild creatures that the legislative Act creating the Park had mandated to be conserved. Even Park Rangers were trained to hunt down those animals naturally inclined to feed upon the emerging new herds of deer and elk. Superintendent Toll, in 1924, offered his opinion that served as Park policy that if issued today would have angered the nation's vast armies of environmental organizations, or worse filled the court dockets with temporary injunctions. "It is my opinion that predatory animal control should be continued in this Park. I would consider it advisable to reduce the number of mountain lion, coyotes and bobcats to the lowest practicable numbers." The slaughter continued but the success of the program soon required a reworking of that peculiar agenda for wildlife management. By 1930 as the number of predators had significantly diminished, the balance of nature was upset as the elk herd's miniscule genesis had swelled to 446 animals by 1932. From that time on the number of deer and elk was on a steep curve upward as their numbers eventually reached near uncontrollable proportions in the early 1990s.

The policy was rescinded, too late for the predator that never again regained its place in the animal kingdom within Park borders, but the new program to strike a more acceptable ecological equation was even more horrifying to those who truly loved all forms of life regardless of the fact that their great numbers wrought havoc to the home range. Rangers now were redirected to reduce the size of the elk herds, and in the year 1949 alone more than 450 elk, possibly deer as well, were eliminated by one means or another. This modified control program lasted well into the middle of the 1960s with much of the dressed meat given to various public institutions as well as being trucked down to Camp Carson near Colorado Springs for use in its mess halls. Predator control had reaped the whirlwind and the tempest still blew upon us in the 1990s. I can assure you that Park Rangers were hesitant to pull the trigger on an animal that earlier they were sworn to protect and would have preferred not to be assigned this duty. One told me, "When I got my sights on an elk or deer, and he looked at me with those big eyes, ---brother it was awfully hard to shoot." Wiser judgment eventually took charge and Park officials began a careful biological study of long range consequences of this former policy as well as others. Present policy seeks to establish a more natural balance within the Park, so far devoutly wished but not as yet achieved. It has come full circle in less than 100 years, from none to overcrowding an unsupportable range. A quick solution, that few favor and which is fraught with cries of insensitivity, is to send in the hunters again, Rangers or a new breed of *sportsman* bounty hunter. 'Why not relocate them back to Yellowstone or other larger ranges?' is offered as the answer, but that would be beyond this National Park's resources, --too expensive. Foolish as it may sound, and this is not to suggest a diminution of the powers of the Great Spirit, others would enlist the services of Native American medicine men to call down upon the Park a series of killer snow storms, a scythe of starvation, to cut down and cull the herds. I should point out that this last suggestion, novel and potentially as effective as a convoluted variety of cloud seeding, could prove disastrous to humans as well for modern man is not as conversant with nor adaptable to the forces of unleashed natural phenomena as recent history in the United States has demonstrated. There is another covey of trendsetters championing loudly their own solution that brings white knuckles to parents of small children and domestic pet lovers. "Bring back the wolves," is their solution that obliquely redirects authorities to a better understanding of the leveling and balancing forces of nature absent of man's meddling. One of my friends questioned a recent Park policy, that he charges *tampers* with the fish population's own inherent method of survival by natural selection, whereby one less pugnacious *native* variety is favored over three more *exotic* species that have become dominant through aggressive adaptability. I only commend these issues to the advice of former Rocky Mountain National Park Chief Naturalist Dorr Yeager, an early advocate for the coyote. I suspect his words spoken in 1934 are as relevant now as they were then. All of us, professional and amateur, seek quick solutions to prove theories that might not stand up to the test required of good stewardship for land and all dwellers thereon. Ranger Yeager urged, "Leave the two species alone and they will strike a balance, for at present times the deer and not the coyote need control." A recent advertisement for a commercial product said it more pointedly. "Don't mess with Mother Nature!" That advice echos the French naturalist, Michel de Montaigne's counsel. "Let us a little permit Nature to take her own way. She better understands her own affairs than we." But let's get back to Horseshoe Ranch.

Willard Ashton had become familiar with the work of an architect whose new theories for designs of buildings were radically different to what a nation evolving out of America's edition of the Victorian Age had come to expect. Of course he was interested in constructing an architectural feature that would gain the approbation of his family, friends and strangers, but his primary concern was to erect his new summer home and lodge in a way that was appropriate for the location he had selected. The architect initially selected, Frank Lloyd Wright with offices in Chicago and who later become internationally famous, drew up plans and sketches in 1908 for this lodge that Mr. Ashton called The Horseshoe Inn. To be situated upon a stunning site with panorama vistas from its 8,500 foot elevation, Wright's plans pictured a large resort hotel for 100 guests in a one story, flatroofed, construction of more than 288 feet in length. The designer stressed that it should be modern in every detail for the times with a cascading stream, Fall River, flowing beneath guest rooms spanning above. The editor of the newspaper thought the original plans exciting. Reporting in the June 4, 1908 edition of *The Mountaineer*, one of the predecessor's to the *Estes Park Trail*, his news dispatch opprobriously equated the current inventory of pointed roofed lodges to something comparable to the Greek mythological grubby Augean Stables. "The plans have produced a building which seems a part of the beautiful landscape rather than a mar upon it as is often the case with summer hotels." A lodge was constructed in 1908, not using these plans perhaps as too costly, incorporating the original ranch home into its northwest section. However I suspicion

Mr. Ashton thought it much too avant-garde, not in character to the mountains with which it would intricately be associated. The editor was disappointed as The Horseshoe Inn, reared in a meadow of forty different species of wild flowers, was another wooden, two storied, *regular* structure. A beautiful building despite the judgment of the local press, it was erected through the labor and inspiration of Willard, his brother, and craftsmen of the building trade such as Robert H. Lindley, a plumber recently arrived from the Midwest for this job. His nephew, Maurice B. Rockwell of Estes Park, continues to practice the trade with noteworthy professionalism. Situated seven miles west of Estes Park, facing northeast on the south side of Fall River, it was immediately west of the present parking lot in Horseshoe Park where now autumn visitors regularly queue up to watch and listen for the bugling elk arduously herding up their mates. Some records indicate many small ranch structures about the premises predated Horseshoe Inn as well as clear evidence of irrigation ditches tracing their serpentine paths through the rich black soil to aid a more intense agricultural use.

Through a large swinging gate, the lodge's name together with an imprint of a horseshoe, the construction date and the initials of the gate's builder set into a concrete support, the first guests arrived in the summer of 1909. Water and good soil allowed for a *kitchen garden* attended to by Mr. Ashton whom guests reported "was a gardener of no mean abilities," and upon the guests' dining tables regularly were found fresh vegetables such as potatoes, onions, radishes lettuce and beans. There were many fun times at Horseshoe Inn with uncrowded, unhurried trails to tread while observing the millions of bright red, blue, orange and yellow blooms the guests could touch and capture on their Stanley Photographic Plates. The Ashtons provided to their guests, as the lodge brochure advised, "an instructor for birds and field lore," as guided field trips were regularly conducted to "teach Nature's Lessons." Guests enjoyed the magnificent aspects of this broad park through which the river lazily flowed. The rough road from the village ended at its doorstep where the staff gave warm welcome at the front vestibule and carried in the bags to a beautiful interior colored in hues of nature close about. Only a very rough wagon road progressed south, up to the divide separating Horseshoe Park from Beaver Park, although guests from Stead's Ranch regularly rode over on horseback to spend part of a sunny day with friends at Horseshoe Inn. As an interesting side note, this road was later improved by citizen effort as bazaars to raise money were held in tents at Deer Ridge Junction, of which site I will discuss later in more detail. But sadness was to seek out the Ashtons when Willard and his second wife Cora buried their small child behind the lodge, the result of an accident on a horse.

Over the years the lodge was enlarged to four story proportions and a three story annex was attached on the south side. Finally a trout stocked lake embellished the premises to the north of the main entrance. To the northwest of the Inn was a large barn and livery stable that was shared with the Marches of Fall River Lodge. Horses were assembled by the hitching rack in the meadow just south of Fall River, where a guest was instructed on how to mount and handle one of the fine string of horses managed by Burt Vetters and Phil Jenkins. Not forgetting the magical setting of Lawn Lake and his enjoyment of the rugged cabin in which he and his family had lived for a few days of pure joy, Willard constructed a Swiss appearing satellite lodge in 1910 to serve fifteen guests. Called Lawn Lake Resort at an elevation of 10,800 feet in the Mummy Range, it was strategically positioned on the eastern shore of the lake. I am not completely certain whether this was an enlargement of the older cabin, in which they had enjoyed a few nights of inexpensive lodging, or a totally new structure. Its operations lasted only into the early 1920s when it was demolished. Included as guests were those harboring allergies who spent the entire summer there until frost came to the lower regions of the Estes Valley. One guest was Pieter Hondius, Sr. to whom I have made earlier reference. This quaint little chalet should not be confused with the Lawn Lake Shelter cabin constructed in 1931 by the National Park Service.

Willard's daughter, by his first wife, was Ruth Elizabeth Ashton, born in 1896 in Roxbury, Massachusetts and who many years after graduating from Mount Holyoke College in South Hadley, Massachusetts enrolled in a graduate program of botanical studies at the school we now know as Colorado State University in Fort Collins. It was there she met her husband to be, Dr. Aven Nelson, President Emeritus and founder of the Botany Department of the University of Wyoming. Her introduction to the Park's flora came early in her life at Horseshoe Inn and was reinforced in 1930 when Ruth served as the Information Clerk at Rocky Mountain National Park. She authored informative articles about flowers that increased visitor awareness and appreciation of their colorful presence especially those who sought a more botanically understandable explanation. Ruth Ashton Nelson's love of flowers, later encouraged and fortified by summer retreats with her father in Little Horseshoe Park, resulted in her authoring a number of splendid treatises on wild flowers, her most popular literary work entitled *Plants Of Rocky Mountain National Park* was later published by the Rocky Mountain Nature Association in cooperation with the National Park.

In 1915, Willard sold 120 acres of his land, including Horseshoe Inn and Lawn Lake Resort to the first automobile dealers specializing in Cadillacs in the region in and around Fort Collins, Colorado, Harry C. Bradley, and Claude C. *Pat* Patrick of Fort Collins, Colorado. The Ashtons retained 40 acres in Little Horseshoe Park on the northwest corner of Deer Mountain, where in present times serves as a resting area for herds of elk and a training ground for young bulls who learn in mock combat the techniques to gather their own herd of cows. By fall season, the mature bull swains are locked in combat for supremacy, announcing their amorous qualifications in the crisp air with high pitched squeals for attention. The Ashtons constructed several cabins with hot and cold running water, the largest of which contained a large stone fireplace that was perfect for a rainy day or an evening of fellowship when the outside temperatures crisped the night air. A large four-car garage was added that housed on its second floor a dormitory for family and friends. Vexed to learn that a new connecting road leading to the south from Horseshoe Park would bypass his dwelling, it was incumbent upon him to build a long access road that presently functions as a hiking trail. As increasing age and long years of hard work had reduced Willard's vigor to find him less able to care for his buildings and acreage, he was desirous of preserving this little valley for the enjoyment of the public and was not willing to sell to private parties. In 1933 he sold his remaining holdings to the National Park but retained life tenancies for the use of the buildings. In a letter written after Willard's death, Cora Ashton restated the reasons why her husband loved this land from his first visit. "This place was his heart's delight and he loved the rains, the hail and the snow, --the solitude, where he found much peace." After he died in 1947 and on August 21, 1956 at Cora's death, the tenancies terminated. A fragment of his *delight* built in Little Horseshoe Park still exists to serve a National Park purpose as a private parking place for participants in nature programs conducted by the Rocky Mountain Nature Association.

All lodge and hotel owners stressed their modern conveniences to convince the traveling public that, even though they were high in the mountains, there still were social graces such as electric lights, hot and cold water and a full plate of recreational pursuits. More particularly, and to erase any sense of aversion in the minds of city dwelling travelers that the accommodations would be tents provisioned solely with dressed game hung in adjacent trees, Horseshoe Inn owners routinely pronounced the elevated level of service to be expected. "We have rooms that are just like home and especially you will enjoy our home-cooked food. We are in the National Park, 7 miles from the village on the High Drive, on the American plan, home cooking, rooms with bath, and hot and cold water in every room." Pat Patrick bought out his partner in 1919 to assume sole ownership with his family. The late Dave Stirling, well known local painter of these mountains and alter ego of Pied Eye Pete with whom he engaged in picturesque dialogue, journeyed west in 1916 from Corydon, Iowa to begin a lifetime career in oil painting. He cultivated a technique to create unique artistic impressions that instantly captured the imagination of the tourist as well as selling scads of pictures. In July of 1921 Dave was asked to be in charge for the summer of a gathering place within Horseshoe Inn known as The Casino. He served his customers light lunches and soft drinks as well as exhibiting his paintings for sale. Later in a tent cabin located close to the present day parking lot on the westernmost curve of the highway in Horseshoe Park, he marketed many of his one of a kind paintings of the National Park. Many other artists of a multitude of disciplines spent many enjoyable hours and days occupying rooms at the Inn that overlooked the lovely landscape of the lake that had been excavated in the meadow, and stocked with thousands of trout, for recreational diversion as well as to supply the large dining room with a best-selling entree.

Regular guests for evening dinner were the Fred Payne Clatworthy family, but never on Sunday as dining at the National Park Hotel in the village on that day was reserved for Mrs. Clatworthy's treat to her family. A brief profile of the noted Estes Park photographer might be appropriate at this time. I am indebted to his daughter Helen M. Clatworthy who provided me with much of the information about her family. Named *Fred* for his Baptist minister grandfather Frederick Clatworthy and *Payne* for John Howard Payne of New York, the lyricist for the All-American tune *Home, Sweet Home*, Fred Payne Clatworthy was born in Dayton, Ohio in 1875. The family name, in derivative form from its English equivalent Cyteworth, still remains affixed to the street sign that leads to his former home in Estes Park. As his father frequently shifted the family domicile, young F. P. as he came to be known attended a number of private colleges including Denison University in Granville, Ohio. Dutifully obeying the family's admonition to become a *professional man* and perchance to foster a more harmonious relationship within the ranks of his elders, he graduated from Chicago Law School in 1898. His real interest in life besides riding his bicycle --an early devotee to cycling that remained into his adult years -- was photography which very soon would occupy the rest of his life as his law practice was limited to only a few years. Although photography was an occupation not then elevated to the professional status it claims today, it well suited him ever since he was given his first camera in 1887 for the family trip to England during the Queen's Jubilee year. Becoming a consummate camera craftsman, clicking his bellows-like black box on everything that drew his fancy, while at Denison University his photo subjects included every buildings and all of the activities of the students including their graduation ceremonies.

With his certificate to practice law filed away and the beck and call of the open road drawing him westward, he and his chum Sidney Foote, cameras on board, headed west on their bicycles eventually to reach Magdalena, New Mexico. This was not a destination of choice but brought about only because their mode of transportation dictated a change. Because of unrepairable mechanical breakdowns, their wheeled companions of too many miles were replaced. To youth with a mission, nothing was impossible if adaptability was put into practice. Two abandoned, nearly wild, burros were commandeered from the wide open, cactus strewn, desert. With burros loaded with food, camping equipment and their indispensable cameras, the pair and new partners visited the Grand Canyon and most every other scenic area all the way to Catalina Island, California. Though the beasts were more dependable, the long eared contrarians certainly had ideas of their own concerning speed and working hours. The young men were captivated by the beauty of the great canyon and with the seashores prompting Fred to commence filling albums with photos that held great promise for his chosen career in photo-journalism. Copies of a number of them he sold to appreciative new acquaintances enabling him to provide for himself on the trip and to return to Chicago with the same amount of money with which he had commenced his odyssey. His introduction to Estes Park occurred on a second trip West, in more style on the seat of a spring wagon. After traveling all about the state, he knew that the West was where he belonged. Consecutive trips through Colorado on a bicycle from border to border convinced him that he must leave Chicago and to this resolve purchased an interest in a farm near Loveland, Colorado. For whatever reason, Fred, and his sister Linda who later became Head Librarian at Denver University, arrived in Estes Park in 1904. Acquiring land on East Riverside Drive in Estes Park, some of which is still owned by members of the family and a portion of which now is bisected by the new Moccasin Bypass, they erected a tent cabin that later grew into Fred's home. Fred is credited with baptizing *Moccasin Pass* with its title for in that ravine south of his home and on his property he discovered Indian artifacts and an erected set of tepee poles. Theorizing that earlier moccasin clad peoples had passed this way, he thought the name appropriate. Linda had her own cabin constructed, Linda Vista, that she enjoyed until her death at the age of 55.

Immediately plunging into the activities of the community leading eventually to his becoming Estes Park's second Mayor, he established in 1905 Clatworthy Studios at 115 West Elkhorn Avenue. The studios occupied the historic first publicly supported public school house in the village, moved a few lots west to make room for the new bank in 1908, is now identified as the Pioneer Gift Shop. The little store he distinguished with an English sounding title, *Ye Lyttle Shop* and for years he and several of his children sold bits and pieces of tourist oriented oddments of varying description. Most business people in the community preformed many tasks and sold an assortment of unrelated merchandise to gain sufficient income to survive. F. P. was no exception as this young photographer recognized his precarious position in a small mountain town that effectively closed up in the wintertime when tourists departed. It is said that in Fred's Ye Lyttle Shop one could purchase everything from Indian baskets and rugs, curios, riding equipment, Kodak cameras, film, rustic willow furniture, animal skins, fresh eggs and produce from his farm. He sold his own black and white, hand tinted if preferred, photographs of the Estes Valley that were highly appreciated by lovers of nature. In fact even today many of those intricately composed photos can be found in prominent positions upon the walls of present day Estes Park establishments and homes as well as in historic journals. I was informed that Fred conducted an incongruous business out of the store, known as The Zippy Laundry Service, where a customer's package of laundry dropped off on Monday morning, and sent by stage and train to Denver for processing, would be ready for pickup at the store the following Friday. Innovation, determination, individuality and professionalism were traits of Fred Payne Clatworthy all of which culminated in a well deserved reputation as one of the finest and certainly the most celebrated photographer of Estes Park. He shared friendships with and extended professional courtesy to the other premier photographers of his day such as Pop Francis, W. T. Parke and Joe Mills.

In 1910, at the age of 35, he married Sarah Mabel Leonard from Binghamton, New York, ten years his junior and the daughter of a country doctor. To them were born Fred, Jr., Helen and Barbara. Later he built to the rear of his store another structure, still standing and formed of red tile blocks, in which he developed his own exposed film as well as performing this service for others. This film developing business, called Over Night Service, advertised *In at 8 P. M. Out at 8 A. M., Let Expert Mountain Photographers Finish Your Mountain Prints*. The business flourished and later was taken over by Fred, Jr. In the wintertime F. P. and Mabel, as she preferred to be called, lived near Santa Barbara, California where Helen was born in 1915. By 1921 the family relocated to a permanent winter home in Palm Springs, California adjacent to the Cahuilla Indian reservation with its resident Aqua Caliente band that greatly interested F. P. all of his life. From these addresses between 1923 and 1935 he ranged widely in search of beauty and geographic phenomena, capturing them on slides to augment an increasing schedule of lectures. He experimented with improved methods of photography, in order to better capture the moods of this universe as well as projecting his own awareness of their beauty. This led him to professionally perfect, by innovated use, the process discovered by the Frenchmen August and Louis Lumiere at the beginning of this century. This process essentially consisted of a 5 x 7 inch glass plate, coated with tiny green, orange and purple grains of potato starch. On to this plate natural light, concentrated through the camera lens, activated the elements on the plate, resulting in the mixing of starch grains to the extent that the image produced was in full color. F. P. was able to purchase boxes of these plates for one dollar a plate and, through this chemical reaction and his own trained eye for composition, produced a fantastic mixture of vibrant colors. The splendid wilderness subjects momentarily captured in his lens were immeasurably enhanced to near three dimension quality. The final product, an Autochrome, had a profound effect upon the public, especially businesses that sought to attract customers through this medium to their particular products. A sizable number of his conventional pictures and Autochromes were prominently featured over succeeding years in the *National Geographic Society* magazine, in advertisements of the Santa Fe, Burlington and the Denver and Rio Grande railroads, and as far away as in posters on the steamships of the Matson Navigation Company.

Although he was aggressive in promoting tourism to potential visitors to Rocky Mountain National Park through his lectures and articles written for tourist publications, it was the sale of photographic scenes of this region to thousands of people at his store that endeared him to those who sought and received a professional remembrance of the Estes Valley. Prized collections of his special photos of mountains and valleys included scenes of and around the lodges of Rocky Mountain National Park. Thousands of them are pasted in albums of many former visitors who clearly remember their lodge residence within the Park through a photo by Fred Clatworthy. Helen perceived her father's favorite subject of all was the Grand Canyon, while his choices of Colorado themes for artistic contemplation and composition through the lens unquestionably were Wild Basin and Long's Peak. Deeply respectful of the Estes Valley and this National Park, Fred's work was admired, as was he, as his photos of monumental character and beauty contributed immeasurably to preserving for posterity those precious images of the West that to him was the best part of America. He died in 1953 in Estes Park and is buried in Fort Collins, Colorado. A pause before one of his photos quickly brings to mind the dedicated life of a reluctant lawyer, turned photographer, who championed his case for outdoor beauty's conservation before a jury of thousands of men and women who rendered a favorable verdict to his professionalism and hard work.

Esta Snedaker Patrick was born in Lucas, Iowa, married Pat Patrick in Chariton, Iowa in 1904 and they became residents of Fort Collins in 1907 where they made their place of residence prior to the purchase of Horseshoe Inn. Mr. and Mrs. Pat Patrick, recognizing the beauty of the setting for their Inn, were clever in their use of green and yellow colors in the lodge. I feel comfortable in my belief that, because of Esta Patrick's perception of color, nature's palette of hue and chroma was presented in bold strokes in the decorations throughout the lodge. Her brother, William Snedaker the construction engineer, enlarged the original Inn in 1917 with a four story addition containing a larger dining room and three floors of additional guest rooms. As it grew in size, its attractive proportions drew many compliments for its appearance and functioning practicality. In the expanded lobby, new guests in the late 1920s while registering at the front desk took in with their eyes three harmonious shades of green painted over the formerly yellow walls that a newspaper reporter aesthetically described "rivaled nature in the result, a color just matching the silver spruce." The tree-like motif was carried into the ceiling as the supporting beams with a color, reminding one of pine green trees, complemented the furnishings designed to enhance a comfortable illusion of nature. As examples of the motif, in front of the long folds of curtains in shades of yellow were table lamps of matching colors. The wicker furniture as well was finished "in shades of aspen green after the first frost" and yellow decorations throughout all of the rooms and hallways sought to resemble in creative symmetry the aspen leaves that quivered with a rustling sound near the front door.

Horseshoe Inn guides conducted groups as large as thirty or forty people on hikes and trail rides, often concluding with a wiener roast at Dave Stirling's new studios at the eastern end of Horseshoe Park. Dave even provided a dining room for them at his studio referred to seriously, but with a twinkle in his eye, as Bugscuffle Ranch. As if on command from a member of the local Chamber of Commerce, the deer and a few elk came close to the dining room windows at sunset to watch the diners while they themselves were closely observed munching on the tender shoots of Dave's landscaping. Hiking was an important recreational activity enjoyed by lodge guests of all ages. When the National Park commenced to receive its first 31,000 visitors in 1915 there were one hundred twenty-eight miles of trails, countless numbers of which were constructed originally for forest fire control and to better access those remote regions deserving prompt attention. The work had been done largely by residents of the Estes Valley, by lodge owners and most certainly by the guides who depended on them as a means for income. The most prominent fire trail in 1914, the Table Mountain route now known as Flattop Mountain Trail and eighteen and one-half miles in length to Grand Lake, began its steep ascent west out of Mill Creek Basin on a wagon road chip-chopped out by Abner Sprague and Horace Ferguson for access to their saw mill for wood shingles. Others trails were those to Fern Lake, Storm Pass, Bierstadt Lake, Lawn Lake, Bear Lake, Loch Vale and of course the truly historic and challenging ascent of Long's Peak. These were greatly improved by the National Park Service because their original design was proving inadequate for the 101,497 visitors who entered the Park in 1919.

Washington's elected officials thought local people should continue to pay for trail and road improvements, reasoning that the greatest benefit from their use would redound to them from increased tourist visitations. Since only five miles of roads in the Park at that time were federally controlled, the others by the State of Colorado, Congress was prohibited from expending public funds on non-federal roadways even though the state roads within the Park's boundary had fallen into a sorry condition. Left to private enterprise to aid Big Brother with road work in Moraine Park, Glacier Basin and on the Fall River, lodge owners together with owners of summer residences contributed the most in time, talent and treasure. Times were hard for the Park in its formative years, and as an example only three hundred dollars could be scrounged out of the budget for trail improvements in 1917. Park officials scraped up every dollar they could find to do their part but, inasmuch as Rocky Mountain National Park through 1919 had but a mere $10,000 each year to operate all categories of responsibility, roads and trails could not be maintained to its required standards. Finally in 1920, after a lot of push and shove from locals -- and Congressmen who had stood under the dedicatory banner receiving the plaudits of a nation for their perspicacity, the appropriation was increased to $60,000, a truly paltry sum unworthy of a National Park with such potential for so much good for so many yet unborn. Congress felt compelled to practice *pork barrel* politics where they could gain more votes. *Who really cared for a mountain park stuck way off in the boondocks?*, and, *there are more important matters of public need than recreation!* was their rationale. The lordly attitude was simply, "**We** gave you the Park, now **you** pay for it." Total federal appropriations to Rocky Mountain National Park in the eight years from 1915 to 1923 were only $126,643, while the appropriation for Glacier National Park was $195,000, Yosemite National Park received $300,000 and for Yellowstone National Park it was $361,000, --**each year!** Something was definitely wrong. The politicians didn't take this new addition to the National Park system seriously until 1923. I will discuss this fact in a later chapter. The State of Colorado during this period of time was not cooperative either as there was a long fight to transfer title to its roads and cede jurisdiction to the federal government within the National Park. This too was resolved but not without a battle, and spilled blood figuratively speaking.

However the depression was grinding on in 1929, 1930 and 1931 with the absence of many tourists who had little extra cash to spend on such personal budget items as a summer vacation in a mountain lodge. A few lodge owners were only too glad to sell out, although in hindsight when they realized their actions were somewhat premature as the economy would rebound within a span of five to ten years, they had second thoughts. The Horseshoe Inn owners were the first of their industry within the National Park to sell. Before the close of the 1931 season, a shrunken register of guests still enjoyed the lodge at a low cost of $9 per day including meals. The Patricks were not the type to raise the price as the volume declined, but they knew that to continue on with decreasing revenue and accelerating costs was an impossible feat of juggling best suited for a circus performer. Since it was clear that only the government had access to money in its sponsorship of a full spectrum of bootstrap programs the names of which would tongue tie the brewmaster of alphabet soup, the National Park Service and the Patricks came to terms for sale at an agreed upon price of $32,500. When the lodge was scheduled to be razed the following winter of 1931-1932, the Patricks removed the best of the furnishings for subsequent sale either locally or in Fort Collins where they lived in the wintertime. By the end of October, 1931, the lodge and its 120 acres of property were turned over to National Park officials. Residents of the community were not certain what their reaction should be for they could not see beyond their own economic problems and assumed that this hopefully was a one time occurrence. They reasoned that with the return of the tourists, like the swallows in other lands, the other lodges in the Park would once again be open for business when the snows melted and the horses were brought in again to fill the stables of Fall River Lodge, Stead's and all the rest. There was a serious question though whether Moraine Lodge would reopen with the death of its beloved owner a few years earlier.

In compliance with plans of the Department of Interior to rid Park interiors of as much privately owned land as possible, the Inn must be removed and the land returned to its virginal state. Members of the community were possessed of a sadness associated with frustrated anger over the loss of a landmark hotel as they witnessed Park employees burn down Horseshoe Inn in the winter of 1931-1932. A hush has fallen across the meadow where only foundation remnants and cement gate post holders exist of a very fine lodge that once shared the long grass and flowers with the creatures of the Fall River. Its own horseshoe symbol was turned upside down and a life of twenty-four years of service spilled out into its own ashes to bring bittersweet nourishment to the flowers that bloomed again the following spring.

Horseshoe Ranch, 1905 (F. P. Clatworthy)

Horseshoe Inn Expands In Size, 1915 (EPHM)

Guests On Front Steps of Horseshoe Inn, 1918 (RMNP)

Horseshoe Inn From Bridge Over Fall River, 1927 (RMNP)

Horseshoe Inn Vehicle On
Fall River Road, 1921
(Mills)

Fred Payne Clatworthy,
circa 1940s (EPPL)

Elk Imported To Estes Valley, 1912 (EPTG)

Elk Find Home In Future National Park, 1914 (Mills)

Ready For Trail Ride From Horseshoe Inn, 1920 (EPPL)

The Ashtons, Middle Front Left, Picnic circa 1920 (Mills)

Final Addition To Horseshoe Inn, 1917 (EPHM)

The Help At Horseshoe Inn, 1920 (EPPL)

Office and Lobby, 1920 (EPPL)

Lounge At Horseshoe Inn,
1920 (EPPL)

Lobby Of Horseshoe Inn,
1920 (EPPL)

Dining Room, 1915 (EPPL)

Pat Patrick, 1925 (EPPL)

Esta Patrick, 1925 (EPPL)

Horseshoe Inn With Pond Addition, 1928 (EPPL)

MORAINE LODGE

Mary Imogene Bates was born in April of 1844 in Orange, DeKalb County, Indiana. As she was a bright girl and her folks knew that she had obtained whatever basic education there was to grasp in this small farming community, Imogene, as she was called, was sent to live with her uncle Duncan Reed of Milwaukee, Wisconsin. Mr. Reed, who later would become a United States Senator, enrolled her in the private school under its head master Mr. O. M. Baker who later became the president of the publishing house for *Webster's Dictionary*. There she met a fellow student, Willard Owen Greene, a native of Vermont, and together they socialized, romanced and enjoyed each other's company while participating in programs of the local Episcopal church. Like many young people, they were smitten with a first love and were married in 1860 when she was but 16 years of age. The Civil War had started and they took active positions of support for Union causes and young Willard enlisted in 1862 to march south with the Wisconsin Infantry group of volunteers. He became seriously ill with typhoid and, showing great pluck and an equal amount of courage, Imogene persuaded the military to allow her and another to pass through Union lines and into Confederate territory to bring her husband back for medical treatment. She succeeded in her risky endeavor thus establishing her credentials for nursing instincts that she practiced all her remaining years. The first National Soldiers Home in America had its origin in Milwaukee and her husband, with health restored, was installed as its Superintendent while she, now a commissioned Army nurse, was made its first Matron. For two years she nursed 'her boys' as she called the disabled veterans who limped home from the divided nation's unsuccessful attempt to destroy itself.

They resigned at the end of the war to begin a number of small businesses, apartment rentals, picture framing, catering as well as acquiring real estate that was to grow in value and gave to them financial stability but not connubial bliss. The Greenes established on a tract of land Fraternity Hall that served as the headquarters for many fraternal organizations. A series of other real estate investments were made but it only exacerbated growing domestic troubles and led to disharmony, discontentment and a divorce in 1894. The couple had two children Marion Lucretia, born in 1873, and Willard Charles born in 1877 who alone survived Imogene. Marion, who became Marion Greene Hoyt McMahan, had a daughter, Eunice who married Reed Higby of Estes Park to whom I shall refer in my discussion of Fern Lodge. After becoming single again, Imogene began to travel extensively with the Women's Relief Corps to forget the past and discover a world that she had denied herself while raising a family and earning a living. Though dates conflict when researching her life, she apparently traveled to Denver, Colorado then south on her first real vacation sometime between 1896 and 1897, free of responsibilities for the care of others. On May 14, 1898 she renewed her association with the Rocky Mountains when she once again detrained in Denver. But this vacation on August 8th in Colorado led her northwest to Lyons where she boarded the stage coach for the rugged 28 mile journey to Moraine Park. In enthusiastic letters from her room at Sprague's Hotel, she wrote that this valley was "the grandest place yet!" While staying with the Spragues she was invited to dine at Elkanah Lamb's home and the Elkhorn Lodge to awaken an awareness to the life of a lodge owner. She regained her old zest for life when she climbed up Eagle Cliff across from her cabin, went picking huckleberries and raspberries and rode horseback with Abner's sister. After years of long hard, dirty, work and stress associated with caring for the sick and wounded and the lingering baggage of anger, doubt, guilt and melancholia carried from her divorce, in Moraine Park she relearned how to laugh and relax. Full spirited and inwardly alive again, enthralled at everything she saw especially the flowers, she profited from a resurgence of joyful experiences in an uncrowded atmosphere devoid of the smell of antiseptic.

She remained with the Spragues for six weeks at a cost of between six to nine dollars a week including food, and the use of a horse for another dollar a day. Abner Sprague wrote about how Imogene procured her lifetime investment in Moraine Park. "Mrs. MacPherson came to spend the summer but like so many others, becoming enthused with the beauties and possibilities of the region, desired to obtain a place she could call home, a place of her own on a tree covered mountain side." A tract of land had previously been filed upon for a homestead, but for some reason the young claimant, Mr. J. Pringle, gave it up prior to his receipt of a patent. Imogene was eager to purchase his interest because it was the exact place where she often took walks and enjoyed sitting on a large rock on the hillside to gaze out to the snowy peaks and dark wooded mountains in all directions. The tract contained 160 acres with a small cabin in a little glade, for all of which she paid $200. Her cabin, high upon the hill opposite Sprague's Hotel, she named Hillcrest and by exhibiting patience and demonstrating her intent to remain by improving her cabin during the next few summers, she received a patent to her land in 1903.

Typhoid fever, of which she had had her share of unhappy experiences with her former husband as well as nursing soldiers who had returned from the swamps of the South, at the turn of the century was virulently active in southern Colorado and taking a toll in lives. During this period of time she nursed the wife of an old friend from Milwaukee who earlier had moved to Rocky Ford, Colorado. Though the sick woman died, William D. MacPherson of Scottish descent and a Rocky Ford lumber dealer, was grateful for all of Imogene's effort. Their friendship over the next few years grew into marriage in 1903 afterwards they resided in Rocky Ford until 1908 with frequent summer excursions to her Hillcrest cottage. During this period of her life, she worked very hard in that community's Woman's Club activities and expended hundreds of hours in establishing a fine local library. Her original intent was to use the rough cabin as a vacation home, but then she came up with a broader vision that her husband encouraged and in which he aided by providing lumber. Relying upon her business experience in renting apartments and catering --a form of tourism she rationalized -- the thought occurred to her to build a lodge where she could shelter, feed and entertain tourists. I'm certain that Abner Sprague also gave her every encouragement and advice since he was in the business himself, knew there was more traffic than he could handle, and genuinely liked this middle aged woman. She possessed what he thought it took to succeed in running a lodge -- determination, ambition and an adaptable intelligence to prevail over harsh conditions -- when many other men and women of her age and single status might have taken the next seat on a returning stage coach to a more finished matrix of civilization.

As a new resort began taking shape in her mind, the first building was erected below Hillcrest in the summer of 1905. The lodge grew rapidly with cabins, livery stable, main lodge and a dining room called Saint's Rest taking their appropriate position below her original Hillcrest on the lower slopes of Eagle Cliff as ancillary structures followed through 1908. It was now time for the MacPhersons to make their permanent move to Estes Park in 1908, to the resort that was four and one-half miles west of the village and at an elevation of 8,000 feet. Calling her resort Moraine Lodge because it commanded a marvelous view of snow capped mountains across a broad river valley bordered in a frame of two heavily timbered moraines, it welcomed the first guests in June of 1910. Imogene was a woman of education, charm, empathetic to human needs and willing to share her world with all of God's creatures in equal partnership. She sought to live her life in complete artistic expression. With these penchants and abilities she toiled to assure her guests of an experience that would improve their minds, rest their nerves and enrich their souls in collaboration with gloriously unspoiled nature all about. Albeit she was the wife of *Mr. MacPherson* as he was routinely known, the Moraine Lodge was hers and she ran it absolutely only allowing her husband to clerk at the front desk. It became one of the most unique and attractive hotels in the Park area and was described as such by a local newspaper reporter in 1913. "Probably the finest view in Moraine Park is that obtainable from the Moraine Lodge, conducted by Mrs. W. D. MacPherson, half way up the hillside forming one of the boundaries of the Moraine Park. The Lodge is a congregation of rustic buildings, cottages, and tent-houses, located at the end of the road, where the trails begin, surrounded by dense pine woods."

It was especially noted for the food placed on its tables, which was the exclusive dominion of Imogene. The lodge, like so many of the others in the beginning of the Twentieth Century, was equipped with its own herd of fine Jersey cows, saddle horses and guides for those desirous of further pampering. At Moraine Lodge one found a group of log cabins, rustic buildings and tiny chalets shaded under the pines. The porches faced out upon Moraine Park and encouraged the occupants to stretch out in a comfortable chair, feet on the railing, and let their minds drift with the passing fleecy clouds. Imogene was affectionately known to friends and family, including lodge guests, as *Mother* MacPherson, whose concern for others earned her that term of endearment. In an advertisement in J. Y. Munson's *Estes Park Trail* three years into its operation, Mrs. MacPherson anticipated an event and opted to acquaint her future guests of her lodge's proximity to it. "We **are** in the proposed Rocky Mountain National Park." In 1916, after the National Park was an actuality, Imogene artistically stressed -- as was her way of communication -- the first class trails under construction. "The trails lead into the very heart of a region that glows with beauty where trails for horseback riding thread their way into still deeper vastnesses." Guests also were encouraged to play tennis and practice their golf swing in the meadow below the lodge, and she, like so many of the early lodge owners, focused on the curative effects upon the body provided by a vacation in the new National Park. "Here is Nature's great reservoir of strength. Here is the great restorative of tired nerves."

Each of the lodges had their own personal charm, reflecting the character of its owners, their locations and the recreational pursuits encouraged although there was a similarity to all of them. This paragraph in Imogene's ear-

99

ly brochure set the theme for her resort, as a place where her guests learned of nature in an attitude of religious inspiration. "There is motoring, horseback riding, exploration parties equipped for several days with pack mule carrying the food and bedding, tramping along the new trails growing wider daily under the Government Engineer and fishing, golf and tennis. You can just rest under wide porches looking into the high mountains with their eternal snows. On your trips you frequently see deer, mountain sheep, beaver, and many other native animals. And with all, a cozy little individual sleeping house at night. Where could more beautifully exemplify the word of the tired Psalmist on the weary plains in summer, when he cried of old, 'I will lift up mine eyes unto the hills whence cometh my help.' Here, indeed, is a rest for the weary, even on this side of Jordan, and a vast and beautiful playground to lighten all the heavy hearts of the world."

Her vitality was not contained just within Moraine Park and her resort. Taking a leading position with the Rocky Mountain Hotel Association and always active in the local Chamber of Commerce, she found the time and energy as well to organize the Estes Park Woman's Club in 1912 in which she served as its President from 1912 to 1920. In 1915 she wrote several articles for that organization, one of which beautifully described what she could see out of her window in Moraine Park as well as an historical synopsis of pre-Park days. "The area now called Rocky Mountain National Park and Estes Park, Colorado the red men of the region believed as desirable as the happy hunting grounds. It contained many thousand acres of grassy intervals, ranges of snow-capped mountains, great forests of pine, spruce and aspen, many hidden lakes, waterfalls and rushing rivers. It was the haunt of the deer, mountain sheep, bear, hill buffalo, elk, antelope, and many fur animals, while the lakes and streams teemed with fish --a veritable garden of Eden to the red men, and to this day you can see the old frame of one of their tepees beside the streams." However her marriage sadly ended in the winter of 1919 while vacationing in Los Angeles when Mr. MacPherson contracted pneumonia and died. Imogene, still possessed with the strength, pluck, resilience call it what you will, returned to reopen Moraine lodge for the summer season of 1920 and carried on to reach even greater goals of service to her guests, many of whom were as close to her as her family.

She promoted a music camp at the lodge and, as many prominent educators and literary people patronized her establishment, she also sponsored their lectures for her guests and those who stopped by for evenings of intellectual stimulation. The patronage of authors of her day as guests was a prime objective of her promotional efforts at the lodge, and many were found in residence who frequently prepared inspired journalistic works replete with references to the flora and fauna of Moraine Park. One such author was Professor Lawrence A. Wilkins of Columbia University who while as Imogene's guest completed his seventh book on languages. Her neighbor was the famous newspaper publisher from Emporia, Kansas, William Allen White, who summered nearby. He had purchased his vacation home in 1912 from an earlier cottager, W. E. Higgins who himself had purchased the gracious cabin erected between 1900 and 1908 from Professor Olin of Kansas University. Her guests were fortunate to have this culturally animated, gracious, woman as their hostess who held strong convictions and created a forum for expansive impressions on all subjects. When one was asked what she was really like, promptly rejoined, "My picture of Mrs. MacPherson is that of a cross between Whistler's Mother and Carrie Nation."

"We are at the west end of Estes Park in Rocky Mountain National Park," appeared in the 1920 lodge advertisement, "rustic and distinctive with modern improvements, private baths, good food -and *a plenty*, and our auto meets the four daily auto stages at Estes Park." The rooms and cabins were gas lighted, equipped with shower and tub facilities, and at the lodge were telephone and telegraph services. She made every effort to provide comfort for her guests and at the same time making them aware of the vast reservoir of wilderness experiences beckoning to them at their door step. The little ditty in her brochures over the years reflected her warmth of sincerity. *Come in the morning, come in the evening. Come when you're looked for, come without warning. And welcome you will find.* Through the years she enlisted the services of several competent managers to assist her, including George M. Derby of a local family whose name was prominent in lodging and livery endeavors throughout the Estes Valley. In 1921, Mr. Derby, as manager, advertised the philosophy of the lodge this way. "Moraine Lodge catering to genteel people at city prices, is a resort that is just like home," and for around thirty-five dollars per week, or $5.00 a day and meals included, art, music, lectures and Mother's warm hospitality were tossed in for no extra charge. This constituted Moraine Lodge as a real, *high toned* bargain with which no one could, or ever did, argue.

A spacious new assembly hall of log architecture, opened to the public on July 14th, 1923, contained a tea room and business office on the first floor and a large hall on its second story. At the dedication ceremony, the hall was festooned in gay attire, the lodge's staff stood smartly in the respective uniforms of their assignments, rank and position, and guests as well as many others invited from the surrounding community trooped in. Mother MacPherson extemporaneously gave a brief history of her lodge, and her manager detailed the festivities to follow. The orchestra struck up an impressive medley of music equivalent to *Pomp and Circumstance* and eighty couples, many in costume, stepped smartly across the polished floor led by her long time summer neighbors Mr. and Mrs. Charles Scott of Kansas whose home, the Scottage, still functions as a family summer compound near this building. The revelers then went down to the Tea Room where they toasted Mrs. MacPherson's continued success. But her mortal accomplishments within five years would be examined by the keeper of the Mansion higher up than even Long's Peak. On March 19, 1928, while again in Los Angeles in pursuit of increased business through a large travel agency named *Ask Mr. Foster*, Imogene MacPherson was struck down by an automobile in front of the Figueroa Hotel. Within a few days of unsuccessful medical treatment, she died at the age of 84 after having made plans to return in the spring to reopen the lodge.

I think her first love, other than for people, was for flowers that she thought more correctly and clearly reflected God's beauty and greatness. She enjoyed talking about her colorful companions of the mountains with their intricate classifications and was pleased to impart to her guests some of their legends and how they acquired their names. I believe that her love for flowers expressed in profound prose revealed her appreciation of God's rich endowment of her world that was interpreted by this special person to her guests. Here is an example from which you may gain sensitivity to her thought processes. Let it be her elegy. "That vegetable life that produces the most beautiful blossoms and the most delightful fragrance, we call flowers. Those indigenous to the soil, we call wild flowers. For their beauty of bloom and fragrance we cherish them, overlooking their greatest value to both man and beast. Yet whatever contributes to the pleasure of the eye is a boon to humanity. A youth and maiden were walking along a steep river bank where the maiden espied, growing near the water's edge, a beautiful and rare flower of heaven's own blue. Turning to her lover she said, 'behold the most lovely blossoms.' He at once gallantly climbed down the dangerous incline to get it for her. He plucked it, the earth gave way, and he sank beneath the dark waters. As he was sinking, he raised his arm and threw the blossoms at her feet, crying 'Forget-Me-Not.'"

I'm certain that Imogene will long be remembered as a strong spirit with a beauty from within reflecting outward to all those with whom she shared her beautiful Moraine Lodge. Abner Sprague, her first friend in Moraine Park, contributed his own remembrance about Imogene's warm heart. "Nothing rude can be said of Mrs. M. Imogene MacPherson as a friend or neighbor. She was interested in the welfare of all with whom she came into contact." Upon her death she was survived by her son Dr. William Greene and two grandchildren, one of whom was Mrs. Eunice Higby of Skyline, Wyoming. Eunice, with her former Park Ranger husband, returned to operate Moraine Lodge for the 1928 season, even installing a gasoline service station at the lodge. Then it was leased in to J. Russell McKelvey 1929. In its last year of operation in 1931 there were still more than 100 guests each day enjoying the old lodge and surrounding cabins who thought the rate of $7 per day with meals in Saint's Rest dining hall, or $36 per week, was very reasonable. In February of 1932 it was purchased from Mrs. MacPherson's estate for $30,125 by the National Park Service and all structures removed, except for one. The 1923 assembly hall, now in refurbished finery, remains as the Moraine Park Museum to welcome in new guests of Rocky Mountain National Park to gain an educated, and perhaps emotional appreciation of its grandeur. Mother Imogene MacPherson would especially direct your attention to the flowers near the museum, that are as lovely as she was in life.

Homestead Cabin, 1901 (CHS)

Moraine Lodge, circa 1910 (CHS)

Cohasset Cottage, Moraine Lodge, circa 1910 (CHS)

Saints Rest Dining Room, circa 1915 (CHS)

Main Lodge And Dining Room, circa 1920 (RMNP)

Moraine Lodge And Long's Peak, circa 1922 (RMNP)

Cabin Erected At Moraine Lodge, circa 1910 (RMNP)

Recreation Hall Erected 1923, (RMNP)

Imogene MacPherson At Moraine Lodge, 1924 (RMNP)

Horseback Riders At Moraine Lodge, 1920 (EPPL)

CASCADE LODGE

Before proceeding with Cascade's abbreviated history, a recounting of the chronology of one town hotel and a reference to two others will exemplify the early lodging industry within the Village of Estes Park and serve as a preface to Cascade's origins as they all were interconnected to some degree. A town hotel was important to a community as it served a different purpose for a growing community other than for the tourists who preferred to base themselves higher up in the parks of Glacier Basin, Moraine and Horseshoe Park. Over the years of Estes Park's relatively young life, both sides of Elkhorn at one time could boast many pleasant hostelries that served as dining rooms, sleeping accommodations, places to meet your friends in good conversation or cook up a business deal. It was not uncommon that at a back table a scheme was hatched to block all entrances into the village on a ghoulishly exciting Halloween night. The old timers still living in town can recall many hotels and the stories each could tell. I suspicion that many of the kitchens in those little watering holes referred to pages from the *Tried And True Recipe Book* then being promoted as a fund raiser in 1920 for seventy-five cents from any member of the local chapter of the P. E. O. There were the Hupp, Hupp Annex, the Park, Prospect Inn, the Jay, the National Park Hotel, the Josephine and the Riverside to name but a few. All, as hotel property, are gone except the Hupp Annex, and it serves more as a rooming house with tourist shops partially built into its original front veranda. There also was Brown's Tea Pot Inn.

Mrs. L. L. Norton for years had been successfully operating her Brown's Tea Pot Inn, a light refreshment business of genteel propriety, very popular for the ladies of the village, while the gentlemen preferred a more robust recipe of refreshment called *three fingers of red eye* available further down the street. Her establishment was located on the north side of Elkhorn Avenue a few doors east of the building now known as The Old Church Shops. Mrs. Norton added on to her tea shop in 1915 a three story hotel building, described as possessing "twenty-five attractively furnished rooms, fitted up with all modern conveniences." She delineated what awaited the public's patronage when she described the construction under way. "The rooms would be strictly European Plan, electric lighted and have hot and cold water in each room." The hotel within a few years would be renamed The Aksarben by gypsied Nebraskans, its new owners the Eisenhart family, who had rolled their mechanized wagon downtown to enter into the hotel trade. They couldn't forget their Nebraska, hence named their hotel a reverse spelling of their native state. In 1921 they sold the Aksarben and perhaps rolled their wheels west to Ainrofilac, --I mean California. The firm of W. S. Magers from Denver and Mr. Magers' friend Dawson purchased the hotel and promptly changed the name of the establishment to The Sherwood Hotel.

Josephine Hupp, known as the leading hotel woman in the Estes Valley, arrived in 1878 from Michigan where she was born in 1857. She came to Colorado as the bride of Augustus Blinn and after his death in 1891 she married John Hupp's son, Henry, in 1893 whereupon they moved to Estes Park. Hank Hupp was given the title by Charles Edwin Hewes, lodge owner and resident poet, of *Our Butcher* as he for years was associated with the Boyd

Market on Elkhorn Avenue. Josie Hupp and Hank's sister Ella built the Hupp Hotel on the southwest corner of Elkhorn and Moraine in 1906, and in 1908 purchased another hotel they called the Hupp Annex situated on the northeast corner of the same intersection. They later sold their first building to Nina Higby, renaming it The Park Hotel, and the Hupp Annex no longer was anyone's annex. It stood on its own foundation as the new Hupp Hotel that we see today. This hotel, on the approximate site of John Cleave's home and store, had a number of tent cottages out behind and under the rock cliff for the summer overflow of tourists. Its wide porches and verandas enclosed its south and east walls where guests could enjoy the cool breezes wafting down Main Street. The Hupp was one, if not the only one at the time, that remained open throughout the year and its corner restaurant was a popular gathering place serving abundant meals associated with good fellowship. Many of its rooms were occupied by employees of various enterprises in town. Josephine Hupp contracted with C. B. Anderson, probably the namesake of Anderson Lane in Estes Park now known as Big Horn Drive, to build a small hotel she modestly had installed over the front door the name, The Josephine. She sold it to the Lewiston Hotels Company in 1920, later reacquiring it in 1926 only to sell it again in 1930 to Ted Jelsema, when it was renamed The Riverside Hotel. In 1956 the top floor of the Riverside Hotel burned but a portion of the lower level remains and is presently occupied by the locally acclaimed Wheel Bar.

As I am mindful of the local hotels, their owners and all of the pioneers who established Estes Park and held it together through all of the difficult times of growing into the Twentieth Century in a high mountain valley, I cannot consider this book complete without a pause for a remembrance of a great lady whose pioneering talents had little to do with buildings, but rather music and a big heart. Hazel Baldwin was piano accompanist of the first rank at the local theater that featured the latest silent movies in early Estes Park. Mrs. Roy Baldwin died recently and I am certain is making beautiful music to an audience, larger I hope but no more appreciative than the many town folks and visitors alike who listened to, and learned from her piano renditions that were always appropriate to the occasion. Hazel, before her marriage, called the Hupp Hotel her home and while there acquired many lasting friendships with the other young employees who persevered to fill important positions within this community. The Park Theater first opened its doors under the neon lit white tower in 1914. After Hazel's arrival that year from Loveland, Colorado, she became employed through the good offices of the management of the Lewiston Hotel to play accompanying music for the silent films featured. "What was it like living in town in 1914," I asked her? "I loved living in the mountains for though I was born in Elbert, Colorado I was raised west of Colorado Springs. Living here was nice in a way, awful at other times when some winters we didn't have electricity for the lights. The power plant ran by a waterfall and, since we didn't get much rain or snow some winters, there was no water to power the plant that Mr. Baldridge ran for Mr. Stanley, both of whom were well respected and always had time to help the people of the village. Also we didn't have much drinking water that year. When I first came to town you never saw a car, just horses."

I asked her about what it was like to play in the theater for silent films, before the *talkies* came in. She screwed up her face and thought for a minute, then a smile crossed her wise face. "When I went to the theater in the evening, I played some jazzy music for a while until the picture started. Then I followed the picture," and her artistic hands moved to a melody she alone heard that day when we visited. "I just looked at the picture and went along as they did. I played a lot of my own music that I had memorized. We had two shows each evening and I got back home at the Hupp Hotel about 10:30 P. M. where I also worked during the daytime prior to my marriage in 1919." One of her favorites films of 1927 was titled *The General* and I can just imagine how her fingers flew over the keys in a series of marching rhythms that kept the audience on the edge of their seats. *Picture shows* cost only twenty-five cents and the theater was always at least one-half full as there was not much to do in the evenings after a dinner at the old Manhatten Cafe. "It was hard to get up here from the valley in the early days," she remarked to drive home just how isolated it was before 1915 as the closest community was twenty-five miles down the treacherous road. She added more facts to our dialogue with nostalgic realism. "When I came there were only stages with horses, and there was only one church, the Community Church, as it represented all of the various divisions. We all had fun at the Odd Fellows Club, rode horseback everywhere and burned wood and coal to keep warm." Hazel, after the silent movies ceased, taught piano and conducted music classes for the children of many of the local citizenry including Helen Clatworthy and Enos Mills' daughter Enda. Hazel and Roy built their home on West Riverside Drive in 1920 and they lived there all of their lives. "I always enjoyed playing the piano for everything and everybody," she told me as we moved off to another room to view her fine old piano on which so many budding local musicians *played their lessons for Mrs. Baldwin.* And the town enjoyed her as the community's citation she received after her final retirement announced. "Among the altruistic people of the village who quietly go their way doing good for the community and usually receiving slight recognition is Mrs. Roy Baldwin. Whenever music is needed, she can be counted upon. Sometimes she receives a small remuneration but more often all she gets is thanks and occasionally these are overlooked. We in Estes Park are fortunate that she is amongst us, and we want to remind Mrs. Baldwin that her efforts are appreciated." We'll see you later, Hazel, after the curtain descends on our last performance.

Magers and Dawson, who had plans for a hotel within the new Glacier National Park, occasioned to cast their eyes enviously on a prime location that looked with far vision to the entrance gate of the new National Park being constructed in 1920 and 1921 in Horseshoe Park. The Glacier National Park project was shelved and by May of 1922 a plan for another new hotel, Cascade Lodge in Horseshoe Park, was announced to the public. It would be located at the east entrance into Horseshoe Park, south of the road, on a portion of artist Dave Stirling's Bugscuffle Ranch property on which he now operated his Jazz Bird Studies of art. On July 13, 1923 they sold their Sherwood Hotel to Josie Hupp who continued to own the Hupp Hotel down the street under the management of Anna May Derby and her husband William. She retained the name Sherwood for her new investment to remind the tourist that, though they were not physically within the mighty forests of the new National Park, they were but a few miles away. The new Cascade Lodge's plans of 1922 disclosed a log, stone and stucco building containing an immense lobby, dining room and thirty guest rooms, all with baths. It would face out upon the Fall River near where the waters cascaded down to the smaller valley below, thus its name, Cascade Lodge. In addition to the lodge building, cabins in a half-timbered motif would be constructed. However by 1923 only four cabins and only a portion of the main lodge had been completed. When the next announcement of the lodge's progress was made, the large lodge had been downsized to twenty rooms and its scheduled opening delayed to July 4, 1925. The lodge was certainly in business when it was disclosed on July 17, 1925 that the Rocky Mountain Biological Station of Denver University would hold its second summer school of classes for college credit in botany and zoology at Cascade Lodge from July 25th through August 27th. The lodge was chosen because its location, five and one-half miles west of the village and at an altitude of 8,500 feet, proved highly satisfactory "for the study of meadow, stream beds, beaver ponds, mountain slopes, timber lands and regions above timberline."

Finding it difficult to keep her three lodging facilities staffed and properly managed to her standards, Josie sold the Sherwood in 1926 to Canyon City, Colorado interests that planned to remodel the large building into "an up-to-date picture house." That never took place for in 1927 the keys to the front door were delivered to Mr. Joseph Ewing of Greeley who owned another lodging facility in his home town. Between 1927 and 1955 there had been no less than eight successive owners and the maturing guest house was certainly confused as to who paid its bills. Mrs. Norton had started this whole fee simple paper journey that was completed on September 16, 1955 when another Nebraskan, Robert Venner, became its final owner. Apparently not sanguine to return to the name Aksarben, he temperately changed the name slightly to The Sherwood Inn. However, as was the case with so many other wooden structures in mountain towns of Colorado, the headlines of the *Estes Park Trail* shouted out its epitaph. "FIREMEN PREVENT SPREAD OF SHERWOOD BLAZE TO ADJOINING BUILDINGS ON ELKHORN AVENUE." The Venners having returned to Lincoln, Nebraska in the fall of 1955, after ordering that workers redecorate the interior of the premises and perform extensive remodeling, sadly learned of the calamitous blaze of February 14, 1956. Observers knew that painting was underway and suspicioned that "it was caused by combustion from the paint cans and rags that were thrown into a closet at the time." It was Valentine's Day, and their hearts were truly broken in an untoward way. If it had not been for a recent five inch snow fall and the ice that coated the adjacent wooden structures lining that section of the business district of Estes Park, the horror that lurks in all firefighters' minds of whole towns being devoured by flame would have been the cataclysmic result. Sherwood Inn never was rebuilt, its space on Elkhorn Avenue being taken by a new building housing gift shops, that sold neither tea nor red eye.

In the early 1930s Anna May Derby acquired the Hupp Hotel after Henry Hupp's death in 1931 and Josie's death in Loveland in 1932. Early resident Cleone McNight, who had lived at the Josephine Hotel, remembered *Mother Derby* as she was called in the 1920s and 1930s as a very kind and caring woman. Her recollections included the fact that Mrs. Derby had the longest hair braids she had ever seen. "That hair, wound in braids about her head must have weighed a ton! She frequently had headaches and wanted to cut off her hair, but Bill protested. After he died, she cut all that long auburn hair off and she had no more headaches." She certainly must have been quite angered over her husband's refusal, but back then, even more than now, women wore their hair in long tresses that the men folk appreciated. Anna May at that time however might have agreed with the sentiment expressed in the local silent movie then playing at the Park Theater in the village entitled *Don't Ever Get Married* by Marshall Neillan, a comedy masterpiece of the times. Previous to her Hupp Hotel acquisition however, Anna May purchased Cascade Lodge. Ownerships and inter-relationships between lodges and hotels with common or successive ownerships involving the same persons was a generally accepted way of business life. Fishing, hiking, porch sitting and especially horseback riding from the livery stables at Cascade were very popular activities. The seventy-five guests who occupied the lodge rooms and cabins at $6 per day including meals with the weekly charge reaching nearly $35, as well as other Park visitors were always welcomed by a member of the family, Ralph Derby, and the very competent liveryman Harry McCaslin who owned and rented out the horses stabled at Cascade. There was nothing better than to saddle up for a long ride up Fall River Canyon or over to Lawn Lake and look forward to a bountiful dinner served by Anna May's competent kitchen and dining room crew of young people. A break in the narrative is in order to discuss more about the horses and their owners both of whom were fixtures at the early lodges as well as lining Main Street of the rapidly growing village of Estes Park.

A tourist came out in the early days on a bus to stay at least two weeks and he or she needed a horse. People expected to ride a horse in the West for that is what the news and entertainment media had preached to them. The number of liverymen grew to well over thirty in the 1920s and 1930's, with at least seven located right on Elkhorn Avenue. In the 1990s, as one horseman confided with some degree of hyperbole, "The tourists come to Estes for a day, and the next day they're half way to California. They don't give any time for anything, certainly not for long term rentals of the horses!" A liveryman in the 1920s and 1930s after trailing his average string of thirty horses back to the Estes Valley from winter pastures near Loveland, Lyons or Longmont, was on the lookout for returning summer residents and tourists. One of the last active liverymen, Otis Whiteside who will be mentioned often in these chapters, disclosed his technique to gain an edge on his competitors. "Every morning about 7 A.M. we saddled up a real nice horse and put on our best clothes. When we saw smoke coming out of a chimney on the hill north of town that had a lot of rentals, we were right at that door to sell them a ride. If you did that today, you'd get him back tomorrow. You see, we advertised on horseback and handed out our cards. We wanted to be the first one up that hill to get the summer people. We also hired a man every night to go up to the Crags Lodge and try to get business. While we held the kids or played cards with their parents and other guests, we always handed out our cards advertising our horses. Then the next morning we brought the horses, ready to go, up to the rack just west of the Crags and loaded up." Some liverymen had exclusive contracts with a lodge as did Otis and his Silver Lane Livery wranglers with the owners of the Lewiston Hotel. Those not as fortunate had to bedazzle tourists off the street by any means necessary to get them on one of their horses, thus it was not who had the best horses but who had the best salesmen. It became obvious that standardizing rates and recognizing an accepted code of business practices and professional ethics would be best for all, and in 1934 the Estes Park Liverymens Association was incorporated. "To keep the prices standardized so that you're not cutting each other's throat," Otis explained was the reason the organization started. "We worked hard together and kept out bad practices, and if one fellow needed more horses for a job the others all pitched in to help him out." In modified form, the organization still exists for the dwindling precious few who remain to compete with go carts, miniature golf, and *no license required* fish ponds whose *wild trout* attack at the first cast of a hook well baited with popcorn.

What did it take for a horse to catch the eye of the liveryman intent upon adding to his string? Men and often women were very careful in what animals they purchased. Of course the first requirement was gentleness; then good confirmation. Otis described his ideal horse to be "one that carries his groceries right with him," which means he can work every day and not get thin. A horse can't be blemished with splints from strains that would indicate it had been overworked as a colt, and, as simplistic as it may seem, a livery-man always checked a horse's teeth for indications of age and health. To elaborate on this point, when a horse is quite young it has four short teeth close together. Then at age three it has six, one more on each side. At four it sheds two baby teeth and gets its first two permanent ones. At the age of six the animal is known as a full mouth horse and has all of its permanent teeth with black appearing centers. Starting at age seven, and as the horse ages, the black centers successively disappear to become entirely white. Over the remaining years of its life the teeth grow longer, hence the expression *long in the tooth* for age, and they become smooth with long use to earn for the animal the opprobrium, smooth mouth. When you are examining a pro-spective acquisition to your herd and see a white centered, long and bucked toothed critter smiling at you as its owner pronounces - -"there's a lot of years left in Lightning" - -, back away pardner for that is an old horse. I must be fair to the horse for though the average period for a horse to remain in ser-vice was ten years in the Estes Valley, some unusual members of the breed still were carrying the dudes after 25 years, that is if their owners served them North Park hay. Although most riders forty or fifty years ago knew how to ride a horse, even the big and strong horse recently brought into a liv-eryman's inventory, ninety percent of current riders won't admit that they know very little about the fine art of horseback travel. Otis Whiteside gave out with a hearty chuckle just thinking about those *experts* who visited his stable. "When I questioned them about if they had ridden much before, they always came up with some tale of having grown up riding on their grandpa's farm. But when they started getting on the wrong side or couldn't pick up the bridle reins right, you damn well knew something was wrong! I couldn't call him a liar you see, but offered him another horse saying 'I have a better horse for you.' You have to be careful, for liability insurance in the '30s only cost $15 a head for the whole season but now it's real expensive."

But rides from Cascade Lodge ceased in its thirteenth year of existence as fires and horses don't mix. In the spring of 1935 the community of Estes Park had been plagued by a series of devastating fires, and such fate awaited this lodge to stunt its history. Over the weekend of June 7-9 of 1935 twenty-three young women of Sigma Phi Gamma, a sorority of business women from Fort Collins, had enjoyed a splendid time together unaware of the fact that their small convention would be the last for this lodge. Bill Crenshaw, an employee engaged in cleaning one of the nearby cottages, noticed on the morning of June 12th a trace of smoke emitting from the roof of the lodge. A fire obviously was in progress but the lodge had no telephone by which to cry out the alarm. He raced down the eastern slope for about a mile to the nearest phone at Park Ranger Jack Moomaw's government house and telephoned in the alert to both the National Park fire crew and the Volunteer Fire brigade within the village. The fire had such a start and generated so much heat from a lodge constructed almost entirely of wood with few defenses, that it was completely destroyed in a few hours. One hundred twenty-five young men of the CCC work force, camped to the south of the lodge across Fall River and actively engaged in controlling within the National Park the Blackhills Beetle, immediately responded and kept diligently at their hopeless task long after all other firefighters had returned to their stations. The only source of fire protection available to the local fire fighters was one elderly fire truck. It was reported that, because it was so slow in climbing the grade from the east, by the time it arrived to a fully engulfed inferno of hot embers everyone in town had passed it on the road to await its appearance over the brow of the hill. An old friend of mine, now deceased, remembered seeing the fire from Deer Ridge that day. Her picture album had this poignant paragraph under a photo of the smoky ruins. "We saw this fire from Deer Ridge but when we got down there, this was all that was left. Through the smoke we can see some CCC boys who are helping to put out the fire. The main building was destroyed but the cottages and other buildings nearby were not touched. Good-bye, Cascade Lodge!"

All fixtures and furnishings were lost. Mrs. Derby announced that, inasmuch as she had only $6,000 of the total cost of $30,000 for the reconstruction covered by insurance and the national climate of financial despair still lingered in the Estes Valley, she would not be rebuilding. Some of the cabins still remain for use by present day tourists, although their days perhaps may be numbered. Mother Derby returned to the Hupp and aggressively pursued her talents as a caring and competent hotel woman. She in 1947 revealed her attitude toward her profession which she long had practiced. "We gave first class service, good accommodations and had an excellent table." Who would expect any thing more?

Hupp Annex and John Cleave Home Behind, 1908 (Private)

Brown Tea Pot Inn, 1916 (CHS)

Estes Park Village, circa 1912 (CHS)

Estes Park Village, Hupp In Lower Right, 1910 (Clatworthy)

Horses Run To Their Liveries in Estes Park, 1920 (EPHM)

Town of Estes Park, circa 1925 (Sanborn Souvenir Co.)

#1 Lewiston, #2 Sherwood, #3 Park, #4 Hupp, #5 Josephine, #6 Sam Service Residence, #7 Sam Service Store

Cascade Lodge and Fall River, 1925 (EPPL)

Main Floor of Cascade Lodge, circa 1930 (EPPL)

Cascade Still Burning, 1935 (Mary B. Totten)

Two Liverymen, Otis Whiteside and Bill Robinson, 1993 (Private)

A Days Work That Reduced The Herds, circa prior 1890 (Webermeier). See Commentary On Page 86.

CHAPTER VI - THREE LITTLE TRAIL COMPANIONS

Fern Lodge, Forest Inn, Bear Lake Lodge

Only A Little Mountain Lake,
So Peaceful And Serene,
A Master Piece Of God's Handiwork,
And Fairer Than A Dream,
Surrounded By Majestic Mountains,
All Garbed In Spruce & Pine,
Where Nearby, Snow Is Sparkling,
In The Brilliant Sunshine.
No Artist's Hand In All This Land,
Can Paint This Lake So Fair,
As The Divine Hands Creations,
Fashioned It, And Put It There.
No Tongue Can Tell Or Words Express,
Of Treasures Held In Store,
In Hidden Spots Of The Rockies,
There Are Charms By The Score.
Henry H. Viestenz, 1921

About the same time as the National Park was created, there were three little lodges that struggled out of the remote regions of the Colorado National Forest to serve as destination points for hikers. Two were on lakes, the third by a pool. In the beginning of tourist days in the front range of the Rockies there was a need for starting points from which to commence a climb as well as a warm bench by a fire when the trail, cold and wearisome, wended its way back as the rays of the sun became defused in the dew of an approaching time of mountain silence. Then as now, a soft chair and a table filled with food were often as important as the hiking, fishing, a slide down a snowy hillock that originally drew in the traveler. The three were Fern Lodge, Bear Lake Lodge and Forest Inn all sharing similarities that made for notability. They were petite, if one can attach to log buildings a somewhat human quality, at one time all owned by the same person, were originally situated on trails instead of major roadways and more importantly the ground on which they were built was always owned by the public.

FERN LODGE

The first one I want to discuss must begin with an introduction of a strong minded, physically dynamic individual who had much to do with its origin as well as exploring and naming lakes and other natural features that we enjoy today. Dr. William Jacob Workman was born June 28, 1852 in

Knobnoster, Missouri and at sixteen entered the University of Missouri Medical School for six months then withdrew to tour the country with his father. After later studying medicine at nights under the direction of a medical preceptor, he received his medical degree from Washington University in St. Louis in 1873. His marriages were many beginning with Katherine who passed away after but a few years of marriage. His second wife, Emma, bore him three children, a son Milo and daughters Dessa and Alberta Grace. Missouri had not been kind to him; an accident caused him serious injury and his patients constantly were in arrears in paying his fees. By the time he elected to move his practice and his family to Ashland, Kansas in 1887, he was owed more than $25,000 and his impaired physical condition reflected a deathly pallor on his large frame draped with a spare 126 pounds. "The warm climate of Kansas was certainly better than Missouri mud," he would later certify, but I surmise that plenteous quantities of good food proved to be helpful to returning health since his body within a year had filled out to 208 pounds. But then sorrow would catch up with him again with the death of Emma at the age of 25 years. He plunged on with his work, seeking to forget his grief, if one ever does, by hunting and fishing with his son. It was while on one of his outings in Indian Territory of Oklahoma that he discovered in the Cimmaron River bluffs a silica that provided the essential ingredient for the first use of gypsum plaster. A company was formed, Workman's Concrete, for the manufacture of building materials and commercial Plaster of Paris, that brought to him financial security. When on a business trip back east, he looked up an old college sweetheart now a widow, Lulu Ripley Oliphant, and they were married in 1888. For her in Ashland he constructed a huge home entirely out of gypsum, and for the next five years was a potentate of progress for the community.

In 1893 as bad luck would follow good times, Lulu's health became impaired and they traveled the country in search of a place of residence where she might regain her health. They both liked Denver and in 1902 purchased a home and he launched into a new medical practice. As was his nature, he explored the regions of his own environs intent on making an investment in the mountains. His interest in Estes Park developed after a previous visit in 1898, and around 1902 or 1903 he purchased a tract of land from Abner Sprague. Sharing a friendship with Enos Mills, they were participants in an exciting episode of true mountaineering in 1906 when they volunteered in a search near Mount Ypsilon for the body of a fellow climber, Lewis R. Levings, who fell August 2, 1905 off the pinnacle of that mountain. The story told is that they found the body wedged tightly and irretrievably in a cleft of the mountain, and ascertaining its permanency resolved to protect it. A truly remarkable feat took place as they carried up heavy sacks of dry cement and, with snow melt for water, entombed the body in its location free of desecration by bird, beast or the ravages of time. The tale has never been fully authenticated as is the case with so many heroic accounts passed down by word of mouth, but, if true, points out the abilities of these men and their compassion for a fallen fellow contender of the sublime spheres. I am inclined to believe the story true as Louis Levings parents, upon their deaths, left instructions for their own ashes to be scattered on Twin Sisters Mountain at a place in direct sight of Mount Ypsilon. In 1929, when the cement was seen to be deteriorating, the remains were reinterred 700 feet above Spectacle Lakes close by where iron plates rather than cement would keep Lewis secure until his time came for further ascent to the heavens. Workman built a hunting cabin about 1908 that later was used by visiting dignitaries of the Park Service when it became publicly owned. In 1910 he homesteaded additional land in the northwest portion of Moraine Park, later selling some of the land in smaller lots for summer home sites, a few of them still stand in private ownership and termed by the National Park Service as *inholdings*.

A vitally active man, perhaps restless, certainly inquisitive of nature, and prone to this bias by his very nature, he was lured further up the animal trails to the west of his new homestead in a disposition for exploration. Intrigued with one special locale on the eastern approaches of a tree enshrouded blue-green lake, he gained permission from the U. S. Forest Service to build a cabin. Workman and his joint explorer, a Mr. Turk whose name some report was spelled Tur_c_k, came up with a name for the lake. As the green trees draped its shores in the illusion of a fern frond enshrouded by shaded mist, it was suitably dubbed Fern Lake. Dr. Workman and a small crew felled and fitted up logs for a cabin in 1910 to face out upon the lake so that from an ample front porch he and his guests might watch the fish surface on placid waters in search of fresh hatches of insect life. As they worked, adding row upon row of fresh smelling timber to the building, the warm yellow sun rays turned red to became lost behind the mountains hugging the western shore. His personal *headquarters* was named appropriately Fern Lodge. The main lodge was essentially completed in 1911 with oiled paper covering the windows, and doors the doctor called *Arkansas Style* that essentially were heavy blankets hung on wooden frames over the openings. Within a short period of time the papered over openings were enclosed with many-paned wooden windows and wooden doors hung to thwart the unwanted four footed denizens of the forest seeking more cushy lodging without the formality of an invitation.

Upon entering into the lodge, guests caught sight of a large dining table. But this one was different. A huge stump stood in the middle of the room, fitted up with a center core revolving cylinder around which, and also attached to the stump, was an oblong pine table top. Balanced on the top of the revolving mechanical device was a slightly smaller pine table top rigged up to its outer edges with pine knot handles for human propulsion. It essentially was a giant lazy susan. It revolved over a dining table capable of seating twenty-one at one time and on which whirling platform food from the kitchen was placed for self service. I am advised that it revolved in both directions, for second helpings, and for many years a veritable feast awaited those weary travelers after their long, strenuous hike up to Fern. The roof of the main lodge was architecturally significant for the times. Because Workman did not have the equipment to fabricate wood shingles, ten men were hired for six weeks to hew out specially designed logs into a pattern he knew would endure severe winter testing. The logs, hollowed out, were then fitted like tiles one with the concavity up the next down, covering the edge of the first and the next in the series, thus imparting a handsome, watertight, appearance to the crown of his lodge. The type of roof design was called *hog trough*. The floor of the lodge was also admired by those who reached this bastion of the back country as it was made of cross sections of logs, sawn smooth and laid flat, with pounded dirt between the circles in a parquet appearing motif. Fern Lodge, joined by additional tent-cabins, tents, and later an assortment of log cabins, were scattered about the eastern flat prominence of the lake. To have William Workman as a friend was comparable to knowing the lord of the manorhouse as no effort was spared to share with his guests the abundance of his mountain kingdom. To reach this lodge in the early days it was necessary to hike or ride in by horseback over a four mile trail, steep and rocky, from a roughed out parking lot in Moraine Park. Then in subsequent years, from the camp at Bear Lake that gave every indication of maturing out of its adolescence, a blazed and widened trail progressed to Fern Lodge then descended Fern Creek canyon to the lodges in Moraine Park completing the popular circular trip hikers appreciate even today.

Pleased with his efforts, he and Lulu went off for a vacation to Europe. However upon their return she became ill again, this time with pneumonia and which disease claimed her life in 1913. At the same time Dr. Workman was himself hospitalized with a ruptured appendix. Dr. Workman recovered, but as he was a man not content to share his dreams and enthusiasm for Colorado only with friends or the trees of the forest, he married again in 1915. Florence, a nurse from Denver, and he became parents to two daughters, Wilma and Dorothy. Long after his sale of Fern Lodge, his eagerness to fish continued with no slackened effort, and with these two daughters and fortified with a lunch box, Florence remembered, "went off for the whole day, --every day, from morning until night, and he supplied the whole of Moraine Park with fish!" How he arranged being away for three months from his Denver patients to enjoy the wilderness and serve as a superb host for his guests, always amazed his visitors and fellow lodge operators. His wife said, "He was a general practitioner for 9 months a year, but from June to September he went up to Estes Park, and his patients in Denver --could just go!" Although maintaining no office in the Estes Valley, he never shirked his Hippocratic Oath and treated friends and strangers alike who called upon him for assistance. As an avid fisherman, every opportunity was taken to try his luck coupled with a *scientific* approach for success to net his clever adversaries. Always hiking the back country with a bamboo pole and creel as his constant companions, it was only natural for his destinations to be piscatorially inspired. When once asked if he had ever climbed Long's Peak, he replied with scornful mirth, "Why should I, there are no fish up there!"

An adventurous visionary, hard working, devoted to friends and family, he was invested with a form of poetic license that resulted in memorializing the names of his friends, family and products of his whimsy which he deemed worthy for honor. Henceforth, on our maps we see examples of this prolific christener of geographic perspectives. Although possessed of a strong personality, it did not carry over into personal ego. Thus, we find nothing that bears his own name, except the marker at his grave. Lake Odessa was his variation of his daughter's name, Dessa, that he deemed more musically apropos in tone for a body of lovely water. Lake Helene was first called Helmary Lake after his friends, the sisters Helen and Mary Stidger of Denver, whose father George owned a cottage in Moraine Park. Grace Falls bears the middle name of another daughter, Alberta Grace. He turned to the high mountains which were the apex of his fascination, and let his mind create. From his musing emerged names like Notchtop and Little Matterhorn Mountains and several favorite fishing holes up Forest Canyon, jointly named with Julian Hayden and Abner Sprague's brother-in-law Ed Andrews, like Arrowhead and

Inkwell Lakes. He perceived another body of water that reminded him of Bear Lake, hence named it Ursula, for Ursa the bear. Whether the Park officials deciphered a similarity as did Doctor Workman is left to speculation, yet they surmised that its name must have been produced out of a rich imagination. As imaginations are in need of quiet scenes for contemplative thought, Lake Ursula thus resurfaced as Dream Lake.

Straightforward labels were hung on other landmarks in tribute to achieving citizens he knew or impressions made upon him when these geologic features were first noticed. However, one took some head scratching to come up with an acronym to appease two neighbors of influence in the community. Those lodges most closely associated with the good doctor were Stead's and Brinwood. Dora Stead and Sally Reed, co-owners with their husbands of that pair of Moraine Park resorts, having observed Dr. Workman nominate much of the scenery after others particularly women, approached him with a request. Could he name a lake after them? Not eager to engender the wrath of several of his neighbors although the suggestion was more in the nature of a playful challenge, he rose to the cast as a fish to the fly and agreed. There was a problem, however, as there was but one lake remaining to name, and he had two ladies to please. Granted Sally had been a Park resident far longer than Dora, Dora was more assertive of her opinions, --just ask Alberta Sprague. His solution was to name that last lake, Saldora, to which joint attribution they were well pleased. Now for Fred Dille, mountain man, scientist and trapper, the lake below Saldora Lake had earlier hung on it the name Dille Lake. These were appropriately changed by Park officials years later believing that such solitary pools were deserving of a better opportunity for remembrance, so Saldora Lake became Loomis Lake for an even earlier builder at Fern Lake than Dr. Workman and Dille Lake was retitled more woodsy-like to Spruce Lake. As to Fred's reaction to the change, we don't know as he had left these parts of the woods to go trapping in Alaska. But if Dora and Sally had been around--! Well! They would not have gone down without a fight, I can assure you. I was confused when reading old records of the lodges to see the name Marguerite Falls. Where was it? I find that the good doctor was at it again. He was willing to make changes and modify his decisions previously made; an illustration of that trait is seen in the first name for the magnificent group of waterfalls on the trial to Fern Lake. He first baptized the water Lulu Falls after his third wife. Then the falls or perhaps only one segment of them was renamed, Marguerite Falls, in honor of a friend's wife, Marguerite Turk. Later the name for the whole thundering cascade of foaming white splendor was shrunk by others to its present name, Fern Falls. It is even more confusing when one examines a topographic map of the area and finds the name of Marguerite Falls designated for another crescendo of water above Fern Falls, on a tributary northeast of the lake and east of the trail. I'll let you work out that solution.

The permit to operate the lodge, after the girdling National Forest came under the jurisdiction of the Department of the Interior, was sold by Dr. Workman in 1915 and assigned to the Higby Brothers. Their family, including their mother Nina W. Higby from Brewerton, New York, later owned and operated the Park Hotel and the National Park Outfitting Company on Elkhorn Avenue immediately east of the old Presbyterian Church in Estes Park. When the Higby Brothers, Cliff, Reed and Lester, operated the lodge, followed later by Frank Byerly, it was a destination many sought out despite its near inaccessibility for the more faint hearted. At Fern Lodge a guest always signed the large red leather guest book, giving their name, place of residence and time of arrival possibly as an act of final success. The masthead on the lodge register gave clear indication of what to expect from a journey to this hidden retreat, and it was repeated at the top of each page in the lodge register perhaps as mental reinforcement if you didn't first accept the advice offered.

9550 feet above the sea
FERN LODGE ON FERN LAKE
You Are In One Of Earth's Beauty Spots,
Enjoy It. Have A Good Time.
Visit Lake Odessa elev. 10,000 Ft, Marguerite
And Fern Falls, Sprague And Tyndall Glaciers,
Continental Divide, Halletts Peak elev. 12,725 Ft,
Stones Peak elev. 12,925 Ft,
Tourmaline Lake And Lake Helene.
Guides -Pack Saddle Horses -Camping Equipment.

In thumbing through the well used book, now in possession of a former visitor, you can read the names of people from all over the United States as well as interesting places of the world. The guest register was not started until July 27, 1915 when the Village of Estes Park listed its population at 500 residents, and the first name in the book reads 'Herbert Kitelle, Huron, South Dakota,' who with his wife and two children occupied one of the tent cabins. Aberdeen Kitelle was only 3 years of age, and the next day Mrs. Mary Washburn of Denver, 72 years old signed in. Trekkers of all ages found Fern a good stopping place on the trail. Incidentally, the rates were fair at $1.00 per night per person. I enjoyed reading the comments of the guests and will relate a few of them to evidence the importance to the hiker of Fern Lodge in the years of Fern's stewardship to the tourist. "Those were some eats!" "We all came in on snowshoes." "Left Estes Park at 2:15 P. M., arrived at Fern Lodge at 5:15 P. M. and left for Grand Lake at 4:30 A. M. to return via Squeaky Bob's and Fall River." "Fishing good." "Raining like Hell! Brr!, thanks for the fire." "All the way on skis, then we went up Flattop." "We say tobogganing is King!" "All one happy bunch." "This is surely a clever place and worth the climb." "Small pieces of ice were still in Fern Lake and quite a bit of snow making it hard walking to Odessa Lake in June." "At last we have arrived. Such a distance, but is worth it to see the beautiful scenery around here." "This is such a cute cabin and we certainly appreciate the shelter as it is snowing and rather cold." "Thanks for the hospitality as we were caught in a storm." And finally, and I guess summing up all the comments, "Thrilled with the beauty of Fern Lake Lodge."

Some believe that the history of skiing in the Estes Park area had its prelude with the ski trip to Fern Lodge by Alson Chapman and Julian Hayden on April 1, 1912. Others attribute its overture to the terrible snow storm that blanketed this area in December of 1913 with more than six feet of snow falling without respite as the roads into this valley became impassable. That necessitated the residents to strap about anything onto their feet in order to move about during the period of weeks, often months as they were confined like early day prisoners with no mail, little food, and water that came from chopping holes through the ice. After waiting for two weeks for help to come from the valley towns, some of the robust citizens skied down to Lyons, more than twenty-two miles away, to pick up the mail and supplies. After that remarkable winter of 1913-1914, the recreational activities of the winter were dictated by skiing, learned as a lesson of survival. Younger townsfolk readily took to skiing and other winter sports and investigated a suitable center for such recreational pursuits. Fern Lodge was the only building high enough in the mountains adjacent to Estes Park village with sufficient snow and suitable terrain for making those lengthy slides on correspondingly long skis thought *divine* by the ladies. Becoming a favorite destination point for the winter outings of the Colorado Mountain Club, The Rocky Mountain National Park Ski Club and the Estes Park Outdoor Club from 1915 and into the 1930s, the lodge often served as many as 500 guests each winter.

Fern Lake was the site for the first of the Annual Winter Carnivals usually held in February or March of each year that began in 1917. It kicked off with an inaugural toboggan slide down Crags Lodge's drive and on up to Fern Lodge with over 100 merry makers shouting their approval for an event "that would last forever!" That first four day Carnival was a complete success with the season of 1918 enrolling even more participants. The Superintendent of the new National Park pitched in with a crew to improve the ski runs and made his personal contribution before the roaring fire of Fern Lodge with an evening lecture entitled *The National Park & Winter Sports*. This program somehow in the 1990s takes on the aura of the imperfect anachronism when Hidden Valley Ski Area was removed from the National Park around 1990 as an inappropriate activity. Several listed on the lodge register during those early winter ventures were Superintendent L. C. Way and future Superintendents including Edmund Rogers. Also a young woman signed the register with her cousin on February 17, 1917, members of the Colorado Mountain Club from Denver. She was Miss Agnes Wolcott Vaille and he was Roger Wolcott Toll who also would become the Superintendent four years anon. They no doubt had a glorious time in the frosty air that hung over Fern lake as their squeaking skis through fresh snow joined the other fun seeking sports enthusiasts on the trail to the ski hill that descended from Lake Odessa. The lectures at the 1920 Winter Carnival encompassed everything from one by the Park Superintendent on *The Objectives Of The National Park*, to another by artist and Park Ranger Dean Babcock reviewing *The Flora Of The National Park*. There even was a beautiful talk by our previous acquaintance, Agnes Vaille, whose topic for those gathered in the great fellowship room of Fern Lodge was *Red Cross Work In France*. In a tragedy of long lasting consequences for Agnes, Herbert Sortland, Walter Kiener and the Denver and Estes Park communities, Agnes was to meet her death on Long's Peak only five years later. Herbert died in attempting to locate her, and Walter the guide would forever bear his self imposed guilt in scars from fingers and toes lost to severe frostbite. The then Superintendent, Roger Toll, had erected a shelter house at the point on Boulder Field where Agnes froze to death awaiting rescue. That shelter house is now gone, but the conical stone building nearby, designed by Arthur Fisher of Denver, was erected the year following Agnes's death by F. O. Vaille, her grieving father. The beehive shaped stone structure, resembling in some way a dwelling of an ancient people of southern Italy, remains as a monument to

Agnes' brave spirit partly molded by her numerous winter trips to Fern Lodge.

Education coupled with healthy outdoor exercise was the usual order of the day for these hearty Winter Carnival snow enthusiasts who made the final push to Fern on skis or snowshoes while pulling their toboggans in from Brinwood Lodge, a distance of five miles. There were just as many women as men in the merry band, in fact the festivities just wouldn't have been the same without the giggles, taunts and shrieks of the pretty girls clad in long skirts who were as eager as the men to compete for the prizes offered by local businesses. For all ages and both sexes, this was to be, and was, a fun filled fantasy. There were others, more innovative, who came on up with neither skis nor snowshoes, with these robust young dandies boldly expressing their manliness by signing the register, 'came in without snowshoes!' as the gaggle of gals nearby cheered them, adulating over them as 'wonderful!' Food and supplies were carried in by brute force on skis and snowshoes, but only the strongest and most deft skier in 1925, Ranger Jack Moomaw, would be entrusted with the astonishing task of carrying in the crates of eggs, unbroken. Because of these popular activities, skiing, snowshoeing and all of activities associated with the season, the Park constructed a ranger station on the north side of the lake in 1924 that remains in use today. However, because of the relative isolation of Fern Lodge and its difficulty of access, the Colorado Mountain Club of Denver shifted its events to Grand Lake in 1934. The local Estes club remained loyal to Fern until the end when the lodge would no longer stand high on the hill to warm them at its friendly fireplace. This same group of men and women, their children and those who newly joined this Estes Park colony of iconoclasts, never could get enough of winter sports. During years in the 1930s, 1940s and up to 1951, they hauled snow down from Trail Ridge Road to a north facing slope of Old Man Mountain just west of the village where they fashioned a ski jump for all participants daring enough to throw themselves into the air on long wooden slats to the cheers and taunts of less courageous onlookers. I should point out that these events took place not in winter but in June of each year. Ted Mathews of Estes Park, who worked at early Hidden Valley Ski Area and continued in his exuberance for the outdoor life by climbing Long's Peak at least 46 times, was one of those who flew with ease down the track and into the air with utter abandonment of care or worry. He, and others of a mold now broken, were the kind of men and women who made this Estes Valley the marvellous place it is today. Yet it will never be like it was, --free spirited, light hearted, compassionate and uncomplicated. Can you imagine men, women and children of today tramping up five miles to a little log lodge to slide down a hill on a toboggan or on crudely made skis, then to sit upon the bare floor to listen to lectures on flora, art and the Red Cross? I wish that it could be that way again, but most youth have passed through the one way gate of sophistication, desirous of high fashion ski wear, expensive snow boards and full access to deafening concerts wrapped up in slick packages.

By 1917, the ownership of Fern Lodge had passed to the partnership of Byerly & Rodgers. Then Frank W. Byerly of Estes Park, after his divorce from his first wife and after his marriage to Mrs. Edna B. Bishop from Kansas, rumored by the town gossips to be "a wealthy woman," became its sole owner. A corporation, Front Range Hotel Company, was formed in 1922 to operate this lodge. Frank H. Cheley was elected a Director and Edna Bishop

Byerly was named its Secretary. They erected a saw mill utilizing a huge water wheel on Fern Creek for power, sixteen feet in diameter, but their efforts to saw lumber required for new cabins proved unsuccessful as the waterwheel was incapable of generating enough force to rapidly spin the saw blade. It was abandoned and hand tools took over to first add to the main lodge. Later, between 1922 and 1924, sleeping cabins were constructed up behind the lodge, some as small as 10 by 12 feet in size, others 16 by 24 feet, and one huge four unit guest facility with proportions of 12 by 72 feet. In 1926 it is interesting to read that the presidential mantle of the corporation no longer fell across the shoulders of Frank Byerly but *Mrs.* Frank Byerly and a year later the chief office of the corporation devolved to Mrs. Edna B. *Bishop* having retaken her former name for undisclosed reasons. Alliances and circumstances changed frequently high in the mountains, like the weather, or like partnerships seeking gold which mineral findings later proved out to be iron pyrite with a beguiling deceptiveness of glitter. For the succeeding years left to this resort facility it was operated by Edna and her sons James and Charles. This lodge was a very popular one for local Estes Park people and those who lived throughout the National Park. Many of the lodge owners and town business people, on an infrequent day off or in company with some of their guests, marked down Fern Lodge as a prime destination, not because that region of the Park was so special, which it was, but more especially because of the great reception they would receive from the owners or managers who considered this little log facility the finest facility in all of the Park, regardless of size or rustic appearance. When lodge owners died off, such as Joe Mills, Roland Reed, Abner Sprague, Imogene McPherson, Steve Hewes and Donald Patrick as well as the scions of local business the likes of Charles Hix, Sam Service, Elizabeth Foote, Casey Rockwell, Josie Hupp, Fred P. Clatworthy and Cornelius Bond, new generations ushered in a quality of benign indifference. Newcomers were less concerned with the past than for future economic success, apathetic to what had been the very essence of the community, of what would never be again. Pioneer citizens who came here to live out their entire lives now were meeting new residents who had but a vague awareness of what glue had held the little village together in those early days. Most of them never did understand, or wanted to, as they were to move on in a few years and the significance of Fern Lodge was to blow away in smoke and dusty memories, lost forever.

Lunches continued to be served to the hikers who ranked this decaying antique a fine midway point in a day's hike from Bear and back down to Moraine Park. A former hiker recalled, "I remember the smell of wonderful homemade bread in the lodge as I walked about on sunken tree trunk rounds embedded in the floor." The small lodge store provided fishing tackle and lures, camping gear, candy, coffee and miscellaneous sundries forgotten by those eager for a day on the trail. Machines were adjusting much of the adventurous spirit of the feet, confining them to luxurious confinement of a high spirited automobile as it sought out landscapes now more accessible on Trail Ridge Road. Also vacations did not last for a month or longer but comprised whatever could be crowded into a frenetic two-week period. The quotient of fractional division of a tourist's allotment of time permitted to places such as Fern Lodge quickly was approaching zero as fragmented family holidays heralded the demise of this lodge. Use of the lodge for overnight accommodations, even a dinner or lunchtime stop, had rapidly declined. By 1938 the lodge was no longer open in the winter season except for the few who obtained permission from the owners such as Park Rangers in need of additional services while on patrol. Later more posh ski areas came on line in other parts of the country, and the traveling public was influenced to be more mobile with more comforts. Then a severe body blow was struck as war years again approached lessening tourist demand for joyful recreation. As one era opened another closed. Dr. Workman after selling the lodge, raised wheat on a ranch he retained in Ashland while his wife and last batch of girls remained in Denver. Later they all moved to Boulder where his daughters attended the university and his remaining summers of his life were spent in Moraine Park, fishing and painting pictures in oil and water color. In 1943, together with his compatriot of the valley between the moraines, Abner Sprague, he died to climb up that great ladder to even higher mountains and lakes that hopefully the new *superintendent* would allow them to name.

Fern Lodge remained open throughout the forties and fifties in the summertime serving as a location where one could purchase light refreshments and fishing supplies from the attractive hostesses hired by Edna Bishop, some who became famous. One young woman who greeted the guests with a big smile and adlibbed for them a song accompanied by nothing more than the mountain wren perched nearby in envy, was song stylistic Judy Collins, then from Denver. Miss Collins never forgot the beauty of Fern and in 1966 she returned to scatter her father's ashes in the cool shade where she often had experienced tranquility. I hasten to point out that this was not the first time that ashes were deposited at or near Fern Lake despite Park policy that discouraged it even though its officials understood the sincerely decent reason for such action. Carrie Cassidy Fuller, a native of Colorado and a true lover of the National Park, requested that at her death in 1943 her ashes be scattered therein. Her husband and children checked into Fall River Lodge, took a hike, and soon checked out one summer day in 1943. Later a granite marker, surreptitiously set in the ground, was discovered near Lake Odessa, the neighbor of Fern Lake, on which was inscribed her name and years of life. Also on the stone were these words. "Her Sweet Spirit Rests In These Her Native Peaks." Later the marker disappeared but then was located, thrown into the lake by uncaring vandals of the same ilk to whom I shall later refer. After its recovery, it was set high in a rock out of the Park boundaries, yet in full view of her beloved mountains.

As time went on the lunches were discontinued and only light snacks were sold. Most hikers had their own brown bag lunch tucked into a bright colored, high-tech backpack requiring only a cold drink, coffee or perhaps an ice cream. Eventually the National Park officials deemed that a use for this little lodge had long past, that its cost of maintenance was out of proportion to its worth, and with the advent of increased looting and deliberate vandalism a final decision must be considered. The concession lease, purchased by James Bishop in 1952 from his mother, expired on December 31, 1958 and would not be renewed. Old Fern Lodge was padlocked for the last time in 1959 and all ancillary buildings to the lodge, such as the dining room added to the original lodge, cabins and storage facilities, were removed in 1964. After a detailed study, The National Park Service confirmed after much empathy for the past that the original lodge should remain closed and locked but preserved for a 'Trailside Historical Display Of Back Country Hotel Facilities Of 1915.' Through a window, wayfarers on the Fern Lake Trail could peep in and see it furnished in rustic attire as it would have appeared back in 1915. A suitable sign was proposed to denominate this historic sight with an adequate explanation. For one reason or another nothing was done, possibly the result of budgetary constraints, and the old lodge stood empty no longer possessed of a purpose for existence. It died in soul and spirit at that time. Much of the rustic furniture was removed and now can be viewed in the Moraine Park Museum. Even though the doors remained locked, vandalism increased from 1969 to 1973. Forcible entry constantly was gained during the long winter months. Those remaining fragments of period furniture, and even structural members of old Fern, were cremated in the fireplace by an expanding segment of the public that didn't give a damn for the past, intent only upon satiating a greedy appetite for promiscuous destruction that to their warped intellect was an attack upon *the establishment*.

The National Park Service made one more effort to stave off obliteration, and covered the still beautiful roof with plywood while working towards further preservation that might bring about a minor renaissance in its new role as an interpretive center. Alas the pirating vandals had found a winter home and were not content until they had plundered the last vestige of dignity from a bewildered trail troubadour now badly crippled. If an old stone fireplace could talk, what would it have said as it witnessed the indiscriminate destruction of some of its weathered friends -- twisted hickory chairs, pine tables and quaint wall adornments, even the parquet flooring -- by craven men and women whose earlier generations would have fought them to the death to prevent this desecration. But the old fireplace stood mute, too old to fight back, enduring ultimate debasement as it was forced to reduce to ashes such long time companions. It knew its own time for further humiliation was near. The stones in the hearth where its heart that beat faintly, were picked out and taken home as souvenirs or scattered about, not in Stonehenge solemnity nor with any design to solemnize the past. If the *pickers* could not get a piece of the old lodge they settled for the government sign on the broken door that warned them not to enter. My tale began with such exalted purpose for this lofty little lodge, and ended in brutishness of selfish citizens deserving of punishment in the pillory. A study conducted by the National Park Service about that same time reflected harshly but accurately on the arrogance and selfish ethics of a citizenry now relegated to a campground existence where rules are difficult to enforce. Those campers needed the lodge owners' caring attention to soften the accelerated ego of the city dweller thrown into a foreign experience often producing abominable conduct. One statement of that report is enough to make my point. "Campers in campgrounds repeatedly violated campground rules, despite reprimands, suggesting that the campers believed the rules were either unnecessary or interfered with the recreational activities they sought."

On March 31, 1976 Ranger Bob Haines recorded in picture and words the end of a wonderful little resting niche of the forest. When he entered the decrepit front door he saw what brought out profound anger and sorrow. "Litter on floor and in fireplace; roof logs scorched by overheated stove pipe; floor log sections burned; writing and initials covered the walls; and front door latch broken. The structure had taken a beating!" That day the structure, or what modern man and woman had left of it, was burned to the ground. I say only the remnant of the structure, the husk of the former green stalk, was burned. Fern Lodge had long gone away to another land, if there is such peaceful soil in a world gone mad, where old log buildings might be appreciated and not forgotten. Dr. Workman might even now be putting it all back together again, as it **was** a great headquarters for fishing, fun and friendship. Yes, Fern was the place to visit, both in summer and winter when the Park was young and spirits soared in more simple activities such as skiing on crude contraptions or sitting in front of the huge fireplace at the end of another day of peace and mental prosperity of life, now as hard to find as the ptarmigan sheltered in a safe blend of rock and turf. The poem that commenced this chapter was entitled *Fern Lake*. Now you know what inspired these words.

First Lodge And Tents At Fern Lodge, circa 1912 (RMNP)

Lake Odessa Adjacent To Fern Lake, 1920 (Mills)

Ranger Guided Trip Lunches At Fern, 1920 (F. J. Francis)

First Cabin At Fern Lodge, circa 1915 (RMNP)

Snowshoe To Fern Lodge, 1917 (Mills)

Skiing From Fern Lodge To Lake Odessa, 1917 (Mills)

Winter Sports At Fern Lodge, 1920 (Mills)

Fern Lodge In Winter, Skis By Door, 1917 (F. J. Francis)

Interior of Fern Lodge Showing Flooring, 1964 (RMNP)

Revolving Dining Room Table, 1920 (EPPL)

Dining Room Building Added circa 1930 (RMNP)

New Cabin At Fern Lodge, circa 1930 (RMNP)

Hog Trough Roof And Fern's New Porch, circa 1930 (RMNP)

Fern Lodge Is Vandalized After Closure, 1976 (RMNP)

Fern Lodge Is Burned By Park Rangers, Winter-1976 (RMNP)

FOREST INN - THE POOL

Although this little lodge occupied a small segment of the public domain within the forest for nearly as long as Fern Lodge, its purpose and usage was much less intense primarily due to its location. There are few records to reveal its life on Fern Trail and thus my account of it is brief, yet it remains in the memory of many now absent as the finest experience they ever had in Rocky Mountain National Park. There was excellent food, a truly secluded location, no automobiles to intrude into the night sounds that were close by, and the friends made there were really special. Although a distant nine miles west of Estes Park, it lay but only three and one half miles up the Fern Lake trail from the much larger resort facilities in Moraine Park such as Stead's and Brinwood that commanded destination patronage. For many it was but a stopping off place on the way to somewhere else, difficult to establish a large clientele, and had an extremely limited function once the trail that was its artery of life became icy and clogged with snow. But to the few you stayed for weeks or the whole summer, it was really heaven, never once desirous of moving to another lodge where lots of activities were planned. To see a mother deer exhibit her new fawn to you by your cabin door, or witness the elusive bobcat leap in the air for no reason other than to express joy at being free, was enough to draw guests back year after year. Who needed a car anyway in such a near private paradise when only your feet were required to propel you along a trail. Probably no one remembers it unless you hiked or road a horse to Fern Lake from the Moraine Park side and climbed fifty yards up the steep hill on the north side of the trail. Yet this beautiful little lodge fit perfectly into the rocks and trees in aesthetic harmony at the crest of the hill as if designed by a band of fairies of the night seeking shadows for their creation. Its small but loyal band of devoted guests always gave evidence of absolute contentment as they sat in comfortable chairs out on the large porch sipping on a cool one, and watching the sweating hikers trudging past the entrance path.

The Higby Brothers, possessing the permit for Fern Lodge, obtained a second authorization from the U. S. Forest Service prior to 1915, licensing 'the establishment and maintenance of a summer hotel and resort for the accommodation of the public.' The permitted area took in no more than three acres of a hilltop overlooking Fern Creek. It was near to the bridge crossing a flow of water, the prologue to the Big Thompson River symphony tuning up in Moraine Park as the added strains from brooks and springs blended into the river's resonance. The beginning Higby venture was simply called *The Pool* in reference to the rock encased basin of aquamarine colored water where spawning fish flung their speckled bodies against plunging madness of white foam in a predestined drama for access to quiet waters of their birth. When that portion of the Colorado National Forest came under the jurisdiction of the Department of the Interior at the creation of the National Park, the permit expired on December 15, 1915. Up until that time, the *accommodations* at the site, and this calls for a liberal interpretation of that word, consisted only of two wooden walled tents for travelers' use as simple yet adequate resting places out of the elements in route to Fern Lake and beyond. The Higby's sold their interest in the permit to that same partnership of Byerly & Rogers who received a new permit from the Department of the Interior on June 23, 1916 and were directed to carry on the embryonic enterprise, generously described as a *summer resort*. Despite the fact that the new owners had little leverage with the government after purchasing the permit knowing that the permit could be terminated, the National Park did not intend for anyone to lose money on the venture and were sincere in having constructed a place of hospitality for a new group of Americans who now found themselves trekking about in a vast new National Park with limited visitor amenities. Cliff Higby, one of the brothers and a renowned guide of these regions, later changed his vocation. From guiding tourists on mountain trails, he became a Minister of the Gospel in Wheatland, Wyoming to guide souls on other trails of divine inspiration.

Frank D. Tecker had his origins in Antioch, Illinois and like many of his age and disposition yearned to go west, and also like so many others the dampness of the Midwest around lakes and rivers had impaired his lungs. Moving to Colorado in 1900, he filed on a homestead tract near Stratton where he met Fannie Byerly and where they were married. In 1902 they purchased a ranch near Parks, Nebraska, entered into ranching, and parented two sons, Max and Ned. But it was their daughter-in-law, Inez Tecker, who would be of the greatest assistance in their future undertaking. In 1916, Frank and Fannie made their first visit to the Estes Valley and the upper Moraine Park on a vacation and of course were interested in seeing Fannie Tecker's brother, Frank Byerly, and learn about his recent purchase. Mr. Tecker was particularly impressed, not as to the quality of the accommodations that left much to be improved upon, but because the secluded setting on the heavily forested hill fired his imagination as to what this tent facility could become. Remaining to assist in the camp's operation for the summers of 1916 and 1917, the Teckers purchased Mr. Byerly's interests at the end of the season who by 1917 was its sole proprietor. On January 16, 1918, Frank and Fannie secured their own operating permit from the government. They might not have purchased it at that time but for the fact the Teckers had had a serious disagreement with Byerly over how the facility should be run, and a mutual agreement was deemed in the best interests of all. Also, Frank and Fannie visualized a more noble blueprint for the property than a simple tent camp resting place, but this ambition required an infusion of more money for construction and needed fixtures than Byerly apparently was willing to spend. Byerly, who was always dabbling in many ventures, all at the same time, was only too glad to sell his camp to one of his own relatives regardless of the fact they were not then on the best of terms. The little facility, hopefully to be crowned with a gracious lodge where guests would have a quality, yet still rustic experience, was deserving of a name that spoke more eloquently to what it would become. It would be an inn within the forest, and to this resolve they named it Forest Inn.

Some of their enthusiasm for the tent camp could have been sparked in part from a 1918 plan of Park Superintendent L. C. Way to build a road all the way up to the bridge that spanned Fern Creek at The Pool. Mr. Way and his wife regularly frequented Fern Lodge as he was a winter sports promoter for that region. The new road could only enhance the use of Fern Lodge, enlarging recreational opportunities of Park visitors and business potential for

Forest Inn. Mr. J. D. Stead of Stead's Ranch thought the plan feasible and contributed the sum of $200 to make it happen, soliciting Frank Tecker to do the same speculating that the new road would benefit both of their businesses as Fern Lake country would be more accessible. That road prospect was shelved by National Park officials and then the Teckers's dreams for their Forest Inn facilities at The Pool suffered a severe setback that would test the most hardy of constitutions. In the second season of ownership, with ink on their plans for expansion hardly dry, Forest Inn burned down on June 5, 1919 as the result of a lightning strike. Only one cabin, a kitchen, storehouse and a smattering of tents survived. With such a blow to their finances, they postponed their grand scheme. The remaining structures, as limited as they were, served for the next eight years as their only source of tourist income. Managing to cobble together a small dining room onto the kitchen and a few basic tent cabins while operating under the most adverse personal economic strife, they still managed to serve in the years through 1922 at least 500 people annually. Hikers and parties of horse riders from the surrounding lodges in the meadows below stopped by for lunch or dinner or choose to occupy a welcoming tent after a wonderfully wearying day out on the trail. I'm certain that much of Forest Inn's small triumph was the consequence of a strong partnership the Teckers had established with the land and their resolve to attain goals often appearing as a Don Quixote windmill of monstrous magnitude when winds roared down Spruce Canyon to rattle everything in its path, except their determination.

Every year thereafter, the Teckers sought permission of Mr. Way's successor, Roger W. Toll, to enlarge Forest Inn. Toll was practical enough to ask them, as ranchers, what they knew about running a resort. After due assurance and an analysis that such growth would not impair competition unfairly between Park controlled resorts and others within the village, the Washington office gave successive approvals. By 1926 visitors would find fourteen tents, concrete floored and side boards four feet high, 11 for guests and 3 for the help, spotted about the top and northwest facing hillside. All but one of them were ten feet square and that super tent attained dimensions of fourteen by sixteen feet. One former employee remarked about their comfort. "They were good for sleeping but you needed plenty of covers, and with each comforter having a six inch wide cotton edging sewn on for sanitation purposes." Guests and help together ate their meals in a twenty foot square tent adjacent to the 16 by 20 foot kitchen cabin and the register was on a table in the 16 by 24 foot lobby tent. Guests were hopeful of securing one of the two most recently erected large log cabins, a single and the other a three room designed structure that fitted its 36 by 12 1/2 foot foundation into the side of the hill overlooking the stream cascading down rocky waterfalls not far below.

The main lodge, 34 feet wide and 60 feet long with large many-paned windows, a balcony and huge fireplace, was built in 1927 and 1928 on the top of the knoll. It replaced the large tents that had served functionally although not artistically as the dining room and lobby. It became operational the summer of 1929, the last season for a while when tourists still had extra cash for a holiday before the financial crash that succeeding Fall. In 1931 Fannie died and their daughter-in-law Inez stepped in to provide invaluable assistance although her record keeping proved a concern to National Park personnel who were charged with the duty of deciphering pages of her reports that defied clear understanding. During the Depression, Forest Inn had its own crash with proportionate despair when in early May of 1933 the lobby end of the lodge collapsed under heavy snow. Mr. Tecker, then in Nebraska on his ranch, returned to Moraine Park and struggled up the snow packed trail to view the damage. The weight of the snow had forced the roof down to push out the west wall while concurrently pulling in the ends of the entire structure. He returned again on June 14th to commence its rebuilding. Over the years, through the summer of 1935, other cabins including one four room beauty were added to replace some of the tents. Yet the tide was running against Forest Inn. With less use, hard times, pressure from the Park officials to improve the facilities and Fannie no longer there to share in the management, Frank was finding it even harder to strike a positive economic balance. The National Park Service made a decision to again implement its stated 1932 policy of lessening commercialization in the National Park, including Forest Inn. In September of 1935 Park officials concluded, "The Park has too many operators operating on a small scale and it would be best to eliminate as many as possible and those that remain should be required to maintain an establishment that is worthy of National Park cooperation." It therefore ruled that Forest Inn, on a scaled down basis, could continue so long as Mr. Tecker remained in the business but he would not be permitted to sell the business to others. Because of Forest Inn's short summer usage portending a limited future, authority was granted only for 'limited improvement,' and after 1938 neither new cabins nor other additions would be endorsed. The Inn continued on in good service to those guests who much preferred its seclusion over a ride into town for the gaiety that others craved at the shops and amusement centers.

Guests were fed in part with ranch products from the Tecker ranch trucked out in the beginning of each season and supplemented by such items that he could procure in the immediate area including dairy and garden products available in the Estes Valley. Guests from other lodges hiked up to Forest Inn for a chance to sit on the front porch with a cup of coffee and enjoy the freshly baked cakes, bread and cookies for which the lodge was locally famous. Mrs. Helen Hallowell of Mount Pleasant, Iowa in that period of Forest Inn's history was a teacher and attending summer school at the university in Boulder, Colorado. She gives us a glimpse into a treasured past as she remembers. "Dad Tecker, as he was called, was a good story teller and his Nebraska steaks which he served at his Inn were the best. He was a good naturalist, making you appreciate nature when he led you on daily hikes. The side screened-in porch was a cooler. One evening a bear smelled the chocolate cake and broke in. Dad Tecker threw pepper in his face and the bear left. Chickens were dressed on Friday and put in jars and then into Fern Creek, as it was the coolest place, to keep for cooking the weekend's big meals. The live chickens were kept in coops and pulled to the tops of trees at night, out of reach of animals. I remember one morning a weasel got an old hen and it ran down the mountainside with me in close pursuit. I won. We had the chicken for lunch."

Horses were widely used to reach Forest Inn and there was no shortage of this popular means of transportation for those less inclined to pit their tender, city bred, feet against the unforgiving rocks of the trail often pulverized into a slick aggregate. In the 1930s one could find an available stirrup on trailwise horses stabled in the village of Estes Park and at nearly every lodge in the vicinity of the National Park. If the lodges did not have their own string of horses, they contracted with others to provide them. At one time in 1934 there were approximately a thousand horses that could be rented, many from liveries on Elkhorn Avenue to which they were released at the end of the day to trot, empty saddled, through the busy traffic to find a friendly feed bag at their regular hitching post. However, Mr. Tecker had but one horse, affectionately referred to as Tecker's Old Grey Mare, who responded to the name of Lady, especially if she knew a gentle rub on her nose was at the source of a beckoning entreat. If she were lonesome or yearned for an extra ration of oats, she knew where she could go. Often the Reeds, of Brinwood Lodge, would find Lady in their oat bin, in good equine company and with a full stomach. She knew her mind and was appreciated for it despite the fact that Mr. Tecker had to fetch her back home, often long after the trail had grown dark, to the hoots of the owls expressing their delight at Lady's latest escapade.

People preferred to walk the three and one half miles of trail, the only means for gaining access to the lodge, from the Brinwood parking lot down in Moraine Park to a quiet retreat Mr. Tecker advertised as a lodge 'where you won't be disturbed by phone, radio or mundane affairs.' Any messages received at the telephone company's office on Moraine Avenue for those not possessing phone service, were hand delivered by a young lady, Margaret Baldridge, who lived next door. She welcomed a chance to increase her delivery charge from the fifteen cents she routinely assessed for in town messages to the five dollar bill she was handed by a guest at Forest Inn. Many notable people registered at Forest Inn because of its complete isolation, and it was not until the later years of operation in the 1950s that a telephone was found about the premises. In 1949 the rate for cabins and tent cabins, as there were no rental rooms in the main lodge itself, cost only $5.25 per day per person, including meals, and if you had private bath facilities the rate was $7.50. The rates included a unique experience, probably impossible of acceptance to most present day vacationers. After guests were met in the village by an automobile, of sorts, and brought to the end of the trail at Brinwood, they walked in, with the luggage pulled on a skid behind a pack horse, our friendly grey mare Lady. She was proud of her responsibilities as she tossed her pretty head and waved her mottled tail in a welcoming salute. The Inn was closed during the war years of 1943 through 1945 as the American public was more concerned with more serious matters than hiking a trail in the National Park. But by 1946 they were back and in 1948 Forest Inn was accommodating seventy guests at one time with a season from the first part of June through the middle of September.

But in 1953 Mr. Tecker was tired out in his 86th year of life, and pursuant to the National Park policy he was encouraged to give up his little hideaway. His last year of operation was 1952. His entire sales price to the National Park Service, as hard as it is to believe, was $14,000, --for everything! The lodge in the summer of 1953 hosted only ghosts that flitted through the shadows in empty rooms and an occasional hiker who ventured up the hill from the Fern Lake trail, curious about the history of the lodge that now stood mute and deathly quiet. Its green asphalt roof was beginning to fall away to become confused in the lovely litter of brown cured grass, Oregon grape leaves, and pine cuttings harvested by chattering squirrels in preparation for another winter ahead. Mr. Tecker moved away to more gentle climates and died on September 12, 1963 in St. Francis, Kansas at the age of 96 years. His long life was invigorated by the life shared with his guests, --his friends, up near The Pool, all of whom he enjoyed and complimented for selecting his Forest Inn as their National Park experience.

In 1959, with an allotment from the Department of Interior of $1,000, Park crews demolished the remaining fourteen structures complying with the National Park's policy then in full swing by Superintendent Lloyd, of 'protecting the visitors and conserving the natural features of the Park.' So for $1,000 dollars vigorously applied to the demolition of more than forty years of an old man sharing with the hikers his piece of isolation, it was all gone. Only the memories now hang heavy in the silent woods as one stoops down to pick up a small fragment of weathered wood, a forgotten piece of green roofing, a rusting nail or a lichen covered scrap of foundation that attest to the fact that Old Man Tecker once lived here long ago. Some say that when the wind is just right and you are all alone, you might still hear the rustling sounds from the darkened forest of Frank once again patiently leading Lady home. One former guest in artistic nostalgia wraps up this saga of a piece of history that once offered a resting place for travelers on the knob of the hill. "I found the gold we all seek in the leaves of the aspen trees on the ground looking for all the world like golden coins. They were glistening in the sun after one of those short morning rains. The rainbow that came over the mountain ended right below Forest Inn in the Big Thompson Valley."

First Dining Room At Forest Inn, circa 1920 (RMNP)

Tent Accommodations At Forest Inn, circa 1920 (RMNP)

Tents Converted To Tent Cabins, 1929 (RMNP)

The First Modern Cabin Replaces Tents, circa 1929 (RMNP)

Largest Guest Cabin, circa 1930s (RMNP)

Trail Up To Forest Inn, circa 1930 (RMNP)

Forest Inn And Front Porch, After Closure 1955 (RMNP)

Main Lounge In Forest Inn, circa 1940s (Private)

BEAR LAKE LODGE

Little is known of Mr. A. E. Brown, but for sure he had vision and compassion for the steady influx of new visitors to the Bear Lake region in 1914 and 1915. Tourist facilities at Bear Lake were nearly non-existent and he thought the travelers to the lake deserved some measure of comfort, at least a tent and a warm meal. On January 16, 1915 the United States Forest Service issued a one year permit to Mr. Brown for the first use of the Bear Lake area as a lodging site. His permitted use was more grand in scope than even he had conceived of, as it read "You are authorized to construct, use and maintain a summer hotel building, tents and other improvements." The fee of $15 charged for use of the two acres of public land on the eastern shore of Bear Lake was certainly reasonable. The Forest Service offered the low fee as an inducement for this businessman to invest his own money in a remote area without much more than a wide trail to reach his proposed camp. Curious visitors in the summer of 1915, discovering this impressively sculpted region of the new National Park descriptively referred to as Wild Gardens while the southernmost portion of the Park was, and still is, designated Wild Basin, were in need of overnight accommodations. Stephen E. Mather, the Director of the National Park Service, issued on May 5, 1916 a new permit to Mr. Brown, allowing him to continue his struggling new efforts at Bear Lake for the good of the public. As costs do increase, even for a licensee in the wilderness with little more than a hopeful gleam in his eyes to succeed, the fee for the new permit was increased to $25.00. For this slight increase in fee, an additional use was allowed, horses, that in later years would be the prime activity of resident guests.

The new permit, in addition to the livery opportunity, reauthorized the first permanent building that as yet was only in the conception stage. "This permit provides for a summer resort and camping ground for visitors or tourists and for pasturage for visitors' stock, a log house, 12 by 15 feet for a kitchen, and tent houses as may be necessary." The government officials were defining two words, *tourist* and *visitor* into two separate categories although the words could be interchanged without violating the rules of syntax. The tourist was classed as someone here for an overnight stay, and the visitor defined as a person just up for the day. The permit again was on an annual basis to extend only to December 31, 1916, yet Brown had the temerity to expend his resources knowing that his investment might all be risked with one year's throw of the dice. The first log house permitted was erected close to the eastern shore of the lake in the summer of 1916 at a cost of $500, and an additional log house, 16 by 20 feet, soon followed the next spring to serve as the recreation hall for what now was identified on the maps as Bear Lake Camp. It proved to be too costly an undertaking for one man, and Brown took in a partner, the same Frank W. Byerly, selling to him a one half interest. By 1920 the records reflect that Mr. Byerly had succeeded to the sole ownership of this somewhat primitive, yet important, tourist inn on the southern terminus of the Fern Lake trail.

In 1920 a one inch pipeline was constructed to bring in water from springs seeping into and around Bear Lake of which the largest one was located on its north slope. Access certainly could not be neglected if the camp had any chance to succeed. That same year Frank Byerly worked to improve the Bear Lake Road so that the fifty guests then using Bear Lake Camp would more easily reach it in some measure of comfort and trucks would be able to provision the camp with needed equipment for expansion. A fifty-five horsepowered diesel fired boiler was installed to the east of the recreation hall and electric lights now glowed, however dimly, across the azure blue waters of Bear Lake causing the wild creatures dwelling nearby some alarm at the intrusion into their security of darkness. As additional buildings became authorized, the first log structure previously erected adjacent to the lake shore was moved to a higher location on the south sloping hillside where many other structures would later be assembled in preparation for a collateral use. In 1921 a 36 by 60 foot building for a dining room and guest facilities was approved by Director Mather and by 1922 a more expansive hotel and camp permit was granted in recognition of increasing popularity of the camp now assuming more permanent proportions. This spacious building, later to be known to guests and employees by the sobriquet *Upper Lodge*, was a substantial single floor log edifice with a large round fireplace centered in the middle of its western section. To this crackling magnet were drawn many delighted young people from a soon to be established boys camp, and guests alike, who enjoyed the camaraderie of friendship and a narration of rugged mountain tales. These yarns were enhanced by shadows cast from the firelight escaping an ornate screen to dance above the pealed log beams serving as horizontal masts for camp symbols and intricately woven Navajo tapestries.

Frank Byerly's Front Range Hotel Company, formed in 1922 to manage Fern Lodge, now included an asset no longer called a camp but raised in stature and renamed Bear Lake Lodge. For several years Mr. and Mrs. Frank H. Cheley had conducted a summer school in the Estes Valley to train boys in the lessons learned from observing and identifying with nature. Commencing with January 1, 1924, the permitted area was increased to twenty acres at an annual fee of $500 for a term of five years with an option for an additional five years. Mr. Cheley, then a company director, voiced his opinion that this location on the shores of Bear Lake under the rocky crags of Hallett and Flattop Mountains was a far better location for his boys camp, and in the spring of 1923 the Cheleys entered into an agreement with Byerly's hotel company to sublease a portion of the enlarged permitted area for their new school. He immediately commenced the construction of double sized dormitories around Upper Lodge, each expensed out at between four and five thousand dollars, together with accessory structures. Timber for the school offices and dormitories would be logged from the immediate area, much of it removed from the western and southern shores of Bear Lake where in 1900 a devastating fire had laid waste great stands of ancient Englemann Spruce and fir trees. This fire, started by a careless camper, burned for the entire summer and was extinguished only upon the onset of the early storms of winter.

A two tiered log administration office building, 36 by 45 feet in size, was erected closer to the small and very rough Bear Lake parking lot. This new headquarters building, named *Tipi-Wakan* and later nicknamed *Lower Lodge*, came equipped with the traditional Goliath sized fireplace and hearth architecturally designed into its western wall. The building of weathered logs that many said "had the look of belonging to the area," consisted of two levels.

The first floor was occupied by a small store, gift shop, soda fountain and offices for the lodge, while the top elevation consisted of one large room capable of holding dances and other recreational events. It later was redesigned into a lounge where tempting viands of various strengths and ingredients were dispensed in a convivial attitude of good fellowship. The covered porch provided a fabulous view of Long's Peak and its smaller sisters of the front range where more senior aged guests enjoyed the comfort of a rocking chair to observe at sunset the curious animals, their antenna-like ears relaxed in the lodge's non-threatening habitat, nibbling their way up the hillside between the many cabins and tents. The porch also afforded guests a first glimpse at new guests approaching on the road to check in at Upper Lodge. Speculation heightened, with all eyes riveted on one of the new arrivals, when he or she had *that look* that might suggest a famous person, such as a real movie star, hopefully from a Western. Cheley remodeled Upper Lodge to add a new kitchen capable of serving an enrollment of fifty, perpetually in motion, boys and their six leaders all of whose appetites were huge, and their eating habits voracious to approximate a busy bunch of beavers in a grove of aspen trees on a summer evening.

Construction at the school site was at fever pitch in the Spring of 1924 that planned to open its doors for the first session that summer. Mr. Cheley, titling the school *Bear Lake Trail School for Boys*, admitted boys to "A Summer Camp For Boys That Is Different" who were at least ten years of age and no older than seventeen. Before and after the construction of the log cabins and dormitories in 1923 and 1924, many of the lodge guests and all of the lodge employees -- as well as parents of campers up for a visit during one of the school's two terms from June 27th through August 25th --occupied a long line of white tents and tent cabins. The solitary lights positioned along the earthen walkways near the lodges, and the uniform lighting system of single bulbs strung all along the long white rows of tents, was likened by an early guest "to the appearance at night of a 'company town." But the close association of all of these groups of diverse personalities from differing backgrounds resulted in lodge guests and Cheley campers, young and old, learning from one another while merging intergenerationally their recreational and learning experiences to the benefit of all. Mr. Cheley's philosophy, especially for his boys camp, was that there is a need to help boys grow in manhood through the experiences of the great outdoors, and that young people learn most if they share first hand, learning by doing things themselves in association with the right kind of adult leaders. In reporting the inauguration of its first season, a local reporter was upscale and optimistic. "The camp should be well patronized by discriminating parents from the start." The young enrollees were taught many useful crafts for outdoor living including a course in surveying. From the camp tuition of $225, or $400 for both terms, there were sufficient resources to provide excellent staffing including Leslie Eichelberger as the official guide, and a full blooded Indian identified only by his nom de plume, Chief Wankon, who "interpreted the wilderness" clad in authentic native dress.

On June 28, 1926 Camp Hiayaha of the Bear Lake Trail School for Boys opened for its third season, with an enrollment of seventy-five boys, swollen beyond original predictions. A companion camp, designated Camp Chipeta and situated at Scotts Heights on the border of the Y. M. C. A. Camp, opened in the late spring of 1926 with an initial enrollment of 25 girls in the tribe. Under the directorship of Miss Katheryn Fravel, of the physical education department of the Minneapolis Y. W. C. A., the advertisement for Camp Chipeta announced it to be "A vigorous camp for vigorous girls." This was not the first girl's camp in the region. An earlier edition, for girls and young women between the ages of six and twenty, was operational years before, called Camp Eloise and named for one of the two Boyd sisters who owned it. It operated on the south end of the village, close to the site of the present hospital, where nearby a ski hill built and operated by the Liedman family served the local community long before Hidden Valley was constructed. Cheley's boys' school operated for only a few years on the Bear Lake property until land was acquired south of Estes Park to which both camps were permanently located. They still operate, greatly increased in size and scope, owned by Frank Cheley's descendents, under the name Cheley Colorado Camps.

Since I am on the subject of young people's camps, I wish to spend a moment or two on another camp, the Rocky Mountain Boys' Camp, as it was a vanguard for organized youth camps in or near the National Park. On 120 acres of the Mill Creek Valley and described as being located "on the south slope of the Thompson Moraine at the base of Steep Mountain," approximately ten log buildings were constructed in 1919 and 1920 by Martin Fagerstedt. The camp's owners, Presbyterian minister Reverend Harrison Ray Anderson of Wichita, Kansas, Charles Shaffer Evans of Harvard College and Colville Cameron Jackson of the University of Chicago, enrolled for its inaugural summer season in 1921 twenty boys between the ages of twelve and eighteen. Water was piped three-quarters of a mile from a diversion high up Mill Creek to provide hot and cold water for the wash basins and showers. Most of the campers, arriving by train to LaSalle, Colorado, made their homes in Chicago, St. Louis, Kansas City, Wichita, Cambridge, Massachusetts and Wooster, Ohio. The owners had competent financial advisors such as John Timothy Stone, prominent in Y. M. C. A. affairs, Dr. Thomas Wood of Columbia University and Tracy Drake, president of the Drake and Blackstone Hotels of Chicago. Objectives of the camp as outlined in its literature were "To give boys a fine home in the Rockies, knowledge of the mountains by at least two trips a week on the camp horses and in its cars, and to stimulate their minds and to develop their spiritual natures." Visitors were impressed with the huge fireplace in its main lodge, the Navajo rugs and animal skins hung on the walls, the library with a piano and Victrola, overstuffed furniture and the "ninety-two pairs of cretonne curtains" covering the windows in all of the buildings. On its property was a baseball diamond, tennis court, basketball court and the first swimming pool in the National Park. The camp premises encompassed much of lower Mill Creek where the fishing was excellent in Hallowell Park, named for George C. Hallowell of Loveland who lived in a rough shelter in 1892 near Mill Creek where he summer pastured his cattle. The boys enjoyed the opportunity to learn the game of golf at the local course in the village but were not allowed to shirk the religious aspects of the camp as they attended services conducted at the Y Camp and the local village church on Sundays. It was a stimulating experience for the boys and their counselors. They joined in efforts to perfect photographic skills in a fully equipped dark room, built furniture in the completely equipped carpentry shop and assembled a radio receiving station. In their spare time they did not

131

overlook the requisite skills important to theatrical arts, as they wrote and acted in their own plays presented to the vacationing public. Not knowing the exact cost, but assuming it was a camp for boys from richly endowed families, my suspicion was vindicated when I read that "each of the twenty campers was provided with his own horse." Horseback trips each summer, as part of the curricula, included one traversing over five hundred miles to range over six days throughout the adjacent mountain ranges and as far away as Cheyenne, Wyoming. Well into the depression years of the 1930s the National Park recorded the camp's presence, eventually ending when part of the site was configured into a working camp for less affluent young men, yet just as motivated and talented, when the federal government established its second Civilian Conservation Camp in the Estes Valley.

By the summer season of 1927, Bear Lake Lodge, now warmed by steam heat, was operated strictly as a tourist lodge with Cheley's camp having been relocated. Further additions to the larger buildings were made including a sandwich shop in Lower Lodge for visitors on their way to adjacent mountain trails, up for a day of fishing or possibly just to sit on the front porch idly cloud gazing as troubles were not permitted at Bear Lake Lodge. Also the lodge owners saw a greater need for more horses and plans were made for a stable and augmented livery services. The lodge sold to the day visiting tourists as well as resident guests lunches, books, curios, tobacco, ice cream, fishing supplies, clothing as well serving beer, wine and spirits in the upstairs lounge. As I previously reported when discussing Fern Lodge, Frank Byerly had married Mrs. Edna Bishop and she was anxious to get into the management of Fern Lodge and Bear Lake Lodge. No one is entirely clear about what happened but after Edna Bishop became Edna Byerly a parting of the ways resulted and the gracious hostess named Edna Bishop emerged on top as President of the operating company for the permitted franchises of both lodges. The Bishop family, that included her two sons James and Charles, concentrated their efforts primarily upon Bear Lake Lodge and hired a manager, often a woman, to manage the Fern Lake facility. Fern was kept supplied by a string of burros in charge of Edna Bishop's employee, Hull Cook, that hoofed up from the Moraine Park side. Early hikers well remember those burro trains as did the horseman who used the trail as many of the creatures had lost the ends of their ears to frost bite. Presenting an oddly grotesque appearance to their queue strung along the dusty trail, those on foot readily gave way while the horseriders had difficulty controlling their mounts that reared in alarm. However when special supplies were required, such as furnishings and heavy goods, horses were employed that originated from Bear Lake Lodge, including carrying up bed springs on the backs of horses all the way on that steep, twisting, nature intrusive trail. Nothing was impossible in those days. A former employee said it was a lot of hard labor, and "the labor was usually by brute force and awkwardness."

Bear Lake Lodge was well promoted for everyone's use, vigorous or those who preferred a lazy vacation, as the Bishops stressed the location of their resort that boded well for all guests. "In this glorious environment, the guest, young or old, finds answer to every mood and desire. On its pine-studded shores, and so delightfully a part of a wonderful environment that visitors respond immediately to the urge to *live among the scenes they came to view*, is Bear Lake Lodge." The long, deep porch attached to Lower Lodge that was, as Edna hypothesized, "located on the spot which held the old trapper spell-bound," was exalted as an unsurpassed vantage point from which those, who like the trapper, "preferred to gaze in silent wonder at the majestic sweep of the continental divide, keen eyes softening with approval as they rested upon that exquisite mountain gem, Bear Lake." Who patronized Bear Lake Lodge? The Bishops had their opinion. "Someone who knew the feel of the hills and the urge to leave hot, depressing valleys and the tension of crowded cities behind," matched the fingerprint of their guests. Edna knew her family possessed the experience to provide every creature comfort without, as she wrote, "discording the wondrous harmony of nature," and in so providing the resources of Bear Lake Lodge they afforded every opportunity "for the seeker of recreation to renew again the deeper appreciation of Nature's values." Those crisp evenings, the scent of the trees, and with no untoward sound but hushed water gently slapping the shore urged on by the night breeze, was verifiably sleep inducing, an indescribable elixir for good health, sound sleep and complete enjoyment of nature at its very best.

Edna Bishop often hosted gatherings of town folks in Upper lodge for, in addition to its purpose as the dining room, kitchen and registration lobby, it served as a gathering place for her special occasions. One of these annual get-togethers was dedicated to the Volunteer Fire Department members, and their wives, to whom she was most grateful for their alert and watchful services rendered to her at the lodge, a location eleven miles distant from a dependable water system for fire fighting. The local newspaper usually recorded the event as "Mrs. Bishop served a splendid chicken dinner to the fire company gathered about the huge fireplace while toasting their shins." The successors of this valiant band of pyroquenching experts continue to man the hoses and equipment grown more costly and complicated, and to whom I express my gratitude for their dedication and success. The Bishops completed the last three miles of the Bear Lake Road that culminated at the lodge, a road commenced under the leadership of Abner E. Sprague. Now guests of both categories could reach the lodge by automobile without fear of losing their oil pan to a high center ridge of rock. The lodge gained its own phone line, a continuation of the one that had been extended out to reach Jack Woods' camp from the village. That line originally extended over to Grand Lake and was primarily for the use of the National Park. However, because none of the line was underground and heavy snows and downed trees wrought havoc to this basic form of communication equipment, the telephone line was moved over to the Fall River Road. It was the responsibility of Bear Lake Lodge employees to keep their phone line working as well as their water line that piped in drinking water from the springs. Also, as the lodge had its own sewer system and power plant, the duties for maintenance personnel were extensive requiring considerable expertise. By the 1930s the main power plant was fired by heavy fuel oil and backed up by an auxiliary electricity generating unit fueled by gasoline. As more cabins were constructed through 1940, all with private baths, the capacity of the resort was brought up to thirty-four guest rooms capable of sleeping 65 guests during a typical two and one/half month operational summer season.

In the beginning of the Bishop's operations, and for many years thereafter, ice for their resort was cut from Bear Lake in the winter and early spring. The lodge had in its small inventory of vehicles an elderly, yet powerful and ever dependable, Oldsmobile touring sedan, respectfully christened The Silver Streak as inspiration to the continuation of its faithful cast iron heart that knocked to a capricious cadence. Old Silver was regularly driven out upon the frozen lake, hooked up to a block and tackle, to drag the large ice blocks to the southeastern corner of the lake where they were wrestled into a sawdust filled log cabin. In later years Jim Bishop, who had received an engineering education at the University of Colorado, came up with a device for use with the power plant to freeze spring water into large cakes of ice. Thereafter, in addition to the tourist business in the summer, he was also the commercial ice man who sold the ice produced to other lodge operators in the National Park since refrigeration and frozen locker services were still strangers in the Park or in its first years of infancy. One of the employees, who remains a resident of Estes Park, was Burwell Spurlock, Bur to his friends. He was hired by Edna Bishop, after dropping out of Harvard Law School in May of 1931 to head west in his Model A Ford Roadster. Bur had previously been a summer employee of three years standing at the Y. M. C. A. summer camp in Estes Park and, although it was too late in the season to regain that employment, learned of a position available at the Bear Lake Lodge. He grabbed it and remained a valued employee for the Bishops for the next three summer seasons, at a time as he said "the Park was trying to get rid of everything privately owned in the Park." I'm sure that some of the activities of Bur and his fellow employees did not contribute to a warm, avuncular, relationship with the hard working and undermanned staff of Park Rangers. To illustrate this point, on one occasion the Bear Lake summer staff had the audacity to drill holes into a large rock on the north side of the lake onto which they installed a diving board for after hours frivolities. The lake was at its deepest point over on that side and it was great fun, after a full day of toil and fearful neither of life and limb nor governmental admonishment, to hurl one's tired body into the bone chilling snow melt supplied waters. When I asked Bur what it was like, he shook his head as if to question the sanity of his actions sixty years before. He exclaimed, "God it was cold water!" and his teeth clenched together as though it had just happened. The Park personnel found out about the lake's adornment and by the next summer there was no more diving into that water of 36 degree temperature as the diving board had been decreed prematurely obsolete by edict of the grand poobah, the Superintendent. For certain there would neither be any more swimming in or across Bear Lake even if a row boat was in close proximity as the employees proposed in an effort to compromise.

Prior to changes in Park policy, boats were frequently used on Bear Lake and for that matter the lodge had its own flotilla of row boats for the use of guests. Although the fish often were long, skinny and devoid of any plumpness as a consequence of inadequate natural food and severe temperatures associated with the oxygen poor altitude, it was not the size of fish that was important or even if you snagged one at all that endeared the lake to guests. The lazy paddle about an inspiring lake surrounded by unsurpassed alpine splendor, warm sun lulling you into welcomed lassitude, and a quest rather than the quarry, was all sufficient to make it a noble venture fit for any captain of this little armada. But the prime activities for guests were horseback riding and hiking. Mrs. Bishop advised her guests expansively in her pamphlet replete with artists' sketches of the lodge and mountain scenery.

"Government trails, leading from Bear Lake, beckon the hiking explorer into age-old canyons, where perhaps another mountain lake springs into view, nestled there among the whispering pines, or shadowed by towering peaks. Trails as you choose, for those who love to loiter along the way, others that challenge the experience and rugged endurance of the mountaineer, are adventures to be re-lived for years." Bear Lake then, as now, was the jumping off point for many of the premier trails to those high lakes and mountain apogees where all cares and contrived worries of the mind were left back home and hopefully forgotten. Only the next turn of the trail that promised a view unsurpassed was uppermost on the minds of guests of Bear Lake Lodge. "There's **my** cabin!, and I can see those people from Illinois sitting out on the front steps of Upper! I wonder if they can hear me? ----Whooee!!", was a common enthusiastic whoop from a guest who sat munching a sandwich near the false summit of Hallett's Peak. About the only concern a worshipper of these wilderness recesses had was to avoid a Clark's Nutcracker bird or Gray Jay from approaching too closely in feigned friendship planning a quick assault upon elements of your lunch sack left unguarded. The weather was never a concern to a guest when a climb was under discussion. The only rule was to get to the top and off of the mountain under discussion before noon and don't stand under a tall tree or by a large rock as a storm approaches. Many writers frequently referred to bad weather hampering some aspect of outdoor recreation. I agree with Enos Mills concerning this issue to flaunt my contempt for timidity that often leaves one prostrate with doubt and indecision when it comes to getting on with one's life. Of course, my bravado must be tempered with good sense. Mills said, "There is no bad weather, just different kinds of weather."

Employees at any of the lodges were expected to assume many tasks and wear a variety of hats, as they were hired to use their initiative without being asked to do so, and apply good common sense and unflagging energy and loyalty to insure that the whole system somehow worked. To enlist too many on the payroll for such a short season would have proven pecuniarily disastrous to an owner. This lodge had avant-garde equipment for its day in addition to their electric light plant. "The rooms are steam heated, shower baths conveniently nearby with lots of hot water," and the kitchen efficiently functioned with "a steam table and dish-drying equipment." Being too high at 9,500 feet for gardens, the Bishops daily sent their truck to Denver markets for fresh meats, fruits and vegetables. The water supply from springs was "soft, pure, sweet and completely protected from any possible contamination," guests were assured. At Bear Lake Lodge in the 1930s there were the four members of the Bishop family, now including Jim's wife, and approximately nine non-family employees comprising a good mix of university students, black and white, male and female. The staff were excellent employees as well they should be as Edna had personally selected them. Some employees applied from surrounding states, especially from schools in Oklahoma while others matriculated up from the University of Colorado where in the Fall, Winter and Spring seasons Edna served as a housemother for fraternity and sorority houses on the campus where her younger son Chuck was a student. If you can survive that kind of experience you can do most anything and at the same time become an excellent judge of character. Bur Spurlock remembered the chef. "The chef was black, from a frat house in Boulder, and he was a damn good one! The food was good! It had to be good to satisfy a frat house!" Through the years employees served as cabin maids, waiters, waitresses, clerks in the little store, soda fountain jerks, and horse wranglers. Two of the best in the horse business were Paul Smith, who was rumored to drive a truck in the off season for a group of bootleggers, and an older man in charge of the livery activities, Peck Connors. The stables they ruled with firm, courteous and helpful hands and were tolerant of the playful antics of Jim Bishop's dog Duke that barked a farewell to guests sallying forth up the Flattop Mountain trail, saddles adorned with lunch packets and yellow rain slickers. The horse trips were promoted by the Bishops in this tantalizing sign positioned in a prominent location in the lodge. "Saddle horses, wise to the trail, provide the most enjoyable of all recreations at Bear Lake Lodge. Trails lead in all directions and those for inexperienced riders are short and easily traversed. The longer, all-day circle trips, on the move after a *daybreak* breakfast, lead, thrill after thrill, into regions where Nature reigns in the sublime silence of the eternal hills. At noon coming none too soon to appease keen-edged appetites, the most delicious coffee ever spreads its tantalizing aroma around the open, pine-wood fire, and thick, juicy steaks, broiled to tender perfection, disappear with almost ravenous relish." How could a poor city slicker resist this provocative palaver that caused their own juices to run in anticipation.

There were two other vehicles in addition to the faithful Oldsmobile. Gasoline was supplied from a pump on the premises, a compulsory commodity for sale at most all lodges accessible by road, inasmuch as guests were unwilling to drive the twelve miles back to town for a fillup. A road wise International Truck served to haul wood, rocks, supplies from Denver and transported shrieking children in cowboy hats who thought it their stage coach surrounded by hostiles. As to the Chandler sedan, with the name Bear Lake Lodge boldly painted on its doors, it presented a more respectable visage to the guests greeted in the center of town at the transportation center. Mr. Spurlock recalls one of those dedicated Bear Lake Lodge habitue', a woman from the plains, he met at the bus terminal. "This woman from Kansas, like so many of our guests, was a repeat customer year after year. She was resolutely loyal about her attachment for Bear Lake Lodge. She knew that the lodge didn't open up until the middle of June because there still was ice and snow about the lake and it was cold at that altitude, so she would sit around in hot Kansas, a fan blowing over a keg of ice to keep cool, awaiting the lodge's opening. Then she'd rush out to spend the whole summer."

Edna Bishop never missed a summer since 1916 when she first learned of the fine vacation potential of the National Park, moving here permanently in 1918 and was actively associated with the Bear Lake and Fern Lodges for more than thirty years. As records must end and equipment wears out, she likewise would find her health declining in the early 1950s. She died in September of 1956 in San Antonio, Texas at the age of 72. The Superintendent of Rocky Mountain National Park in 1958, after a full assessment of the necessity for lodge improvement through what he considered too many years of deferred maintenance, elected to terminate the lease at the end of its present term, December 31, 1958. Mr. and Mrs. Jim Bishop returned to the lodge the following June to dispose of the interior furnishings of the lodge, selling many of those memory resplendent fixtures to local residents who determined to keep the name of Bear Lake Lodge alive, at least in the security of their own homes. Upper Lodge was moved down to a local private recreational vehicle camp ground, but everything else that could be considered belonging to the old Bear Lake Lodge including quaint Lower Lodge was demolished by Park personnel shortly thereafter and the site reshaped and reseeded to a previous conformation.

The final chapter to our story ends on August 7, 1976 with the death of Jim Bishop. The warm friendship of the Bishop family still pervades the brisk air as you walk on the hill high above beautiful Bear Lake, now resplendent with tall trees hiding the scars of a wild fire so long ago. Long is absent the laughter exuding from the many guests who were fortunate to have been recorded in the old lodge guest book through the years. This lodge, like all of the others scattered within the Park, lived up to its motto, "Live among the scenes you came to view." The late Dan Griffith, early day lumberman with his father Albin, harvested the fire blackened timber that was used in much of the log construction of this lodge. He summed up his pleasure of having been a resident of the Estes Valley when the lodges were at their peak of popularity. His words echo back to a time when broad opportunity, naturalness, clear skies and uncrowded trails were golden to him and his early Twentieth Century contemporaries, including the owners of our little trail buddies Fern, Forest and Bear. "I feel that I was born at the right time and certainly in a rather select place. There were boundless opportunities in this environment that just simply no longer exist. I certainly had the freedom of some early years, able to walk around, to fish, to hunt and to go into wild areas. I think to awaken mentally to the great gifts of nature has helped me to learn to work and to assume quite a bit of responsibility. Someway or another it has been a part of me, and I am grateful that it occurred at the time it did." In a former visitor's sentiment expressed about the lodge, in which I perceived a quality of *wishing it were otherwise*, I shall close this brief account of Bear Lake Lodge. "It was a relaxed place of refuge, not too upscale. There was an atmosphere of the Old West that you didn't find at large hotels or in motels. But now its gone and that's sad."

Original Bear Lake Lodge, 1915 (RMNP)

View From Lodge And Fishermen, 1915 By W.T. Parke (McDC)

Second Lodge And Damage From Fire In 1900, circa 1920 (RMNP)

Tent Accommodations At Bear Lake Lodge, circa 1920 (RMNP)

Upper Bear Lake Lodge, circa 1922 (RMNP)

Interior Of Upper Lodge, circa 1940 (Private)

Barracks Of Bear Lake Trail School, 1923 (RMNP)

Bear Lake Trail School Site and New Buildings, 1924 (RMNP)

New Cabins Replace Tent Accommodations, circa 1930 (RMNP)

Livery Stable At Bear Lake Lodge, 1947 (RMNP)

Lower Bear Lake Lodge, 1924 (RMNP)

Interior Of Lower Lodge, circa 1940 (Private)

Brinwood, Fall River Lodge, Deer Ridge Chalet

The Tourist Comes From Off Afar,
From Heated City & Scorching Plain,
The Flight Is Checked At Estes Park,
Where Nature Smiles On Fair Moraine.
Then Cast Your Eyes On Either Side,
To North, South, To East, To West,
From Snow-capped Peak To Gulch Below,
Then Choose The Hotel You Think Best.
A. R. Ross, 1943

BRINWOOD RANCH AND HOTEL

Horace Ferguson of the Highlands Hotel, had several children one of whom was Sally, his second eldest. While living in Longmont she met the Assistant Postmaster Charles Lowery Reed, and they subsequently were married in October of 1886. The couple alternated between living at the Highlands Hotel and back in Longmont where Charles would hold positions as Postmaster, Longmont Water Superintendent and finally as an insurance agent until 1908. During this period of time four children were born, two sons Roland and Charles, Jr. and two daughters Louise and Mabel. Charles, Sr. and Sally had *done their courting* at father Ferguson's resort and thought they might enter the guest business on their own, and thus moved back to the Estes Valley in 1908 to their final and most fulfilling careers as lodge owners. By then many more tourists were seeking out the mountains as the result of the improved roads that led up from Loveland and Lyons, in great measure the result of the Stanley Steamers that manipulated their cargo of excited passengers alongside the Big Thompson River. In fact, in the summer of 1909, the Estes Valley was host to more than 4,000 visitors prompting an old timer to remark, "It's getting so you kin hardly spit without hitting one of those flatlanders!" He would have had given up his habit entirely if he had lived to the summer of 1932 when the 4,000 had grown to nearly 283,000.

Charles and Sally purchased 290 acres in 1909, including a tract homesteaded by Sally's brother Hunter Ferguson, and commenced to build the large main lodge of their resort in 1910 ably assisted by Sally's brother James. It was situated six miles from the Estes Park post office, adjacent to the west line of Stead's Ranch, on a high bench of timber and meadow immediately east of the present Moraine Park Stables. The view was marvelous overlooking the valley of the Big Thompson that wound its many silver-blue threads of the purest water methodically and unhastened through wide beaver engineered willow dams. The lodge comprised two stories. The office and lobby occupied the east end of the first floor, the kitchen attached out behind, and the dining room on the west end of the first story with its large windows posi-

138

tioned to best watch the sun descend behind Long's Peak and the deer that sought shelter after a final drink at a rivulet of quiet water. On the second floor were rooms for guests, as well as the quarters for Mr. and Mrs. Reed immediately over the lobby from which vantage point they could hear the arrival of wanted guest, or unwanted strangers who might be intent on matters other than signing the registration book. The lodge was called Brinwood for the mountain, named for Brinton Woodward, Chancellor of the University of Kansas in the mid-1890s who owned land on its south slope, that crested high above them to the north. By the summer of 1911 they were open for business. One note about Mr. Woodward, who vacationed for years at Sprague's Hotel, is worth repeating. One fall, having elected to remain until the aspens and mountain shrubs turned gold and red, he remarked to Abner Sprague how the growth on an unnamed mountain changed in color from green to gold and brown and laid down in layers due to the heavy frost. He said it took on the appearance of a large pile of thatch. Abner agreed and followed through to dub the mountain with its present name, Thatchtop Mountain. Louise Reed Hayden years later recollected the opening of Brinwood and how her family's lodge benefitted from the fiery demise of another hotel that same year. "This was a great boon for business at the new Brinwood Hotel that just opened, for the Brinwood opened with guests from the Dunraven Hotel." Louise Reed first married Albert Hayden, and upon his death fell in love with Al's brother Julian, called Jude, and they were married. The Hayden name is remembered in our mountain geography by a number of geological features including Hayden Creek named by Abner Sprague in honor of both of the brothers. Louise, as a girl, occasionally went horseback riding with Enos Mills to examine beaver dams in the high grass meadows of upper Moraine Park. He grandly explained to her his vision as his eyes swept over the vast expanse of openness that would soon take on a new name. "One day you'll see 10,000 people in the National Park in a single day!" He was right in forecasting an increase in usage, but his numbers were grossly understated. Oh, that there were only that many, for my fishing possibilities might show a distinct improvement.

The senior Reeds, known affectionately as Grandpa and Grandma Reed to family and guests alike, spent part of the fall and spring in Moraine Park, while the really cold months found them much lower in the valley towns. Their alarm was raised on October 3, 1915 after a sawdust pile at the Hidden Valley Mill, west of their home, caught on fire. It burned slowly and was difficult of containment because of its near inaccessibility to water and fire fighting equipment, and eventually burned itself out after consuming great quantities of timber. Their private dwelling for their personal use when the hotel closed for the season was next constructed in a draw that now leads up to the west end of the present Moraine Park Campground. On the east and south sides of the lodge, running their entire length, was the ever present front porch that all lodges constructed as an outdoor living room, up and away from ground dampness, chiggers and children's scarey creatures that went *bump in the night*. Several cabins were placed on the grounds to the north of the lodge and other buildings were located below the present road leading westward to the Fern Lake trailhead, such as a ranch house, barn, garage, parking lot, and the stables strategically positioned down wind from the lodge. Local newspaper editors theorized correctly that real news items for a young newspaper were few so they sought advertising revenue which was their life

139

blood. The two categories occasionally became cleverly merged into one, an arrangement economically beneficial to all as undisguised ads were written up as *news*. In 1913 this story appeared, no doubt the inspiration of the Reeds as all the lodge owners justifiably sought to promote their businesses in the short holiday season of the Park. "Located at the gateway to Moraine canyon, six miles from the Estes Park post office, is a modern little hotel known as The Brinwood. C. L. Reed & Son, the proprietors, have built up this resort into one of the most attractive in the Park. Among special features appealing to guests are the new and modern hotel, with hot and cold running water in all rooms, and the numerous tents and cottages. Guests are met at Estes Park with the private automobile of the hotel. The Brinwood is the starting point of the trails to the beautiful Fern, Odessa, and Cub Lakes, Fern and Marguerite Falls and The Pool and Sprague's glacier. During the past winter the proprietors have made numerous improvements in the resort, in anticipation of an unusually busy season."

In the next few years was erected a guest facility northeast of the lodge, in the shape of a semi-circle, containing six rooms. To the west of that building were two long rectangles with more rooms for tourists, some provided with private baths while most shared the *facilities* down the hall. This was a *strictly modern* hostelry with no traipsing outside to the crescent adorned little two seated apparatus. If anyone ever shared in its use at the same time, it was the absolute extreme act of fellowship. I remember such a quaint place of contemplation wherein the owner gave the user advice in a poem on the back of the wood planked door. I think it read, "Please let us know when the paper is low, so no one will shout when the paper is out." People remember the darndest trivia, yet it was significant at that time to an impressionable youth. Further up the hill to the north was a log building for the young female staff including the waitresses. I'm not certain where the young men took lodging, possibly in tents hidden about in the trees and certainly in a room or two down with the horses. I am hopeful they had a real cabin, but then boys are different and their lifestyle even back then proved exhilarating to say the least for management. Since you can't get away from your relatives, and the Reeds were no exception to that rule, they built two other buildings where the relatives lived and were put to work in the summer as a way of leveling the ledger. However the main lodge rooms were the most sought after as Roger Low, a grandson of Charles and Sally Reed, advised. "In the lodge the best rooms were located down at the west end of the structure, where they had private baths, and everything!" To the northwest of the main lodge was a large dance hall and soda fountain with dimensions of 62 by 32 feet. But in 1925 when rooms in the National Park were at a premium, and never enough to meet the requests of those recommended to the Brinwood by guests of prior years, that ancillary edifice dedicated to high stepping and a cooling dish of ice cream was sacrificed to became The Annex and remodeled into additional guest rooms. An ad in the 1920s evincing the growth of Brinwood and its amenities that now placed it in the grand category of *hotel*, softened the most obdurate heart and made resistance economically unthinkable. "A home-like hotel situated in beautiful Moraine Park, the gateway to one of the main approaches to the Continental Divide, in whose shadows lie Fern and Odessa Lakes and Marguerite Falls and many other spots of beauty. Hot and cold water, electric lights, good meals, telephone, telegraph, auto and horse livery, two daily mails, fishing, tennis court, swings and quoits, all for $4 to $6 per day." Although the lodge was called Brinwood, the guests at the lodge at the opening of the 1919 season opted to call it Honeymoon Lodge as nine newly married couples carefully signed the registration book within thirty days of each other with a 'Mr. and Mrs.' in shaky hands.

In all there were 29 buildings, in assorted sizes for this many purposed lodge, now advertised as Brinwood Ranch and Hotel. Their construction was of log and frame and nearly all erected prior to 1926 although there were a few small additions made up to 1938. The lodge had a guest capacity of 90 to 100 and employed 30 seasonal persons to operate the ranch between June 1 and Labor Day. The employees gathered aspen for the cooking and water heating while pine was used for the fireplaces. Logs of dimensions as long as eight feet were dragged in from the forests to be sawed into firewood, with some very hard pieces requiring dynamite to split them. In the lobby was a huge fireplace that always burned during cold or rainy weather, and the children secretly slipped in a piece of pitch that alarmed the older guests when it exploded with a great noise to delight merry eyes peeping from around the corner. It is interesting to read of summer employees from other states being required to license their personal autos with Colorado plates. After dinner in the lobby-lounge, when guests draped themselves over comfortable chairs or on the mountain lion skin in front of the fire place, was the culmination of a full day on the trail or in the stream. Their sagas in degrees of importance, though to the storyteller his or hers deserved primacy for attention, were re-lived, acted out and retold to any who would listen if one were courageous enough to barge into a heated card game or interrupt the participants battling away at ping-pong for the soda pop prize. Upon adjacent walls were exhibited, as was the case with most of the lodges, other artforms of the nearby wilderness that proved educational to young and old. The activities often consisted of ranger naturalist talks and wildlife movies. "Of course Charles Eagle Plume came and talked about Indian lore and did dances," the Reed's grandson Roland Reed, Jr. remembered, "including throwing a blanket over a single woman, usually a school teacher, and both would dance around with the blanket over their shoulders." Mr. William Hallett, of whom I have written previously, a friend of all of the Reeds and who was their guest at Brinwood, delighted the guests out by the front porch with his trick of feeding the chipmunks by having them climb up his arm and on to his hat where he had placed peanuts around the brim.

The hotel had its own garden, and also raised pigs and dairy cattle for milk for its own guests as well as selling the surplus in the village. The lodge was very proud of its produce and dairy products, and advertised, "Fine wholesome milk and cream from our own dairy of tested cows and fresh vegetables in large varieties, partly from our own garden, are served in abundance." However caring for domestic stock near the haunts of predators had its problems as bears killed several of their pigs. Adjacent lodge owners now and then had complaints about one another because of the wandering stock. Stead's raised beef cattle and there often was a battle to keep Stead's bulls from wandering down to check out Brinwood's dairy cows, to the extent that shots often were fired at those bulls as a deterrent to their amorous intentions. The horses, as well as some of the cattle, frequently were given names of former guests whose mannerisms bore a strong resemblance to those beasts mouthing a clump of blooming wild flowers. A horse more senior in age, which was equated to the older guest who could always be depended upon to appear every summer, was designated 'Old Bob' and a rounded Holstein, that won the honors for being the best producer, was called 'Old Lady Walker' although I don't feel courageous enough to delve into the reason for such attribution. I don't believe any of Brinwood's pigs had human identity tags for the reason that it would have been difficult to single out any one person for such questionable honor as there were so many who met those porcine specifications, especially after the chair was pushed back from the usual feasts at Brinwood.

The Brinwood promoted horseback riding and was well known for its breakfast rides described effusively in one of its brochures. "For the early risers we sometimes serve breakfast out in the woods. How those flapjacks and scrambled eggs with bacon do hit the right spot, especially after an early morning horseback or auto ride from the hotel. The sun peeping over the lower mountains, and the higher peaks being tinted with the shadows of the morning light is a sight soon not to be forgotten." All day rides were promoted to Lawn Lake, Ypsilon, Trail Ridge, Fern Lake, Bear Lake and Loch Vale, with food being taken into locations for the guests when they arrived on their horses. It was said that the food never tasted as good as it did cooked out-of-doors near high alpine lakes. The food always included crisp bacon, scrambled eggs, bread and butter and coffee. Roland Reed, Jr. as a young man was a participant on many of those rides. "I can still smell the aroma of the bacon drifting thru the trees, and the smell of the coffee in the crisp cool air was mouth watering." Several of the rides were as long as twenty to twenty-five miles in length over the Mummy Range or all the way to the sublime lakes east of Grand Lake. Others were shorter such as along the north bank of the Big Thompson River to the Forest Inn and up the shaded trail to Fern Lake Lodge where the riders had time to cool off their feet in the lake while nibbling a snack arranged for them.

Under the guidance of Shep Husted, Estes Park's premier guide who worked for most of the lodges at one time or another, organized trail hikes and horseback trips were conducted for groups that once included a climber known only as the 'Alpine Fly.' A few of those excursions ventured far over the Continental Divide to spend a few days at Squeaky Bob Wheeler's Camp Wheeler in Phantom Valley, then continuing on to Grand Lake. One year Shep's flock were the first party of the season to climb Specimen Mountain where they saw a large number of the mountain sheep. It was said that Squeaky was in his best voice and served a delicious breakfast of the elusive trout that Shep had caught 'while resting,' for Mr. Husted was that proficient with the fly rod. A brief word about Squeak, as his friends called him. Robert L. Wheeler, received his nickname because of his high pitched epithets when he became angry, which was seldom, or excited, which was chronic. Also his malady was in part attributed to the after effects of a severe case of bronchitis when he was eighteen years of age. Squeaky, a native of Michigan, first came to North Park, Colorado in 1885 to work on his brother Luke's ranch where he lost two fingers from his right hand. Moving south to Grand County, he volunteered to serve in the Spanish-American War in which his cousin, General Joseph 'Fighting Joe' Wheeler, gained fame. At its cessation he returned in 1902 to Grand Lake, some say in an effort to forget the carnage of the bloody battles in which he dutifully participated as a soldier. Others say his Second United States Volunteer Cavalry unit never got further south than Jacksonville, Florida. *Squeak*, as his friends called him, never disabused those who believed that his Torry's Rough Riders had chased all over San Juan Hill. It is not important whether he went overseas or not, the fact that he volunteered to serve his country in whatever capacity he was assigned is what counted. Homesteading on an unclaimed tract adjacent to the North Fork of the Colorado in 1907, then known as the Grand River, he established Camp Wheeler. The camp catered to dudes and served up a variety of tasty food however dubious the content. His remote kingdom he enjoyed referring to as his Hotel de Hardscrabble and it still echoed with the clangorous remnant of gold seekers who divined that wealth would be found in the next pan or scoop of Grand County soil near Lulu City, Dutch Town or Teller.

Squeaky Bob's resort was little more than a collection of tents, possibly tent cabins, for his guests, and was very popular despite the fact there was no road for wheeled vehicles to reach his camp in the early days. There never were locks on the doors as his accommodations were provided for people on an honor basis even when he was not there to welcome them. Tacked to the doors of each of the units was a sign evincing a scrap of his attitude for life. "Blow your nose and clean your shoes. Use all the grub you need and leave things as you find them." Although some said he was immaculate in every way except for his language, there were others who perhaps knew him more intimately who said that Squeaky never changed the sheets, just scented them with talcum powder. This was a management *technique* often practiced by hotel owners in the boom town of Leadville. Because of the dearth of available beds for the thousands of miners without even a packing box to call home, each bed served as a resting place for three shifts of miners per day with no time to practice the niceties of basic sanitation guidelines. No one objected to the quality of Squeaky's meals served in camp, often concocted out of a secret recipe of porcupine meat with an overlooked quill as a surprise, because when you finally arrived at his place after a very rough trip, you were too tired to complain and very hungry. He was well acquainted with his portion of the mountains as far up to the continental divide to the east, and named the little lake just west of Milner Pass, Lake Irene, after two eastern girls who had the spunk and cast iron stomaches to spend a period of their vacation at his camp. When someone asked a former neighbor by what authority did Squeak have the right to name a National Park lake, he received the answer, "Since Squeak stocks the lake, he has every right to name it."

One of his early guests who spread his fame in the East was President Teddy Roosevelt, rumored to have savored Squeak's food, especially the venison, *baa'r* meat and big horn steaks in the little restaurant he called Cafe de Paris. The President thought the source of the meat was big game, although anything was possible, and predictably it was small game or whatever hopped, flew, crawled or trotted by the kitchen door. Also he was a true raconteur, a story teller and comedian of the first order, whose Bulldog, chronically at his side and often observed with a derby hat cocked over one eye, thoroughly appreciated the stories judging by his wide toothy grin. You enjoyed yourself so much that any criticism over the meal or cleanliness of the accommodations was forgotten in front of a fireplace hearth where Squeak regaled the assemblage with gleeful anecdotes evoking gales of laughter that filled the starry night. You literally fell under the spell of this lovable little man whose door was always held open to all. Around 1926 he sold out to Lester Scott who, after removing most of the tent cabins and constructing new ones, he renamed his acquisition Phantom Valley Ranch only to sell it again to Irwin Beattie in 1941. As the National Park boundaries pushed further west, Phantom Valley Ranch was eventually absorbed by its purchase and removal in the 1960s. Robert Wheeler long before had drifted away to bring decent merriment to others wherever he next set up camp. When he left because of a heart condition, he equated his move to the habits of wildlife. "I'm in the winter of my life now, and like the sheep I had to come down from the high country." I would suggest that if you run into him, somewhere, bring your own change of linen and save room for a slice of chipmunk pie.

Getting back to Brinwood, every mountain lodge had its antlered monument on the front lawn, including this lodge. This activity is now prohibited by the National Park as everything is to remain natural and undisturbed with such discards providing necessary calcium for the little creatures who recycle them back to the soil. But back then many guests returned at the end of a day in the woods armed with one or two elk or deer antlers to add a new layer to the pile somewhat like a tree developing a new ring of growth. Their symbolic gesture ritualized another successful season for both the creatures who produced them and for another year of Brinwood guests who gathered them. Brinwood had a wide reputation for its delicious and appetizing meals that were said to be "prepared by first class women chefs." Guests in the 1920s and 1930s at most of the lodges stayed from two to six weeks as the father brought out his family for the entire summer to return as often as he could. Summer residents informally adopted their assigned waitress as one of their own during a long summer season, coming to know their servers not as employees but as daughters. The Reeds personally choose everyone of them and advertised their quality by stating "We employ only high class college girls and teachers in our dining room." Roger Low, whose mother Mabel was another of the senior Reeds' children, worked at Brinwood and remarked that the guests "were good tippers." Rates in the 1920s started at $3.00 per night per person, including three meals a day and by 1931 the 90 guests paid up to $8 per day with the highest weekly tariff per person, with bath and three meals per day, being $48. Grandma Sally Reed commanded a considerable drawing power for Brinwood as her culinary abilities as its cook extended over most of the years of the Reed's ownership. Her reputation spread beyond the confines of the Park with diners driving all the way up from valley towns thirty-five miles away to eat at Brinwood. Brinwood was a regular stop for locals entertaining their friends for a dinner in the National Park. Although in her later years when other chefs were hired to prepare the food, she insisted that it be in strict accordance to her rules and high standards. Delegating part of the kitchen duties to qualified personnel was one thing, but she alone attended to all of the food purchasing, even after she had attained the age of 85 years.

To supplement the diets of her guests and to provide for food rich in vitamins especially produce, the Reeds raised potatoes, peas and beans, on their property. Many of the female guests participated in a variation of a Nebraska *husking bee* without the corn, a tribute to Sally's persuasive talents for a more productive use of the big front porch as one remarked. "Some of the guests used to sit out on the front porch and shell peas. Pretty good to get the paying guests to do some of the kitchen work! Those women guests would sit out on the front porch in those rocking chairs and shell peas and snap beans while looking at the moraine and Long's Peak. You couldn't ask for any thing better, could you?" Fishing was excellent in the meadows in front of Brinwood if you could gain the courage to bait a hook with a squirming worm extracted from the hip pocket sized King Edward Tobacco can. However if you were more of a purest, a gray hackle or black gnat fly served the same purpose, but be prepared to get tangled in the willow branches that were alive in their graspiness. Another talent Sally Reed had was her unique way of fishing, obviously learned from her father Horace, as she didn't like to get her feet wet. The guests watched from the porch at full attention as Sally and her sister Fanny, up on holiday and dutifully put to work, rode their horses out into the river and beaver ponds for some early evening fishing the results of which were placed on the buffet table, browned and with a wedge of lemon.

Roland Reed, Jr., whose father helped organize Estes Park's American Legion Post 119 in 1920 and was its first Commander, noted that early day settlers did not want the National Park to take over their back yard and believed their lives emotionally as well as economically threatened by potential government control and regulations. But times were hard after the financial crash of 1929 and into the early 1930s and many lodge owners, including Brinwood, sold out to the National Park in March of 1932 for $56,585 but received a 20 year operating permit. It was extended in 1951 for a few more estimable years while a study was conducted in 1953 to establish the need for such concessions and their impact upon the natural resources. The study disclosed no further need for such resorts as the requirements of the traveling public were *adequately* provided for outside the Park's boundaries. The lodge was given a five year final extension to wind up its operations and turn over the keys to the National Park Service. Stead's, the closest neighbor, didn't sell at that time, but the Chapman ranch on which the first post office for Moraine Park had been established more than fifty years earlier, also sold out in March of 1932 for $23,630. The Chapmans moved into town and started a lumber yard near their home on west Elkhorn Avenue which home now serves as a business selling Christmas ornaments. A member of the Reed family was present to witness the beginning of the end for historic old structures left standing after the National Park was created, when in 1932 he witnessed government employees burn to the ground the Chapman's family home. He was bitter about the direction taken by the National Park Service, but to me it was obvious before the enabling legislation was only days old that this had to be the direction for the new National Park in keeping with the purpose clearly expressed in language that left little for interpretation. "It seems to me that there was a great pressure not only to get all commercial ventures and ranches out of the Park but to obliterate any thing that would cause people to remember the past history of the area," Roland Reed, Jr. professed. He illustrated his point. "They changed the name of Brinwood Mountain to Beaver Mountain. Beavers don't live on mountains! Where the hotel and ranch stood, we now have a concession operated to provide horseback riding for tourists. This was a service that the Brinwood provided! As I stand here today where the hotel had been and breathe the repugnant air of the corrals, which hold horses 24 hours a day, my blood boils. Anger rises within me as I think that they tore down a great facility that brought great pleasure to many people and replaced it with a stinking, smelly set of corrals and buildings. Our horses were allowed to go out to pasture at night and our corrals never smelled like the present ones. For whose best interest is this?"

There was much similar sentiment expressed by most of the lodge and summer home owners who saw their investments surrendered to future camp ground sites that now perhaps place more demand upon the resources of Park officials and impact much more of its terrain than ever did the lodges. I do not take a stand on this issue for it was settled long before I was born and its full implementation was under way long before I found myself in residence in the Estes Valley. Whether the decision was a wise one in Rocky Mountain National Park, I cannot say. I am but an historian but would do a disservice to cause a reader to assume that the policy for preservation of nature, but not its historical human association with nature, rode into the Estes Valley on a white charger to unanimous cries of *Hallelujah, All Is Well*. It didn't, as there was an outpouring of complaints of concern to Chambers of Commerce, Congressmen and whomever would listen. The local newspaper in 1932 expressed the fear of the Town of Estes Park towards the federal government's plan of development of the National Park and for further encroachment upon private lands. "The existence of the Village will not be permitted to stand in the Park's way of this development," it editorialized. Before the expiration of that lease term for Brinwood, Charles Reed died on March 15, 1944 at the age of 85 years. Sally, her son Charles and his wife Belle Brandt Reed, kept to the high standards of the Reed family while keeping the doors open for three more years during a time when registrations were reduced due to the war.

The lodge with its remaining years of the government lease was sold in February of 1947 to Estes Park residents, Fred and Marti Steffens and Gil and Carol May, who incorporated under the name Brinwood Ranch-Hotel, Inc. They continued the tradition of operating a quality resort as their advertisement declared. "Brinwood--where the road ends and the trail begins. With all the comforts of home and but a few moments drive from Estes Park. It is secluded at the foot of a great ridge, the habitat of the mighty Big Horn Sheep with Long's Peak and the Moraine in the foreground." They sought and received a permit extension until December of 1958 when the doors finally closed, but not before a fight as we shall see in my discussion of a sister lodge. In 1960, in exchange for the salvage, Fred Steffens performed the sad task of tearing down the buildings. As I drive the road leading to the Fern Lake parking area, I find myself glancing up to where Brinwood once occupied its lofty position. I feel a twinge of loneliness when I no longer smell the home cooking, hear the laughter from the front porch or see another breakfast ride head up the trail with another generation of young and older buckaroos, possibly Old Lady Walker's grandchildren.

Road To Brinwood, 1915 By F. P. Clatworthy (McDC)

Brinwood Hotel, circa 1930s (Private)

Entrance To Brinwood Ranch, circa 1940 (RMNP)

Brinwood Hotel, 1949 (RMNP)

Charles And Sally Reed, 1898, (EPPL)

Dining Room Of Brinwood, circa 1920s (CHS)

Lounge At Brinwood Hotel, circa 1920s (CHS)

Reed's Summer Home At Brinwood Hotel, 1958 (RMNP)

Big Horn Cabin, 1958 (RMNP)

Annex, Formerly Recreation Hall, 1958 (RMNP)

Saddling Up At Brinwood Livery, 1952 (EPTG)

Front Porch of Brinwood, 1958 (RMNP)

FALL RIVER LODGE

Dan March, a Canadian by birth and living in the Province of Ontario, journeyed south to Greeley, Colorado before the turn of the century where he found employment as a blacksmith. In 1907 he and his wife Minnie migrated to Estes Park in search of relief from asthma and hay fever, a story we have heard so often from other lodge owners. The journey from Greeley took two days in a wagon pulled by faithful old Halley up the new road along side of the uncontrolled Big Thompson River. Mrs. March, in a reverie in 1936 recounting the wonderful times she had enjoyed, chuckled at that first trip, forgetting the unpleasantness. "How well I remember that old Big Thompson Canyon road, so narrow, and the turnouts every so often that were none too wide. I can see Halley yet rearing on her two hind legs every time a car passed us. The cars of those days were Stanley Steamers, the grades were too steep for gasoline motor cars then. It is a good thing for many of us that we did have to use the Steamers, as their whistle was a timely warning on many occasions where the road was so very narrow and it looked a long way down to the river." Within two years their relief was so complete that in 1909 a tract of land in the western end of Horseshoe Park was purchased from Mr. E. E. Raymond, and by 1911 their love for the land had increased to the extent they homesteaded an adjacent 125 acres. Their location was south of the road that turns off to the Lawn Lake parking lot, near the Fall River and east of the entrance into the present Endovalley picnic area.

It was not easy constructing a new home in 1911, recessed into a remote canyon where the only flat ground was swampy and full of willows, yet the presence of water and suitable building timber made the location promising if hard work was practiced. And work they did by first draining a tract of the land on which they built a cabin and a barn, then set in posts for the fence to contain their livestock. In 1912 the cabin was enlarged to more comfortable quarters, but the wood ticks, mosquitoes and pack rats made housekeeping an adventurous and wearying undertaking. It was that year they nearly had their first guest in their home, one who was uninvited, as a young man struggled to ford Roaring River in his bright shiny Steamer by bouncing off tree roots and unstable rocks. Their visitor however was only looking for a place to fish, and in turning his vehicle around in the narrow defile he left flecks of black paint on rocks and trees to mark his departure. The Marches had planned on farming, but it was at that time that Dan and Minnie got the idea for a tourist lodge, reasoning that if this man would dare to sacrifice a prized possession for the sake of wetting a fly in Fall River, there might be a whole lot of others willing to pay for an improved experience. Mrs. March explained. "Since our first summer in the park we had visions of a hotel in that quiet valley. Those visions never left us, and as the summer wore on, and the winter's wood piled up, we talked and thought of hardly anything else. When winter set in we found ourselves quite alone up there. Mr. March spent most of that first winter drawing plans for the hotel. I used my time sewing rag rugs." Winter evenings could be very long and discouraging with only the sound of the west wind moaning in the Blue Spruce and the alarming cry of the coyote hunting the unwary snowshoe rabbit by the light of an ice ringed full moon. Making plans as we all do can expand the vistas of the mind, freeing them at least temporarily from the commonplace duties that often are forced upon us from which we can not shirk. Living in 1912 and 1913 in an austere yet not unfriendly environment proved the worth and fiber of a pioneer and these challenges the Marches took in stride. As an example, just to get to town for supplies was an all day event, that is if the weather cooperated, and that was rare. An arrangement with Mr. Thomson who operated the fish hatchery half way between their home and the village made it unnecessary to go further for their mail as he was kind enough to keep it for them at his home. But when spring broke through their self imposed isolation, first the Pasque flowers then the pussy willows, the world looked brighter and certainly more encouraging.

In 1912 the new Fall River Road was rumored to be built right over the top of the divide, passing in front of their front door to pierce their property. That just might have been the catalyst for their new lodge still in the embryonic stage, but when Minnie learned who was to comprise the construction crew moving in to build the base facilities in July, she was reticent to open her door. The state and county highway departments were leading the way in a remarkable effort to join the east side of the Rockies with its western neighbors, and the best source of cheap labor, convict labor, had its source supplied from the state prison in Canon City. Imagining being murdered in her bed, she was soon disabused of her alarm and prejudgment as she found the men were decent human beings, kind and considerate. In fact before they moved their camp and equipment further up the route of construction, they had become friends with the Marches and gave Minnie gifts they had fashioned for her out of silver and abalone shell. Although these men worked diligently to build the first three miles of the road, the balance of Fall River Road to the summit was completed under contract with a private construction company. All early settlers in the Estes Valley had a common response when asked about the toughest time they ever had with weather, and to the following statement the Marches were in full agreement. "It was that awful winter of 1913 that started in December, the big snows! that was the worst experience." The Marches, too, found themselves blocked by the snows, and the convicts came to their aid. By rigging up a sled of logs to a team of large horses, they broke a trail open to their cabin, dug them out on December 14, 1913, and helped them reach the safety of the village more than eight miles away. Minnie remembers riding her horse with the cow tied to the horse's tail. "At 10 o'clock in the morning we started for the Village. I rode in the saddle on Halley's back, and at times the snow was so deep I had to almost stand in the saddle to keep out of it. The big sorrel team broke trail for us all the way to the Village. We arrived there about 4 o'clock in the afternoon and for the next week we lived in a real community Village if there ever was one."

The road out to Horseshoe Park, named for the its semi-circular pattern of mountains that hemmed it in on the north, west and south, was a rutted, bumpy, rock strewn torture trail. It ended in a lush green meadow covered with periwinkle blue Columbine flowers below Horseshoe Falls and quickly assumed proportions as a popular picnic spot for town folks. Arapahoe Indians referred to the 1,000 acre Horseshoe Park by a name that translated out as *In-Lodge* because of the abundance of game located within its confines, while Deer Mountain to the southeast was *In-Butte* because this high ridge, blocking out the first rays of the morning sun, closed up the valley. Further up the road today tourists can view a torrent of foaming water gracefully arching its way through a cleft of rock. In the Marches' time this was called Upper Horseshoe Falls, but Dan thought this too confusing as each waterfall was deserving of separate recognition. He renamed it, as it is today, Cascade Falls. Dan blazed the first trail up to the falls and later Park personnel spanned the crown of the falls with a bridge. But in 1933, after two girls survived a fall through its weakened boards to plunge into the pool 40 feet below, the bridge was permanently removed. Roaring River, spanned by no bridge by which to travel to the March homesite and spawned from entwining arms of outrushing waters from Lawn, Ypsilon, Crystal Lakes sheltered in the icy grip of the Mummmy Range, energized Horseshoe Falls. Over the years these falls lost their name to obscurity, even their peaceful significance as a destination for a Sunday drive with the family. High powered vehicles, gears grinding and attached baggage rattling, drove by in a cloud of deteriorated granite dust conveying thrilled *autoists*, as they were called by horse people, to Grand Lake over the new Fall River Road upon its completion in 1920. Old Horseshoe Falls was effectively destroyed in the Lawn Lake flood of July 15, 1982 reducing it to its lowest common denominator, water zephyring over bare rock bereft of its evergreen canopy of branches that had composed it into a canvas of green shade and sequestered pools of watery sunlight dappled blue. Now its skeletal, denuded form is scientifically studied as the conduit for the broken dam high above its clouded waters, and nearby is positioned a sign describing its blemished basin euphoniously as The Alluvial Fan.

In reading of these early lodges one is overwhelmed how quickly they were erected with such limited help, usually a family venture, and with no heavy equipment other than a strong team of horses and arm powered tools. It was back breaking work, often resulting in damage to one's health as history records. But if you had dreams, as the Marches did, you had no chance to reach them unless you were prepared to work in the worst weather possible in the Estes Valley, historically in the springtime when heavy wet snows blanketed the high parks such as Horseshoe without warning. Their first task before anything else was possible was to clear the land, grubbing out willows and draining the marshy soil infested with blood sucking deer flies. Large rocks that had rolled down from the hillsides to project out at weird angles from the best building sites, had to be moved, often by splitting them with water poured into holes and left to expand in freezing temperatures. On April 1, 1915 the first spade cut cleanly into the ground in outlining the foundation on the tract first acquired from Mr. Raymond east of the homestead and work progressed as Dan shaped and carpentered hand hewn logs harvested and dragged in by horse power to the construction site. After continuous sweat and toil by both of them and others conscripted from the limited local pool of labor, the first building of their resort at an elevation of 8,600 feet was ready for its first guests on July 4, 1915. A promotional tract stated simply what to expect, and for the first time revealed the resort's name, "Spend your vacation at Fall River Lodge, where there are modern conveniences and reasonable rates."

In 1915 excitement was very high, on both sides of the issue. The new National Park had been approved and cheers rang out from those who saw more government money flowing in as well as an increase in tourist traffic.

Rocky Mountain National Park translated into a commitment to get the local economy moving again as world wide fears associated with the war raging in Europe threatened the involvement of America and its resources. But however sincere were the Park proponents' intention to carve a National Park out of others' private playgrounds, opposition was always simmering on the back burner. What was to be the direction of such enthusiasm, and would business people within the Park's boundaries have to adjust their lifestyle to accommodate expected changes? These were tough questions that are still perplexing even seventy-eight years later as recent conferences between many eschelons of county and Park officials now ponder, not the impact of human development **within** the Park but rather those activities **outside** that could influence the mission of the Park. When the new Park was formally dedicated on September 4, 1915, many American flags waved briskly in the picnic grounds just southeast of where you now find the Lawn Lake parking lot. It is interesting to read that the ceremony, while within the boundary of the National Park at which throngs gathered under the gigantic National Park banner stretched between two pine trees, was situated close upon the property owned by the Marches. I am confident that they were in attendance listening to eloquent speeches of praise and hope with mixed signals of their own eagerness tempered with uncertainty.

Throngs of people parked their buggies and steamers nearby before 12 Noon on this overcast September 4th day to partake of the refreshments being served. Some even arrived by the taxi service of Elmer Jones, including the family of local resident Ted Mathews, who thoroughly enjoyed the ride out to the festivities in Mr. Jones' polished black touring sedan. The actual ceremony commenced at 2 P.M. with all speeches limited to five minutes, a task of momentous proportions for politicians seated on the front row in dark business suits. After a rousing performance by the band from Fort Collins that echoed off the surrounding hillsides and a sprightly rendition of *America* from local school children, congratulatory telegrams were read by the Dedication Chairman Enos Mills from Secretary of the Interior Franklin K. Lane and President Woodrow Wilson who were unable to attend. Representing the National Park Service was Steven T. Mather, Assistant to Mr. Lane, who in turn was followed to the podium by Governor George A. Carlson, a Republican and critic of Democratic federal policies. Having earlier promised not to say anything in his remarks of an untoward nature to mar the dignity of the auspicious occasion, he failed to keep his word and laced the Democrats for reasons only known to a recently elected office holder. Following the governor was Mrs. John Dickerson Sherman of Chicago, a true influence for the National Park as the Chairwoman of the Conservation Department of the General Federation of Women's Clubs. She was honored for her organization's valued assistance in raising a nation's awareness for preservation of rapidly disappearing public lands, uniquely qualified for National Park status. As a side note, Mary Bell King Sherman was no stranger to the Estes Valley as she and her husband, an editor of a Chicago newspaper, in 1911 owned a portion of Elkanah Lamb's ranch and she was a frequent participant in winter sports at Fern Lodge. But, like Mr. Mills earlier, she was to have her life sadly end in 1935, the result of an bus accident in Washington D. C. on October 19, 1934 from which injuries she would not recover. Next on the agenda were Congressmen Charles B. Timberlake and Edward Taylor who took their bows as political figures do by accepting all the plaudits and benefits that flow from rewarding their home state with a governmental appropriation. F. O. Stanley spoke briefly, holding his miniature American flag, and then was honored for placing Estes Park on the auto maps of the nation. Two other notables of the commercial world, voicing pronouncements for much success to the National Park, were Thomas Patterson and T. B. Stearnes.

Enos Mills's articulate and emotionally moving remarks that were the highlight of the festivities, expressed his philosophy towards all National Parks, especially this new jewel in the crown of America's effort to save the past and present for future generations. "A National Park is a fountain of life. It is a matchless potential factor for good in national life. It holds within its magic realm benefits that are health giving, educational, economic, that further efficiency and ethical relations and are inspirational. Without parks and outdoor life, all that is best will be smothered. Within National Parks is room, glorious room, room in which to think and hope, to dream and plan, to rest and resolve. This is the proudest moment of my life. I have lived to see the realization of a great dream come true. The day is at hand when these wonderful hills and matchless valleys are to be the playground of the world." I often wondered what thoughts were in the mind of the oldest participant at that laudatory event of welcome to Rocky Mountain National Park. Mrs. Mary M. Sprague, at the age of 84 years, occupied a seat of special honor as the proud representative of the pioneers and their courageous spirit of discovery and foresight without which this day of dedication might not have been possible. Her days of pioneering ended with her death in 1917. The Marches' dream as well had come true and all was well as the bright new National Park had immediately garnered guests for them. The dawn of September 5th now gave promise for success, and they were satisfied that all of their hard work would be amply rewarded with economic prosperity and continued happiness.

The following summer the old kerosene lamps at the lodge were rendered obsolete when they engineered a combination water and power plant with an ample supply of electrical energy sufficient for both Fall River Lodge and its older neighbor Horseshoe Inn. For its time, this was quite an engineering feat that coupled necessity with recreation as two six foot deep depressions were excavated in front of the lodge building into which the water, after producing electricity and being partially diverted into water lines, was allowed to flow. Fall River waters were never used for drinking water or to propel the power plant for the reasons the beavers and water borne debris were not the purest ingredients of drinking water and further the lodge and location of the power plant were higher than the river. The source of water for everything at the lodge was Roaring River west of the lodge, diverted 800 feet above Horseshoe Falls from which it fell to build up a great head of water as it entered the small hydro plant and water intake pipes leading throughout the resort. The Marches' efforts were so thorough that they included a high spraying fountain by the driveway that led to the front door of the lodge. In those days nearly everyone was purchasing a Stanley Steamer for trips to the National Park with many of them parked under the shade of an overhanging Ponderosa pine at the lodges in Horseshoe Park. Dan and Minnie succumbed to the auto influence and bought one, effectively retiring old Halley permanently out to pasture as a companion to the children of the guests, to which pleasant duty she whinnied no objection. Now the drive to Greeley was re-

151

duced from two days to a few hours. Approximately thirteen cabins of one and two room configuration were added in 1921, to the north side of the main lodge building, whose foundations still can be observed nearly hidden within the shadows of the trees now grown tall. An additional tract of 70 to 80 acres was purchased in 1923 from Pieter Hondius, Sr. in front of the main lodge structure that Minnie said was "to give a larger front yard," and it did as the lodge now occupied between 227 and 240 acres of deeded land depending how the survey lines were run.

In October of 1923, Dan March died in Greeley, Colorado at the age of 61 following a long illness and Mrs. March argued that the hard work in cold windy, inclement weather had shortened Dan's life span. Dan March was an extremely hard worker, an excellent resort owner, loved the land and sought to make it even more beautiful from the first time he looked out over the willow clad river valley. His passing greatly saddened his many friends as they read his obituary in their paper on October 12th. "His strenuous physical activity, never considering the limits of his strength, together with an attack of flu that he could not completely throw off, resulted in an illness that lasted nearly four years culminating in his death." Messrs. Bond, Service, Lester and Stead were his pall bearers and he was buried in Greeley as was often the case with so many of early Estes Park's leading citizens as until only recently was it possessed of a cemetery. In November of 1924 the National Park Service purchased from Mrs. March nineteen acres of unusually large aspens bordering the Fall River at the extreme end of Horseshoe Park located at a point where the Fall River Road starts its climb up the big hill. This is now Endovalley picnic grounds. It was acquired as reported "to enable campers to get an early start for the trip to Grand Lake or for those to camp who come over the Fall River Road in the late afternoon," and a road into this acquired tract was constructed for public use in 1925. Another 20 acre tract also was purchased at that time by the National Park Service from Pieter Hondius, Sr. adjacent to and on the west side of the National Park's utility area. Although it was to serve as the location for another public camp ground, it does not appear that this happened. Further reasoning for the acquisition of the new camp grounds, bluntly recognizing an early Park management problem, was "to make the four camp grounds in the Park so desirable from the campers' viewpoint that there will be no necessity of parties camping alongside of the roadways or on private land where they are not wanted." That was a very clear statement of policy. No more, 'wherever you want to park,' camping along the byways of the Park. Regulations were taking hold as the annual number of Park visitors was rapidly reaching a level of 250,000, exceeding even the attendance at older National Parks. Now that the hidden paradise of Lord Dunraven had been discovered, those embryonic vacation seekers, vanguards of the hordes to follow, must be regulated with respect to their freedom to wander about acting out their parts as a new breed of explorer.

After Dan's death Minnie continued to operate the lodge, and from 1924 through 1940 other buildings, including a barn, wranglers' cabin, employees' quarters and a recreation hall perched on the southwestern shore of the lodge's lakes, took their places on the very scenic grounds of the resort. In 1925 when Minnie reopened the lodge, she found a snow shoe family in residence, and there were Chinese pheasants running about that came from who knows where to share the warm summer days with the guests. It was recorded in the newspaper one time that Mrs. March, while looking for something different for decorations, found short logs that had been cut by a beaver near the lodge. The news related, "She made them into lighting fixtures, with five evenly sized pairs selected that were made into very interesting fixtures to be installed in the dining room. The logs still display the teeth marks and where the beaver pealed them." Minnie certainly made every effort to associate her lodge with its surroundings.

The Marches for many years had been friends with Mr. and Mrs. Sam Service, as Sam was the groceryman in the village and Minnie's continued friendship endured to attain another status. Sam Service, born in 1860 in County Antrim, now one of the six administrative regions of Northern Ireland, immigrated to the United States as a small child in 1863. Sam did not forget his nephew and niece, Sam and Libby Buchanan who had remained in Ireland, as he later brought them to Estes Park and where Libby became a Chapman and the postmistress of Moraine Park signing her daily accounts register simply as L.B.C. Sadie Boyd was born in 1869 in Charlevoix Michigan and married Sam in Sterling, Colorado. Subsequently moving to Lyons, Colorado, Sam was fully occupied in the quarrying industry as well as operating a general store. Only twenty-five miles from Estes Park and without the view of the mountains that had lured them further west, the magnetism was too much for them. In 1902 they purchased the general store of William T. *Billy* Parke who would remain in the village to become prominent as a premier photographer and operator of the Kodak Film store. Service's Store was the place where locals went to socialize and functioned as the gathering place to get the news of the day. If one didn't want to talk, there was the ample front porch on which to sit and whittle away on a hunk of wood that might have fallen off one of the many wagons that now were frequent sights on a previously quiet street. The Services purchased an adjacent lot on which they erected a handsome home where the fireplace was always in use. "It never went out!" locals exclaimed in a stance of cost consciousness at the extravagant use of coal. The Service family frequently sat out on their large front porch, an appendage that brought exclamations of astonishment when later it was "totally glassed in!" They witnessed the ebb and flow of increasing numbers of humanity whose constituent members played out their new roles on the busy stage known as Main Street, never referred to as Elkhorn Avenue by locals.

After a lingering illness, Sadie Boyd Service died on November 22, 1931. Grief and loneliness are troublesome comrades with which to live, and for Sam, an outgoing man with scores of friends, he needed a flesh and blood companion with whom to share his remaining years. After a respectable period of being a widower, Sam asked for Minnie's hand in marriage and to the surprise and delight of their many friends, one Saturday morning in October of 1935 they drove to Greeley and were married. After a wedding trip to Banff and Lake Louise, they continued on to California to spend the winter. They returned in the spring of 1936 to remodel and enlarge the lodge and await the new crop of tourists who had begun to return when the dark days of the depression gave evidence of brightening. The whole community was well pleased with this respected couple in hitching themselves to the same wagon, and before the first tourist checked in that season their friends feted them one evening. Passed down the public grapevine, the newspaper editor was tipped off and published news of the *secret* event to a community eager for some humor after distressing news of business failures. "History was made last Monday, the 25th of May, when friends and neighbors of Mr. and Mrs. Sam Service, Park residents of long standing who were married last winter, were subjected to a charivari at their summer home at Fall River Lodge. More than a score of resort and hotel owners in the Horseshoe Park district, old timers who have known the honeymooners for many years, and others, proceeded the presentation of *gifts*, such as rolling pins and dish cloths, with noise, catcalls and hilarity as they surrounded the lodge." Whether it was because Sam had the first telephone in the village after acquiring the store in 1902, I can not be certain, but the telephone number now for Fall River Lodge was listed as Estes Park No. 1.

In the summers of 1936 and 1937 the lodge regularly hosted, on a daily average, 75 guests. Minnie was an expert in the kitchen and Sam by the great fireplace recounted his adventures in early day Estes Park, his tales peppered with humor of his encounters with Estes Park's first citizens. For all of the attention paid to the guests, the cost was only $6 per day including meals or $40 for the whole week. Sam's store, that was broadly classified somewhere between a shooting gallery and a chautauqua prayer meeting and now identified as the Coffee Bar on Elkhorn Avenue, was the hub of the community where gossip, good and bad -- *interesting stuff* it was called -- was exchanged in front of the large stove and where it was not unusual to have the discussion gain steam into a strong debate, and go beyond. Minnie had been a resident for nearly as long as her husband, who had been Mayor of Estes Park, and it was sincerely hoped that they would have many more years to share together in the Fall River valley as they greeted the tourists with tales of what it was like *back then*. However, Sam died suddenly in 1937 and Minnie for the rest of her life referred to herself as Minnie March Service out of respect for the two men in her life whom she had loved and who had loved her for her fine qualities as a wife and hostess. Her positive personality was a valuable asset to the community of Estes Park as all considered this pioneering woman "a very gracious lady."

In the late fall of 1941, after a last party at the lodge for all her friends and particularly those in the resort business with whom she and her men had toiled together to shape the Estes Valley into the unique summer resort that it had become, she sold all of property in Horseshoe Park to Mr. J. Russell McKelvey and his wife Florence. The lodge, and cabins blended into the surrounding forest, then had the capacity to comfortably house 90 guests requiring a staff of 30 employees during its regular summer season from June 1st to September 15th. As was usually the case with the lodges except for Long's Peak Inn, the dining room was staffed by female college students while the boys attended to their duties as dish washing, supplying wood to cabins, assisting in the maintenance work and assorted chores, or working as bell hops, a position unique for rustic mountain lodges within the Park. What most guests did not know is the fact that throughout the summer, kitchen bacon grease and fat drippings were saved in crocks until the end of the season. Then, through the application of a Fall River Lodge *secret recipe* guarded as well as the *Coca-Cola* formula, next year's supply of kitchen and laundry soap was produced in bulk form and stored upon a shelf for the next season. This certainly was an early application of sound environmental practices continued from very early times, however one former employee emphasized the strength of its cleansing properties. "It sure was strong. If you left a towel in that stuff for more than thirty minutes, it was gone!"

Possessed with its own small lakes, the pleasant appearing recreation building provided guests a splendid opportunity to watch rafts propelled by the young men courting the midwestern school teachers who were well represented in the lodges during the month of June. Occasionally canoes were observed upon the lakes, supplied by Dr. Zeckel who regularly towed his small fleet out from Chicago for his enjoyment and that of other guests. The recreation building, known as The Pavilion and often The Rumpus Room, was a one story affair, having the comfortable appearance of a hideaway upon a Wisconsin lakeshore, and it was equipped with a stage on the east end and an excellent dance floor. In addition to being the venue for shuffle board matches, energetic Ping-pong battles, songfests and marshmallow roasts near the large indoor rustic fireplace, every Thursday night and often twice a week as requests prevailed there would be found colorfully attired square dancers gracefully whirling about the floor their faces shining with broad smiles as well as glistening beads of perspiration. Picnics were held on the hill top south of The Pavilion after which the kids would head off to the river, to the livery stable, run screaming through the ancient trees in an attitude of wild Indians, or do whatever kids did when turned loose after a *required* appearance. The older women enjoyed the view associated with a wide arcing ride on the tall swing where their dresses were caught by the prevailing western breeze. Many of the men folk rolled up their sleeves for a spirited game of horseshoes or grouped together to tell stories about the battle they fought to net their *trophy* fish that had to be in excess of thirteen inches according to the scale taped to the top of the old wicker creel. Of course the pond that released this leviathan dweller of the willows was never revealed. As a point of detail, the swing was later replaced by a gazebo that could accommodate more guests for a splendid view up the Fall River canyon. The only structure known to survive the final demise of Fall River Lodge is that little gazebo, still serving the tourist trade at Rockmount Cottages on the road to the Y. M. C. A.

Despite its pastoral appearance in the pines, there was a virus of vitality about the place that infected all at this resort. It was constantly being energized by Russ's dedicated attention to detail and his application of reasoned yet sympathetic practices, and by Florence's vibrantly cheerful personality who sought to make every day at her lodge a quality and fun filled experience. As a personality person, she was ever alert to the requirements of her guests, and always showed them a smiling face despite the many hours at her tasks. Of course, no good lodge would be complete without a stable and horses for the less conditioned for vigorous hiking. Daily trips included Lawn Lake, up Fall River Road to visit William *Miner Bill* Currence's home and his mining activity, or to trod the dozens of trails originating at the lodge's hitching rack south of the lodge. The beavers never let the lodge owners forget that this country first belonged to them, and their many dams upon Fall River perpetually threatened the stables, corral and utility buildings with flood waters to require constant vigilance and an occasional stick of dynamite strategically placed.

Russell McKelvey had previously been engaged by the Marches at Fall River Lodge as their assistant manager, then as the manager of Moraine Lodge in 1929 where he employed his mother as its front desk hostess. He was versed in the hotel business in Florida, dabbled in land ventures in and around the Estes Valley, and from 1931 to 1934 managed the 53 acre site at 8,700 feet known as Hotel Mountainside for Chicagoans Charles H. Woods and B. E. Paige. That small hotel and its surrounding land, now called Mountainside Lodge and in an awe inspiring location, now comprises the western section of the Y. M. C. A. Center that for many years has been its owner. Immediately before his acquisition of Fall River Lodge, he was in his seventh year as manager of the Lewiston Hotel when it burned to the ground that memorable September afternoon in 1941. By the time he became the owner of Fall River Lodge he was a confirmed and competent hotel man, and the McKelvey family's first full year of operation at Fall River Lodge commenced in 1942. Inasmuch as so many of the lodges had already been purchased by the National Park, Russ stressed obliquely in advertisements that this lodge was not under government supervision, a statement that perhaps piqued Park officials who viewed their responsibilities differently than did those lodge owners whose tenure predated the creation of the Park. "We are privately owned," he said, "and operated within Rocky Mountain National Park, with comfortable, modern accommodations in the lodge or cottages. There are a wide range of activities and splendid riding country." On one of their picture postcards was an assurance to future guests that relaxation for the whole family was attainable at their resort. "At Fall River Lodge, there's complete release from the normal and routine chores for the entire family, including mother." By this wording, it might be presumed that a mother was not considered within the full embrace of the noun, *family*, which certainly was not the case with Florence and Russ McKelvey who adopted all of their guests as a full and voting members into their own family. One former guest remarked about the quality experiences and much fun she had when the Marches and McKelveys owned the lodge. "It was a popular resort. The gracious manners of the hosts and hostesses of Fall River Lodge through the years, together with the tasteful and rustic elegance of the lodge's appointments, coupled with its lovely location, all combined to make many friends for the lodge."

Horseback riding was considered an essential component to a healthy mix that made for a complete vacation package. Up to the time of the McKelvey purchase, a string of at least thirty horses were stabled at the March-Service lodge and successively owned by the liverymen Burt Vetters, Phil Jenkins and his brother. Art Card and his younger brother Bill purchased the horses, tack and supplies at the time of the lodges's sale to Russ and Florence. A young man, William E. Robinson from Denver who resided with his folks only a few blocks from the former Colorado Womans College, became a friend of Art Card who had the contract to supply the college with horses for the equestrian needs of its students during the fall, winter and spring terms. Art, who had recently purchased the Stanley Livery in Estes Park, decided to employ his knew 14 year old friend at his town livery during the summer weekends of 1941. When Art also took over the Fall River Lodge livery operation, Bill was asked to work for him for the summer of 1942 and where he would remain for the next eighteen seasons. Robinson had seen the ranch once before from high atop Trail Ridge Road when returning by way of Estes Park from a vacation with his parents. While descending into Horseshoe Park he caught sight of the beautiful set of buildings nestled into the north side of the Fall River and exclaimed to his folks, "Some day I'm going to live there!" As Bill and I shared memories, he thought about that statement while looking at an old post card exhibiting the lake in front of the lodge with guests gathered about the front steps. He added to that statement from his youth, "Yes, I said I would live there one day, ...and I did!" For the first ten seasons he bunked in the old March homestead cabin with Bill Card, the brother directly in charge of the horse operations at the lodge and who was like a second father to young Robinson.

Robinson, although having assumed most of the management of the livery operations by 1946, did not purchase all of Art Card's interest in the horses, tack and supplies until 1951 at which time he became fully in charge of the horses under contract with the McKelveys. Employing three additional wranglers, he competently tended to the requests of the lodge guests for pleasurable rides throughout the National Park. Russ McKelvey printed each year a little promotional tract entitled *Fall River Lodge and Ranch News,* mailed out to all former guests and by which he promoted the upcoming village and lodge activities and frequently Bill's talents as a horseman. In the April, 1954, edition, after a busy season in 1953 when nearly a million and a half visitors had entered the Park's entrance stations, he made an important announcement to the family of guests who had come to know and value their friendship for their trail boss. "Bill Robinson, our stable boss, will be on hand for the 1954 season to furnish good, dependable saddle horses, and guides if you wish to take longer trail trips. *Better Breakfast Rides* is the theme of another tune that will be perfected and recorded by the time you arrive at Fall River Lodge this year. If you've ever been on a breakfast ride, we don't need to sell you on this feature of ranch living. Whether you are an expert horseman or a beginner, Bill has the right mount for you. Just tell us the time you wish to head for the trails, and your horse will be waiting for you at the stable. Bill, by the way, was married in January to a lovely young lady from Wickenburg, Arizona." When Bill and Fannye Kingston Robinson returned in 1954, they lived during the summer seasons in the chicken house he had remodeled that was more than adequate for two people in love as they remain nearly forty years later in their more capacious and comfortable home west of Estes Park.

During the McKelveys' duration of ownership, the season for business of the Fall River Lodge and Ranch like most of the lodges extended from the first week in June to the middle of September and food service was always on the American Plan of three meals a day. The lodge's central building grew into three stories in height with the second and third floors dedicated to rooms with private bathrooms for thirty-five guests. Sixty-five additional guests were housed in the fourteen cabins that also were equipped with full bathrooms. The Marches built most all of Fall River Lodge's structures, except for a few utility and employee housing to the south and west of the main lodge. The only major additions by the McKelveys took place in 1946 when a large wooden structure, left over at the completion of Bureau of Reclamation activities when Lake Estes was created, was moved onto the property. It then was converted into a four room guest cabin and placed on the former site of a tennis court that had fallen out of favor with the horse and fishing legions constituting the majority of the lodge's invitees. The other major change occurred when Bill and Russ's chief of maintenance and brother, Paul McKelvey who lived in and operated Prospect Inn with his wife Audry, spent the winter of 1948 enlarging the lodge's 45 seat dining room with a 600 square foot extension on its west end. The enlarged dining services naturally required the attentive efforts of many employees, including young J. D. McKenna whose prime responsibility to management was unique and the envy of all the others. Obliged to provide a dependable supply of fish to the chef who early each morning advised him of the number, size and variety of trout he required for the evening meal, J. D. headed out to fish. It was a mission fraught with more difficulty and strategic planning than one would imagine. To catch a sack full of *keepers,* he was compelled to trudge ever higher into the Mummy Range, including Crystal and Ypsilon Lakes, as the result of an accelerating imbalance in the ratio of fishermen to fish. While on the subject of fish, one would ask why the fish could not have been obtained from the lodge's own lakes. Those waters were essentially fish rearing ponds, under the jurisdiction of the Colorado Game and Fish Department, whose wildlife officers stocked them with hundreds of small trout fingerlings each spring and fed them twice a day until fall. When the lodge closed at the end of a tourist season, the officers drained the lakes and allowed the now fourteen inch long, and fat, trout to enter Fall River to repopulate the heavily used portions of the river meandering through Horseshoe Park. No one was allowed to fish the ponds including the lodge staff. However, I have it on good authority from sources who have pledged me to eternal silence, that human shadows in fishing poses by the small lakes on what were euphemistically termed *midnight forays* were not uncommon apparitions of the night air.

Two other duties delegated young J. D. resulted in tests to his courage and footwork as their hazards, management concluded, balanced somewhat the scales of equity in job assignments. Thus, as an additional benefit to cabin guests, he was required to arise at 4 A. M. each morning, before departing to fish, and get their wood stoves fired up thus assuring warmth when the inhabitants awoke at a more timely hour. Frequently when new guests first arrived in the late evening and were not advised by the desk clerk of J. D.'s rounds in the darkness, the next morning the young man provided a ready target for shoes and heavy objects as those guests believed this intrusion into their key-less front doors the act of a curious bear or even worse, a burglar. The worst duty mandated to J. D. had an unintended association with those bears, an animal species that thoroughly frightened him. To further even the score for what many assumed to be a leisurely day of fishing, the evening garbage run was decreed to belong to our young seventeen year old friend who was observed performing the assignment with a marked degree of animated alacrity. One evening, gripping firmly the two handles on the 35 gallon container, he briskly proceeded down the semi-darkened path to the secluded garbage rack one hundred feet behind the kitchen. Generally succeeding in scaring off the eight or ten bears that considered this area suitable for dining and relaxation, he assumed he had again triumphed in man's dominion over the beasts on this dark and fog enshrouded evening. Just as he lifted the container up on the platform, one bear, still lurking in the mottled darkness of a sickly glowing light bulb suspended from a tree limb nearly, slowly reached out at the same time to relieve the container of its bent lid. After a robust shout and without letting go of his malodorous burden, the young man turned wildly and dashed back to the kitchen, --right through the unopened screen door. After four years of employment, J. D. left to seek an indoor job in the big city, with strong lights and no zoo. In the early 1940s when bears were particularly bothersome around the lodge, Park Rangers including the late Bill Grove were required to live trap the trespassers. After painting a bright white mark on their rear, an action thought demeaning to a bruin growling in disapproval, the usual procedure was to truck the animals up Fall River Road to the last turn before the final climb to the pass, unload the offenders and by shouts and arm waving, the bears usually descended down into the Poudre River drainage no longer to be observed on this side of the mountain.

Russ, Florence and their daughter Kay, who was always to be found about the premises usually on the back of her favorite horse, always considered their tourist facility as a family oriented establishment as their brochures announced. "Fall River Lodge and Ranch welcomes you and your family. The lodge blends into the mountain surroundings. It is big, beautiful and typically Western in architecture, cloaked in warm friendliness and informality." The first floor of the lodge was the central focal point for guest activities. Ascending the front steps after acknowledging the greetings of those seated about the front porch enjoying the brilliant sunshine and usually clear blue sky, a new guest entered the spacious and attractive lobby. This room, serving a multiplicity of purposes in addition to a place for registration and initial welcome by management, was the assembly point in the evening for movies, card playing and where a noisy game of Bingo was regularly called. The large stone fireplace's toasty warmth beckoned the newcomer to take a seat and relax. The furnishings were appropriate for a mountain ambience with wildlife pictures, antlered deer heads mounted on the walls and the usual scattering of Navajo rugs to assist a guest to make a transition from an urban setting to one more in tune with the *Wild West*. In a small room, tucked away to the right of the crackling embers, was the friendly Nick Nack Nook where gift items could be purchased, reading material secured and light refreshments available, especially for the youngsters who **must** have an ice cream before bedtime. The adjoining sunroom offered a quiet scene of sanctuary for reading, post card writing or just a cozy refuge where the new adventures of the day could be placed in proper prospective as sleepy eyes campaigned against the effort to plan the next 24 hours of fun.

In every chapter I have emphasized the importance of horses and their wranglers to a guest's enjoyment of an extended vacation at one of the lodges. Horses were no less important at Fall River Lodge when in the 1940s they were rented by the week and month, seldom by the day and never by the hour, as guests came to the mountains for a lengthy stay, some of whom spent the entire summer. A horse was assigned to them according to their desires and abilities, considered *their horse* just as if they owned it, and many of the guests were as informed about the back country as many seasoned wranglers. No one else rode that horse except the one assigned to it, and if that person elected to sleep in and not ride one day, the cost remained the same at $25 a week to $90 per month. The liveryman and his employees fed and cared for the horses, pasturing them between the lodge and the Endovalley Campground, frequently on the south slope of Mount Chapin. Every morning at six or seven they were rounded up to be fed a ration of grain for energy and saddled up as all of them were expected to be ready each morning unless the wranglers were advised to the contrary. In the early days, guests knew how to ride, hence the string of horses could be counted upon to be tough range horses with a lot of life in them, --working horses that would not brook an amateur sitting their saddles. Bill Robinson remarked, "If one or two people weren't bucked off on an early morning ride, it was considered a pretty calm day for in the early 1940s those ranch horses were strong and tough!" He smiled just thinking of those saddle sore riders who stood extra tall in their stirrups when returning to the corral just before supper, adding this final tribute to their endurance. "When that trip returned, several places were set up, --in a standing mode, for those who had hit the ground." A limited number of wranglers in the 1940s were required since ninety percent of the guests were proficient in the saddle, required no guiding service, preferring to ride their particular range without any direction or constraints from the staff. The only exception to this rule of individuality were the Wednesday morning breakfast rides, frequently into Little Horseshoe Park, when all participants went together strung out along the trail to their destination of bacon, eggs, flap-jacks and hot coffee around the open fire. Later, as times changed and vacations became shortened, guests were found not to possess the same riding skills, nor knew the surrounding countryside, thus necessitating more gentle horses, closer supervision and guide services.

Bill, as was the business practice of most liverymen working under contract with lodge owners, hired his crew, purchased his feed and tack, rented his pasturage and paid for discounted meals obtained in the employee's dining room. Horses were rented and rides booked by Bill usually within the lodge as he quickly came to regard the guests as his personal friends. Each day he rendered an accounting to Russ by paying him all of the daily proceeds, later to receive back all but ten percent of the gross receipts as the consideration for an exclusive privilege to operate the horse concession. In later years he, as did most of the other liverymen of the community, looked to the children --especially the girls who were the best riders -- as his bread and butter customers when older guests came to prefer more diversified, possibly less strenuous and time consuming, activities by which to gain a first class vacation encounter justifying one postcard mailed home per day. Of course the women usually got together once a week to join in group ride as a compromise to their husbands' pronouncement "I don't know why you came out to this horse place if you didn't want to get on a horse!" But there were others, perhaps playing with some levity combined with a measure of truth who suggested this trooping together was but a continuation of separate gossip sessions where now all could be present to defend themselves. Some of the men enjoyed riding but their number dwindled as most, who were not content just to read and rest up from their demanding schedules of earning a living, much preferred fishing the then stocked waters of the National Park.

As was the case with all previous lodge owners, time was running out for old Fall River Lodge. More demands were placed on the McKelveys by the National Park Service, as new regulations greatly impacted their opportunity to make a reasonable return on their investment. But more especially the atmosphere that for so long had been collegial in a private and public partnership to educate and entertain the visitors to the Park, now assumed a relationship of adversarial neighbors with diverging objectives. The National Park was intent on its assigned mission of ridding itself of another fly from its single stew pot while the McKelveys saw no reason why their hostelry could not coexist on a broader holiday menu for those preferring a closer presence within the Park in comfortable and convivial accommodations. But an end to the lodge was becoming obvious to Fall River Lodges' host and hostess who were surrounded by a powerful and more politically acceptable land owner that considered them unwanted, unneeded and an unacceptable intrusion into the public's domain now on an unstoppable course to total naturalness. Fall River Lodge was purchased by the National Park Service in 1955 for $160,000, succumbing to pressure for it acquisition at which time it still catered to 100 guests on its 240 acres. It is somewhat ironic that nearly contemporaneously with the removal of this tourist facility, demands for more tourist amenities necessitated the Park's construction of a new visitors center. The McKelveys continued to operate the lodge for a several more seasons pursuant to the agreement negotiated with the Park. Title passed after the final payment was made on December 1, 1959 and its doors closed for the last time.

At that time the National Park Service also owned the Brinwood and in May of that year the Department of Interior, pursuant to its Mission 66 program to make more accommodations available for projected large crowds of future visitors, solicited bids to operate one or both of the lodges. Applicants were required to meet strict qualifications as would be expected for the obvious advantages of operating as concessionaires within the monopolistic confines of any National Park. But what made this particular business decision nearly impossible for any potential bidder were the costs to improve outdated utility infrastructures. Brinwood's improvements alone would cost, by official National Park Service's estimates, at least $56,000 and for Fall River Lodge the expense would be more than $100,000. As further quid pro quo for a proposed twenty year lease, any future concessionaire must pay a fee of $1,500 per season plus a percentage of the gross sales. As expected, there was not a land rush of prospective applicants to acquire the leases. Applicants justified their less than sanguine response rationalizing that a short season of perhaps 12 to 14 weeks, burdened by those front end costs, would not bode well for an economically successful season. With no *acceptable* bids being received for Brinwood, and the offer of Mr. McKelvey for more reasonable terms having being rejected, the landscape soon would be less cluttered with two more out of place tourist facilities made redundant by government decree from which there could be no successful appeal. Russ McKelvey was not bitter, rationalizing that he had been treated as fairly as he could expect in a time when lives again were disrupted and attitudes polarized by cold war polemics and international political posturing leading to a still unresolved martial chaos in Southeast Asia. Lodge defenders were frustrated after the *Estes Park Trail* reported the news in its headline dated September 25, 1959, "HISTORIC FALL RIVER LODGE HAS MET ITS DOOM." To expend more of their resources in a losing cause, obviously, was unwise. Russ' only real complaint had been that he hoped for but one more year in which to make arrangements concerning his other property outside of the Park.

Critics of this chapter of *encouraged condemnation* should be fair to The National Park Service. By arranging those perceived authoritarian decisions in correct context with the reality of their times, it reasonably might be concluded that they were not buttressed on irrational assumptions nor shaky foundations but grounded on statistical facts. In 1958 Park officials had surveyed the need for the continuation of overnight lodging within the bound-

161

aries of the Park. Because no more than three and one/half percent of the total accommodations available in the Estes Park region were physically located within the Park that year, and often those only experienced a sixty percent occupancy rate in the summer season except for a few national holidays, it was their logic that visitors could best be housed outside of the Park and the land itself restored to its original configurations absent as much as possible the effects of man. "Logic," one old timer told me when I offered that as an explanation for resort removal, "is a mighty poor substitute for a pretty lodge's obliteration." He directed me a quizzical glance as I picked up my notebook to leave and I knew he was thinking how to end our conversation on a positive uptick. I watched him standing in the opened doorway, his head angled to catch a sight of Long's Peak observed thousands of times before. I stood with him, the pink glow of the winter sun painted on its mantle of perpetual snow, as my friend shook my hand. "I'm glad you wanted to talk about those lodges. I didn't think anyone cared...," his voice trailing off. "Those places were great when they were here and we had wonderful times in Fall River Lodge. One day those federal guys might look back in their retirement, like mine, and wonder if they were correct." In 1960 the old Fall River Lodge was torn down and the March homestead's removal followed in 1966. It is apparently forgotten by most, remembered only by the few who still walk the old haunts down by the willows that have luxuriated to nonpenetrative thickets to crowd out by their yellow-green curtain the laughter of those now long gone men, women and children, --especially the children, who sat in those rocking chairs and witnessed the passing of wild life, and good times. Some might harken back to a Sunday morning's old fashioned sing-a-long led by Doctor Crabbe, President of State Teachers College in Greeley, when voices joined in religious harmony in tune with all of nature to welcome back the sun to Horseshoe Park.

Russ and Florence, now deceased, are buried in Greeley and their daughter Kay, after studying hotel management at Michigan State University, married John Eckhart and now reside on their guest ranch near White Sulphur Springs, Montana. With some nostalgia mantled in undisguised irritation, two women presenting a program years later about the Park's lodges said, "How wonderful it would have been to have left suitable markers telling of the homesteaders who crossed the mountains to build these lodges and ranches and maintained them through rough winters for the enjoyment of many." I have heard that the Chief Interpreter of Rocky Mountain National Park may have just such plans in mind and I know that all will benefit from his sincere though long overdue effort to remember a valuable segment of the history of Rocky Mountain National Park. The Fall River Lodge property has been returned to its earlier configurations as if man, --and woman, had never occupied these now silent grassy knolls and hollows filled with emergent growth. But their memory still permeates the premises and lingers to blend with the music of the flowing water and wind moving Dan March's willows that have grown back to feed a new generation of beaver.

I asked Bill and Fannye Robinson, what was unique about Fall River Lodge? Their answer was prompt in coming. "It was the families," Fannye said, to be echoed by Bill who embellished on her succinct answer. "The guests, their children and their children, we have kept in touch with for fifty years. This was a family place, and when I walked into the lobby in the evening it seemed they were all there, as games were being played, the music, the fire cracklin'...." The friendly face clouded over with a vision of that last year and his voiced grew husky with understood emotion, and he swallowed hard. "You see, it was my home for a long time, and I couldn't go back when it closed to see it demolished." In looking back at her days on the upper Fall River after overcoming so much to provide pleasant accommodations for thousands who called Fall River Lodge their second home, Minnie March Service, in her 90th year of life, offered her critical evaluation of more modern visitors with which so many Estes Park residents today can identify. "Now people travel these boulevard roads, climbing to the top of the world with no effort whatever. I often wonder, as they look down on Horseshoe Park, as they must, if they can possibly have time to enjoy the wonders and beauty which lie in this little valley. I'm sure they can't realize the beauty, the splendor, the immenseness, of even our little Horseshoe Falls. They may see it from afar, but they miss the best part in their hurry. They never get the thrill of 'nature in the raw' as one gets on the trail to Lawn or Ypsilon Lakes. They can never enjoy the beauty of a Hairbell, nor a Shooting Star, nor a Mariposa Lily nor a Columbine. I don't believe they even know the trees, nor the jagged rocks which form our peaks. And that makes me wish once more for the good old days of the horse and wagon, the kerosene lamp, the fields of flowers, the *side-wheeler* telephone, the buckets of raspberries to make into jam, and the old kitchen stove in the little log cabin. I think I'd like it just for a while, --not too long. How about you?" Mrs. March Service, after moving in 1956 to San Bernardino, California to live with her sister, died at the age of 94 on December 8, 1963 to join her men high above Trail Ridge Road.

I shall conclude this bit of history on the sentiment expressed by a guest in 1934 upon being asked what it was like to stay at this mountain inn. "That **was** a beautiful lodge! As I stood looking at it, the flag was flying. And with that beautiful snow-capped mountain in the back, I just thought it was paradise." And as the word *paradise* is defined in the dictionary as "a place of great happiness, a place of great beauty," so was this place on the Fall River.

March Homestead Built In 1911, 1951 (RMNP)

Fall River Lodge And Recreation Hall, circa 1920 (Private)

Horseback Riding From Fall River Lodge, circa 1920 (EPHM)

Lounge At Fall River Lodge, circa 1930s (Private)

Sam Service And Minnie March Service, 1935 (EPPL)

Bill Robinson Entertains In Lodge, 1952 (Robinson Family)

Breakfast Ride, 1950 (Robinson Family)

Fish Fry At Fall River Lodge, 1955 (Robinson Family)

Lobby And Lounge Of Main Lodge, circa 1940s (Private)

Enlarged Dining Room, circa 1950s, (Private)

Cabins At Fall River Lodge, circa 1950s (Private)

Typical Guest Room At Fall River Lodge, 1940s (Private)

Kitchen Crew, circa 1950s (Robinson Family)

Housekeeping Crew, circa 1950s (Robinson Family)

Last Guests, 9-15-59, Russ & Florence On Right (Robinson)

Lodge As It Appeared In Final Season, 1959 (Robinson)

DEER RIDGE CHALET

Although Deer Ridge Chalet was not known as a lodge that met the specifications attributed to the others described herein, it is deserving of recognition for its status as a more modern version of a stage coach station that would always be affiliated with the early lodging industry at the principal crossroads within the Park. So many vacationing tourists paused at Deer Ridge Junction for one final look around, perhaps a last minute purchase of mountain memorabilia, to remember their splendid holiday time. "Anything else you need?" exclaimed father to his brood. "Get it now at The Chalet because it's a long way to the next stop," he urged. A family clambered out, selected a last souvenir, candy bar, visited the loo and in general bid fond adieu to the Estes Valley before setting forth up the dizzying heights of Trail Ridge Road on their journey through unsurpassed natural drama in a tundra dream world environment. Also Deer Ridge Chalet was significant as memories of those who stayed at the lodges contained pleasant thoughts of an all too brief visit to the store for a postcard to send to friends *laboring in the vineyards* of a midwestern summer's heat. The vintage hackneyed message often conveyed their sincere sentiment as they wrote 'having a wonderful time, wish you were here' to those with envy who questioned 'where did they get the money for such a vacation when they should be home taking care of business?' And then that climb up to the top of the tower for a fantastic picture to dazzle their flatland relatives.

Who could hardly forget the soda fountain, rock shop and rubber tired miniature train that carried happy children on a circle trip in full view of Long's Peak and its assembled family of granite faces beaming down their approval. And of course there was the dining room of shiny pine wood furniture, decorated with tiny covered wagons, wood carvings, western bric-a-brac, attended by denim skirted waitresses with friendly smiles who might have been your kids' school teachers from Nebraska. A seat at the friendly lunch counters was popular and, though patrons did not present the best posterior presence, they knew they were in real America as customers rubbed shoulders, and knees, with all varieties of humankind. As the years have rushed past we all treasure those bygone days when life was more gentle and laid back and your only needs were more basic, such as 'please pass the ketchup bottle.' And by the way, the food associated with that condiment was great! It was a meeting place for hikers and motorists from the lodges in Moraine Park and especially Fall River Lodge in Horseshoe Park. The many horseback riders tied up their mounts and strode in with feet shod in new cowboy boots, intentionally scuffed to look otherwise, to take a seat at the lunch counter for light refreshment and perhaps a cool brew. The highway junction now just doesn't look the same to those who enjoyed the milling about of the horses, people, dogs, burros, kids and whatever exited from those thirties, forties and fifties vintaged vehicles eager to browse through the thousands of items for sale. Those lodge guests who had been in residence for more than a week delighted in a climb up the tower to prove their credentials as true mountain experts to some Texan who wondered if those large, antlered, shaggy beasts were another genus of longhorned cattle.

Orville W. Bechtel homesteaded this tract of land before the National Park was established. It was at the end of a bumpy road, a location he considered the best vantage point from where to compose a picture of the front range. As a semi-professional photographer, he had a hunch that others equally would value a photo remembrance of the visit to Deer Ridge summit eight miles west of the village, and for that purpose he constructed a small twelve by sixteen foot rectangular log building. As today one reaches the junction where the present road divides three ways at the T shaped intersection, Mr. Bechtel's little store was on the northwest corner, west of the road that rises out of Horseshoe Park. It was in this rough textured native lumber outpost that he sold his own photos, film and enlarged pictures by others of the natural scene that spread out so panoramically in all directions. It was not easy to get his business opened at the beginning of any season as Mother Nature often had entered in a conspiracy with Father Winter to extend his time of snowy solitude. In fact the season of 1921 experienced a delayed opening after a heavy spring storm on April 14th deposited more than four feet of heavy, wet snow to collapse roofs on Elkhorn Avenue. But by the time the first tourist flivver clattered its way to Bechtel's door, he was ready. In their eagerness to talk to him about his life in the mountains, watch the pine squirrels, deer and small herds of elk wandering about in their now protected status, as well as take pictures with their leather box cameras, they realized that they had forgotten to bring along any food. Thus over the years he added to his business line an inventory of soft drinks and small food items for the tourists who had reached Bechtel's photography store unprepared.

Before 1920 the main entrance into the new National Park came in by way of Moraine Park, then the road meandered around many curves, up and over hills to effectively terminate at Deer Ridge Junction. Trails were made by nomadic animals up to Hidden Valley succeeded by a wagon road to timber operations and saw mills that were actively harvesting timber and rough sawing lumber for some of the early lodges. The rough road connecting from Horseshoe Park was very poor and was used mainly by the horse riders from Fall River Lodge and Horseshoe Inn. Deer Ridge summit, essentially the end of the road for vehicles whose owners valued the continued existence of their shiny black motor cars, was at an elevation of 9,176 feet later to become more accessible when the High Drive branched off from the Beaver Point junction on U. S. Highway 36 to extend further west. The view of the many high mountains was incomparable and, since the road to Bear Lake as we now know it was not completed until 1927, it was a destination for those with a good camera, or even those who were content to stand in awe at what nature had chiseled out of the ice and rock millenniums before. An advertisement, in the style of a news item, was published in the local newspaper. "At no point in the Rocky Mountain region can there be seen such a superb array of craggy snow covered peaks. Deer Ridge is a privately owned tract of land and is thrown open for your special enjoyment. At the Chalet lunches and refreshments are served and the finest collection of photographic enlargements, prints and post cards are to be had. Deer Ridge is the most beautiful beauty spot in the Rocky Mountain National Park and you should arrange to make the High Drive trip and pay them a visit." One distinguished visitor took up the offer, registering his family for one of the six little cottages that were now available to the public. He was William Howard Taft, former President of the United States and then Chief Justice of the United States Supreme Court, a position he valued more highly than the Presidency.

On February 22, 1924 a ski course was constructed on a northwest slope of Deer Ridge close to the Chalet and described as "a long course that landed on Ashton Flats," property controlled by the former owner of Horseshoe Inn. From the Chalet, cross-country ski touring was promoted west up to the beaver ponds and beyond to the end of the primitive road in Hidden Valley. Mr. Bechtel offered to erect a small shelter building on his property further to the east, rent free, for the following fall as a warming shelter for the skiers. He even installed a stove for the brand new, first in the state, Colorado Ski Club, formed by the Estes Park Group of the Colorado Mountain Club on January 29, 1924 at Stanley Manor in the village. After increasing numbers of vehicles arrived in 1924, banging and bumping along the southern flanks of Deer Mountain and north of Beaver Meadows with small tanks and large appetites for gas consumption, O. W. installed a fueling station in May of 1925 southeast of his store as a further inducement to visitors. Statistics fluctuated as to the actual count of National Park users as the numbers depended upon when the count was made, by whom and for what purpose they were revealed to the public. This figure usually was given for those visitors who came before *the close of the season* that traditionally ended around Labor Day or a little later according to when the first snows sealed off the highway pass to the west. In 1925 the season ended on October 2nd as the first measurable snows accumulated to close down Fall River Pass and the National Park *officially* recorded 224,211 visitors. The Rocky Mountain Parks Transportation Company closed its books that year after busing more than 9,867 passengers over 'the top of the world', as some in lofty idioms described their experience,

O. W.'s business was becoming an active one, too much for one man to handle, and it attracted a new investor from the hot plains of eastern Colorado, in fact a whole family of investors. Gustave Schubert, a baker and cigar maker, and his wife Emma Thale Schubert made their home in Brighton, Illinois. Mrs. Schubert, called *Bomma* Schubert, and her husband had seven children. The oldest child, given a strong German name like his father, was Emil Otto Schubert and his younger siblings were Wilbert, Edward, Adele, Bertha, Hilda and Florina known as Muggy. Moving to Mitchell, South Dakota then to Denver, they settled down on farm land near Roggen, Colorado, and where Bomma was later widowed. Exactly how she and her children learned of Bechtel's place is not entirely clear, but sometime between 1925 and 1927 the family purchased all of Mr. Bechtel's interests on Deer Ridge. All of the children spent time at the new property assisting their mother in varying degrees, but it was Emil, Bertha Anna, and Adele Emily affectionately known as Toots who became the legal owners and operators on an equal basis in 1927 or 1928. It is necessary to point out that Deer Ridge Chalet, as the Schuberts fully titled their enlarging business, was not located on the west side of the road but on the east side, or the northeast portion of that *T* intersection to which I have earlier referred. O. W.'s buildings remained in different uses by the family with some of them being moved to the east side of the improv-

166

ing highway emerging from Horseshoe Park. Back then as the road was improved leading towards Hidden Valley, the intersection at Deer Ridge Junction took on the characteristics of a *Y*. At the top of the *Y* was the filling station, and bearing the Conoco flying red horse symbol, that was managed by Art and Mary Rowland, and to its south stood the Deer Ridge Chalet's stables. Known as Budge Rumley's Deer Ridge Chalet Livery, between 15 and 20 saddle horses owned by Budge were available for rent for trail rides. Budge's real name was Virgil, the brother of Clarence Cyrus Rumley. Cy Rumley's own Beaver Point Livery, located at the present site of National Park Village South, was a camera point for tourists who enjoyed stopping by to watch the horses heading off into the National Park and photographing his large white barn with the cowboy figures, silly names and brands painted in a comical display of Western life. He, like his brother, provided many tourists with just the right horse for their first ride up into the Park until his unnecessary death in 1948. At Budge's livery he sported a spoked ring that captured the fancy of younger buckaroos where they could ride the small horses tethered to it around a ring and scream their approving delight as the little creatures trotted briskly in a circle. On the west side of the road, across the road from the main buildings, was a large parking lot and usually full.

Bechtel's store was remodeled into a rental unit, left where it was, but all other commercial activity was removed east of the *Y* to the other side of the roadway. The first building of the new Chalet was constructed in 1927 and was enlarged in 1932 as another building was attached to it for marketing souvenirs, gifts and a great assortment of curios. The oldest building then was made into a rock shop where interesting specimens of nature's best were very popular for purchase. Everything sold in the gift stores at Deer Ridge Chalet was representative of what was to be seen in the National Park, with no cheap nicknacks like rubber hatchets ever offered to the public. Behind Schubert's main store were six to eight cabins, heated by wood stoves, but no bathrooms. They were available for lease by the day, the week or the whole season. By 1930 or 1932 the cabins could accommodate about 25 guests for $5 per day and approximately $30 per week. A larger cabin, known as Bomma's Cabin was built and used exclusively by her. Until her death in 1941, she enjoyed *supervising* her grown up kids and the many other little ones belonging to appreciative guests.

Electricity for years was provided by a gas powered generator before Deer Ridge was reached by public power, and the water source arose out of a well in the westerly portion of the 227 acre tract that required extensive piping to the premises. Though the emerging resort was possessed with many modern contrivances, modern sanitation fixtures were not amongst them. There was but one outhouse, albeit it a gigantic one. Equipped with five seats on one side for the ladies and five more on the other side for the gentlemen, it was situated out behind the buildings from which no scenic view was possible yet accorded an opportunity to be closer to wildlife. There was one shower for the guests and one for the employees who lived above the store, although it was rumored that Bert and Toots had their own portable bathtub secreted away for their personal use in their quarters attached to the main building. Rank did have its privileges, even high up in the mountains.

Not usually kept open in the winter, the newspaper in September of 1930 announced that Mr. Merrill S. Bunnell would manage part of the premises for the entire winter. This decision to remain open in 1930 was invoked for those making the trip up to see the increasing number of elk and as the news article reported "to watch the road operations in Hidden Valley as the Trail Ridge Road was of considerable interest." To those who appeared, he sold hot sandwiches and hot drinks. After following tour bus company owner Roe Emery to Estes Park from Glacier National Park in 1919, Mr. Bunnell later became the owner of his own electrical business in the village. Though duties were not assigned, as all the family pulled together to share the responsibilities, each of the Schuberts had particular talents that they applied to the venture. Emil was the greeter and a good mixer, Adele was excellent in the kitchen working over the coal stove and large lazy susan, but Bert it was reported "was the brains behind everything" and the family member really in charge. She made the decisions for the growing number of enterprises at the store all based on her business judgment and practicality. To illustrate this point, Pat Schubert Webermeier shared this story with me as a slow grin spread across her face. "Around the Chalet we had millions of chipmunks, and so we sold a brand of peanuts to the tourists so they could feed the little creatures. One day, when working under the old building, we found a huge pile of unopened peanuts that the chipmunks had stored. The pile was three feet high!" I asked Pat what they did with the peanuts. "Well, Bert handled the finances, and so she said to gather them up and sell them again. And we did!"

Guests well remember the large doe deer that for more than twelve years gave birth to a set of twins, and each year just like clock work returned with her fawns to wander around the cabins soliciting compliments for her progeny as well as a tasty munchy that was most appreciated. Emil always fed her and over the years most anyone that wanted to was most welcome. In the 1930s burros carried children all over the Chalet grounds and often were tempted to ride right into the store for a special treat. Children thrilled to the activity of hanging bacon strips in the trees, then perch on the ample roof of the outhouse for the evening appearance of the bear families that regularly sought out such treats and anything else negligently left outside that was nourishing. A fifty foot tall observation tower was completed in 1933, enclosed and accessed through the gift shop, then a new one was erected to replace it. Larger rooms were added on in 1940 including the beautiful dining room in stylized western motif with all the trimmings to put you in the mood for a real chuckwagon dinner. On the porch of the gift shop building frequently could be found the Blackfeet Indian Charles Eagle Plume, a friend of the family, selling Navajo Indian rugs and discoursing upon the contributions of Indians to civilization. He often put in an appearance about the premises to add to the authenticity of the atmosphere where Navajo goods were prominently displayed and hypnotically swayed in the breeze to tempt the tourist. Routinely Navajo men and women voluntarily came to the Chalet to dance and weave, especially the women who beaded clothing, from which activities they garnered good incomes all summer. "They weren't employed by us," informed Pat Webermeier, "they just appeared on the front porch throughout the weeks of summer and were enjoyed by our guests and visitors." Some of the Schuberts were caught up in the spirit of Native American culture by wearing costumes and painted faces to the extent that the tourists were unable to determine whether those in feathers, buckskin and paint were *real* Indians or *play*

Indians. Members of the family thought Ed Schubert looked more like an Indian with his paint and bonnet than the real thing. Eagle Plume latter acquired the Perkins Trading Post ten miles south of Estes Park and operated it as the Charles Eagle Plume Trading Post until his death on September 8, 1992. His story and the history of that trading post can be found in a book entitled *JOY - The Life Of Charles Eagle Plume.*

It was a natural stopping place for the tourists, open for breakfast at 6:30 with freshly baked pastry produced by the two full time bakers, and closing at 7:30 in the evening after the last dinner was served during a season that commenced on Memorial Day and ended just after Labor Day. In 1945 Emil, Bert and Adele sold their interests in the Chalet to their younger brother, Edward and his wife Eleanor who expanded operations with additional services and conveniences offered to the public. Several more cabins, larger in size, were erected, one of which was occupied by members of the family. Eleanor took charge of kitchen and dining room management, staffed of course by many loyal young men and women. Their daughter, Pat, was mighty handy with the ice cream scoop at the soda fountain while father Ed managed successfully its expanded gift shop. His abilities as a purveyor of merchandise were obvious as my question concerning the success of the gift shop received the answer, "It was a gold mine!" For years the National Park Service had been attempting to purchase Deer Ridge Chalet so that the Federal Bureau of Roads could redesign Deer Ridge Junction. More than one and a half million visitors annually passed by Deer Ridge Chalet in the late 1950s to continue their journey up the Trail Ridge Road or return to Estes Park by way of the new road that now accessed the National Park on the east at Beaver Meadows Entrance Station. Negotiations had broken down, and by 1959 Deer Ridge Chalet was controlled by Deer Ridge, Inc., a family corporation owned by Ed and Eleanor Schubert and their daughter and son-in-law, John and Pat Webermeier. Condemnation proceedings commenced that year. Despite appeals and protests as to the procedure and the evaluation placed on the property, the government in 1960 acquired the 227 acres of the Deer Ridge Chalet, including all of its improvements, for $270,350. Don Griffith, a member of one of Estes Park's earliest families, participated in the last chapter of the Chalet. While appreciative of the significance of the National Park, years later he was still angry over the condemnation proceedings. He said before an historical association, "How can you set a value on what the Chalet did for those who worked there and what it did for those people who built it?" Several of the newer cabins constructed in the late 1940s and early 1950s were purchased by local people and moved to the hillside just west of Marys Lake. One of its first structures, Bomma Schubert's home, was moved down to a new location where the Webermeiers established a very successful tourist complex called National Park Village North that was recently destroyed by fire, including the old rubber-tired train. However Bomma's house to the south of that facility survived and still stands gazing querulously up towards Deer Mountain where it used to share in the merriment of summer holidays nearly forgotten.

However Deer Ridge Chalet would gain a new breath of life at an altitude 1,500 feet lower in association with an ancient Order of builders. The local Masonic Lodge, formed in 1959, needed a home of its own finding the nearly unheated local golf club in the winter somewhat inadequate for its ritual and fellowship. It acquired twelve acres on the south side of Estes Park in

1960, later selling off slightly more than nine of the acres, and prepared to receive a former mountain dweller into its brotherhood. Through negotiations with the National Park Service, several of the larger Deer Ridge Chalet buildings were either given or sold for a small price to the Masonic Lodge No. 183. The dining room, gift shop and other smaller buildings, were moved by a Greeley, Colorado company down through the Park entrance to Beaver Point, south past the former site of The Highlands, east to Highway No. 7 and north again to be situated upon a newly prepared foundation. The wooden units were carefully tied together by Don Griffith and a crew of talented local men in an effort to preserve the appearance of the old Chalet yet made functional in its new mode of service to the community. Windows in the dining room were closed up to become the lodge's club room and the gift shop became the kitchen and fellowship hall. It stands there today in a fresh coat of brown stain serving the fraternal needs of a dedicated association of local citizens.

All of Bomma's children are gone as well as Pat Schubert Webermeier' hardworking husband John. But Pat, and two of her children, continue the fine tradition of serving tourists at their National Park Village South complex adjacent to the highway that thirty-three years before carried its old predecessor to a new home of less hectic relevance. I think O. W., Bomma and her hardworking children would be pleased to know that a segment of their hard work remains. Even though the view to the west is not as grand, a herd of elk remains close by to give their curious approval. I recently asked Pat, "What **was** Deer Ridge Chalet to the tourist?" Her answer was positive. "It was a natural stopping area. We had good home cooking, sold no cheap curios, the horseback riding was gorgeous and the original buildings and furnishings we had were so unique. Everything closing in around Deer Ridge was so new, modern, but our Chalet preserved for the tourist something of the past." She, and many of those who had their lodges and concessions removed from the National Park boundaries, thought that "it was terrible that people could be kicked out of their business." Then she reflected upon the whole drama after the curtain had come down, and voiced an opinion that had matured beyond past resentment and anguish. "But what happened probably was for the best, for if the government would have continued to have commercial places like Deer Ridge Chalet all over the Park, it would have been destroyed."

It **was** a wonderful little stopping off place, with a magnificent view from the tower. There were friendly people to top off your National Park experience with good food, quality gifts and occasionally a second hand bag of peanuts for the chipmunks beseeching you to replenish their pile. "Yes," as Pat put in the last word, "everyone loved their experience at Deer Ridge Chalet, --well everything, except that outhouse."

O.W. Bechtel's Store, circa 1920s (Webermeier)

First Store Of Deer Ridge Chalet, circa 1927 (Webermeier)

Emil-Bert-Bomma-Adele-Wilbert Schubert, 1930 (Webermeier)

Hilda Schubert And Steed at Deer Ridge, 1940s (Webermeier)

Budge Rumley, Left, and Schubert Sisters on Right, 1930s (Webermeier)

Kids Loved The Burros at Deer Ridge, 1935 (Mary B. Totten)

Bomma's Cabin, circa 1930s, (Webermeier)

Ed Schubert, Right, and Fellow *Indians* In 1930s (F.J. Francis)

Charles Eagle Plume and Schuberts In Early 1930s (Webermeier)

Dining Room At Deer Ridge Chalet, circa 1940s (Webermeier)

Lunch Counter & Gift Shop At Deer Ridge, circa 1940s (Webermeier)

The Staff At Deer Ridge Chalet, circa 1950s (Webermeier)

Deer Mountain and Deer Ridge Chalet, circa 1960 (Webermeier)

A Synopsis Of History
And
Policies To 1962

When Leaving The Park,
We Turned Our Backs Upon Its Enchantments,
The Sun Never Shown More Brilliantly.
The Flowers Never Blossomed More Beautifully,
And The Waters Never Chanted More Hypnotic Music,
All Luring Us To Stay.
Carrie Adell Strahorn, 1878

Since 1909, sentiment had been gathering to establish a new National Park in Colorado. The U. S. Geological Survey of 1912 by Robert B. Marshall pronounced that this area was deserving of National Park status, --even giving the Park its official name. Finally, legislation was introduced into both Houses of Congress in 1913 by Representative Edward Taylor and Senator Charles Thomas of Colorado but they never made it out of committee. Reintroduced in 1914, Senator Thomas's bill quickly passed the Senate without debate, but it was in the House of Representatives that politics came into play. Outgoing Democratic Governor Ammons and Republican Governor-elect Carlson pledged that the State of Colorado would complete the Fall River Road from Estes Park to Grand Land as an inducement to create the National Park. Supporters of the Park in 1914 lobbied Congress on a personal, one on one basis, and Frank W. Byerly of Fern Lodge exhibited his personal set of stereoptican color slides of the scenic features of the proposed Park as the clincher before the House Public Lands Committee. He said, "If you could see pictures of it you couldn't vote against it." After the original acreage for the proposed Park was reduced to appease the Forest Service and accommodate ranching and mining interests, and after eloquent rhetoric voiced by Congressman Taylor of Glenwood Springs, Colorado, the legislation passed the House. President Woodrow Wilson signed the enabling Act on January 26, 1915 formally establishing Rocky Mountain National Park. The Park's first boundary enclosed 229,062 acres but over the years its size would increase to 263,880 acres by 1975 with smaller expansions made through the years since then to present times. Those addenda included Gem Lake, Deer Mountain, Twin Sisters Mountain, the McGraw Ranch, the Never Summer Range and Kawuneeche Valley on the western slope to name the most significant.

The Rocky Mountain News, ever since its founder and publisher William Byers described this region in 1864 as "a very gem of beauty," was still casting garlands of respect to the broad valley of the Upper Thompson as evidenced by its New Year's greeting to subscribers in January of 1915. "The people of Colorado have many things to be thankful for at the beginning of this new year, but perhaps none of them means more to the future of the state than the creation of Rocky Mountain National Park." I wish to quote from two documents that should be taken into consideration as we examine the direction the National Park has taken. The first is extracted from the underlying Act creating the National Park, that I highlight as **The Purpose**. *To conserve the scenery, the natural and historic objects and the wild life therein and to provide for the enjoyment of the same in such manner and by such means as will leave them unimpaired for the enjoyment of future generations.* The second quote is from the *Book of Administrative History* on the Park's first fifty years of existence, that I highlight as **The Problem**. *Throughout the Park's eventful history, administrators worked to resolve a basic dilemma: How to preserve the wildlife and scenery in their natural state and still allow tourists to visit and explore the region. Included in the problems growing out of this dilemma were wildlife management, winter sports development, removal of private inholdings and concessions and the extension of Park boundaries.* The public forests for many years had operated through a Division of Forestry with Forest Reserves serving as predecessors of the system of National Forests under the Department of the Interior. Then in 1905 the United States Forestry Service was created as a division within the Department of Agriculture. The various National Parks initially were each a separate unit under the Department of the Interior, as was the situation at the time of the establishment of Rocky Mountain National Park. Mr. Franklin K. Lane, Secretary of the Interior, appointed Charles R. Trowbridge, a Minnesotan by birth, Acting Supervisor of Rocky Mountain National Park on July 1st and his office opened on July 10th on the south side of Elkhorn Avenue across from Sam Service's store, later removed to a side street. Although Mr. Trowbridge was not known for his prowess in matters of forestry and recreation as at the time of his appointment he was a member of the Secret Service stationed in Salt Lake City, he did his best with the limited resources with which he had to work and was expert in training rangers and explaining the purpose of the Park to local interests.

Richard T. MacCraken was born in Washington D. C. His parents moved to Denver while at the same time homesteading 160 acres near Mount Olympus in the Estes Valley about 1902. *Dixie*, as he was known to his friends, was working for a company in the nation's capitol when he heard of employment possibilities in the National Park recently created back in his home state. Contacting political figures as well as a friend who was a ranger for the State of Colorado, he never mentioned his goal to become a Park Ranger to his parents until the appointment came through. In 1961 he spoke about their parental reaction. "When I wrote my folks and told them I was coming back, it was a wonder that my father didn't disinherit me. He didn't think there was any future in the thing as the salaries were terrible. I never regretted one day that I made that move." Dixie, appointed on August 9, 1915 as the first Park Ranger and a comedian of the first rank, remembers his initial reaction to working with Mr. Trowbridge. "I thought old Trowbridge was an old F. B. I. guy. Now I may be wrong, but he didn't know any more about a mountain than I do about the Virgin Islands." Although he eventually married Helen Bowsell of Washington D. C., he said at the start of his assignment "I didn't think I'd ever be married then being a Ranger. I didn't know any woman I thought would ever live with a Ranger in the sticks some place." At the time he went on the payroll he was only twenty-two years old with an education as a structural engineer. His salary was $2.50 per day, $900 per year, and he provided and maintained his own two horses and his pride and joy, a Model T Ford automobile. When questioned about his low pay Dixie answered, "If you complained, they said you shouldn't think about yourself. It's for the love of your country." The government furnished him with a cabin at Mill Creek Ranger Station and all the fuel he needed. Sympathetic to his fellow man, he regularly left his door unlocked so that weary travelers in need, caught outside in a storm, could gain access for safety, food and comfort. He was truly a compassionate man, well respected and admired. His uniform was "not like they have today," he advised, "but I had a western hat with a hat band that said **National Park Ranger** and I was supposed to have a gun on my hip. In the winter I wore anything to keep warm." Although his salary was penny-pinching and the duties generous to the extreme, Park rules were minimal to non-existent requiring rules to be made up as new situations presented themselves. Innovation and resourcefulness were requirements to be the first National Park Ranger, as his commission read *This is to certify that Richard T. MacCracken is a Ranger in the Rocky Mountain National Park, and has the authority to enforce the rules and regulations governing this Park.* That was it. He was a Park Ranger. Make the best of it.

Two other Park Rangers, Frank Koenig and Reed Higby, were appointed after the first summer to join in patrolling the Park's premises that consisted of a quarter of a million acres, 128 miles of trails, and fifty-five miles of roads all but five belonging to the State of Colorado. Frank named many lakes and mountains, including one lake, Hazeltine for his wife and Mount Ramsay for his father-in-law. One of Dixie's duties he remembered was "to guide the big shots around" while he paid his own way that frequently cost him a dollar more per day than his salary provided. A fourth Ranger, Howard G. Beehler, was hired in 1916 as the only Park Ranger on the western side of the Park and stationed near Grand Lake. He became so adept at winter patrolling in the back country and enforcing the regulations that he was known to the locals as the *Timber Beast*. It is interesting to read that none of the Rangers, other than their Supervisor, were married, but then the Supervisor's salary was much larger, $1,800 per year. The first summer of operation Supervisor Trowbridge estimated that 31,000 visitors had entered the Park, although other records reveal more than 46,000. Since no entrance fees were charged during the first years of Park operation, only four Park Rangers counting noses, and in the first few years there was no automobile entrance station on the west side, who knows what was the true visitor tally. It is safe to say that enhanced attention was focused on this new natural wonder with unlimited recreational possibilities that quantification in the higher estimates had the ring of closer veracity. On August 25, 1916, the National Park Service was organized within the Department of the Interior to supervise the ten National Parks then established and comprising four and one-half million acres, with its first Director Stephen T. Mather in command.

Former Army Captain Lewis Claude Way, in the business of cattle ranching near the Grand Canyon and a former Forest Officer in northern Arizona, was employed in October of 1916 replacing Mr. Trowbridge and given the title of Chief Ranger In Charge. While possessing the same duties, the next year found him designated as Superintendent, and thus would be known as Rocky Mountain National Park's first Superintendent. As with all new administrators of new enterprises, *Captain* Way, to which moniker he preferred to be identified, proved to be controversial right from the beginning. In a highly publicized effort to promote the use of *his* Park, he, or more probably it was the *Denver Post*, employed a pretty girl cloaked with a primordial alias *Eve* to live in the Park all alone, clad only in her leopard skin. The news articles said Eve was "to live off berries and fish caught by hand," while unbeknown to the public she was actually ensconced in warm, comfortable quarters at Enos Mills' Long's Peak Inn. Her activities were serialized and avidly read in newspapers and magazines and Dixie MacCracken was detailed to look after her, a duty that he thoroughly disliked as he didn't believe that this beautiful Park needed such fraudulently cheap publicity. He recalled his responsibility. "I was the guy, the ranger, who was taking her clothes and meeting her about a block from Long's Peak Inn somewhere on the trail, and she'd change her clothes and go stay at Long's Peak Inn for several, maybe three days, and then she'd suddenly disappear on signals to me and she'd be over at Fern Lake or some place in her leopard skin. Well I came in one night, --I guess I was tired or something, and I blew my top to Way. I told him of all the stinking things to have to advertise the Park by, something that we knew wasn't so! I really told him off! For some reason Way never liked me after that. I found out that he was in cahoots with the guy who was writing the story for the *Denver Post*." The newspaperman was said to be Mr. Al Burch, literary editor of the news organ who owned the rock foundation now seen on the hill, behind the Estes Park parking lot on Elkhorn Avenue, called *the ruins*. Dixie asked for a transfer, then opted to get into another conflict and joined up in the war effort for service in France.

Even though no entrance fees were charged, there were more than 800 beds available at the lodges within the Park with an increasing use quite apparent. The year of 1916 had estimates of total visitors to the Park of between 47,000 and 51,000 with licenses issued at $25.00 per year to guides whom the lodges employed to acquaint their guests with trails that led into the back country. The first licenses were issued to Shep Husted, Cliff and Harry Higby, Charles Hewes, Glenn Mills, Harold Dunning, Edward Rowland, Sidney Golden and Emil Johnson. The first of many Winter Carnivals was held at Fern Lake in 1917, with 463 participants in snowshoeing, tobogganing and skiing events that recorded its initial casualty in a broken leg sustained by Eleanor Hondius. That same year Ranger Beehler and Captain Way located a 'camp site' within the Park on which would be constructed the Grand Lake Lodge by A. D. *Gus* Lewis of Estes Park, owner of the Lewiston Hotel, that first opened for business on a limited scale in June of 1920.

One of the early Rocky Mountain National Park pamphlets of 1917-1918, by its wording promoted both the National Park and Estes Park. The inducement to visit the ' two parks,' not necessarily to explore the greenery of the recently opened up out-of-doors but to spend some of the visitors' own green, strongly suggests it was the product of the local free enterprisers and officials of the recently incorporated Town of Estes Park. The National Park barely had enough money to put a uniform on the few Rangers recently hired as the authorizing legislation had placed an annual spending cap of only $10,000 on all Park programs 'unless otherwise authorized by statute.' The pamphlet verbosely described, correctly or otherwise, what a visitor could expect to find in the village and the Park after the Bear Lake Road had been extended to Mill Creek Road largely the result of Abner Sprague's efforts in

1918. "The new Rocky Mountain National Park and Estes Park are adjoining. They embrace a very wild part of the Rocky Mountains. In this region are sixty peaks twelve thousand or more feet in height, several peaks thirteen thousand feet, and Long's Peak, more than fourteen thousand feet. In this rugged region are glaciers, deep canons, two hundred small lakes, hundreds of brooks, and many larger streams. There are forests of pine, spruce and balsam. Groves of aspen and other trees. There are a thousand varieties of wild flowers, and more than a hundred species of birds spend the summer in this wild region. For several years there has been a rapid increase in the number of wild animals of the region. Mountain sheep are the most conspicuous, and they have become very tame. There are many deer, and elk, bear and mountain lions are still scattered in the wild places."

Its next paragraph reveals how National Park policy has changed over the years, especially the abundance of trout and the gathering of flowers. It made every effort to allay any fear those from the cities might harbor as they contemplated a vacation in a *primitive* area to the extent that it would be foolhardy not to bring the wife and kids out to the Park. "The region is almost as primitive as it was a hundred years ago. The only changes that have come are the good roads that have been built to the interesting places. The Fall River Road in the National Park is one of the most wonderful motor roads in the world. On it you can motor to perpetual snow, and pick flowers in the shadows of the snowbanks. This road is being constructed to the crest of the Continental Divide, and it will be completed before long into Middle Park and the Grand Lake region. Everywhere the trails, some winding into deep forests; others zig-zagging up to dizzy heights among the clouds. Some trails lead to mysterious places where fishermen find hidden pools with waiting trout. There are no poisonous snakes in the region, and the wild animals are not dangerous. The mosquitoes do not bother. If you would find a region wildly beautiful, natural, and quite unspoiled, these two parks combined offer almost any sort of outdoors that can be imagined or desired. Trout are stocked in every stream and lake, the roads and trails are marked, and the people are accommodating. There still lingers the spirit of the pioneers." The pamphlet's last paragraphs were the real kickers to persuade price conscious shoppers that Estes Park's merchants were *down home and friendly folks*. "In the village of Estes Park, which is easily accessible, are shops of all kinds. At them you can purchase camping equipment, auto supplies, Kodak films, pictures, and in fact about the same merchandise which you find in the city stores. The prices are very reasonable, and the stores and business places are permanent. Autos and horses are for hire at regular rates which are somewhat less than other resorts charge. There is a free information bureau in Estes Park which has been established by local folks for the purpose of assisting anyone who desires information about the region, its hotels, cottages, roads, rails, etc. In the region are scattered nearly thirty comfortable hotels. Each is conducted on somewhat different lines. The rates quoted are all American Plan. No matter what sort of accommodations are desired, you can find what you want at one of these hotels. Everything from the most modern and complete to the very modest country place may be had. Visit the carnival and ski tournament in February. Conditions are ideal for winter sports."

Auguring a brisk tourist season for 1919 with great possibilities after the cessation of hostilities in Europe, Captain Way began to wage his own war. By a contentious action without formal bidding nor any public hearing, he awarded only one transportation franchise to Rocky Mountain Parks Transportation Company for the transportation of visitors within the Park. F. O. Stanley, hotel owner and author Clement Yore, and especially Enos Mills, vehemently objected. They considered the National Park Superintendent's attitude a slap at local enterprise, a step backwards and tainting the Park with special privilege. Mr. Mills, having his own small transportation system to convey his guests through the Park, resented a monopoly effectively denying him and others free access to the roads of the Park. He vowed to fight this radical change of public policy in a Park for which he had labored so tirelessly to establish. This was at the time that most of the Park's roads still were controlled by the State of Colorado, and hence the National Park Service did not want a fight with anyone until the matter of the jurisdiction over the roads was resolved. The Park tried to make peace by allowing hotel owners to take their guests in and out of the Park without a permit, but Enos was not appeased and filed suit in court to break the monopolistic sanction. His case was dismissed when Judge Otto Bock decreed the matter was within the exclusive jurisdiction of the Department of the Interior. After the close of the 1919 tourist season, opposition became somewhat dormant except for the verbal assaults by Messrs. Stanley, Mills and Yore that continued more or less unabated. However all of the other 26 hotel owners broke ranks with this trio to chorus their approve to the Park's transportation plan. These owners, operating in a loose confederation, appointed Crags Lodge proprietor Joe Mills to ascertain if there were valid complaints of any hotel owner to the Park's plan for conveyance of their guests about the Park. None were proffered. However there were growing numbers of local business people who were not necessarily against the plan to keep out of the Park unauthorized commercial *rent cars* as they were termed, but angered over Captain Way's attitude that some said "bordered on arrogance and empire building." One could understand their suspicion of Park activities after reading the *Estes Park Trail* news item dated August 27, 1920. "Mr. Stephen T. Mather, Director of the National Parks Service is at the Lewiston Hotel. Mr. Roe Emery of the Transportation Company and Captain Way, Superintendent of Rocky Mountain National Park and his wife, have been among the guests who have been entertained by Mr. Mather at a dinner." Although the National Park won the lawsuits and prevailed in the process of the subsequent appeals, the situation cured itself within a few years when statistics revealed only about 15% of the visitors used the Park's designated system preferring their own means of transportation. Whether the franchise was revoked is not entirely clear, however the public roads reverted to free and unfettered use by all although supervised by Park Rangers.

I want to examine the history of the Fall River Road. Its origin paralleled the birth of this National Park, without which they both might never have materialized. Certainly the road itself, standing on its own merits, would never have received state funding without the incentive of federal participation in the National Park's designation. This road had first been spoken of as early as 1895, and in 1912 the Supervisor of Arapahoe National Forest asked that a survey be conducted to Milner Pass. The road was deemed feasible and interest grew on the eastern side of the Pass, especially in Estes Park and Loveland. Newspapers of Estes Park and valley towns proclaimed in their efforts to urge the state to fund the project that "it would all be below timber-line," a prediction grossly inaccurate. When supporters on the western side of the divide were able to learn of the road's projected route, they were horrified and angered as the survey line denoted it winding up Fall River, but diverting to the north to descend to the Poudre River to Chambers Lake and returning to Fort Collins! A scenic route to be sure but it was not the one to hitch the east with the west as the businessmen of Grand Lake were given to expect. Grand and Larimer County commissioners teamed up to straighten out this matter, and fast, succeeding in directing the twenty-one miles of new roadway to its original destination, Grand Lake and U. S. Highway 40 beyond. The construction commenced in 1913 after the State Highway Commission, created in 1909, declared that the contemplated new road from Grand Lake to Estes Park would become a state highway. The first segment commenced was the improvement of the old wagon road traversing ten miles of trees and meadows from Grand Lake to Lulu City under the direction of Grand County's contractor, Richard McQueary. After some discordance had been resolved concerning the bearing for the eastern portion of the roadway, its costs and who would foot the bill, convicts were moved in by late July of 1913 as the initial designated work force. The road enthusiasts had hallucinations of Mercury footed workers hacking away at fever pitch, pumping up the locals to believe that "it would be finished by next summer season." Far from it, for no more than thirty-eight convicts at any one time and using little more than picks and shovels were fracturing out the first three rocky miles of pioneer road for the next two years just to reach the first objective of Cascade Falls. The road from that point would take the form of a serpent weaving its way in search of its quarry, in this case Fall River Pass that was positioned at eleven thousand eight hundred feet in elevation.

By 1918 all of the basic grading leading up the western slope to Milner Pass' 10,800 foot continental watershed was completed. Records of the State Highway Commission reveal that from Milner Pass to the connection with the eastern division of the highway near Chapin Pass, "the road would lie within the Atlantic sloping drainage of the Cache la Poudre," with crews engaged in preliminary timber clearing in the summer of 1918. The Highway Department, as well as the two counties involved, assumed that the connection over the top would be below the height of Berthoud Pass, around 11,500 feet, and 'below timberline' as their newspapers had heralded. However in 1919 an inspired decision was made, through the leadership of the National Park Service and the prompting of the Denver Tourist Bureau. Turn the road to the west, increase the elevation of the crossing by six hundred feet and out over the tundra, and follow a portion of the Indian Trail Ridge pathway that the Highway Commission called the *high line* all the way to Fall River Pass. The views of the front range would be unsurpassed anywhere by this change those visionaries predicted although the maintenance consequences would be significant. Whether by following the original lower road alignment might have resulted in the highway being kept open all year is questionable but worthy of contemplative thought, and much hindsight for which many amateur *experts* qualify even today. On September 14, 1920 the contractor for the western section, Dick McQueary, drove to Estes Park from Grand Lake and the Park Superintendent, Captain Way, motored from Estes Park to Grand Lake, then to Denver and back home. This inaugurated the Grand Tours featured by the

177

bus companies that began the following summer.

In the first few years when drivers started up this twisting ribbon with no guard rails or other reassuring devices, there were many accidents and bus drivers frequently were required to be accompanied by one of the limited supply of Park Rangers. The local newspaper in 1920 was offering advice for safe and courteous driving with practical and homespun advice offered for the times. "The importance of the auto is being recognized today in appropriations for road building. Much has already been done. The opening of the Big Thompson road this spring gives autoists a fine double tracked boulevard to the Park. But the increase in auto traffic is accompanied by an increase in danger to travelers served. The driver in the canyons must always be ready to meet the expected emergency. Go on the principle that the other fellow is an idiot with a wobbly steering gear. Don't let anybody walk when you have an empty seat for it becomes an exciting adventure every time you overtake pilgrims on foot. Why not establish a reputation for Estes Park as the place where autoists pick up pedestrians instead of knocking them down. And finally, the autoist who stops on a hill and puts a rock under a wheel, should always remove that rock before going on his way."

Now that Rocky Mountain National Park was a part of the family of venerated Parks, an effort was made by the National Park Service to encourage the public's use of improved roads throughout western United States that led to the National Parks and Monuments it administered. In anticipation of the completion of the transmountain Fall River Road, in the summer of 1920 a road journey was arranged in association with local Chambers of Commerce to promote visitations of the Parks in western United States. Hundreds of autos were scheduled to make this first unified journey in a symbolic linking of all of those National Parks. Emotion ran high for local citizens as now the village will be joined to the whole world! Lodge owners licked their chops in anticipation of revenue from motoring tourists that was only a running board away. Estes Park played an important part in such activities as the Estes Park newspaper reported. "A procession of autos left Denver Thursday morning, August 26th, for Estes Park on the first stage of the official Park-to-Park highway tour. The party was headed by Mr. Stephen T. Mather, of Washington, D. C., Director of the National Parks. It was piloted by Mr. A. L. Westgard, the official pathfinder who had just recently completed the 5000 mile circuit of the national parks in a trip of fifty-five days. The official ceremonies marking this epoch-making development in our system of national parks began with a banquet at the Brown Palace hotel in Denver. Mr. J. D. Stead, president of the Estes Park chamber of commerce, and Mr. Joe Mills went to Denver Wednesday to be present at this occasion. Eight governors of western states were among the guests at the dinner. This highway, which connects twelve national parks with their varied attractions, should prove a great attraction to auto tourists. The Park-to-Park Highway association is planning a campaign for federal appropriations for the improvement of the poorer sections of this road. With proper financial aid this should become the most wonderful scenic route in the world. It is expected that there will be 250 cars in line by the time Glacier National Park is reached. The official party, opening the Park-to-Park highway, arrived in Estes Park the night of August 26, 1920 and had dinner at the Crags Lodge. The party left Denver at 9:30 in the morning and had a luncheon at the Boulder Chautauqua grounds.

About 150 business men of Boulder attended the luncheon. On the 27th they had luncheon at the Northern Hotel at Fort Collins, and 125 being present. They reached Cheyenne in the evening, where dinner was served to 200 guests in the Masonic Temple. Captain L. C. Way left the party here to return to Estes Park, but Mrs. Way continued to tour the Yellowstone National Park. The route of the party is from Rocky Mountain National Park to Glacier, Mt. Ranier, Mt. Lassen Volcanic, Crater Lake, Sequoia, General Grant, Yosemite, Zion, Grand Canyon, Mesa Verde, and then back to Denver, a total distance of 5,590 miles. Mr. Stephen T. Mather, Director of the National Park Service, had to return to Washington to prepare the official estimates for the annual report, but will rejoin the party on the coast. On the return to Denver, an organization will be completed with delegates from every city along the route for the purpose of getting publicity for the highway and securing congressional appropriations."

The Fall River Road now completed needed a suitable entrance where fees could be collected as well as to clearly impress upon the mind set of motorists that they were accessing a protected area with special regulations. Land in the west end of Horseshoe Park for the new entrance station was given by Dr. and Mrs. Homer James while construction material for this facility was donated by Mr. and Mrs. Frank L. Woodward of Denver in 1920. The attractive gateway included an archway under which autos would pass, reminiscent of one at the northern gateway to Yellowstone National Park. In subsequent years, as the Park's boundary moved eastward, the entrance station was relocated several miles in that direction to where it stands today, unfortunately now minus its log offices and Ranger quarters joined together by that picturesque arch. The visitor count by 1921 had passed the 115,000 mark, of which nearly 86,000 were from Colorado, 30,000 of whom cautiously and with measured trepidation urged their coughing and smoking autos around twisting hairpin turns of the new Fall River Road eager to see what their tax dollars, and cheap convict labor, had produced. Affixed to each of the windshields at the entrance station was an octagonal sticker that gave advice on the safe means to negotiate the new roads:

Speed Limit - 20 MPH.
Keep Out Of The Ruts.
Sound Horn On Turns.
And, Horse Drawn Vehicles
Have Right Of Way.

In opening the road every Spring, snow removal was always a monumental problem first performed by hand shoveling, then by steam shovels, scrapers and later with the application of more modern mechanical contrivances. Prearranging for the snow removal took much study and inventiveness including planting explosives at known locations of large drifts and deep accumulations of ice and snow in the fall after the road closed for the season. In late Spring of 1922 two tons of T.N.T. were detonated in as many as five or six episodes in an area known as Old Faithful where great slides rocketed down the south side of Mount Chapin blocking the road on a regular basis. The most noteworthy chapter of road clearing heroics commenced in October of 1924 as thirteen boxes of dynamite weighing 650 pounds were situated at those stretches of the road surface where snow and ice depths of nineteen feet in the winter of 1924-5 were anticipated. On June 1, 1925 Park employees held their breath, and certainly covered their ears, as the explosives were detonated all at once creating a trench six feet deep, fifteen feet wide and three hundred feet long to remove one thousand cubic yards of snow at once. The steam shovels moved in like hungry crabs, claws grasping at shredded ice, loosened rocks and thawing muck. These were followed up by workers hired to hand shovel the sides of the opened track, a task of promethean proportions fraught with the danger of cave-in at any moment. As a testament to the success of their efforts and courage, the road was opened to the tourists that season on June 14th, six days earlier than ever before. To give the crews protection for late Spring storms, a sturdy little stone building was erected just to the east of Fall River Pass. The stone mason, Carl Piltz who had arrived from Wisconsin in 1902, built it, and before his death in 1926 had constructed many stone buildings in the Estes Valley as well as over 325 fireplaces including those in most of the lodges. As an example of its use, the late Park Ranger and Estes Park businessman Bill Grove recounted this episode. "Lyn Coffin and I drove up Fall River Road one winter day in the 1940s to find out what had happened to the National Park's telephone line to Grand Lake. About at Miner Bill's cabin was all we could go, and getting out we tramped on snowshoes through deep snow towards the Pass. After cutting steps in the hard packed snow and locating only the chimney on top of the store building, the rest of it lost in deep drifts, we repaired the line and returned to the rock shelter cabin to spend the night. The winds blew so hard that you could barely stand up and the sound of the moaning wind was eerie and deafening. The next morning --and I will never forget the sight so help me!, there was a deep drift of snow **inside** of the cabin, extending from the door to the cook stove, that had been driven with such force, --right through the key hole!" This shelter proved lifesaving to many until the new Trail Ridge Road made Fall River Road's eastern section and the little rock shelter house redundant except as scenic relics of historical significance.

It was not just automobiles that were disturbing the tranquility of the Park in the summer of 1920, for the quiet composure of the canyons reverberated with the roar of an airplane engine. Although the plane did not land within its Park borders, it buzzed about its perimeter as its power to climb was insufficient to intrude into the collection of soaring snowy peaks. Flights lifted off from Stanley Field in the village, piloted by former Army instructor, Lieutenant Frank Yager of Florida. The passenger, seated behind the pilot in his Curtis 160 horsepower plane, was treated to an itinerary that included flights over Marys Lake, Sheep (Rams Horn) Mountain and Moraine Park at an altitude of 3,000 feet that ended with a low pass over the village. Albeit the flights were nearly injury free, Mrs. Alberta Yore did sustain a minor jaw injury when on one occasion the aircraft was unable to get airborne at the end of the improvised runway. But when the plane deposited its first passenger, Mrs. L. Virginia Locke, safely from Estes Park to Denver that summer in only fifty minutes, it portended commercial flights into the village to see the Park. In the village's efforts to move into 1921 on the wings of fabric and wood, the local golf course's Number 7 fairway was selected to serve a double purpose, the most bizarre being as a runway. This was all possible because many of the town's nabobs and members of the Chamber of Commerce held the majority of seats on the Board of Directors of the golf course. But after the two-engined plane from the Saint Louis *Post Dispatch* newspaper, here on some promotional spiel, had great difficulty getting airborne on its return flight because of the short runway and 7,500 feet of elevation, commercial flights were abandoned. After one last fling in 1944, when a flying service out of Fort Collins, Colorado examined the economic potential with negative receptivity from a changed public that had become more environmentally oriented, some of whose homes were now much closer, old Number 7 reverted to its preferred purpose of hiding duffer's golf balls in the rough or guiding them beyond a row of sturdy pine trees.

Captain Way left the National Park's service in 1921 to return to his cattle business in Arizona. At the time of his departure, some said "he did not leave a friend in town." I believe that it was not his fault that matters were rocky in Rocky, more probably it was only his showy and decisive style of administration that rankled so many. His successor, Roger W. Toll from Denver, was an active member of the Colorado Mountain Club and frequent visitor to Fern Lodge. He was truly a breath of fresh air for all, especially those in the village who thought *their new Park* was being taken away from them by the rough treatment accorded them by *The Captain*. Superintendent Toll was a practical romantic and a firm believer that the Park certainly was an analgesic for ills of the body and mind if one would only look into its pan-hypnotic terrestrial soul. Upon his arrival he penned these insightful words to quicken the step and inspire the most jaded of conscience. "Surely if one can ever grasp the infinity of time and space it is here, standing on the peak and looking off to the vanishing horizon. It has been said that great views create great thoughts and great thoughts create great men. Mountaineering in the broadest sense promotes the health and strength of the body. It teaches self reliance, determination, presence of mind, necessity for individual thought and action, pride of accomplishment, fearlessness, endurance, helpful cooperation, loyalty, patriotism, that love of an unselfish freedom, and many other qualities that make for a sturdy manhood and womanhood." Statistics often capture our minds to the extent that we make comparisons with them rather than examine the totality of the subjects for which those numbers were prepared. However, the following statistics do lend credence to the fact that this region of Colorado, called the Switzerland of America, was eminently qualified for its designation as a National Park. Within its boundaries that rise from its lowest point of 7,200 feet, visitors can delight in the fact that this National Park contains billions of flowers, millions of trees, thousands of wild animals, and hundreds of rivers, streams, small brooks and alpine watered tarns. Also, there are mountains galore, at least 56 snowy peaks of over 10,000 feet of elevation. Of these there are 35 over 12,000 feet, 15 over 13,000 feet and of course that stone faced denizen that creates its own weather complexities, Long's Peak, standing out on many distant horizons at 14,255 feet. It is a grizzled, snow crusted, craggy, dangerously beautiful mountain that we, who live here, never fail to study the first thing in the morning before determining the direction for another day of life.

In March of 1919 the $10,000 expenditure limitation was removed and in the same year visitor statistics proved that Rocky Mountain National Park was the most popular of all the National Parks. Though appropriations for Rocky Mountain National Park thereafter slowly increased, it was in 1923 after nearly 1,231,000 visitors had visited all of the National Parks -- many of them to this Park --that complaints grew vitriolic about how badly Rocky was underfunded and in need of support from Congress. Congress responded to some extent and appropriations were modestly increased to permit needed improvements, deferred since 1916, including a new Park Administration building completed in 1924 on Moraine Avenue in the village. Appropriations increased to more than $115,000 for fiscal year 1925 when nearly 225,000 visitors passed beneath the entrance arch and through the gates, and through the remainder of the 1920s appropriations averaged $93,000 per year.

In 1908 Enos Mills constructed what he called Timberline House, a small but adequate hostelry patronized by those intent upon climbing to the summit of Long's Peak. Located at the base of Battle Mountain not far from where Jim's Grove is now located, it occupied a site at an elevation of 11,400 feet. Neither large nor elaborate, it sheltered and fed perhaps thousands of people from all over the world during its short life-span in its spartan facilities. Hikers were grateful for its availability in such a hostile environment when winds of tornadic amplitude rushed about this mountainscape as if demon possessed. Providing a barn for the horses of those parties who deigned to begin their ascent of the Peak after riding up to a higher level, Timberline House was no larger than 12 feet by twenty-four feet in size. Divided so that on the southeast end there was a kitchen, dining room, living room, store room and office in close confinement, its northwest half contained sleeping quarters in even closer association. The sleeping quarters were little more than twenty-four inch wide shelves, stacked in three tiers, one above the other. There were certainly no box springs nor any form of padding, only a blanket, and a pillow if you were fortunate to get one before the supply ran out. The early settler, guide and writer Harold Dunning, a regular at Timberline House while piloting climbers, remembered his lack of sleeping experiences. "You were not expected to sleep for two reasons. First, who in sam hill could sleep on a board, half froze, except a corpse! Second, there was always someone yelling, singing, fighting, complaining, cussing, preaching, pounding, or slamming the door!" When morning mercifully came and overnight guests splashed their faces with ice cold water, drying off on a rough textured fragment of towel that served as their personal toileting habiliment, they were raring for their breakfast of sizzling bacon and eggs washed down with hot coffee. The cook, who frequently served double duty as manager, most often was a big jolly Irishman full of stories, and complaints. Some of his complaints centered on the eating habits of guests such as the lady from Boston who had made a request for boiled eggs, an impossible task for the hard working little stove that could never attain a boiling temperature for water.

Rates were extremely reasonable at one dollar per night for a bed and seventy-five cents for a meal. Supplies were regularly brought up by pack horses and there was a telephone that connected to Long's Peak Inn several thousands of feet below. Even at such a high altitude, all food and for that matter everything not tacked down had to be contained within strong galvanized metal boxes to avoid the perpetually uneven tradeoff with the pack rats that left an attractive rock or rusty can in place of a pot, pan, food tin or box of crackers hustled off to its personal lair. The wind was treacherously unpredictable, frequently managing to probe like icy shards its cold breath through cracks of the building. At times even the oven was filled with powdered snow as storms deposited frozen white moisture from purple-black clouds enveloping Timberline House and its guests. But it was all worthwhile as upon your awakening you were greeted by warm, glorious sunshine mounting a successful charge up and over the rugged rim of Twin Sisters Mountain. "The sunrises from the Timberline House were the most wonderful ones you ever saw!" Mr. Dunning sentimentalized. Then even more seriously added these words that plumbed the depths of his emotions to a bygone time of unforgettably harsh beauty and camaraderie, an era that has departed like yesterday's sunset. "A night at Timberline brings sights and sounds you never knew before. The birds and small animals lend a part as well. The cloud effects and peculiar noises of the timberline region, the northern lights often seen, and the company of good friends are an experience never to be forgotten." This little aerie for human eagles that defied the weather and the perils abounding above treeline, was abandoned in 1924, two years after the death of Enos Mills. It surrendered to those elements, with which it had engaged in near mortal combat, one year too soon for climbers who would have sorely appreciated its hospitality in the unprotected frozen world of January, 1925.

The beginning of calendar year 1925 Superintendent Toll suffered a personal setback as I alluded to in my tale of Fern Lodge. His cousin Agnes Vaille was making the first winter ascent of Long's Peak on January 11, 1925 together with a guide -- an emigre from Bern, Switzerland -- Walter Kiener. They had made the summit and were descending when she fell. Kiener went for aid, and upon his return on the morning of January 12th found Agnes' frozen body. Kiener had suffered with extreme pain from frost himself as a consequence of which he lost most of his fingers and toes. Another would be rescuer from Long's Peak Inn, Herbert Sortland, following his own rescue attempt, froze to death a short distance from safety. If only there had been a shelter for them in 1925 and all the others who had died before from the effects of adverse weather on the mountain! The first recorded fatality was Miss Carrie Welton, described as *a high toned lady from the East*, who after a successful ascent froze to death on September 23, 1884 at the Keyhole while descending under the guidance of Carlyle Lamb. During Roger Toll's first four years as the Superintendent, five persons lost their lives while attempting to climb Long's Peak. As a result of these tragedies, in 1925 he committed to have erected a shelter cabin at the Boulder Field. Since Long's Peak Inn was no longer operating Timberline House at its site 1,300 feet below the Boulder Field, fallen into desuetude including the removal of its emergency telephone, it was essential that prompt action be taken to meet this exigency. Toll planned that the shelter cabin, six miles by trail from the Long's Peak campground, would be at the highest place on the trail accessible to horses, 12,700 feet, that happened to be in close proximity to where his cousin had lost her life. Work commenced in 1926, and the shelter -- constructed of stone and metal so to avoid any thought of a resident using any of the construction material as fuel for warmth -- was completed in 1927. Its dimensions were eighteen feet square and consisted of two floors with an inside stairway. The first floor was used for dining and lounging while the second floor was allocated for sleeping facilities. A tall metal flagpole, fifty feet from the shelter, was erected to attract lightning away from the building, and an adjacent horse stable completed this outpost of rest and survival. A practical innovation was included for the bunks. A series of sleeping bags, in units, were sewn togeth-

183

er making the heavy package of bedding quite a deterrent to would be thieves.

Mr. and Mrs. Robert Collier, Jr. of Boulder, Colorado were given the permit to operate the facility to be known as the Boulderfield Shelter Cabin, and he and later his wife Dorothy served as the cook, accommodations manager and caretaker for many years. The Shelter Cabin was supposed to be air tight and yet, like Timberline House, every spring it was filled to the ceiling with ice and snow requiring much effort by Park personnel and the Colliers to get it in readiness for another crop of hikers. The winds, residents recalled, "hit like dynamite and then stop suddenly, and drive the powdered snow into air-tight structures." As late as the 16th of June in the 1933 season, it was necessary to bring up the CCC workers just to open up the trails to the shelter house as the snows that winter had been even more formidable than usual, tightly packing drifts into solid blocks of white ice. Robert Collier was a chemistry instructor in the Boulder School District, and when often teaching in the summer time and looking after the couple's young daughter, Dorothy all by herself served as *Uncle Sam's Hostess*, as she was called, from June through September. The Shelter Cabin could accommodate twenty-six people and it was highly in demand as one year's registration list revealed 1,513 men and 370 women climbers in residence. Guides were available and most climbers surmounted the North Face of Long's Peak with the aid of the long, but assuring, cable in an average time of two and one-half hours to reach the peak's apex. The descent was the present trail, down the Home Stretch, then descending the Trough, along the Shelf trail that now has the *Fried Egg* markings and back to the shelter cabin through the Keyhole. When the cable was still in use the record for an ascent to the crest was recorded by a Colorado University student in a scant thirty-four minutes. Supplies were packed in by mule and the Shelter Cabin was connected with Rangers far below by telephone. Dorothy was remembered as a peace maker when tempers flared in the rarified air, and cared for her guests and their horses. She cooked meals, assigned and tended the beds, organized and led rescue parties when needed, and much more while supplementing her family's income from her elevated, rocky perch. Dorothy, years after she had terminated her employment on one of nature's proud pinnacles, said her work was all worth while. "I got the best," she phrased epigrammatically in reference to her guests, "for only the good sports came past timberline a thousand feet below." After ten years of torment from the elements that battered the door of the Shelter House for admission, rocks under the structure began shifting to cause the walls to crack. That, together with the need to shovel out the snow each spring and supply the cabin frequently by overworked personal and low funded budgets, the unit was dynamited by the National Park officials in 1937. A small shelter cabin still stands nearby, erected by the Agnes' father in 1926 to her memory, to which a plaque attached retells the tragedy that all started out with such high hopes and sunny skies.

The placement of the cable to which I have alluded was a concomitant to the erection of the cabin and was near the route of Agnes' descent and death. It would remain for the use of climbers on Long's Peak north route for many years until it too was removed long after the Shelter Cabin was only a memory. The cable consisted of two lengths, one 160 feet and the other forty feet, five-eighth' in thickness, and fabricated from galvanized iron. Carried in by pack train under the leadership of Park Ranger Jack Moomaw

with the able assistance of Glenn Walker and Harry Simpson, it was of sufficient strength to sustain loads of up to five tons. In adverse weather and often suspended from the end of a rope, the men drilled into hard granite the
first of the eighteen supporting eye bolts at the awesome height of 13,500
feet. Completed on September 3, 1925 in just one week of extremely hard
work, with a planned gap of 75 feet between the two lengths of cable, the final 755 foot portion of the summit ascent could now be made in comparative
safety thus reducing the duration of the climb by one hour. In those days a
Park Ranger's duties were not as we view them today, for there were so few
of them and they were expected to perform herculean tasks on their own and
with limited supervision, equipment or funds. One Ranger, whose longevity
of service in one National Park has rarely, if ever, been surpassed, was Fred
McClaren. Born in Lyons, Colorado, Fred came on duty on the western side
of the Park in March of 1921. He continued in his distinguished service until
April of 1957 after which he was to serve as the Mayor of Grand Lake. The
vigor derived from a life principally lived out of doors as a Park Ranger sustained him as he attained the age of 100 on February 5, 1992.

Another category of early Park Ranger was the summer employee
affectionately referred to by the visiting public as *90 day wonders*, an alias
the employee resented because it was perceived as a reflection upon their
qualifications and knowledge. These young men and women, many successful
in other careers, lent their expertise to their government when it was short
handed during times of emergency and budgetary constraints. Many were
school teachers, such as Ben Slater and Bill Grove. In the 1940s, when many
full time rangers were away in the armed forces, substitute rangers were
employed whose enjoyment of their short term duties frequently led to full
time status as regular Park Rangers. They were required to purchase their
own uniforms --but never wear them into the Dark Horse Tavern, perform an
assortment of tough and dirty jobs such as fire fighting, clean up, equipment
maintenance and trail construction, and all for a pitifully inadequate wage.
Seeking to serve their country by any means possible, money was never a
measure of their dedication as their accomplishments spoke eloquently to their
worth. Ranger Slater was an excellent naturalist and interpreter of the forest
and meadows as he led groups of visitors along the trails. Ranger Grove, assigned the task of inspecting guest lodges within the Park to assure full compliance with fire safety requirements, never found anything of which to complain as he confided to me "Gee, those were nice places." Those *wonders*
packed fish in boiler cans on their backs into the high lakes, supervised the
trails, picked up the trash, patrolled the high roads offering assistance to
frightened and confused travelers, and compassionately retrieved the bodies of
climbers and those who lost control of their autos as did the four young employees of Bear Lake Lodge on the winding road. Was it worth it? A retired
business man who had once served in such a capacity, looked up from his
chair and said in no uncertain terms, "I was proud to have been a Ranger!"

I remember especially those pioneer Rangers who cleared snow, fought
pests, thinned elk herds, extinguished forest fires, stocked fish, enforced Park
regulations, built ski trails, apprehended law breakers and uncooperative
bears, spied on non-permitted *rent car* drivers, measured snow depths, drew
maps, laid telephone lines, rescued stranded hikers, *rode shotgun* in tour buses
up Fall River Road, built their own ranger stations, as well as courteously an-

swering visitor questions as absurd as 'when do the little deer turn into big elk.' Their objective was simply to protect the Park's resources, and they did what was required and much more to accomplish their mission. It was a hard, low paying, yet mentally stimulating and challenging position that commanded long term loyalty of decent, hard working men and women from an assortment of educational, cultural and economic backgrounds. I hope those that are gone all inhabit those Elysium fields, the paradise of Greek Mythology, where heroes and virtuous souls dwell after their mortal lives have ceased. A former Chief Ranger, John McLaughlin, succinctly summed up his feelings of what it was to have been a part of this early adventure as a member of the band extraodinaire. "Those were exciting days, vibrant with possibilities and opportunities. It was good to have been a part of the times." I for one am glad that caliber of individual was around when the public needed them, and doubly glad that we have equally talented and dedicated men and women serving the public in this National Park today.

In 1927 the Bear Lake Road was finally completed, Mills Lake and Loch Vale were added to the boundaries of the Park following the land exchange with Abner Sprague, but unsatisfactory negotiations were frustrating to the National Park Service that sought absolute jurisdiction over the Park's roads. After more political machinations by politicians in the State of Colorado, each party trading lawsuits, the United States Supreme Court ruled that the Park had no sovereign authority to regulate state roads within the Park without an abandonment and cessation of jurisdiction by the State of Colorado. The field of battle returned to Colorado where the Federal Government stood with hat in hand and a reminder of previous promises of cooperation by the State of Colorado if National Park status were granted, as it was. That cessation was forthcoming from the state in 1929, but contained concessions for vested interests in irrigation canals, water rights, and storage dams that later would savage the purses, property and persons of the Estes Valley in 1982. Under these constraints, the National Park now was free to pursue its dictated purpose of conserving this component of the public domain that had been legally assigned to it fourteen years before in great fanfare. The year of 1929 saw Edmund B. Rogers, an outdoorsman though then active in the banking business in Denver, became Superintendent, succeeding Roger Toll. Mr. Toll was transferred to Yellowstone National Park as its Superintendent, but lamentably was killed in an automobile accident in 1936 at the age of 53. Mr. Toll's memorial at the summit of Sundance Peak in the Park and erected in 1941, affords the visitor at the end of the high tundra walk a fantastic opportunity to view many distant peaks climbed and named by him. By the end of Superintendent Rogers' first year in 1930, there were 255,874 visitors frequenting the Park and 1,500 horses operated by twenty-two liveries made full use of its trails. Yet this National Park's annual support from the Congress was lukewarm as slightly more than $100,000 was appropriated.

1930 marked the beginning of the end for the lodges within the Park boundaries when Representative Edward Taylor, one of the authors of the enabling act of 1915 and who himself would live only until 1941, sponsored an important piece of legislation. The words were politically puzzling but portended no danger at first blush to business interests within the Park when local readers concentrated, as they were suppose to, only upon the words relating to transportation. The legislation read in part "Extend the boundaries of

Rocky Mountain National Park along physiographic lines so as to permit development of the Park's road system and easier administration of the Park through a district affording relatively easy grades." The acquisition of lands on the both slopes of the Park was certainly necessary to the proposed Trail Ridge Road to enable the road's construction, and no one on the local scene ever thought those lands taken would be theirs. The legislation that same year was followed up by a series of edicts by the National Park Service Director marking a radical departure from previous Park usage policy relative to concessions and the accommodation of visitors on private lands within Park boundaries. Director Horace Albright, examining Congress' purpose for this National Park, appealed to his misinterpretation of local public opinion in an effort to gain acceptance of his anticipated course of conduct. He engaged in the belief that free enterprisers not privy to concessions -- licenses on land within the boundaries of the Park -- were jealous of those who possessed them. He therefore held out a basket of sweets for which he expected the village fathers and mothers to savor and devour in mouthfuls of gratitude. He added, "If cooperation of the community is forthcoming...," then followed language to the extent that there would no longer be allowed any new concessionaires in the Park and that many of the existing ones would be removed. The locals were not clear what *cooperation* meant. He said, "If the businessmen of Estes Park village provided for the needs of visitors...," pointing out the need for local revitalization of the economy taking place, he would follow through and remove competitive forces within the Park that he thought locals agreed had an unfair advantage for the emerging tourist dollar. In essence he would eliminate all concessions except those holding the transportation franchise. What Mr. Albright failed to grasp about this Estes Valley was that all of the people's dependence upon each other, in their joint venture of economic survival, had no boundaries. Village entrepreneurs and those conducting business within the borders of the National Park were engaged in friendly competition from which there was no ill. In fact, the more visitors residing within the Park the better for retail sales within the village. Most lodge owners were close friends, often related, in fact many of them within the Park held prominent positions in service organizations within the village as well as directorships in the country club, hotel associations, chamber of commerce and the local bank.

To be absolutely fair to Mr. Albright whose service to the nation was exemplary, one issue that he and local Estes Park citizenry could agree upon was the need for more winter sports within the National Park. At the preliminary events, prior to the annual Ski Carnival held in the early summer of 1931 on the north slope of Old Man Mountain outside Park boundaries, he praised and encouraged efforts of community leaders to utilize the abundant winter resources provided by the Park. At a dinner on June 26th, he made these encouraging remarks. "I see no reason why Estes Park could not be made into a winter resort as well as a summer resort. It has been done in other National Parks, and we have to find a place for the toboggan slide, ski jump, etc. where it will not mar the natural beauties of the Park." At this year's event chiefly consisting of a ski jumping contest on the afternoon of June 28th, competitors from all over the country, including those seeking a position on the 1932 U. S. Olympic Ski Team, were invited. Local men worked all night on the 27th and into the early morning hours to pack in the

150 truckloads of snow brought down from Fall River Pass. It is enlightening to read that Rocky Mountain National Park personnel shared in the fun of that Ski Carnival and who also participated, with Superintendent Rogers as chaperon, at the Lake Placid Olympic tryouts for the privilege of representing this country in international competition in 1932. After an appearance at the June festivities in 1931 where he was made a life member of the local ski club, Secretary of the Interior Ray Lyman Wilber authorized a search for a winter sports site that resulted in the facility at Hidden Valley. By the early 1940s, skiers by means of a new rope tow powered by an automobile engine were propelled up the mountain thus ending the strenuous uphill climb by pioneering skiing enthusiasts.

In the beginning of its history the Park realized that facilities and services must be provided to the visiting public but that all private facilities should be excluded except so far as may be necessary for the accomplishment of said purpose, including accommodations. The government would not be providing by itself such facilities and services, therefore it sought out concessionaires to provide such services and facilities at reasonable rates under the supervision and regulations of the Secretary of the Interior. One of the first regulations promulgated, I imagine to clearly make known that alcohol and quiet appreciation of nature were incompatible, was that there would be no barrooms located within the National Park. When concessions were first allowed within the Park --there are few now other than Trail Ridge Store and several livery stables -- the government recognized that to provide such facilities and services required a substantial financial commitment. Therefore it resolved to allow the private providers "a reasonable opportunity to make a fair profit." Also, the government contracted to "give reasonable protection to the concessionaire against loss of its investment and against substantial increase in costs, hazards and difficulties in operation." As a point of information, in nearly all Park concessionaire contracts to reinforce the Park's purpose, was set forth this standard provision, termed by its scriveners as *boiler plate*. "Whereas Rocky Mountain National Park was established by Congress to conserve the scenery and the natural and historic objects and wildlife therein, and to provide for the enjoyment of the same in such manner and by such means as will leave such area unimpaired for the enjoyment of future generations." When these providers were necessary at a time when few outside accommodations were available, the Park administrators were very fair and went out of their way to be helpful. After 1930 reasonableness and fairness to permittees was applied obliquely, reflective of the Director's intent to target them for eventual removal. While blueprints were being quietly drawn in low profile for the eventual appearance of the Park unimpacted with private development, Superintendent Rogers in 1931 also was studying the feasibility of the National Park and National Forest Services cooperating to build a twelve mile road north from the future Trail Ridge Road to connect with the Cache la Poudre River canyon on the northern periphery of the Park. His reasoning was that visitors to Yellowstone National Park would be better accorded an opportunity to continue their visit to another National Park and then exit through Estes Park. In his exploratory sentiments expressed about the road bringing in more easily new visitors to see the Park, and consequently spend money in the village, some Park critics believed this was but a soporific economic sop thrown out for heightened revenue potential to assuage a community possessed with imagined fears of Park domination of private investment.

Obviously the new road never materialized for one reason or another, primarily due to financial constraints rather than environmental concerns as the public of 1931 was not as attuned to the plight of nature as the generation of the 1990s. The corollaries of the national depression plagued the surrounding valleys of Estes Park with its first casualty in the lodging industry, the Horseshoe Inn, selling out in 1931 at the same time the new Trail Ridge Road construction contractors were offering employment to many local men cast adrift in deep oceans of economic uncertainty. The thirty-seven mile long Fall River Road was proving difficult to maintain as well as to traverse. Rangers were on a standby basis to drive the autos for hesitant tourists, a roadway intolerant of timid or queasy drivers. In 1926, following a survey run to find an alternative route to avoid the difficult terrain of Mount Chapin, a way was mapped out to follow in part another section of the Child's Trail of ancient Indian passage. By October of 1929 the lower area of the new thoroughfare was under construction by a team of 75 men at work under an agreement with the William A. Colt & Son Construction Company of Las Animas, Colorado. Mr. Colt, at that time seventy-two years of age, previously had been successfully engaged in constructing ditches, road beds for railroad trackage as well as much of the challenging Wolf Creek Pass and Independence Pass highways. His contract required the completion of the long eastern segment of the road, seventeen and two/tenths miles long, starting at Deer Ridge Junction and terminating at Fall River Pass. The cost for the entire Trail Ridge Road was bid between $1,250,000 and $1,500,000 depending upon certain contingencies. The proposed road bed was not then called Trail Ridge Road but rather Long Trail Ridge.

Colt set up his base camp where Hidden Valley Ski Area was under consideration by local ski enthusiasts. Mr. Colt's answer to the question "Why did you locate your main offices there?" certainly proved advanced justification for the ski area's recent removal from the National Park. He said, "I'm having the camp built here because this is the place in the whole area that would be least bothered by snow." Colt's contingent of 185 workers performed continuously in three teams in an ordered sequence of mission. One team operated the equipment, another gathering together their personal equipment after completing their work shift to descend the mountain for rest, and the third team prepared to relieve the team then presently working. Equipment consisted of five gasoline powered shovels, five compressors, three tractors, three mounted blades, twenty trucks and eight horses. The weather during the winter of 1929-1930 was exceptionally mild with only one brief three week period when operations were halted. The flow of manpower was so efficiently managed that by September 30, 1930, fifty-five percent of the work had been completed. Charles Moody from Lyons, Colorado had the contract to supply gasoline for the parade of trucks, loaded with gravel and other road base material, that tilted and twisted their burdens up to the end of the line through the summers of 1929, 1930 and 1931. Little if any material was removed from the tundra area, and only then for shaping the sides of the road and turnouts to preserve as much of the naturalness as possible. An example of W. A. Colt's expertise was demonstrated by the lattice of heavy poles he positioned about to protect the rock cut portion of the highway that is remarkably preserved to resemble supporting pillars for an entrancing portcullis into a castle in the sky. Though he finished ahead of schedule, but still lost money on the contract, he was pleased with his work and was entranced with the sights he saw when on the job. If he had the final say as to the name for the completed roadway he would have given it the more picturesque designation, the Rendezvous With The Clouds Highway.

L. T. Lawler of Butte, Montana won the contract for the next portion of the contract, from Fall River Pass down the eleven miles to the floor of the Colorado River valley. The early Fall River Road on the western side of the pass was only partially utilized by Mr. Lawlor as the road alignment in his contract called for a road to be built for scenic beauty not just one of utilitarian proportions. In October of 1930 he mobilized and motivated his 200 workers on their objective to join up with Colt's group at Fall River Pass. Enthusiasm ran high in Estes Park as locals assumed that the road would be kept open all year, free of blocking drifts. However maintenance expense and fickle weather in the average years ahead would prove their forecast overly optimistic. The winter of 1930-1931 was severe with most assignments greatly hampered or shut down by the end of November, yet by August 1931 traffic could travel up the west side of the new roadway as far as Poudre Lake at Milner Pass. Crews, to their immense credit, on both sides of the Divide exercised great care in removing debris so as to protect weathered lichen covered rocks and the fragile tundra on the road that was to become the highest continuous highway in America. Designed to a twenty-four foot wide driving surface at no more than a 7 per cent grade and spanning thirty-six miles of the most unbelievably glorious panorama of hundreds of panoramic snowy peaks and pinnacles, Trail Ridge Road was completed in 1932. Traversing the challenging ridge for eleven miles at more than eleven thousand feet of elevation to crest out for a length of four miles in excess of twelve thousand feet, it still outshines all other continuous highways in the nation at this remarkable height. Its highest point is near Lava Cliffs, formerly known as Iceberg Lake, to penetrate cloud cover towards the stars at 12,183 feet. A true marvel to the persistence and expertise of man and tolerance of his Creator, the new transmountain highway was sorely needed in 1932 as the entrance gates at the Park now recorded 282,980 visitors. Near its completion, the *Estes Park Trail* editorialized the significance of the new highway and of its stout men who pitted their minds and bodies in a deadly game of chance of immense stakes against horrendous odds programed for failure. "These men are building an enduring monument to themselves in the name of beauty and of the spectacular. There is no other road in the entire world that will compare with it." Those of us, who now enjoy the majesty of man's achievement in harmony with these breathtaking creations of God whose splendid works gave reason and purpose to these human endeavors, can truly respond to the editor's opinion with a strong Hallelujah! Those workers in their gamble met Mother Nature's house rules and prevailed and we, who follow along the ribbon of asphalt and concrete that wraps together the package of unsurpassed alpine splendor that is Rocky Mountain National Park, say thank you so very much!

After Trail Ridge Road was completed in 1932 and completely covered with blacktop surfacing by 1935, the use of Fall River Road was limited by Park authorities. By 1954 that portion of it from Chasm Falls to Fall River Pass was closed to auto traffic. Later it reopened, as is exists today, to west bound vehicles -- uphill traffic -- for a few months in the summer for hiker access to the trailhead on Mount Chapin and for those desirous of an experience bouncing along an old Park road that still impresses those concerned not with speed but with the marvels of daring engineering exploits endowed with scenic qualities. The shelter building on the Old Fall River Road was removed many years later as an intrusion on a landscape scene of unparalleled beauty in which it played out its part in the saga to provide access to its vistas. The true marvel of Trail Ridge Road's whole undertaking was the fact that it was completed at all when times, economically speaking, were so gloomy. However, as I had pointed out previously, such construction provided needed employment for the local men of both Grand Lake and Estes Park who encountered a paucity of travelers in the near empty outdoor hippodrome of summer sport and refreshment. A national bootstrap program of President Franklin Roosevelt's New Deal is associated with the beautiful stone walls securing segments of Trail Ridge Road. The Civilian Conservation Corps, generally referred to as the CCC, sprang up in several valleys of the Park starting on May 13, 1933 as well as many other regions of America. Their arrival was truly auspicious from nature's point of view for the advance party of these raw recruits were welcomed by eighteen inches of snow laying upon the ground at their unconstructed camp site in Little Horseshoe Park. Tents were pitched for the first one hundred fifty-nine young men soon to arrive on the bright red tourist buses. The red buses transported the young men to and from their work of rock wall building on the newly completed highway, also to remote sites for trail building and tree felling with the result that their colorful means of transport and their work with axe and pick earned them the title of *The Woodpeckers*. The Woodpeckers earned an average of $30.00 per month including board and tent, and were required to send back home $25.00 of their pay. As they worked, tourists heard them singing lustily little ditties such as "Another day, another dollar, I get the day and my mammy gets the dollar." They were a conscientious band of young men from whom the country generally and the Park specifically received much in value. In 1934 a second camp was established in Hallowell Park, near Mill Creek. The Horseshoe Camp was only operational in the summer time, while the Mill Creek encampment was designed with wooden barracks and considered a permanent, all year, camp. Mill Creek camp was used until the summer of 1942 when most of the recruits bequeathed their camp back to nature's devices as they enlisted in the armed forces. The total number of enrollees at the two camps reached their apogee in numbers when three hundred fifty-five were at work in 1934.

The next lodge to be acquired was Moraine Lodge, and it was removed except for its recreational hall redesigned in 1933 as the Moraine Park Museum. Superintendent Rogers said that after Horseshoe Inn and Moraine Lodge were acquired they would be torn down "to preserve natural scenic beauty, especially along the new highways, and to make preserves for deer and elk." Sentiment for the old lodges was running high, but no concerted opposition arose as there were still many hostelries still operational within the Park and locals were preoccupied with their own survival in this reign of national depression. Colorado Congressman Charles Timberlake's proposed legislation of 1932 to enlarge the area of the Park backfired. It was discovered that the Stanley Hotel and the Estes Park Chalet, both owned by the transportation company and a firm supporter of the National Park, had been included in the territory to be added to the Park. This just would not do! Estes Park had gone along quietly with the broadening of the shoulders of the National Park and a fattening in its middle by other acquisitions. But locals balked at a government poised to encircle their town and bite off small pieces until nothing was left, and awakened to a nightmare, at its worst, of *The Captain* revisited. After concerted action by town folk, County Commissioners and the Estes Park Chamber of Commerce, the proposal died peacefully in committee. Next the Secretary of the Interior in 1935 *suggested* the inclusion of the Town of Grand Lake as a logical expansion of the Park. More objections from the westsiders and this plan, too, was shelved. But winds of change were picking up volume as those on both sides of the question --*How large should the Park become?*-- formed ranks but held their fire.

Tourists returned in increasing volume in 1936, and with resulting augmentation of traffic over Trail Ridge Road and, though there was a small stone restroom facility then in use, it was deemed appropriate to erect a store, museum and visitor center at Fall River Pass. That building, we now recognize as the store and restaurant albeit in enlarged and remodeled style, was completed in 1937 by the monetary contributions of the Rocky Mountain Motor Company that insured its continuing presence, albeit in changed corporate ownership and name identification, to present times. As the result of this cooperative effort, the company and its immediate successors Ted James and his brother Isaac of Greeley, Colorado --and perhaps even the present owners of the Fall River Store franchise -- gained a potential priority to operate the gift and food concession at this prime location for an uninterrupted period of time. Much later, in fact on July 16, 1965 on the Park's Fiftieth Anniversary, the Director of the National Park Service George Hartzog, Jr., chaired the event that opened to the public the Alpine Visitor Center that we enjoy today. The transportation company, often operating under the name of Rocky Mountain Lodges, Inc., had been providing bus trips for years as its route originated in Denver and up the Big Thompson Canyon to Estes Park, then over Trail Ridge Road to Grand Lake Lodge. Thence, via Berthoud Pass the passenger ladened buses proceeded down Clear Creek Canyon to its lodge in Idaho Springs, to conclude the tour through Denver's Mountain Parks, up Lookout Mountain, through Golden and eventually back to Denver. The trips of 240 miles in length cost between $20.50 to $41.00 per person depending upon how many nights of lodging were requested. Meals were included in the tours scheduled from June 15th through September 20th and were favored by those less inclined to drive the high roads that had few guard rails, walls and little oxygen for human as well as mechanical engines. Time played a part in the success of the bus tours as tourists on a shrinking vacation timetable could sample the phenomenon promoted as the *mountain experience*, for less that fifty bucks a head.

From 1932 to 1938 the National Park Service was to make further land acquisitions while at the same time assuming a stiff posture that alienated it from a large element of the citizenry of Estes Park. The Colorado-Big Thompson Project, then in the planning stages, had a goal of water diversion from western Colorado through a series of tunnels, dams, canals and storage basins to irrigate the semi-arid lands east of the Continental Divide where crops were a major component of the economy. As the most important phase of the project, waters would be diverted from Grand Lake through the thirteen mile Alva B. Adams Tunnel, right through the mountains in which was situated the National Park and create Olympus Dam and Lake Estes. This part of the plan would greatly impact Estes Park, adversely to some extent by increased demands placed upon the village infrastructure, but the overall effect would be very positive. It was perceived by most locals to be a new source of employment in a period of hard times, and as it would provide to the Estes Valley a more stable source of water and collateral revenue other than from the shrinking tourist dollar, it was destined to be a long ranging winner for the small village. The National Park objected, persuaded that the purpose of the Park would be compromised by such intrusion upon these pristine lands while at the same time it was aggressively pursuing its own program of removal of prior human development. The National Park Service was walking a tightwire however as this water project involved both state and federal eschelons of government to procure a dependable supply of water to the thirsty fields parched from previous years' dust bowl conditions of ruinous dimensions.

The Park lost its battle and over time the fears of Park planners were ascertained as grossly exaggerated when no visible signs of the tunnel and support facilities at their completion were detected. But the impact of this multi-million dollar project upon the tourist town of Estes Park, that annually slowed down its rapid summer heart beat to enter a somnolent mode of winter hibernation, was enormous. It would never look back again after the first trucks of workers arrived in 1939. When the project was completed in the middle 1940s, project workers were cast adrift and began looking for work in a valley that they had come to call home. The Bureau of Reclamation had erected a New England-ish looking community of small homes and support structures adjacent to the village, now close to the Rodeo grounds. At the project's finale the main administration building became the present American Legion Post and club rooms, other structures were sold and moved to various locations throughout the Estes Valley, and many workers purchased their homes that previously had been furnished them by Uncle Sam to continue their same place of domicile. People of Estes Park, and for that matter those throughout Colorado and in neighboring states, hitherto had the attitude that Estes Park was strictly a summer resort. But with the coming of the project and the influx of many new faces, Estes Park was discovered to be a good place to live year around as new businesses appeared and older onces kept open longer just to meet increased competition. One resident of the community remarked about the change after the tunnel was completed. "Before the tunnel project came in, there weren't fifty kids in our school system. After that, nothing in our village was the same."

David H. Canfield was appointed Superintendent in 1937 and his outstanding years of service were written in two installments. The first of which ended in 1943 when he resigned to enter the Armed Forces, and the second encompassed the period from 1946 to 1954 after he changed uniforms to again don the National Park's wide brimmed hat of authority. In 1937 and 1938 he inherited the enmity generated by the Park's stance on the water project and its intent to get rid of all lodges and most other concessionaires, now orchestrated from the Washington office of Director Albright. Sprague's Lodge and Brinwood Ranch and Hotel had by then been purchased and were now operating under leases however their longevity as destinations for tourists was in question. The most robust opposition to the Park's policy that certain community leaders classed as 'egregious conduct of buying up the valley,' was strangely the local school board. That board based its opposition upon a platform of decreased operating revenue. It perceived the school district's shrinking tax dollars the direct consequence of the permanent closure of lodges within the Park thereby decreasing the number of parents and children who lived or worked at those places of employment. In short, the school leaders' fear of finances and for the future weighed heavily upon their collective and individual minds. Despite the stalwart efforts to allay the fears of the local citizenry to an increasing presence of the National Park now more flushed with greater appropriations from a more friendly Congress, regional sentiment remained wary of such entreats. An enforced cooling off period came about as World War II preempted the full measure of men, both local men and Park personnel, to fight other battles of greater magnitudes than for brick and mortar. Those battles were against foes who were intent on denying fundamental freedoms to millions simply because of their religion, nationality or based on a warped vengeful attitude to get even for past, yet to us deserved, humiliation in an earlier bloody confrontation for turf, power and greed.

In 1946, after the last shells were expended and nations sought to heal themselves, demand for summer homes and cabins in the Estes Valley, particularly on private lands within the National Park, pushed up the price of these properties. Any thought of cheap acquisition of the inholdings as was the case back in the early 1930s was impossible, and just as well as the federal government had more pressing uses for its money. The soldiers and sailors -- after the glitz and glamour of welcoming parades had disappeared down the hollow of political rhetoric and diffidence --needed employment and housing, and factories required reorientation and retooling to a non-garrisoned economy by federal subsidy. That year Rocky Mountain National Park, again with limited resources and again under the superintendence of David Canfield, was unable to fully staff the entrance stations for collection of the one dollar per car admittance fees initiated in 1947. Many Coloradoans from the adjacent valley communities regularly sneaked in and out of the Park after midnight contending that no charge other than regular taxes should be inflicted upon a public for enjoyment of *their* National Park, nor did they deem it appropriate for gate keepers to count their catch of fish. The first one dollar entry pass was sold by the Park's Northern District Ranger, Jack Moomaw, at the Fall River entrance station. When the purchaser announced he had no further use for the pass, Moomaw promptly handed him his own dollar bill to repurchase it for his personal scrapbook of Park memorabilia.

Despite the near penury of the Park's purse, purists in the National Park Service's office in Washington were again on the attack, believing that overnight accommodations within this National Park did not belong within its borders. They loudly chanted their creed "--extensive human use tended to modify or destroy the peculiar habitat of the area" in influential ears that set Park policy. Superintendent Canfied was not of their frame of mind viewing differently the connection between lodges and the National Park under his administration. His philosophy, articulated to his superiors, was simply, "Hotels in the Park were a necessary part of Park operations so long as each was no larger than to accommodate three hundred guests." His opinion was derived from a considerable period of time personally shared with lodge own-

194

ers and guests who occupied rooms both within and without the Park. His conclusion was emphatic. Park visitors who stayed at these lodges within the Park "gained a better Park experience than tourists driving to the Park from lodgings outside the boundaries." His further evaluation of the parameters of supposed conflict with Park policy was that concessionaires should be granted long-term contracts at the expiration of their current leases. His arguments apparently fell upon deaf or insensitive ears as the Park Service Concessions Advisory Group in 1947 recommended just the exact opposite. It recommended short leases, stiff improvement requirements to gain any renewal of leases, and the eventual elimination of all, not just within buildings, but all forms of overnight accommodations. Did this mean no more camping? With the return of tourists after the war and with no obvious move to modify Park policy, the lodges regained their momentum to enjoy fabulously successful seasons from 1948 to 1952. Then the decline of lodges again set in as the first of the small lodges, Forest Inn, sold out to be razed to its original grassy configuration. In ensuing years the lodge operators under the suzerainty of the Park were advised their lease terms would not be extended beyond two to five years, obviously in preparation for the ultimate resolution of this protracted conflict between man's development and nature's conservation.

On the watch of Superintendent James V. Lloyd, from 1954 to 1961, many vacation cottages were acquired by *encouraged purchase* that belonged to families such as Faulkner, Willming, Wolfe, Husted, Fisher and Godchaux, these mostly located within Moraine Park. In 1956 the National Park Service announced that all of the facilities it supervised must be enlarged and improved in preparation for an anticipated influx of tourists within the following ten years. The program, called Mission 66, had two goals. Firstly, there must be more visitor and interpretative centers, more trails and improved roads, and additional tourist accommodations should be constructed within the National Parks, but this time they would be campgrounds. Secondly, these new trails, service structures and camping complexes were to be located in areas where they could be developed without diminution of the natural features of the Parks. This forward thrust to meet that surge of humanity forecast, before being swamped by waves of new tourists, was simultaneously -- paradoxically to Park critics -- associated with the effort to remove all historic log lodges within the Park from the lists of accommodations available to the traveling public. Thus that year Superintendent Lloyd announced that a new three mile road into the Park, branching off the state highway at Beaver Point, would be constructed. In the planning stage since 1949 after more than 1,032,755 visitors had entered the Park the preceding season, old High Line Road, called High Drive, was no longer adequate nor suitable as it presented a cluttered, mercantile appearance inappropriate for the front door of a National Park. By the end of 1956 total visitors to the Park since 1915 had surpassed the 23 million mark and, in only seven years since planning for the new entrance road had begun, annual visitor count had soared to 1,587,408. A new road definitely was needed, and since annual appropriations since 1915 had risen dramatically from $10,000 to $657,376, nearly 30% coming from boosted entrance fees, the Park was in a better position to generate new improvements. Lloyd was correct in his effort to remove increasing commercialization from the main entrance to the Park, having assessed that the best means to prevent this deleterious first impression was through ownership of the road and its abutting land. A new visitor center was then constructed in a distinctive architectural design of rock and copper-rust colored metal supports. Proving compatible with nature's own adornments although somewhat difficult to maintain, it has proven a valuable asset to the interpretative program for visitors but somewhat too confining for administrative needs.

Friendly pressure was applied to the remaining lodge owners occupying private land within the Park, as well as others who had unexpired leases, to accept early and fair payment for their improvements as an inducement to return the entire premises of Rocky Mountain National Park to its near original appearance. Again, much local sentiment ran contrary to the goals of the government in 1957. The Estes Park Chamber of Commerce challenged the Park's decision to raze commercial facilities, "...in order to restore the Park's natural surroundings," in light of the government's stated purpose to replace the old lodges with picnic areas and camp sites. The local newspaper offered up its challenge to a permutation of human presence within the Park in the form of this rhetorical question. "How will picnic areas and camp sites serve to restore the setting to natural surroundings?" The editor then verbally assailed the National Park Service's Director, Conrad Wirth, with further probing questions. "How much low altitude land does a campground for 400 people require," and "Is it more than the land required for lodges of similar accommodations?" There were other strident voices in the community who could accept the removal of buildings that were intruding upon a true natural appearance of the Park, but questioned their demise in exchange for campgrounds. "We favor guarding and the retention of natural beauty, but not a capricious change from one type of human use to another." The editor phrased his pronouncement for many of his advertisers, though I do not doubt his sincerity, equating the old lodges to a sine qua non of citizens' rights. "We can't quite understand why folks who desire lodge accommodations are to be denied the same privilege of *living in the Park*, for a hundred people living at a lodge create less confusion, less muss and fuss, than a hundred camping out." His statement then may not have been as relevant as it is today when we observe hard working Park personnel coping with burgeoning problems associated with sophisticated and demanding camping machines whose owners frequently make up their own rules. Models of recreation vehicles often are greater in mass than the individual cabins they have replaced, and the ruts and marring left on the soil with associated scattered debris are proving inimical to the purpose for which the projected *quiet camping nooks* were authorized.

In 1958 the policy to deal with concessionaires was firmly and finally restated. All non-federal land lying within the boundaries of the National Park would be acquired whenever possible and in an amicable manner as possible. As justification for this resolution, this National Park Service's statement evinced a clearer hindsight. "The lower regions of what is now Rocky Mountain National Park were settled quite early before any thought was given to setting aside a portion of the area as a national park. Thus, it was fully recognized that much would need to be done in the field of land acquisition to protect the Park in accordance with our basic preservation and public use policies." In 1958 a study revealed, as one basis for the National Park Service's position on accommodations, that fewer visitors were remaining for any duration in or adjacent to the Park and those who sought accommodations that year had an ample supply of non-Park located rooms from which to choose. By 1959 only one lodge and Deer Ridge Chalet, remained within the boundaries of the Park, and they would be removed under the jurisdictions of Superintendent Lloyd and his successor Allyn F. Hanks between 1960 and 1963.

The final demise of the last of the lodges was difficult for many of the old timers to accept as the Park sought a fulfillment of its destiny and regulation interpreted statutory purpose. Two opinions were voiced after the last pioneer lodge was gone that speak sincerely the feelings of two points of view. The first one is more factual although rings with a thrill of completeness. "There are still places in the Park that are not adulterated by man, where the only trails are those made by elk or deer, --and you think, My God! this is something special." The other is quite simple, to causes one to wipe an emotionally moist eye. "They are all gone now. You hate to lose a single friend. Change generally is a wonderful thing, ...but, sometimes its manifestations are difficult for the Old Cowpoke to swallow." We all have our own longings for the past, and I for one can take both sides of the issue and feel comfortable in my ambivalence. But that battle, of what remains and who must leave, is nearly over with only the battle over the preservation of all or a part of the historic McGraw Ranch to be fought out by the press, public and political pulpiteers in 1994. Now all must press on to the future and allow nature's own Creator to shape this place the way He chooses with as few modern human footprints upon its diversity so apparent as to bring dissonance to a melody of a cherished composition in tune with the song of a bird and a whisper of the wind.

Rocky Mountain National Park Dedication, 9-4-1915 (RMNP)

National Park Dedication Speakers, 9-4-1915 (RMNP)
In Center: Mills, Stanley, Taylor, Sherman and Carlson

Camping In Comfort On Long's Peak, 1910 (Mills)

Well Dressed Hikers, circa 1910 (Mills)

Early Camping In National Park, circa 1916 (EPHM)

Food Always Tastes Great On Picnic, 1920 (Mills)

"This Is A Wild Flower Madam," Park Ranger in 1920s (EPHM)

Autos and Picnics Just Go Together, before 1920 (Mills)

Ranger At Deer Ridge Junction, 1934 (Webermeier)

Young Ladies Hiking Club On Glacier, circa 1930s (EPHM)

Park Dedication Guests View Fall River Road, 1915 (EPPL)

Going Fishing, circa 1920s (Mills)

Flight From Stanley Field Over National Park, 1918 (Mills)

National Park Entrance To Fall River Road, 1921 (Mills)

Shelter House High On Fall River Road, circa 1920 (Mills)

First Rest Facility At Fall River Pass, mid-1920s (Mills)

Rock Cut On Trail Ridge Road, mid-1930s (Sanborn Souvenir)

Timberline House On Long's Peak, before 1915 (Mills)

Boulderfield Shelter House On Long's Peak, 1928 (EPPL)

Agnes Vaille Memorial Shelter On Long's Peak, 1926 (Mills)

CHAPTER IX - THOSE OFF STAGE PLAYED A PART

Stanley, Lester, Hewes-Kirkwood, Lewiston, Crags

Nature Seems To Have Reserved Its
Best Efforts In Planning To Beautify
The Earth For Man's Delight And Did
Concentrate Them Upon
The Forming Of Estes Park.
Ansel Watrous, 1911

It would hardly be fair not to discuss in some detail those lodges though located without the National Park that had much to do with the attainment of a mountain resort classification for the Estes Valley. There were many small hotels such as the Rocky Mountain Hotel no longer existing west on the Moraine Avenue road, Copeland Lake Lodge in Wild Basin, Columbine Lodge south of the village on Highway No. 7 now owned and radically altered by a charitable organization, and Lilly Lake Lodge a remnant of which now stands sentinel over the body of water that gave it life. There was the New Rockdale Hotel long replaced by the Estes Park Chalet near Marys Lake, Mace's Baldpate Inn that recently has had an excellent treatise published about it by present owners, and others that were as loved by their visitors as those who registered at better publicized, larger resorts. One day a complete story should be written about all of them, and certainly the hundreds of cabins for rent and cottage camps that sheltered the thousands who preferred a less structured program than was served up by those lodges and hotels that provided everything from horses to dancing, wild west exhibitions to guided tours, and from uniformed waitresses serving soup de jour to steak fries up ye olde streamside picnic grounds. For the sake of limiting this literary work to readable proportions, I will discuss only a few whose owners had a significant influence upon the village, the transportation system, the National Park, or those hostelries that were representative of the times in the life of the village of Estes Park during that important period of 1900 to 1915. All of the Estes Park lodges advertised this one thought that their owners wished to firmly establish in the minds of those contemplating a visit to Colorado. "You cannot see all of Colorado, so why not see that which represents it all, -- beautiful Estes Park!"

THE STANLEY HOTEL

Even before it was built, its founder wove a mosaic of many fabrics whose threads wrapped about a community in such a manner that its birth was welcomed as a deliverer to a village in need of a reasonably defined purpose. Its original owner personified the spirit, dreams and achievement of the community to non-Coloradoans who were drawn here after 1909 because of the publicity of its first manager, Alfred Lamborn from New York State. However the history of this hotel would be incomplete without probing into the Stanley family's love affair with the motor car that gave cause for the improved road system leading to Estes Park we now enjoy. Freelan Oscar Stanley was born in Kingfield, Maine in 1849 and was educated at prestigious Bowdoin College. His parents were middle income farmers and were the parents of six boys and one girl. He and his identical twin brother, Francis Edgar whom he called Frank and from whom was distinguishable only by the discerning nose of their dog, were mechanically inclined, willing to tinker around until something came out of their free wheeling cranial exploration with objects and ideas. Francis was more outgoing of the two, athletic, and a fine photographer as was their sister Chansonetta Stanley Emmons whose exhibitions of her craft have attested graphically to her enduring affection for rural life of New England. Chansonetta, a French word for *little song,* called Netta by her brothers, was nearly ten younger than the twins. When their mother died when she was a teenager, her father and all of the brothers she said "spoiled her," even through her adult years until her death in 1937.

Francis, known to others as F. E., had a strong attachment to photography that, through his interest and the inquiring minds of both brothers, led to them developing a new photographic process in 1886. It was incorporated into The Stanley Dry Plate Company and proved to be a great success from which they greatly prospered. They relocated their dry plate business from Lewiston, Maine to Newton, Massachusetts in 1890 and, with a movement towards individual assertiveness away from their twinship, each erected their own specially designed residences, --F.E. on Hyde Avenue and F.O. on Waverly Avenue. Their relocation to precincts closer to Boston was precipitated by the growth of the business necessitating adjacent railroad facilities to better access the markets. F. E. greatly appreciated bicycling, and though his wife Augusta was a large woman and aghast as to what her appearance on such a device might conjure up in the minds of her neighbors, she was game to give it a try. In a learning mode, her husband lending every form of encouragement as she went wobbling along for thirty feet, she fell once too often. "Never again!" she loudly articulated as her solicitous husband brushed off her long dress. "Never you mind, Gussie," he consoled, "I will build something that we can ride in safety and comfort together, side by side." He also was becoming loath to the moods of horses because of his experiences with them bolting, running away or being general nuisances. While F. O. was perfecting the manufacture of a device to load the dry glass photo plates into cameras, Francis set to work in 1897 on his version of a horseless carriage to be shared with his beloved. The brothers had first observed a steamer auto at the Brockton, Massachusetts Fair of 1896 and seeing how it refused to perform properly, thought that they could build a far better one someday. The idea was always latent in the back of F. E.'s mind, while his brother was much more occupied with the matter of the dry plate company, his music, teaching and making a few violins, a musical instrument that had captivated his interest since he was ten years old. Francis hit upon an improvement upon an adult sized four-wheeled velocipede, and although his first steamer was a small, flimsy appearing, 350 pound flivver, with only a rod for steering, it only cost him the sum of $500. He wrote to his wife, visiting Paris as was the fashion for many Eastern ladies of position, that his vehicle "will be four inches wider and five inches longer than our best buggy." He went on to compare it with those horses that had found forever damnation in his way of thinking. "It will not be afraid of a steam roller, will have no bad habits and it will stand without hitching, --and perhaps that is all it will do."

The little vehicle's maiden steamer voyage took place in September of 1897. Reasonably satisfied with his first effort though some of the neighbor's horses were placed in an attitude of near panic as they broke lose and wildly raced down the streets to the dismay and displeasure of their owners, F. E. made plans to try out his new practical toy on a long road trip on July 8, 1898. He reached as far as Kennebunkport when his steering bar broke causing the little vehicle to hit a wall. Although the steamer was damaged, F. E. was to survive this wreck. Interest was whetted as the news media praised the fact that the little two-seater had gone that far in so short a time even though his final destination was to have been Poland Spring, Maine. Many wanted to see this auto so he exhibited it in Boston where other competing automotive models were on display. In the challenge to see which vehicle could climb a hill fabricated out of wood upon the floor of Boston's Mechanics Hall, F. E.'s little device, little more than an engine and a seat upon wheels, won hands down with throngs of eager people flocking about it to inquire of its availability for purchase. The early vehicles, including some later models, were black with a long round hood that looked like a coffin. The boiler, heated by a kerosene burner working like a blow torch with a small but intensely hot flame, required a period of 30 minutes to attain steaming capacity. The steam produced drove a 2 cylinder horizontally mounted engine that directly activated the gears to the rear axle. When the engine turned, so did the rear wheels, --immediately. With no clutch and but two pedals, the right one for the brake and the left one for reverse gear, a startling discovery was made by a buyer. To his chagrin and pocketbook he learned that the pedal for the reverse gear could be depressed and rearward motion activated even when the auto was moving forward at a lively speed. Another effect of his discovery was that the little vehicle was an excellent tree climber.

Freelan became involved when he realized that his brother's invention had touched a public nerve that just might produce a profitable reaction. As both brothers had a passion for whittling, instead of hiring pattern makers they themselves carved out the wooden forms to serve as pattern molds for the first model. They commenced building models, one at a time, as orders came in for they would not be rushed into mass production. By 1899 they had purchased a factory in Newton, Massachusetts and were producing ten vehicles per day, and though orders were backed up to three months, still they would not be rushed. But if they had any chance to keep up with demand, it was clear that they must alter their manufacturing process, employ more workers, and meet the other requirements that would increase capacity and productivity. Reticent to take these measures as their photographic plate business was requiring more of their time, they sold their auto business for $250,000 to two men who had yearned to get into the auto business from the first moment they had heard about it and observed the steamer's stellar performance in Boston. In 1899 the new organization, a partnership consisting of John Brisbane Walker, founder and owner of *Cosmopolitan* Magazine, and Amzi L. Barber, owner of Barber Asphalt Paving Company, emerged as The Locomobile Company of America. F. O. was generous in his efforts to promote the car for the new buyers and demonstrated its capabilities by driving with his wife Flora Tileston Stanley up Mount Washington in an astounding time of one and one-half hours. After the bloom of enthusiasm to a common interest clashed with two very different styles and personalities, the partnership ended within a month as Mr. Barber continued on with the company to produce machines with the name plate *Stanley Carriages*. However often changing a recipe even slightly can produce a fallen cake, The Locomobile Company instead of steamers began turning out gasoline powered autos. Its fortunes fell on hard times as did Mr. Walker's own auto design, his *Westchester County* model also dissimilar to the Stanleys' invention, as both former partner's companies shared the similar fate of insolvency and receivership.

In 1900 or 1901 the Stanley brothers bought back all that they had previously sold at a severely discounted price, redesigned the vehicle to retain steam as the method of propulsion, and in 1901 a new model rolled out to the acclaim of the public. Their joint efforts would now be focused upon manufacturing and marketing the best steam powered vehicle in the world. George Eastman, founder of The Eastman Kodak Company, was concerned with the intense competition to his own glass negative plate process he was receiving from the Stanley Dry Plate Company. In 1901 he went to see the brothers intent upon purchasing their company but they were not interested. Their interest soon slackened towards the dry plate business, it no longer was challenging as it increased in profitably without much demand placed upon their resourcefulness. However, by 1903 the auto business was commanding more of their time and inventiveness was back on their minds, but concurrently F.O.'s health became impaired and his appearance exhibited signs of deterioration. They consented to sell to Mr. Eastman for a price estimated to be anywhere from $565,000 to $800,000, a price that would approximate three to four millions of dollars by modern dollar valuation. Kodak's gray box with black lettering, containing 4 x 5 inch post card size glass plates, hit the market bearing the Stanley Dry Plate name over its own and a trademark of a charging knight in armor upon his stallion, sword raised and shouting **On Stanley On!** And that's exactly what happened, for on the brothers went to further develop their steamer. They named it, modestly, the Stanley Steamer, a horseless carriage that operated essentially on kerosine heated water and assorted brackets of lubricants. The auto had a visage "like a flat iron and chugged like a tractor," yet with only a 35 pound two cylinder engine, the little contraption weighing but 500 pounds was capable of achieving incredible speeds. The brothers neither smoked nor drank, enjoyed teasing and were possessed of a passion for speed that would be demonstrated in an avant-garde design of a sports model of their steamer. They hired professional driver Fred Marriott and, in 1906 at Osmond Beach near Daytona, Florida, their steamer set a world's auto speed record of 127.659 m.p.h., even faster than the speed of any airplane at that time in history. While Marriott was racing down the beach he went airborne, ten feet high, and upon regaining terra firma the little machine broke into two sections. Fred was injured, though not seriously, and it was reported that the auto's detaching boiler flew down the beach for more than a mile, "blowing steam like a meteor." Thereafter this vehicle, and similar Stanley auto creations, was called *The Flying Teapot*.

In 1903 he was in search of improved health after earlier contracting tuberculosis, and his doctor had given him only a year to live. Because his

201

illness had reduced his weight to a pallid 118 pounds, it was mandatory that he withdraw from all work, conserve his energy, and the prescription recommended was dry air in a higher part of America. Freelan Stanley, his wife of twenty-seven years of marriage, her maid and his personal steamer auto traveled by train to Denver in 1903 when he was 53 years old. At the station his steamer was unloaded under the gaze of many eyes that reflected a mixture of astonishment, admiration and rough humor. Although somewhat inward to suggest shyness, he possessed a large measure of determination that dictated he accept most any challenge offered especially those thought up by himself. His arrival into Estes Park that summer of 1903 illustrates this attribute. Estes Park was known to many practitioners of the healing arts as a situs for those in search of *constitutional reinvigoration* and he was bent upon driving up to see this Estes Park while at the same further testing his little machine that had not surmounted mountains as grand as the Rockies. The two ladies transferred to the Burlington Railroad for Lyons, then up to Estes Park by the local stage operated at that time either by the Cantwells or the regionally acclaimed Nott Brothers from Georgetown, Colorado. Attentive to details and ever the planner, he arranged to have a young man join him the next day for the trip up the mountain to fetch the water for the boiler in his vehicle. The next morning arrived but not his companion yet, unperturbed, he continued on alone to Lyons to spend the night at Welch's Stage Stop north of town. Requesting one of Mr. Welch's hired hands to accompany him, he was turned down as such a trip in such a contraption was considered a hairbrained idea. The appearance of the driving machine was described by observers as looking like an *upside down canoe with spindly wheels* and Welch would not hazard the life of one of his employees on such a crazy escapade with a sickly looking man in a gray beard. To heck with his health and the fact that he would have to trudge down to a stream to fetch water for the boiler! This was enough of a challenge worthy of acceptance! He bid Mr. Welch adieu and, with cap pulled down smartly and full beard flying, chugged off upon his quest along a narrow and dusty little road that had not previously felt the turn of a rubber tire synchronized to the rhythm of a wobbling gear box. Completing his journey to Estes Park in one hour and fifty minutes, he walked confidently into Sam Service's all purpose general store on Elkhorn Avenue. Using the only phone in town, he shouted, "**Mr. Welch! This is Stanley! I am at Sam Service's store!**" Welch would not give up without further corroboration, and Sam himself was asked to verify the fact that indeed Mr. Stanley had just arrived. There was no malice in F. O. He knew that he had won and thought it was *the decent thing to do* to inform his friendly nemesis -- who had doubted **his** ability to drive **his** auto -- of his arrival. Perhaps he didn't want him to worry, or something like that, or maybe -----. Oh well, we are human and mature years don't change us in certain attributes, just emphasize the traits that have coined our individuality.

The Stanleys moved into the Elkhorn lodge for three months, and by the end of that time he had increased his weight to 147 pounds and felt marvelously renewed. The thin, dry air proved a better remedy for damaged lungs than all the bottles of patent medicine palliatives offered to soothe inadequately diagnosed maladies. When his health improved they returned to Newton, Massachusetts, but he could not forget Estes Park. The family returned in 1904 and 1905 for long holidays in these mountains where his body had been restored and his psyche profoundly influenced. Then in 1906 he erected their white, Georgian style home where they would remain for the next thirty-seven summers to confirm the curative powers of dry, clean air. One incident occurred at this home, amusing to those of us that read about it but not to Mr. Stanley who lived it, that concerned his meticulousness and his personal steamer automobile. The Stanley home in Estes Park had a fine garage to shield his vehicle from the vagaries of mountain weather. Routinely he backed his auto into the garage at the conclusion of each day so that upon his exiting from it the following morning it would be better positioned for whatever the winds and clouds had deposited the night before. On one late afternoon as he was returning to his home, the weather had turned nasty and the rain was beginning to form into shards of ice. Fearing for the paint on the hood of his immaculately groomed steamer and seeking to protect his investment -- as timeliness can be a preserver of fortunes, he drove directly into the garage without turning it about. Closing the garage door quickly, he moved briskly to avoid being drenched. The next morning, seated behind the wheel and without a single thought to the placement of the vehicle as his meticulous side for regularity and orderliness had served him well over the years, he drove forward, --right though the back wall of the garage. Thereafter he had installed in the garage a turntable so that the vehicle could be reversed and thus avoid a similar 'disquieting event' which was his restrained description for this inauspicious event. The house and garage, although now altered to fit more modern lifestyles though substantially similar to F. O.'s times, still peers over the town from the north side of Wonder View Avenue.

Stanley, together with Burton Davis Sanborn, a prominent irrigationist from Greeley and an original member of that city's founding Union Colony organization, purchased Lord Dunraven's interests in 1907 taking title in the name of their new corporation, the Estes Park Development Company. One of the conditions for Mr. Sanborn's participation was that Stanley was to build a hotel and improve the road up from Lyons. Having previously purchased 140 acres of land for a hotel site and after a series of his own sketches and architectural renderings were shown to potential contractors, he settled on the same Georgian style as his home. With Stanley acting as his own architect, work progressed from 1907 until July of 1909 with much of the rough lumber being timbered from fire blackened trees in the 1900 Hidden Valley fire. As a point of fact, the Hidden Valley fire was accidently caused by National Forest Ranger Joe Ryan who, in attempting to burn off the huge piles of sawdust left over from the sawmill operation of Walter Fulton, unintentionally let it get away from him. That blackened timber, cut by what was described as "a sooty bunch of men," was rough sawn near Bierstadt Lake by Reverend Albin Griffith's resident crew of nine men including his sons Dan, and John. In horse drawn wagons it was hauled to Dr. Homer James' single surface planer at the west end of the village for sizing wherefrom it finished its journey to the building site. Finished wood for the interior and exterior adornments was hauled up in wagons from Denver through Lyons on Mr. Stanley's improved road.

The road up to the hotel commenced on east Elkhorn Avenue, between two stone pillars adjacent to which was a large gate house with quarters for Walter E. Baldridge, his wife Winifred Rebecca and their family of three daughters. Mr. Baldridge had been hired by Mr. Stanley on the recommendation of J. D. Stead where Walter, on assignment for a Denver electrical contractor, was wiring Stead's Ranch for the first time in 1915. Two of the Baldridge girls later became prominent in the affairs of the village of Estes Park. The late Wilma Glendenning owned and operated her beauty shop, first called the Jade Beauty shop. Margaret Houston, the youngest and residing in her late parent's white Dutch colonial home on Moraine Avenue, a replica of the gate house but with a modified roof line to accommodate tenants, was the first woman elected to the town's Board of Trustees. Margaret remembers the frequent steamer rides she shared with Mr. Stanley who picked her up at the gate house to continue out to Sprague's Lodge. They visited F. O.'s power plant west of town, to other destinations that would be pleasing to *his young friend,* and wherever else his curiosity carried him. The gate house was later moved to the west side of the hotel where it can still be seen performing a useful function as housing for current hotel employees. The road then gracefully swooped up to the front porch steps of the large building that might suggest in the mind of the reader that in 1909 it was out of place. To the contrary. Those villagers who had lived through the Victorian age of the 1890s, considered it admirably suited to the lofty and picturesque topography it occupied. To prove its acceptance by a community of a few hundred independent thinking mountain people, no words of scorn, envy or small town talk ever were directed its way. Village folk liked it because they liked and admired F. O. Stanley for what he had already done, and would do, for their community. He was to accomplish far more that erecting a hotel where visitors could sleep and eat in style. He built a transportation building in the center of town, engineered and laid out at his own expense a water and electrical system, donated land to the community, organized the Estes Park Bank and became a durable supporter of a new National Park at which dedicatory celebration his support was acknowledged. He hobnobbed with the citizenry at Service's General Store where he often was observed giving the children candy and telling stories to those gathered about the warm stove. Stanley was often heard to remark that if he had started Estes Park he would have faced the front of the stores and houses towards the river rather than their back doors. Present town officials at long last are following his judgment as much needed improvements along the rivers of the community have been made to enhance the beauty of this quaint village.

Mr. Stanley planned on naming his hotel The Dunraven, after the Irish peer who had led the way with his own spa, but thought better of that idea and initiated a referendum for the village residents to come with a suitable name. They were unanimous in its name. Of course it would be called The Stanley Hotel and early advertisements heralded to the traveling public what would be its quality. "The Stanley Hotel is strictly a first class hotel conducted upon American lines, yet offering the same service that would be demanded of renowned hotels in Chicago, New York, London or Paris!" Mr. Stanley would not have it otherwise. Before the hotel was completed F. O. threw across Fall River the Cascade Dam needed to power his new hydro plant's turbine for the electrical requirements at the hotel. Anybody in town could purchase electrical power from him at a very reasonable cost, and they jumped to this opportunity as never before had it been available in the village. Thus the hotel was totally electrified including a large fully equipped kitchen, but a sudden lack of power delayed its formal grand opening on July

4, 1909. That day, as water was released from dam to plunge down through wooden pipes to enter the power plant and spin the turbine, the last section of the pipe buckled and broke as the result of a rock catching in the pipe. The old power plant, not currently used, still can be seen at the west end of old Fish Hatchery Road out the Fall River Road in its original color of paint that matched the hotel it served.

Although the grand opening for the general public occurred on July 4th, the hotel had previously opened to its first convention, a convocation of pharmacists from throughout Colorado, on June 23rd. Arriving at Loveland by train to the strains of a lively brass band, they were driven towards the Big Thompson Canyon in twenty-one, eight passenger, touring cars. Mr. Stanley met the entourage as it reached the mouth of the canyon and, as F. O. enjoyed playing good humored tricks on his friends, he led them up the canyon close upon an overhanging projection on which he had positioned a large stuffed grizzly bear adjacent to the road. This immediately brought the caravan to an abrupt halt. Some of the conventionaires were so sure it was real that weapons were drawn for an imminent shoot out until their error was pointed out by the laughter of those in cahoots, including the ringleader who enjoyed his own prank immensely. *The Rocky Mountain News* described the new hotel with marked hyperbole. "It is simply palatial, equaling anything of its size in the world. It is luxurious and modern even to the great kitchen where cooking is done entirely by electricity. It takes first rank with any resort in the world. Its view of the mountains and its setting rivals Switzerland." The pharmacists were even more eloquent in their praise as mortal F. O. now found himself in competition with the celestials on high. "With a site unequaled in Colorado, and being conceded on earth, nature has combined with the great philanthropist to perfect a dwelling place for man that gods may envy."

The hotel was three stories high, with a full basement, and contained 105 rooms. Painted soft yellow, considered by F. O. as *an eastern color* to match the motif of the hotel's furnishings, it was finished off with a red roof that many thought created the appearance of a European mountain lodge. A king's ransom for those times as it might indicate at a cost of $500,000, F. O. paid cash as he did not believe in using credit nor any form of financing, advice that modern man and woman might prudently consider. In fact when he was producing steamers back in Massachusetts at this same time, he refused to allow a vehicle released from the factory until it had been fully paid, and in cash. You might be interested in two other rules of his auto business. The brothers sold only to customers they analyzed to have the 'right personality for the auto,' --whatever that might be, also, if any customer ever asked for a **written** guarantee, that customer's order was cancelled. To challenge the Stanley reputation or impugn the craftsmanship of their products approached blasphemy, deserving of prompt retribution. Touring buses in the early days transported many of the guests from the trains at Loveland and Lyons to deposit them in front of the hotel on its circular drive. In a two month period in 1911 the hotel was so popular that its Mountain Wagons, powered by 30 horsepower steam engines, shuttled in on their three rows of seats more than 2,500 passengers. As the patrons entered the huge 100 foot long by 40 foot wide front entrance foyer, they first caught sight of a grand center stairway leading up to the sleeping rooms. To highlight an ancillary use for the large front room, during quiet periods when most guests were in their rooms or when the hotel was between conventions, the manager's wife frequently was observed, --surreptitiously of course, rolling the full length of the room in an effort to keep her waist trim and her hips firm. That room, like many others, had soft crimson and white walls with floor coverings woven from English fabrics of coordinated colors and wherein guests could slouch down in soft green leather chairs and settees. Guests enjoyed the music room, furnished and decorated in a Louis XVI design with damask of bright frost and gold, where melodies were played on the massive Steinway piano that had been a gift from F. O. to his wife on opening night. Of course the men were made aware of the fact that this richly appointed room of delicate decor was reserved during morning hours for the exclusive use of the ladies as their writing room. Under no circumstances would anyone be allowed in with noisy shoes, and especially no cowboy boots.

The solid mahogany furniture was of *Grand Rapids* design, all rooms included private baths and telephones, and each stair landing of the grand staircase was equipped with velvet benches. Throughout the hotel were carvings and pillars laced with arches to confirm the fact that no cost was spared in the hotel's appointments. In succeeding years guests could play golf on the hotel's nine hole course, trap shoot, enjoy tennis, take the kids to the playground or ride Shetland ponies and donkeys around the grounds. A rousing game of croquet about the manicured grounds was usually in progress, and many just relaxed out on the screened porches to study the mountains or the flower dotted meadows of the Big Thompson River below. Even a small airfield for small 'aeroplanes' out in the front yard competed with the golfer for the turf as late as 1927. The grand dining room seated 250, and no respectable hostelry would poke its nose out of the ground without smoking and billiard rooms for the gentleman. The Stanley Hotel game room was panelled in solid mahogany, heavily beamed, and had a gigantic fireplace near to the padded benches where ladies, bold enough to enjoy strong manly endeavors through a blue haze of cigar smoke, would be seated to encourage their favorites. Mr. Stanley was an avid billiard player to the extreme and took his game most seriously. One evening when once he missed a shot and a guest had the audacity to laugh, Mr. Stanley turned to the miscreant, cue in hand, and asked the guest to leave the hotel immediately. If one tired from all of the festivities and the staircase proved too strenuous, an elevator was at the guests disposal that worked by water pressure. The manager could always tell when it was overloaded for, instead of smartly rising to the selected floor, it settled slowly to the basement level where the load was lessened with a tip of the hat as several gentlemen graciously made their chivalrous exit sparing the ladies any inconvenience.

A smaller replica of the main building, called Stanley Manor and containing 33 rooms with its own dining, parlor and billiard rooms, was built in 1910 to supply the pressing demand for accommodations. It was recommended for 'single men on vacation without their families.' The *Little Stanley*, as it was termed, first opened the season and remained open later in the fall because it, and not its big brother, was winterized with insulation. An even smaller structure to its east was then constructed, The Casino, capable of seating 600 for artistic performances and its basement level was taken up by two bowling alleys. Many of the local boys earned good wages while serving as pin setters, but they were required to be fast on their feet to dodge the balls and pins that often ricocheted off their shins. Employee quarters bordered the main hotel on the west and to complete the scene adjacent to the Casino was a garage for guest vehicles and the fleet of thirteen, nine-passenger, steamers specially designed for the hotel.

On Main Street a sign advertised The Stanley Stables, just across from the gate house. It was not owned by the hotel but by Elijah R. Rivers to whom Mr. Stanley regularly gave $50 so that children who had no money to ride would not be denied that experience. *Lige*, as Mr. Rivers was called by his friends, was typical of the liverymen of early Estes Park days. Born in Clinton, Missouri in 1875, he was lured to the mountains by the thrill of living when history was still in the making and where there still was a chance to be a part the remaining adventure of the Old West. Settling in Lyons where he was fortunate enough to hire on as a stage coach driver from 1898 until 1907, and understanding the importance of the horse to the emerging tourist industry, he joined forces with businessman J. Frank Grubb to establish a livery in the village. Its proximity to the main gate of the Stanley Hotel mandated its name, Stanley Livery and Stables. Most liverymen owned a string of not less than 30 horses but in Lige's livery, after purchasing his partner's interest, the herd grew to three times that number. He routinely supplied mounts for downtown lodges, hotels and cottages as well as the walk in trade and for the special events of the village. Lige's men regularly led large bevies of horses all the way from the village to the Y. M. C. A. camp for organized rides from the camp to Bear Lake. As many of the dude riders were attending a sit down conference and not accustomed to long horseback rides, more than their feet were tender at the end of the trail. Lige therefore customarily instructed his wranglers never to allow the people to dismount at Bear Lake, for to do so might lessen the numbers inclined to make the return trip. Thus the cry echoed off the mountains as in early cattle drives as they neared the lake 'Keep 'em moving!' Lige reached the end of his earthly trail days in the early 1940s and his widow sold the largest livery operation in the Estes Park to Art Card about whom I have written previously. Later a livery stable occupied a portion of the hotel grounds.

In the ensuing years the Stanley hosted big name bands, concerts, dances, conventions and many cultural events. Before his orchestra's performance at the hotel, Lawrence Welk played his accordion from the back of a truck bed down Elkhorn Avenue, and the renowned violinist Fritz Kreisler performed in concert at the hotel for the famous people, potentates of industry, who were listed in the guest register. There was J. C. Penney who was a regular pool player with Mr. Stanley, and Harvey Firestone. Dr. William Mayo, the Schilling spice people, Jane Adams of Chicago's famous Hull House enjoyed a holiday at The Stanley, and John Philip Sousa even had time to tune the piano. F. O. Stanley had no children of his own yet paid for college educations for hundreds of children all over the United States including some from the village. Local resident Ted Mathews, in 1912 when he was but seven years of age, well remembered Mr. Stanley. His dad, Arthur Claude *Shorty* Mathews, was a freighter out of Lyons prior to his residency in the Estes Valley. This day as Ted rode *shotgun* on the seat of the loaded wagon drawn by his dad's four-horse team, he was handed the reins as they neared the Stanley Hotel's main entrance. There was F. O. and, impressed with Ted's ability as a horseman, handed him "a whole quarter!" Helen Clatworthy of Estes Park also remembered the attention he paid to children when one day in the late 1920s "that kindly man presented to me and my sister Barbara a baby doll." Mr. Stanley's interest in any child's future motivated him to regularly invite all the kids from the village to go with him to the local rodeo, --free, and at other times invited them up to the hotel where they would join him in the music room to listen to a lady play the violin, thereby gaining an appreciation for music. As a child he played the violin and at the age of ten invented a mechanism for the manufacture of the instrument, that in 1921 led to a business endeavor to produce violins in Massachusetts with his nephew Carlton. To be a violinist one needs to have a good eye and deft fingers, and be meticulous to detail. One incident reveals this attentiveness to detail and his sharp eye. The late Henry Dannels, a long time resident whose son is presently the Mayor of Estes Park, recalled an incident when he was hired for some repair work at the hotel in 1919 or 1920. "Mr. Stanley had us doing our carpentry work and he was watching us. We were to put a small piece of decorative moulding up on the third story of the hotel. My scaffolding consisted of a board put out the window piled on the end with heavy trucks. When I finished the little job and was coming down to where Mr. Stanley was standing, he remarked, 'that piece doesn't look like the other moulding.' I said, 'no, it's one-eighth of an inch shorter.' 'Well son,' Mr. Stanley directed while stroking his well trimmed beard, 'if it's alright with you, let's wait until we get a piece the right size.' I remarked to myself, 'three stories high and that old man saw that it was one-eighth of an inch off!" When questioned about his excellent eyesight at the age of 80, F. O. reported that as he aged "I got second sight and didn't need glasses as I had earlier."

Concerned for his wife's safety and enjoyment of the hotel, as Flora had nearly become blind and always wore an eye shade, he never allowed any furniture in the public rooms of the hotel to be moved since she had learned exactly where each piece was located. They often were seen walking about, her arm lightly resting upon his, so that guests were unaware of her affliction. Margaret Houston was appreciative of the kindnesses extended by the Stanley family to her own and frequently took Flora on drives through the community ending up at the Stanley home where the two were served lunch by Minnie the cook on a beautiful pattern of Spode china. Margaret considered Mrs. Stanley her friend, and "a sweet, nice little lady that you would adore." F. O. was not sheltered from sadness that shadows all normal lives. Apart from his distress over his wife's debilitating condition, in 1918 he was hit very hard emotionally when his twin brother Francis E. was killed instantly in his steamer vehicle at the crown of a hill while striving to avoid two oncoming wagons in the roadway. F. O. lost interest in his transportation business in Estes Park and sold out Mr. Roe Emery. By 1925 his steamer production had essentially ceased as the invention of the electric automobile starter and new oil field discoveries made the gasoline internal combustion engine more economically attractive. At the same time, as he neared 76 years of age, he judged it was time to sell the hotel. After several years of negotiations with alternate bidders, the hotel and his 2,750 acres of deeded land except his home were sold to Roe Emery's Rocky Mountain Motor Company in the fall of 1929. That company continued to operate the hotel until well into the 1940s after which title passed through a series of complex corporate ownerships to its present owner, Mr. Frank J. Normali. He has worked very hard to preserve the hotel as a national historic landmark for the enjoyment of both local citizens and the many tourists. Perhaps they deserve less effort to preserve an eighty-five year old structure judging from the fact that so many present day citizens consider the past and its achievements not as worthy for praise as a more expansive yet uncertain view from the distant moon. When the announcement was made in the local paper on November 1, 1929, it spoke of the affection the whole town had for its benefactor. "Mr. Stanley --Estes Park is proud of you and your memory shall not die. You were a man who would not take advantage of any man, nor of the most simple soul, and a man whose love and generosity to a community has made it a common name on the lips of an entire nation." The hotel was never a money maker during Stanley's ownership, nor was it designed to be, as it was a summer only patronized town icon. Of himself and his hotel, F. O. summarized his views on the hotel business, ethics, religion and good health for all of us to ponder. "I would come out here in the spring and bring thirty thousand dollars to operate, and go back east in the fall with ten or fifteen thousand left. But I'm happy. My daily routine is work, fun and temperance of alcohol, tobacco and coffee. My religion comes from the happiness of others. Hope of Heaven and dread of Hell forms no part of my daily life." His longevity of life he also attributed to the fact that he ate one apple every day.

While on vacation at their home in Estes Park in 1939, Flora died at the age of 93 and the following year he died at nearly 92 years in Newton, Massachusetts to join her again at their final rest in Kingfield, Maine. At his death two remembrances of him were offered. The first, by Dr. Ralph Hunt, President of the Board of Trustees of Hebron Academy in Maine where F. O. had taught and richly endowed, was lengthy and exalting. The second, offered by an anonymous local person, was simple in its eloquence and praise. Yet in their diversity of syntax, they unified to expose to the world the character of this quiet, hard working, extremely caring and generous man. Dr. Hunt said, "Sometimes when men are given the genius, they impress you with the fact that they are conscious of that greatness. Mr. Stanley was not one of those. He was one of the finest exponents of democracy that it has been our fortune to know. Humility, frankness, kindness marked this man. Where men value fellowship and fraternity, this splendid soul made a contribution that enriched everyone he met. Where service to those who follow is reckoned, he will be known as a pioneer who blazed an upward trail. Mr. Stanley, musician, student, manufacturer, inventor and friend of youth, has passed on to the other life, where the Master of all good workmen shall put him to work anew." The anonymous contributor simply said, "He enjoyed sitting out in the front of the hotel, interpreting the beauty of the mountain range to guests. He could give a respect for the mountains that nobody else could give you." I raise my hand in a salute to a virtuously successful man who, though possessed with wealth, power and prestige, delighted in helping others, especially the children who would never forget his gentle kindnesses to them.

Stanley Hotel, circa 1909 (private)

The Stanley Manor, circa 1910 (private)

Gate House To Stanley Hotel, 1927 (CHS)

Gates To Stanley Off Elkhorn Avenue, 1930 (Otis Whiteside)

F. O. Stanley, circa 1910 (EPPL)

Guests Arrive In White Bus, 1924 (EPTG)

Main Lounge Looking East, circa 1920 (EPHM)

Main Lounge Looking West, circa 1920 (EPPL)

Dining Room Crew, circa 1920s (Willa Jean Graves)

F.O. Stanley In Cowboy Suit, 1925 (EPPL)

Stanley Rodeo Grounds & Airplane Hanger, 1920 (Mills)

The Hotel, Manor & Casino, circa 1920s (Sanborn Souvenir)

THE RUSTIC - LESTER'S HOTEL - H BAR G RANCH

This little hotel has had three names in its nine decades of life while at the same time becoming transfigured in purpose five times. It all began with Shepherd Newcombe Husted, born on Christmas Day in 1867 in Ohio and later to make his home with his parents in St. Louis, Missouri. His father, of English descent, was a ship's carpenter and from him learned woodworking and became a true craftsman of his trade. Clara Gertrude Crawford was born in Champaign County, Illinois in 1871 and, after meeting Husted near St. Louis, married him on June 29, 1892. Shep, by which abbreviated name he was known, venerated the openness of the mountains, wind through the trees and the isolation from his fellow human beings. He was more comfortable with the wild animals that to him were more honest and straight forward in their goals for survival. Rather than a paved highway, he much preferred the *less traveled* way of the poet Robert Frost, an indistinct trail leading anywhere where honest struggle and achievement on his own terms was still possible. He esteemed the frontier denied him in St. Louis already hemmed in by fences on the soil as well as of the mind and thus to the wide open spaces of Colorado they journeyed in search of a new life. Learning of the Estes Valley and visualizing it a splendid opportunity to acquire some land and raise crops, he was unaware of the fact that such high altitudes yielded few crops except hay, onions, and potatoes. A homestead was quickly claimed and filed upon, but if the records had been seriously inspected they would have disclosed claims to nearly fourteen hundred acres, under his name, his wife's name, and under whatever name sounded reasonable and believable, as was the case with many others of his day. Many early homesteaders to Colorado obviously had read of Dunraven's techniques, or had better ones of their own contrivances that were partly legal and illegal at the same time. After competing claims were adjudicated in the courts, others settled up in acts of violence, while many often were stipulated in agreement by a handshake when both parties agreed not to reveal openly their doubt to each other's claims, family names became identified with tracts of land on which they constructed a cabin to continue living. Such was the case with Shep as on a fraction of his original claims eventually culminated in fee title from the government registrars years after he had settled down in the Estes Valley.

Shep arrived to his claims five miles northeast of Estes Park in 1893 with three wagons, and on a tract of 40 acres of his original claims he erected his home. He drove one wagon, Clara another, and trailed the third behind. It was necessary to bring up whatever he and Clara would need for six months as it was time consuming, expensive and certainly hard work to make successive trips on nearly non-existent roads that tolerated no mistakes in judgment. The wagons were filled with everything he thought he might require, except fresh meat, including tools, wire to make nails and a forge with large bellows. When the home was finished he named it simply *The Homestead* cabin. A second cabin, somewhat larger and subsequently called *Shep*, followed in 1897 into which he moved his growing family. Both of these cabins and most all of the subsequent ones erected are still in use on the property today. Although he became famous as a guide and in later years lectured under the promotional title *A Guide For All Seasons*, he ostensibly claimed his land for farming purposes. His crops proved basic, hay for the stock and potatoes for the family, and, as the questionable expectation for an agricultural kingdom in the high Rockies became apparent in scant harvests, they realistically adjusted to build a resort and reap a crop from a rudimentary yet germinating tourist industry. By the end of 1900 four more cabins were erected and a man, who had previously applied his architectural talent in the village of Estes Park, H. C. Rogers, was hired to design a main lodge. In payment for Mr. Rogers' services, he was given a lease on a small tract of land on which a cabin was erected in 1901. The lease by its terms would expire in 1930 at which time the land, unencumbered by any leasehold or otherwise, reverted to whomever owned the abutting land. There was one interesting provision of the lease, that never was contested. During the thirty year term, if Rogers or his estate ever tried to sell or lease the tract and cabin to another, the lease would not be cancelled as the expected consequence. Instead Rogers, or the assumed new owners or new lessees, would be required to eat all of their meals, not in the cabin but in the lodge with all other guests of the lodge and pay the full price. Whether the penalty was the price for the meals or that the food dispensed was penalty enough since its quality was not revealed, is anyone's guess.

The resort opened on June 18, 1901 as The Rustic Hotel with Shep N. Husted & Co. as the manager and Rose A. Overback from Newark, New Jersey registering as the first paying guest. Her accommodations assigned were listed in the register simply as 'a solitary tent,' and rates charged ranged from $1.50 per day to $8 per week, with meals. Shep and Clara learned to raise fresh vegetables in their garden, milk and cream were supplied from their own dairy herd, and the delicious water for the guests's tables flowed from a spring at a temperature of 44 degrees. The hotel, advertising *The Finest View In The Park*, each day sent its own horse drawn coach to the village's post office to meet the Denver stage that left at 9:30 each morning and arrived in the village at 4:30 P.M. Before the lodge building even was completed, mostly through the labor of Shep, he was spending much of his time guiding tourists and hunting parties through the mountains of which he had become quite knowledgeable and considered an expert. Shep, of course was the guide and, in his brochure written with a self promotional assessment of worth, advised of that additional resource if one chose The Rustic Hotel. "The management has succeeded in securing the services of an experienced and genial guide who will personally conduct, free of charge to all guests, to all points of interest in the vicinity." By 1906 he was nearly financially insolvent as it was rumored he had received poor legal advice, although low rates and his lessening interest in lodge management were certainly contributing factors to his difficulties. Selling the resort in July of 1907 including forty-three acres to the Rustic Land and Cattle Company presided over by Fred Henry, Shep and his family moved into their third home located on adjacent property he still owned. Later that home was destroyed by lightning. His lawyer was W. G. Edwards and records revealed that Mr. Edwards at the time of the sale appeared to have a substantial financial interest in the Rustic Land and Cattle Company. That suggested a possible conflict of interest, but nothing came of it even after Mr. Edwards on July 25, 1907 was listed as the resort's new manager. John Rausch became the chef and advertised to the Estes Park's enlarging population that he "guaranteed good cooking and wholesome food." Financial stability was achieved when the rate was increased to $3 per day or $17.50 per week. In addition to the tents and cabins, the lodge also provided what were described as *sleeping apartments* on the second floor as well as a dining room, kitchen, parlor, smoking room and office.

Shep remained only distantly associated with the resort as his interests were now fully directed to guiding, forest rangering and lecturing on what he knew best, --the wilderness. On one noteworthy trip with which he was associated from July 14 to July 31, 1914, he contracted to provision with food, supply horses and tents, and guide a party of eight, including three Arapahoe Indians from the Wind River Agency near Lander, Wyoming, through the soon to be Rocky Mountain National Park. It was an endeavor originated by either Agnes W. Vaille or her sister Harriet and their father in conjunction with representatives of the University of Colorado and the Colorado Mountain Club of which Harriet was its Secretary. Joining with the group was Roger Toll and the trip had the avowed purpose of uncovering more of early Indian activities within this region and their nomenclature for its geological features. The Indians that provided much useful information were named White Horse, Old Man Sage, and Shoulder-Blade also known as Shovel Foot. The results of their activities can be found in a most interesting report of Mr. Toll in the Rocky Mountain National Park archives. One day a full account of Shep's life will be written, but for now I will but touch on a few incidents from his picturesque life. He was a forest ranger and became a Superintendent of several of the National Forests within Colorado. As a collateral fact, the large national forest within the State of Colorado in the Estes Park region up to 1932 was simply called the Colorado National Forest. Edith Roosevelt, widow of the great naturalist and outdoorsman President Theodore Roosevelt, granted permission for a suitable tribute to her husband's memory, and the name of Roosevelt National Forest was written upon the maps in 1932. Shep's service included nine years as General Foreman for the Civilian Conservation Corps at the first three camps established west of the Mississippi River and situated within Rocky Mountain National Park. But his episodes as a guide are near legend quality in the State of Colorado as are his climbing achievements that remain unmatched. His record for the number of ascents of Long's Peak, at 938, has never been challenged and, on an average, guided parties up that mountain twenty-six times per month. His final climb was in 1936 when he was nearly 70 years of age.

Shep Husted was also known as a horseman and an excellent naturalist, and he held strong feelings about not tampering with the National Park as revealed in remarks he made in 1926. "I hope that they leave Rocky Mountain National Park alone, --just as it is. I've seen too many national parks already putting in a network of roads across them. People drive about in those automobiles and throw their lunch wrappings around on the wild flowers!" One of his friends praised Shep's plant identification talents and technique. "One thing about Shep, ..he knew all the plants. If he didn't know one, the people never knew it." The late Frank McGraw, of whom I have written in the story of the McGraw Ranch, gives another insight into this colorful pioneer. "I worked for Shep Husted for two summers when I was about eighteen and of course anybody that knows Shep knows that he was a great dancer. Dancing was his first love. So we were out on pack trips and wherever we were, if there was a dance within ten miles, Shep would say, 'Now tonight we're going to the dance.' So I'd have to go to the dance with him. We'd ride all night to the dance, then come home and pack up the horses in the morning to go on. Soon as Shep would get up in the morning he'd be wheezy until all the work was done, the meals cooked and the horses packed, then he'd get to feeling' good. He'd feel good until about four o'clock in the afternoon, then he'd begin to get wheezy again and he'd be wheezy until time to go to bed. Then he wanted to lay awake and talk all night. I'd done all the work, but he wanted to talk. He always carried a little bottle of apricot brandy and he'd say, 'let's just lay awake a little while and talk and then I'll give you a little nip of apricot brandy and you'll sleep real good.' And you know, he never wheezed on the dance floor. I recall one trip Shep and I took, and we were with some people who had a dining room table. Some of those people that he used to take out, --they took everything in the world with them! Well, on this trip we had this dining room table and we packed it on a horse for about three days. Finally, one night as we lay talking, Shep says, 'you know tomorrow we get rid of the dining room table.' I said, 'how are we going to do that?' He said, 'just wait, I'll show you.' Well, we had one spooky pack horse and we loaded that dining room table on that spooky pack horse and we started down through the timber, and he rode behind it. He did something to it and away it went. That was the end of that dining room table. We didn't have that problem any more." The late great authoress Edna Ferber, who was guided by Shep up Long's Peak in 1921, wrote of her friend in her book entitled *Peculiar Treasures*. "Shep is made of iron and gold and granite in pleasing proportions. He is tireless, dependable, cautious and wise in the ways of the mountains." In 1941 the National Park was getting too crowded for Shep with more than 685,000 visitors, also his health was failing. His memories were full of joy as well as the sorrow that never leaves one after burying several of his children out on his old resort. He and Clara returned to St. Louis to live with their son Kenneth, and where he died on February 14, 1942. Clara followed many years later in Salinas, California in 1963 at the age of 93 years. A lake in the National Park bears his name also it is inscribed in Larimer County records on a tract of land they once owned that has been subdivided in lots known as Husted Heights.

Charles E. Lester was born in South Hadley, Massachusetts in 1863 and as a young man was attracted by the heady chronicle of the West associated with romance, drama and a chance to attain economic security. Together with his brother Will, they traveled to Colorado in 1886 to stop briefly before continuing on to California in search of whatever gold had been overlooked. But Colorado so attracted them both that they remained and were heard to say, "Here we stay! This is our land, no need looking further." As to what became of William at this time it is not clear, but by the spring of 1887 Charles and Lord Dunraven's agent Theodore Whyte had opened a small store a mile and a half north of Dunraven's hotel. In the summer he split his time between this store and working at John Cleave's post office and business venture at which locations Lester was remembered as an excellent merchant and a kind man who rewarded the local children with chocolate treats. In the winters he managed restaurants for the Union Pacific Railroad in Sidney, Nebraska and Green River, Wyoming. In 1893 his fortunes diverged into a new direction when he married Edna Brush, the daughter of a Jared Lemar Brush who was a prominent cattleman, banker and Lt. Governor of Colorado and for whom the town of Brush, Colorado was named. Mr. Lester devoted his initial married years to a series of commercial ventures including a printing business in Denver and later as the manager of the Imperial Hotel in Longmont. He could not forget the Estes valley and, after talking over its possibilities with Edna, he accepted a position in 1898 to manage Lord Dunraven's Estes Park Hotel. His former associate, Theodore Whyte, became in charge of all Dunravian investments when the Earl quit the Estes Valley to pursue adventures in Europe and southern Africa. The arrangement was most satisfactory, portended a long relationship, and Charles Lester was preeminently successful in his role as Manager of the leading hostelry in the region.

But his bubble burst in 1911 when the Estes Park Hotel was destroyed by fire. A friend spoke about this fire and its disastrous effect upon its manager. "That fire did more than burn a hotel, --it killed something very fine, very beautiful in the heart of Charles Lester, and life was never quite the same to him. Yet on and on he went, making more lovely the lives of all those with whom he walked." But his drive, and his acquired managerial experience over the previous fifteen years, now somewhat muted, would not be restrained in some emotional moratorium of self pity and he cast about for a way he could continue in the hotel trade. The Rustic Land and Cattle Company sold The Rustic Hotel in June of 1912 to Charles Lester and his reappearing brother Will, and as we do not read of brother William's activity at the resort we must assume that he sold his interest to his brother or was a silent partner. Charles took over ownership and he and his wife also were its managers commencing with the summer season of 1913. An advertisement appeared in early June of 1913 spelling out the enlarged scope of the hotel. Though Lester now owned the lodge, this news-ad was Mr. Lester's introduction, and Mr. Edwards' departing swan song to his better suited lawyer duties. "The Rustic, the Select Little Family Hotel, has the most beautiful location in Estes Park, commanding the grandest possible view of the Park, Long's Peak and the Range. Good, substantial home cooked meals, milk and cream from our own dairy, pure spring water and our own livery. There is golf, tennis, croquet and personally conducted riding and fishing parties. Our auto meets the stages at the Village. Literature and full information on application. W. G. Edwards, Proprietor. Mr. C. E. Lester, former proprietor of the Estes Park Hotel, is now connected with The Rustic, and will devote his attention to looking after the comfort and entertainment of our guests."

On June 14, 1913, Flag Day and deemed an auspicious occasion to toot his horn and run up his banner over his renamed establishment, this proclamation was prominently positioned in the local newspaper. "Lester's Hotel occupies the site of the former Rustic Hotel, which has been greatly enlarged and improved for the present season. It is conducted this year by C. E. Lester, formerly of the Estes Park Hotel, which statement is sufficient to insure those acquainted with the Park that they will be well taken care of." A full praiseworthy description appeared in the June 7, 1929 edition of the local newspaper that also broached a news reporter's opinion of Lester's Hotel's capabilities and the quality of service provided by its caring proprietors for the preceding sixteen years. "The hotel itself is rustic, being built with logs, cobbles and red cedar. The main building contains the drawing room with a large stone fireplace, the lounging room, smoking room, writing room and library. There are ten cottages all pleasantly located and convenient to the main building. These cottages are built in rustic style with porches and have from two to four rooms with a fireplace or stove in each one. All guests dine at the hotel in the large, spacious dining room. Guests return year after year and always find a hearty welcome awaiting. The best tennis court in the Park is located there and is one of the most popular pastimes of those visiting the hotel. Good livery accommodations are provided in connection with the hotel and at frequent intervals Mr. Lester arranges excursions to various points of interest including Long's Peak, Hallett's Glacier, Lost Lake, Gem Lake, Hague's Peak, beaver dams and Horseshoe Falls. Mr. and Mrs. Lester are the kind of folks one likes to stay with and nothing pleases them so much as to have their guests enjoying themselves. They are kind, considerate, hospitable and friendly and are never forgotten by their many guests. So when you are in Estes Park, do not fail to call at the Lester's Hotel, for the view you obtain from that point is well worth seeing and you will feel amply repaid for the trip."

The Lester's Hotel was operated by the family until August of 1933 when because of Charles's deteriorating health and the effect of the great depression reducing tourist business, it was sold and the Lesters moved to Greeley, Colorado. In December of 1934 he suffered a stroke and on January 11, 1935 died at the age of 72 years leaving his wife and only child Elmer to survive. Edna herself died in March of 1949 at her home, shared with her sister in Greeley, that had been given to the sisters by their late father. The Lesters lie buried in Greeley, within sight of their beloved mountains, fulfilling Charles's prophesy youthfully proclaimed to his brother in 1886, "Here we stay!" Clem Yore, Estes Park's late resident author and poet, wrote his friend's epitaph that in itself is a classic. The same words could be said for Clem himself who died in the succeeding year. "To me his friendship was a genial, sweet and serene thing, as intangible as a dream, and yet as palpable as a June day. You just knew something warm and kindly was about you when Charley Lester was around. I understand what Publius Syrus meant when he wrote, 'an entertaining companion, on the way, is as good as a carriage.' His five feet have trod the trails of these hills in all directions. His fishing rod has flashed on all our streams, on all our lakes, for he was a mighty fisherman in his day. But mostly will he be known for the loyal friends and royal man he was. Proud, sensitive as a young girl, dignified, determined, and as adamant to his decisions, as the very granite of these mountains. Charles Lester was one of the few men I have met in my life whom I believe was righteous to his core. His word was as good as his bond. He wouldn't have taken a copper cent from any man had it meant misery to another. I shall always see the sparkle of his fine eye, feel the warmth of his hand clasp, ever know that he was my friend, mine, and everyman's, a rare example of what Socrates called the natural aristocrat, and I am a better man for having known him."

The 1930s would witness the ending of so many of Estes Park's finest early day citizens, with one of the best being Clem Yore. His career took many turns, all uphill and requiring an abundance of energy. On his journey of life he was decisive, yet gentle, aggressive but not boastful, and strongly opinionated while in poetic expression he revealed a loving soul of which his community revered in memory at his death. Born in St. Louis in 1875, he obtained a law degree from the local Washington University. Law practice he tried, but then found journalism as his true vocation with employment with newspapers from Seattle to New York, and from San Francisco to Boston. After serving as the City Editor of the *Chicago American* he returned to St. Louis where he married his sweetheart Alberta McCauley Plondke. Two weeks later the couple were in Estes Park where he would remain for the rest of his life. He was not one for exaggeration, and when asked why he chose Estes Park, his answer was crisp yet abundantly clear and complete. "Estes Park met my ideal as nearly as possible as a place where life was worth living." He was an avid Democrat, in party and in his Jeffersonian philosophy, and dedicated to the preservation of the rights of all peoples. As evidence of his allegiance to local citizens, he joined forces with Enos Mills in the fight for free access to the roadways of Rocky Mountain National Park. In his lifetime, although a hotel owner himself, he authored 20 novels, two books of verse and 600 short stories, articles and novelettes. At the time of his death in 1936 at the age of 61, he had just finished his final novel entitled *Hard Country & Gold* that indirectly said something about his own life. The absolutely jammed town auditorium for his funeral, and an elegy orated by his fellow artist Dave Stirling, would have gratified Clem. Truly for him, Estes Park was a creative refuge where his life was well lived and where he mined the hearts of his fellow townspeople in a hard country, and found his gold.

In 1933, Julian Livingston who was prominent in the baking industry in Denver, Colorado and elsewhere, purchased the hotel including cabins, furnishings, four teams of horses and 200 acres of land for only $12,000. Times were hard, the price was right, and Mr. Livingston was advised that the hotel would make a splendid men's club. Instead of a haven for rich men, Mr. Livingston wisely elected to continue the tradition of fine lodging for the tourists at a superb location overlooking the Estes Valley out the Devils Gulch Road. It opened for the summer of 1935, and again with a name change, the H Bar G Ranch. The *H* represented Shep Husted, who was again to return to its management, and the *G* stood for Helen Gates, Julian's sister who would share in its administration. Printed stationery and china place settings arrived at the ranch, adorned with the H Bar G Ranch logo, but when Shep pulled out from participating in his old resort a short time later to continue his work with the CCC, the name remained, as it does today. From 1935 through 1958 it continued as a destination for tourists with the number of cabins increasing to eighteen and furnished with bathrooms now that the ranch's spring had been supplemented by a new well. Most all of the cabins had names attributed to them by Helen Gates that were emblematic of characters of the region or those who had something to do with the ranch. These cabins, as well as the lodge still stand, and you can read the wooden signs on the cabins, such as Shep, Dunraven, Homestead, Rogers, Dave Stirling, Tully for the alcohol imbibing house painter, Squeaky Bob and of course the one called Edwards.

The season extended from Memorial Day through Labor Day and the hotel had the capacity for fifty-two guests who participated in all of the usual excitement associated with a dude ranch, especially long horseback rides and camping trips from its own livery. Every year the kids at the ranch wired up one of the dining room chairs with a current of electricity that regularly sent a guest flying from the table. The merriment and bedlam of fun was not restricted just to the ranch. One episode took place while guests were away on a ride to Gem Lake. William May, President of The May Company and itself the owner of many leading department stores, was a frequent guest at the ranch. One very warm day he was determined that upon reaching Gem Lake on a scheduled trail ride he would partake of a swim. Several others, together with Park Ranger Jack Moomaw, had cooked up a scheme. Just at the time May removed his boots and trousers and jumped into the lake, Moomaw arrested him for 'disorderly conduct, endangering the fish' -- of which there were none --'and pollution of National Park waters.' He was released after a laughing admission of guilt and a pledge of purer conduct.

All guests took their meals in the lodge, and most came for six to eight weeks. Every Tuesday, as surely as the pasque flowers returned to the meadows at Easter Tide, Freelan Stanley had someone drive him out to the ranch where he often spent the afternoon and evening. Even though he had sold his hotel, he returned to the Estes Valley every year, at times without Flora who was too ill to travel. He enjoyed the fine food served at the H Bar G but often was heard to remark that the real reason for his visits was the view. He said, as he rocked on the front porch, that "the view from here is far better than the one from my former hotel." Dave Stirling, the incomparable talented and witty local artist, often visited the ranch for food and liquid refreshment, regaling the guests with musical renditions on the piano in a style unique to himself. Mr. Stirling was an adaptable oil painter, creating matchless scenes of the Estes Valley that are highly coveted today. He said often that "art is nothing but form, motion and color," and he was quite adaptable in his marketing techniques. Once, when a lady visited his studios within the National Park boundary and exhibited interest in one of his renderings, she commented that she was not sure whether the color of the trees would fit in with the color of her furnishings. Dave was heard to remark, "Bring me a sample of your room decorations and I will paint those trees to match them." He was a marvel of talent, energy and rich humor and his agile mind and great personality are sorely missed in the community. And of course Charles Eagle Plume always was in demand to perform at the ranch, usually for the price of a good meal as he was generous with his time. His dancing and paean for, and lectures about, Indians lore and his tales of butterflies, were unforgettable. Eagle Plume was frequently heard exhorting for racial cooperation, "We **can** all get along," a message that another of recent notoriety repeated in Los Angeles with questionable consequences.

Guests were certainly impressed with the scenery and the location of this little hotel, even hotel men from other parts of the United States traveling about to compare what they had seen to what was available in the Estes Valley. In the 1920s a prominent hotel man from Chicago spoke candidly. "I have been all over the world, in Switzerland, Italy or any other quarter of the globe and they haven't anything in the line of scenery that can rival Estes Park!" At the end of the 1958 season the ranch was out of the dude business as Helen was 67 years of age and choose to end most of her exhausting duties of twenty-three years as a resort hostess and manager. Lou Livingston, Julian's son, informed me the ranch was converted "to a camp for overprivileged girls," and two ladies from Chicago named Reinstein and Unger were hired to operate it. Helen remained as the cook and to handle limited duties concerning its infrastructure. The 60 teenaged girls primarily came from Chicago, New York, Kansas City and Cleveland. Their attendance was promoted by color slides shown by the two head mistresses who exhibited them with appropriate palaver about the fresh air and healthy atmosphere as they toured about in search of campers. The H Bar G Ranch Camp for Girls had been in business for two seasons when Julian Livingston died in the Spring of 1960 at the age of 75 years. Mr. and Mrs. Lou Livingston purchased the ranch from the estate and continued the girls' camp with Mrs. Unger in charge through the summer of 1965.

After a brief respite for the family as they regrouped to find a new use for the ranch facilities, it reopened to shelter members of the Youth Conservation Corps while they performed work in the community and the National Park. Then the ranch became the locus for hundreds of young men and women under a program of the Center For Research & Education, an adjunct of the Federal Peace Corps, through 1974. In 1975 the facility entered its last, and current state of mutation. It is now a Youth Hostel reorganized recently into a Hostel for all ages and, in its first year of true dedication to the purpose of fellowship in a home away from home at a reasonable price, recorded more than 1700 *bed nights* of traveling young people from all curves of the globe. Shep, Charles, Julian and Helen would be very pleased that the tradition of their little hotel and ranch continues on in service, not just to the local community, but as a host to the world.

Homestead Cabin Of 1893, Photo Taken 1993 (Private)

Another Cabin In 1897 (CHS)

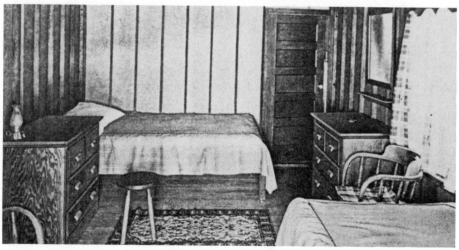

Interior Of Early Cabin Of 1890s (CHS)

Guests Off For A Ride, 1901 (CHS)

Shep Husted On Lecture Circuit, 1930s
(Lou Livingston)

Shep Husted, 1928 (EPTG)

Lodge Men At Rustic, 1910 (EPPL)
J.D. Stead-Howard James-Alf Lamborn-
Stanley-W.G. Edwards

View From Rustic Hotel, circa 1905 By Rogers (McDC)

Rustic Hotel, circa 1910 (McDC)

H Bar G Ranch In 1993, (Private)

HEWES-KIRKWOOD INN

Hewes-Kirkwood Inn, is derived from the names of the brothers Charles and Steve B. Hewes and their mother Mary Hewes Kirkwood who had remarried and taken her second husband's name. Charles Edwin Hewes, the older brother by four years and the individual primarily identified with this old Inn, was born on October 29, 1870 to Stephen Brown Hewes and Mary Catherine Palmer Hewes in Boone, Iowa. His formal education was limited, but through his penchant for reading widely and in depth, no cheap fluff, he essentially was self taught in many subjects particularly literature. His father died when he was but nine years old, and at the age of fifteen he was out on the streets selling newspapers to help support his mother and younger sibling. At age sixteen he embarked upon a career as a railway expressman that would fully occupy his working days for twenty-one years. While in Denver as he had broadened his activities into the transportation and shipping industry, he chanced to take a ride on one of the local stages to Long's Peak Inn in 1906. He immediately came under the spell of Long's Peak, smitten as a lover with the first breath of perfume of a creature devine. In 1936, he spoke about his fascination for the mountain to which he attributed superhuman qualities. "Having lived at the foot, and within four miles, air-line distance of the summit of Long's Peak for close to thirty years continuous residence, winter and summer, the great mountain has assumed a sort of personality to me which is difficult to describe. The nearest I come to it at this writing is, that he is a giant without hands that does things to you if you don't watch out. Eternity, great Mountain, that's you. A summit of Earth well known to the stars."

His second career commenced that summer when he was employed in the summer of 1907 at Enos Mill's reconstructed Long's Peak Inn where, as Charley wrote, "Joe Mills was the manager then and Enos played the *stellar role of the great naturalist*." Certain that one day this area would be on a major roadway, as it is today with the scenic Peak To Peak Highway leading into Estes Park, he succeeded in drawing his brother and mother to Colorado where they all took up separate but adjoining homesteads. No longer would he yearn for any other occupations than mountaineering, lodge ownership and poetry writing that from which he would look to for his income, sustenance and complete happiness. Enos Mills never forgave Charles his dream to build his own tourist lodge as Enos had reckoned in his heart and soul that this valley was his and should not be overpopulated with homesteaders, and certainly not by one of his former employees. In fact, after the Hewes-Kirkwood Inn had been opened for business for a number of years, when Enos learned that several of his own guests had ridden over to Hewes's place for entertainment and a meal, they were asked to vacate their rooms at Long's Peak Inn. Everyone who ever knew Charley Hewes, except Enos, loved him, not affection in the form of admiration, but honest to goodness love and from whom they received a greater measure of that sentiment with no strings attached and with no demands or expectations. His friend, the late Harold Dunning, considered Charley "the nearest Christlike character I ever met." But because of some bizarre reason that no one could comprehend, Enos Mills harbored his animosity for his closest neighbor to the north until the day he died, although Charley did not share that same rancor preferring to love everyone until his earthly life ended. If there were a defense to Enos' behavior, no one discovered it.

Charley's family, consisting of Mary Kirkwood, Steve Hewes and his wife, arrived in August of 1907 on Cantwell's buckboard stage from Lyons to Sam Service's store in the village. Continuing on to their homesteads previously unseen, they arrived by the mail wagon from town to Charley's cabin located at an elevation of nearly 9,100 feet. Steve Hewes described how the main lodge and cabins were first constructed. "Brother Charles and I cut down the logs and built mother's cabin, laying the first logs September 21, 1907, and we moved in Thanksgiving Day that year. We got the cabin chinked on the outside but Charles and I chinked the inside in the dead of winter with the mortar box in front of the old fireplace. I'd mix the mortar and Charley did the chinking, but it was so cold that by the time Charley got the mortar upstairs, it was so hard he could hardly get it between the logs." Over the next few years, by the time the lodge and numerous cabins had been assembled, the two brothers had cut more than 800 trees on their property during the cold, snow numbing ensuing winters. Before applying their whip saws in a concerted effort to fell them, it was first necessary to dig down through three feet of snow to reach the ground near the base of the trees. Most of the timber was harvested on Steve's own homestead tract that never was a part of the lodge's rental inventory. It was located just west of the present Long's Peak Campground and on which he erected his own summer home. The lodge's large living room was designed around the beautiful fireplace, said to have been fitted together, rock by rock, by the strong hands of the true artist in stonemasonry, Carl Piltz. The upstairs included sleeping rooms for the family as well as guests who soon found their way to this new lodge. The brothers also laid claim to adjacent real estate west of the Inn, known as *stone claims*, from which much of the rock for the cabins and fireplaces was quarried. By the time the resort was complete, the main lodge· building was only used for the Hewes' living quarters, their office, and recreation rooms for guests. In an adjacent structure of similar log design, guests took their meals in the dining room with food prepared in the adjoining large kitchen near to where all supplies were stored. Grouped around these two main facilities were at least eleven single and three double guest cabins, a laundry, stables, workshop and employee quarters. After the Inn opened around 1910 its guest capacity, stretched to the limits by popular demand, approximated 100. Although others rendered expert assistance in those early construction endeavors such as John Miller, Bill Brokate and Charley Hupp, in addition to Carl Piltz, Charles Hewes was the boss of the jobs without any question.

A small man of extraordinary strength coupled with an equally large portion of gentleness, he extended a great degree of empathy for people, animals as well as a reverence for the creations of nature that confirmed his firm belief in the creative power of his God. At the beginning of his permanent residency in the Tahosa Valley, for at least ten years he kept accurate measurements of snow for the federal government. To compare present day snowfall with the years Charley kept the records, clearly authenticates an early settler's statement, "We don't have the snow now like we did back then." In the 1980s and including present times, the snow fall seasonal average at

Hewes-Kirkwood's location has been four feet. But when Charley Hewes kept the measurements fifty or more years earlier, his charts showed 21 feet. It must have been very challenging to have lived high in the mountains back then with so much of Mother Nature about you ready to defeat your puny efforts if you gave her half a chance. Henry Dannels in the early years carried the mail to and from Hewes-Kirkwood Inn on foot or horseback, or more often on skis as a branch post office had been established at the resort to serve local residents. The Hewes brothers were guides for their guests, leading them up Long's Peak and to all of the other fascinating destinations within the National Park including Fern Lodge where their names were recorded in the register with interesting comments. In cooperation with the proprietors, the Bitners, of the Columbine Lodge north of Hewes-Kirkwood, and Joe Copeland at his Copeland Lake Lodge to the south in Wild Basin now long gone, they worked very hard to construct a new trail to the top of Long's Peak. These builders considered it shorter, easier and more convenient to their operations than the previous one made by the Lamb family as branches led off to each of the contributing hotels.

As their enthusiasm grew with an assortment of potential services for the increasing numbers of guests, these indefatigable Hewes brothers even had plans to build an Alpine Tavern at timberline where mountain climbers would be given an opportunity to lodge and board over night, or as long as they might wish to stay. This really angered Enos Mills who wanted no competition to his Timberline House. Rather then antagonizing him further, theirs never was constructed as the brothers concentrated their efforts on enlarging their holdings to provide a near wilderness adventure in relative comfort for their guests and an abundance of conviviality with the chief host, Charles Hewes. The resort quickly gained wide acceptability despite its newness and remote location. In August of 1914 the editor of the little newspaper in the village printed his assessment of the Hewes's hard work in his enlightening description of what he termed the *ranch*. "It is one of the newest and one of the most popular resorts in Estes Park, and consists of one thousand acres stretching across the Elkanah Valley from the foot of Long's Peak to the Twin Sisters on the opposite side. Running through the ranch is the Alpine brook which furnishes the water supply and is stocked with 50,000 trout. Amidst a group of cottages close to the Long's Peak trail, stands the lodge constructed of logs with a broad terrace and veranda in front. It has a pleasant view of the valley and the Twin Sisters peaks. There is a large living room with a great granite fireplace quarried on the ranch with the dining room having a similar fireplace. From the raspberries, strawberries and huckleberries found around the ranch, guests are treated with fine deserts. Mr.(i.e. Charles) Hewes is an excellent fisherman, and once on his property he landed 53 trout in four hours. They have their own cattle which furnish the table with an abundant supply of fresh milk, cream and butter."

In 1914 an adopted *member* to the Hewes family took up residence at the Inn. Julia Ann Morrisey, born in County Cork, Ireland, immigrated from her home to the United States in 1907 to seek employment as did many other Irish expatriates of her day whose green isle had fallen upon hard times. Steve Hewes, during the early years of the Inn's existence, at the end of the summer tourist season returned for the winter to his home in Cleveland where he pursued an active career in the insurance industry. By 1912 Julia had secured a position in Ohio with the Steve Hewes family. In the spring of 1914 she accompanied the family to Hewes-Kirkwood Inn essentially for the purpose of caring for Mary Kirkwood. Julia rode on the train to Loveland from Denver, then weathered her first ride in a Stanley Steamer to the village. With the final nine miles completed in the mail stage that delivered her to the Inn, the trip that now consumes less than two hours confined Julia to those bumpy rails and roads for more than ten hours. When asked in 1957 her impression of the region wherein the Inn was located and where she still resided in continued service, she responded with furrowed brows "Oh now, it was a wild place!" Searching her mind, packed with forty-three years of hard work, joys and mind boggling escapades in close association with the enigmatic personality of Charles Hewes, she broke out in a broad Irish smile and exclaimed, "It's home to me, and I guess it always will be." During the winter she and Mary Kirkwood shared an apartment in Denver where Mary could receive more comfortable care. As the business of Inn matured with more than enough summer help employed to attend to the needs of its guests, Steve remained in Ohio most of the year where he become an officer of the Union Central Life Insurance Company and only returned to his summer hideaway for occasional visits.

Julia was a full-blood Irish woman, ample in proportions to the degree that she wore a man's size 10 shoes. Somewhat untidy in her appearance and chastised by management for wastefulness in her generosity with Inn food and provisions for the guests, she nevertheless was militantly loyal, hard working and totally devoted to all of the Hewes-Kirkwood family and their guests. Her love and concern to others extended to the wild life and especially to her dog, Watch. Living most of his life on two legs the result of an encounter with a trap, she carried in her strong arms her faithful friend until he moved up the golden stairs to a renewed life with four good paws. Julia also was Charley's bookkeeper. Though she was aware of the fact that others took advantage of her friend and employer, as finances and making money were not high on the priority list for Charley Hewes, she kept her mouth closed. She also was in charge of the kitchen and, though some said she was not as tidy as she should be and often added a bit too much of the Inn's resources to her culinary offerings, everyone appreciated the quality and quantity of the food. So typical of emigrants to salt and pepper the English language with earthy idioms acquired in a new country under adverse circumstances, Julia frequently used language that would make a carpenter's thumb run for cover. As an example of her vituperative epithets, a former kitchen employee still chuckles years later as he can still see, and hear, this bigger than life woman endeavoring to get the dinners out to the hungry guests on time. "Julia was the only woman I ever knew who when she swore made it sound absolutely natural. It just went with her." She remained in the Inn's employment into its final ownership, and those who knew her extolled at her death her many qualities that had made her life well worth living, and remembering. A former guest summed up Julia's life that had reaped a healthy crop of affection for this wonderful woman out of unyielding rock surrounding Hewes-Kirkwood Inn. "She devoted a lifetime of service to the traveling public." The Inn still remains Julia Morrissey's permanent residence as her ashes upon her death and cremation were cemented into a rock crevice somewhere upon the property, where she can remain nearby in case she is ever needed.

The brothers thought so much of their land in Elkanah valley that in 1921 they set out to incorporate the Town of Hewes-Kirkwood, wherein a number of lots were sold and great plans made that never were completed. The Inn and cabins in the twenties and thirties did not have the luxury of electricity. They were illuminated by kerosene lamps with the fuel in 30 gallon drums brought in by Charles. Glen and Cleo Tallman, who were employees during that time, reported "It was a real chore keeping those Rayo lamps going, the glass shades and chimneys cleaned, and the lamps filled." Water for the Inn, carried up from Alpine Brook, was consumed untreated because its qualities of potability were considered "the icyest and nicest of water." The only refrigeration required was for the milk and meat items to be kept in boxes suspended in that cold, bubbling brook. Fifteen young people were employed, with the boys quartered in a bunkhouse and girls in another cabin called Brookside that, as its name implies, was adjacent to Alpine Brook. In fact all of the cabins, for employees and guests alike, were positioned in the pine and aspen groves so that the sparkling little brook wove its cool arms around each one on its way to join Cabin Creek, and later the St. Vrain. Their pay was $5.00 a week, board and room included, and your *found*. Charley Hewes didn't talk about tips for his employees, however, if money was found in a vacated cabin intentionally left for the cabin girl, or likewise if money were left at the table in the dining room and found by the waitress, an employee could keep it as *found* money. All the employees had one day off, and in the evenings Charley allowed them to drive the nine miles to town in his old Model T Ford to the dances at Riverside. While the boys routinely spent their days off fishing or climbing, with perhaps a line or two scribbled to their parents sweltering in the midwestern heat, the girls often could be seen hiking down to Helen Dings' Kentucky Homespun store to the north of the Inn where she sold on her large front porch craft items purchased in the back woods of Kentucky. Helen's sister was Katherine Garretson and, though Katherine remained a spinster, she gladdened the hearts and stomaches of her large family of friends that frequently visited her Big Owl Tea Room southeast of the Inn as a unique address of social gathering. The tea room is now gone, but who could ever forget the aroma of homemade cookies and cupcakes on plates in the large cheery room with tables dressed up with checkered coverings.

Charley was a small man physically, Gandhi-like in attitude, yet a giant of ability and determination. While his hands were calloused, he possessed a soft, loving heart incapable of containment within his wiry frame. A single man all of his life, he literally gave away the clothes off his back if one needed them. For that matter, if a friend, guest, or even a stranger in anyway showed appreciation for his clothes, food, fire wood, books, furniture, pictures, or money, a gift with no strings attached usually was presented. "That's why he never made any money!" was the sentiment of the community. A friend echoed this opinion by stating, "He may not have been a good business man, but he was such a wonderful fellow! He was a real Christian gentleman to the extent that people took advantage of his big heart and gentleness to the extent that they robbed him." His regular attire was an English country cap, woolen sweater and riding breeches with leather putties wrapped about his legs, but his personality was discernable in a wide variety of roles he played in life unconcerned about his appearance. While very comfortable with a fishing rod, swinging an axe, or constructing a trail up Long's Peak all while reciting poetry, his own or others, his greatest pleasure was derived from reading a book by Socrates or Shakespeare. He was a man full of many moods, mostly joyous. One morning when he heard the radio news revealing a bleak world of apparent mindless hate, greed and war, he refused to give in to pessimism. He stood in the front door of the Inn to watch the warm glow of the sunrise reveal itself around the rough edges of Twin Sisters Peak. As the full orbit of reddish gold cast its first earth renewing rays upon his hopeful face, it elicited a comment that elevated those gathered about. "It's wonderful isn't it, --wonderful!" Wars, pestilence, greed and all of the other Horses of the Apocalypse were forgotten in this quiet moment of unconquerable majesty from on high. Everything just seemed right and this little prophet of glad tidings was ready for another day, with a smile. Another example of his eternal optimism and deep appreciation of nature was revealed during his first winter at his homestead claim, before his brother arrived, where by shear stubborn endurance he protected his claim during the proving up period and would not allow his happiness ever to be shrouded in gloom or loneliness. Remaining alone in a nearly unheated, windowless cabin during that entire winter so the government could not claim any abandonment, years later he was asked what it was like to be alone at his claim. He smiled and said "It was too cold to sleep, but the blue nights, the snow, the pines, --they were too exciting!" He saw beauty and value in everything, including his experiences from which others of lesser stamina would have beat a rapid retreat. His friend, Siegfried Wagner, could never forget this dreamer, a man who was not interested in prestige, comfort nor money. Sig wrote, "He came from Iowa, and was more fascinated by gathering buffalo chips for fuel on the open plains than any gadgets equated with the modern world. At his place, outhouses in the woods were more intriguing than putting in a bath, or electrical outlets. In fact, up until 1942, Charley was not really interested in listening to the radio as the great outdoors was his beloved world to occupy his time. But often people came in droves and shared his love for the primitive, the primeval fascination of his life and of all the majesty it held for him."

As a true worshipper of all of God's creations that he calculated "shared his world with him," his dining table for guests was different. He never allowed elk or deer, bear or rabbit to be killed. Chickens were the exception to rule, although not for himself, and I could never understand why these cackling creatures were browned in the ovens except that they possessed a disturbing influence to the dewy fresh hours of his morning solitude. Charley ate only fruits, nuts, breads and perhaps his *trout pie*, its secret makin's hidden under a crust of pastry. To the inquirer who sought lodging and was concerned with the absence of an internal water system, Charley was heard to answer, all smiling and with no malice, "If you need a bath, dear, you'd better go to another lodge. Let me arrange it for you." Charles Eagle Plume talked about Charley, as a smile played over his face. "Now, I was a deep admirer of a gentle little old man named Charley Hewes who had a place up behind Mills' Longs Peak Inn. Hewes, who was a deadly enemy of Enos Mills, was a lover of mankind and a lover of peace. He believed firmly that if everybody would call everyone else *dear*, there then would be world peace." So imagine the scene when a Texas tourist drove up to the door of Hewes' Inn one afternoon. Eagle Plume shook his head in mirth as he remembered this episode from Hewes' life. "This big Texan drives up to the door, walks in and says 'do ya have a room?', and Charley says to him 'yes dear.' That Texan left promptly!" Most remained at the Inn, content with a sponge bath of heated water on the cabin stoves and, as Mr. Wagner termed it, "admiration for this small wonder of the woods." He idolized his mother, tried to love everyone, and was considered as Christ-like a holy man as anyone knew in the valley or elsewhere. His 800 acres he regarded as 'The Lord's domain,' and religious services were regularly conducted at Hewes-Kirkwood Inn each Sunday evening as his dedication to his Lord. Despite his limited finances, he even considered constructing a church on his property for the use of his guests and all of the people residing in Elkanah valley. As the name Elkanah means, *possessed of God*, Charles Hewes was one of His greatest exponents in his special way.

Charley over the years was consumed in writing manuscripts of prose and poetry that unfortunately no company would publish, not because his writing was poor. To the contrary. It was wonderfully exciting and drew pictures in words that revealed the true soul and spirit of the Rocky Mountains. He used his limited resources to print up his literary efforts but in doing so did not pay enough attention to the business requirements of the Inn and his creditors began to demand payment with no more delays. His friends wanted to help but he was a true believer in Divine Providence and would accept no other assistance. The Inn property had long been mortgaged and, with the accumulation of interest and unpaid taxes, a foreclosure resolved the issue. Sadly, the Inn was closed. The Sheriff physically removed Charley from his beloved Inn as he sat and waited for help from on high that he knew would come, and all his beloved furnishings were sold off. For some reason the woman, who had purchased the mortgage, restored him to his original homestead and others give back to him that portion of the property on which was located his Hewes-Kirkwood Inn. Some of his prayers had been answered and he was grateful and he moved back in and cleared that portion of the property of its debts. However the balance of the Charley's unimproved real estate, south of the Inn and consisting of 640 acres, was purchased at the foreclosure sale. The purchasers were four businessmen of Estes Park, the grocer Fay E. Brainard who owned other property nearby, C. Byron Hall of the transportation company, the liveryman C. Everett May affectionately known as *Granny* because at an early age he always acted older than the other boys of his age, and Russell McKelvey the owner of Fall River Lodge. The land was divided up under the name Hewes-Kirkwood Development Co. and five acre lots were sold off in a new subdivision, now identified as Rockwood Acres south of the Inn.

Most everyone who ever knew Charles Hewes thought him to be a wonderful character, very religious, and generous to the extreme. But many took advantage of his weakness for giving away money, food, property and about any thing else to others more in need than was he. One old timer remembering Charles Edwin Hewes with great affection added, "Charley couldn't make money if he had a mint." That may be true but he coined a new token for lasting love and fellowship for man and all nature as his lasting memorial. Isn't that better than waiting until the cold hand of death erects a marble temple in the cemetery attesting only to one's financial abundance that benefits no one? Former employees said that although "Charley was the most peaceful person we ever knew in life, Enos Mills got so darned ornery with him that for two winters Mr. Hewes carried a gun for self defense." Whether there is more to this tale I cannot say, but when they met later after his death, I hope their differences were resolved to each other's eternal credit. Kid brother Steve, who followed Charles in death on December 22, 1970, might have resolved the issue upon his arrival in the heights as he was an excellent arbitrator in business. Charles Hewes died August 27, 1947 in Longmont, two years after he sold the Inn property to Paul Nesbit, who himself resold it in 1947 to the Reichstadt family. In due course the Inn property was deeded in 1951 to Beth Miller Harrod, a teacher of classical music in Lincoln, Nebraska and a musician of national stature. Miss Miller, before her marriage to Carlton Harrod, since 1942 had operated a music school near the Inn, and when the property was made available to her she jumped at the opportunity to crown her dream for a school of regional musical significance. Today, in 1993, marks the 42nd anniversary of her school on the Inn property, where musicians of many disciplines at Rocky Ridge Music Center are trained and who concertize the tourists in euphonious tones that resonate the granite sounding boards of mountains in harmony. Charles would appreciate the direction taken by his Inn as this *Poet of the Rockies*, as he was known, predestined the school in his important published poetic work entitled *Song Of The Rockies*. A poem on a 1922 post card advertising his Inn speaks eloquently of love of nature and of his home where his spirit dwells free as a song.

AT THE FOOT OF THE PEAK

There's a lofty Mountain reared in the West,
At its foot is a cabin small,
Where I dwell in that peace and quiet rest,
That comes to those who call.
To a mother of sweet and cradling breast,
Who sings when the night shades fall,
This Mountain that rears its mighty crest,
That croons with its waterfall.

Hewes-Kirkwood Lodge, circa 1912 (CHS)

Interior Of Lodge, circa 1920 (Private)

Charles Edwin Hewes, circa 1920 (Harold Dunning)

Early Cabin, Hewes-Kirkwood, By Helen Clatworthy In 1957

Steve Hewes & Fishing Pole-Julia Morrissey Standing, 1918 (EPPL)

Big Owl Tea Room, Katherine Garetson (L), Annie Shreve (R), 1915 (EPPL)

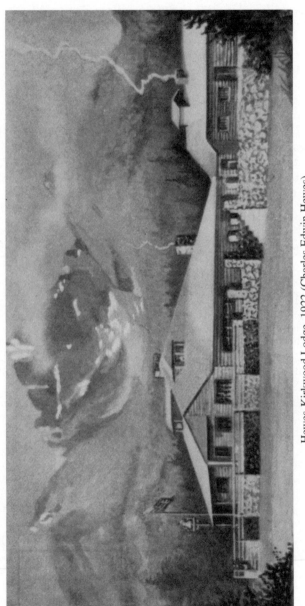

Hewes-Kirkwood Lodge, 1922 (Charles Edwin Hewes)

THE LEWISTON HOTEL

Mr. F. O. Stanley, anxious to promote financial stability for the little village of two hundred citizens and in which he had invested large sums of money, made contact with Sidney W. Sherman, a banker from Grand Rapids, Michigan. Temporarily in residence in the village for health purposes, Sherman advised Stanley of the procedure to establish a bank, and through their joint efforts received Colorado Bank Charter Number 37 in 1908. Organized by thirty-six men and women of the community, all prominent in their fields, their number included many lodge owners among whom were names now familiar to us. They were Willard Ashton of Horseshoe Inn; Josephine Hupp of the Hupp Hotel; Horace Ferguson of the Highlands; Hugo Miller whose ranch grew into McGraw's Ranch; Charles Lester who managed the Estes Park Hotel; Enos Mills of Long's Peak Inn; Charles Reed of Brinwood; Homer James of Elkhorn Lodge and James Stead of Stead's Ranch. Mr. Stanley was installed as its first President and Sidney Sherman was elected Cashier. The bank building, constructed at a cost of $1,400 on an $800 lot at the corner of Elkhorn Avenue and Big Horn then known as Anderson Drive, opened for business on June 16, 1908 with $12,000 in capital and remains an important constituent of the Estes Park financial community.

A. D. *Gus* Lewis established permanent residency in Estes Park in 1912 after having lived in Hot Sulpher Springs, Colorado where he owned property. He subsequently moved to Loveland, Colorado where he became an employee in one the local banks. After being chosen by the directors of the Estes Park Bank to be its second Cashier, Gus and his wife Anita erected their home on a prominence west of the village. By 1914, because of the demand for additional accommodations for business guests to the bank and other establishments in the village, they had opened their bungalow home to travelers as one of the first guest houses in the area. It was described as "modern in every particular, of most artistic architecture and furnishings, located in the midst of tall pine trees in a retired spot far enough away from the main street of the village to avoid the noise and dust." When their home's extra rooms constantly were filled, four tent houses were assembled on the back lawn that increased its guest capacity to twenty-five. Anita Lewis, a busy mother of three children, found time to assist her husband in their guest house as she took charge of food service as well as the entertainment of their guests. By 1915, after a substantial enlargement of the home on its east side, the capacity was further augmented to fifty guests requiring the employment of a small but efficient staff. Gaining recognition by the professional class of customer who patronized the Lewis's Guest House, as word spread of its convenient location and excellent food and as a place of quiet retreat for the traveling businessman, the guest house was raised in height in 1917 so that seventy guests per evening could be accommodated.

In winter of 1918-1919, at the conclusion of the Great War, a decision was arrived at to expand to three stories high and widen it further to the east and north. Gus assigned the management to his half brother, Claude Erwin Verry from Fairmont, Nebraska. Mr. Verry at that time was himself a proprietor of the small Rockdale Hotel near Marys Lake, acquired from Charles Robbins in 1915, which he managed until it was blown apart in the winter winds of 1919. Thereafter the site was sold to Mr. Lewis's hotel company and developed into the Lewiston Chalet. In addition to obliging as a lower priced resource for more economy minded travelers, the Chalet later served as an outdoor pantry for Lewis' numerous tourist operations. On its grounds were grown vegetables, and dairy cattle produced milk for the children and cream for the freshly brewed coffee available at Lewis's guest house. Business was so good and the service widely acclaimed that the sizeable hostelry that we see in historical pictures was the culmination of final additions to the guest house in 1920. It was now listed in the tourist trade publications as The Lewiston Hotel and fully capable of accommodating one hundred and fifty guests. The Lewiston strove to host the rich and famous and performed its job admirably as it promoted its boasted relevance as "Metropolitan elegance in the timbered vastness." Its ad in 1924 was pitched to the breed of visitors it sought to captivate with a splendid view from a terrace equipped with cushy chairs and all the amenities one would expect for $50 per week. "The Lewiston needs no introduction as it has entertained as its guests the most fastidious of the pleasure seeking public. From The Lewiston veranda may be obtained a view of Long's Peak and the encircling snowy range unsurpassed by any point in Estes Park. No expense or thought were spared in the appointments of The Lewiston to place it in the front rank of resort hotels. All rooms in the main building and in many of the cottages are fitted with baths and the furnishings and decorations are of the highest quality." Local residents considered it a "posh place to stay."

Claude Verry introduced the Harvey Girl concept of employee utilization during the years he managed this hotel and the other Lewiston Hotel properties for Gus, as The *Rocky Mountain News* Magazine Section of September 23, 1923 reported. "College boys and girls, especially girls, have found a new and exceedingly profitable occupation to take up their time during the summer vacation months. They have forsaken the bespectacled drudgery of the classroom for the cool greenness of the Rocky Mountain National parks and have assumed for the time being the roles of waitresses, pantry girls, bell hops and truck drivers. And they love it! Each year between forty and fifty girls are employed for this sort of work by Mr. C. E. Verry, president of the Rocky Mountain Lodges, Incorporated. This corporation operates chalets and lodges in Estes Park and Grand Lake and employs, through Miss Eunice Roberts of Keokuk, Iowa, only college students during the summer season. The Harvey system of service is used in the lodges and chalets and within a few weeks' time the girls have learned all the tricks of the trade and become remarkably proficient. And this particular trade is worth while for them as well as for the management, for, with their regular wages and the gratuities they receive from the guests, they make enough money during the summer to put them thru school in the winter. The presence of college girls in the dining room lends a certain atmosphere of refinement that would not otherwise be there. The college boys are employed in the capacity of busboys, truck drivers, dishwashers and bellhops. They enjoy it as much as the girls do and of necessity are kept out of doors most of the time and this in a way makes up for the winter months of indoor work and study." Oh how I wish that the present day students would be occupied as much with indoor activity such as study. The college students had no regular hours, and when their assigned duties were accomplished they were free to hike, horseback ride or pursue other leisure activities. As Mr. Verry reported that "Our employees are happier when they're busy than when they're idle," those long hours for the staff resulted in their separate dormitories being populated with tired young men and women.

A. D. Lewis was an excellent promoter of the village and of his hotel to the extent that within a brief period of time he had formed The Lewiston Hotels Company with offices both in Estes Park and in Denver. His son-in-law, Glen Preston, a garageman of the village, was the company Secretary and by 1921 the corporation had constructed Grand Lake Lodge that grew in size to accommodate 300 guests at rates of $7 per day and $50 per week including food. He purchased the Josephine Hotel on Elkhorn Avenue, then added to his investments the Park Hotel where he had offices, moderately priced tourist rooms and where reasonably priced meals were offered to the tourists in the Lewiston Cafe. A true community leader, his efforts were recognized when he was elected to the position and prestige of the President of the Estes Park Bank in 1922 and became Mayor of Estes Park in 1923. An avid sportsman who saw recreational opportunities an added value for business as well as healthy recreational pursuits for the community, he became an organizer of the new Colorado Ski Club in the winter of 1924.

In every addition of the early newspapers, *The Mountaineer,* the *Estes Park Trail,* and especially the *Estes Park Trail Talk* that was first published by Archibald Taylor on July 2, 1920, there appeared a regular feature that went into a litany of detail about who was staying at which lodge, the categories of activities available, and more in the form of friendly hostelry competition and varnished advertisement who participated in the serendipitous fun and frivolities aimed at keeping the tourists diverted away from hometown heartaches. The guest registers were routinely gleaned by the reporters to see who had checked in, even who a guest might be visiting in town. If you were a *somebody,* or for that matter if the news of the day was sluggish you could be an *anybody*, you could not cache yourself away in your special mountain hideaway without being spotted by a newspaper's reporter. The young newshound delighted in featuring your horseshoe match, quoit toss, promenade on a trail in search of some Indian tree or perchance the visit of your great aunt Nellie as she dismounted from her steed at Grubb's Livery. And if you were truly a somebody, or had given indications of being such a person, your name unquestionably would be found in the hotel column for the week as *a prominent person* registered at a certain lodge or hotel. It was just good business for the lodge owners to see their names juxtapositioned with some one identified as *prominent*, and thus for the tourist industry was the life blood of the newspapermen and vice-versa. Another way of bringing notoriety to a lodge was to raise a guest up one notch from *prominent* to *famous*, and thus a guest never was just a businessman but a *famous* businessman and a guest who came for golf was called *a golfer of exceptional ability*. Even a guest who sold photographs out of his home in Cicero, Illinois was referred to as a *well known picture dealer near Chicago*. To the editors, everyone staying at these lodges high in the Rockies was important. In fact guests' qualities not fully recognizable by their closest associates were discerned immediately by the vox populi. And of course, putting in a good word for the Estes Valley and lodges chosen by these laudatory visitors certainly did not harm the advertising revenues of the printed page. It was not enough for one cub reporter to log in that a prominent musician from Washington was staying at the Lewiston Hotel, he had to go further to report the guest's impression of the view from the porch. "While gazing at Long's Peak from the Lewiston, the prominent musician remarked that the view was wonderful and that the coloring of the clouds over the horizon gave him the impression that dainty fairies have been at work trying to rival the famous paintings of another age." A toast to profound journalism! ---Here! Here!

Within the first few years of the grand opening of the Lewiston Hotel, it was considered **the** place to stay with such kudos as "The Lewiston had the best furniture and was highly furnished, so much better than the Stanley Hotel ever was." Artists, industrialists, educators and politicians made this their place of vacation abode, often for many weeks. Congressmen, Senators and financiers such as John Davison Rockefeller, Jr., considered the Lewiston Hotel their home in the village when on holiday. Californians Charles Bowman Hutchins and his wife, were employed to provide entertainment and nature education for the guests of the hotel and its sister Lewiston Chalet. Hutchins was ascribed the title the California Bird Man for he was an accomplished bird call imitator and a renowned authority in the United States on these winged creatures and their habitat. His evening lectures and daily nature walks, as well as Mrs. Hutchins' musical renditions on her harp and lectures on flowers, were highly regarded by guests and employees as hours well spent in "distinctive intellectual enlightenment." The hotel also was identified with the transportation power play when the first Superintendent of Rocky Mountain National Park awarded an exclusive franchise for commercial tourist transportation within the Park. The Lewiston often hosted officials of both the National Park Service and the Rocky Mountain Parks Transportation Company thereby creating the appearance that A. D. Lewis was playing an active role in their negotiations while they socialized at his hotel. Rising to this suspicion, justified or not, was Enos Mills who wrote an accusatory letter to the public in 1921. "This transportation monopoly, which is interlocked with the Lewiston Hotel Company, has the opportunity to discriminate against other hotels and to favor the Lewiston Hotel. This is exactly what it is doing under the protection of the Park officials." I am certain that these caustic aspersions cut deeply into Gus Lewis who had done so much to promote the business opportunities for all lodge owners and other business men and women of his adopted community.

Possibly because of a sense of indignation at being so roughly attacked or for whatever reason provoked the action, in January of 1923 he sold the Grand Lake Lodge and Lewiston Chalet, then operated under the name of Rocky Mountain Lodges, Inc., to Roe Emery's Rocky Mountain Parks Transportation Company. Mr. Emery was pleased with the purchase and said, "This acquisition will allow for the rapidly increasing business through a circle trip through Estes Park, Rocky Mountain National Park, to Grand Lake and back to Denver." The Lewiston Chalet was renamed the Estes Park Chalet, and its size was greatly expanded to hold 300 guests brought up on bus tours in Emery's bright red buses. By the 1931 summer season, with increased patronage from tourist demand, more than 100 young men were employed to drive the fleet of motor vehicles in the transportation system. Gus concentrated his abundant talents on his Lewiston Hotels Company as the Town of Estes Park was now welcoming to its shops and accommodations more than 218,000 visitors annually. In 1926, because of the demand upon his time in local government and at the larger hotel, and for the reason that he no longer needed hotel and restaurant space away from his primary base of operations, he sold the Josephine Hotel, Park Hotel and Lewiston Cafe in the village. After ridding himself of his other business ventures in Estes Park, the business at the Lewiston began to encourage conventions and rooms were definitely at a premium. In 1927 the Lewiston Hotel was described as "splendidly situated with a magnificent view of the snowy Front Range and Long's Peak. It is attractive, nicely furnished, serves splendid meals and has a homey and likeable atmosphere." The rates on the American Plan ran between $20 to $40 dollars per week per person and rooms were highly in demand because of its location, proximity to the village, exquisite service and outstanding view from its high rocky overlook. That superb location, with wind and lofty isolation from the masses below, would prove the harbinger of its eventual demise.

Gus Lewis promoted the enjoyment of the National Park through walking tours in a coalition with Frank Byerly entitled the Lewis-Byerly Walking Tours headquartered at the hotel. Also from livery stables on Elkhorn Avenue, such as Elijah Rivers' Stanley Livery, Harry Langston's Hupp Livery and Otis and Opal Whiteside's Silver Lane Stables, horses were tethered at hitching posts behind the hotel to await the guests who had signed up at the recreation desk. The destinations most popular were north through the MacGregor Ranch to Lumpy Ridge into Black Canyon to Gem Lake or west to Lawn and Fern Lakes, or south up Deer Mountain where the views into Horseshoe Park were impressive. For the consummate horseman, a ride southwest to Bear Lake rewarded a guest with an experience never to be forgotten. The livery rates in the 1920s and 1930s were quite uniform, stabilized by a liverymen's association that promoted safety, proper care of the animals and ethical standards at the stables in and around Estes Park that sought aggressively to satisfy tourist demands. For an hour's ride it cost seventy-five cents though few rode for such a limited time except for someone seeking to impress those back home in a photo when in truth he or she truly detested the effects of rubbing leather. It cost $2.50 for half a day and $4.00 for the popular all day ride, and if one were really into regular equestrian exercise a mount could be hired by the week for $21. There were always devotees to the school of gluteus maximus reduction by the saddle pounding technique, and a month of torture on your own personalized mammal came to $75. Otis Whiteside, who later held the exclusive contract for renting horses to Lewiston Hotel guests, said "The three story, shingled, hotel was a nice place where anybody would like to stay and be proud of it." He routinely stationed one of his employees at the hotel in the evening and "sold rides to the guests for the next day." When the guest walked out the back door of the hotel and over to the hitching rack, the horses brought over earlier by Silver Lane wranglers were already saddled and ready to go. As reported previously, in the 1930s and 1940s there existed at least thirty full time liveries, five or more of which headquartered their operations on Elkhorn Avenue. I propose to write a more extensive story on these liverymen who contributed so much to the enhancement of Estes Park as a quality resort in the rockies.

Though many of these wranglers are deceased and are not identified in chapters of this book, they deserve recognition. Please excuse me if some are accidentally overlooked or their names are misspelled, as records now have faded and recollections of my sources have dimmed. Members of their Association were Clyde Sheffield, Long's Peak Inn; Chuck Malone, Bald Pate Inn; Everett *Granny* May, Cheley Camps; Harold Alps, Blue Ribbon Livery; Harry Langston, Hupp Livery and H Bar G Ranch; Don Adams, Glen Haven; Marvin Manford, Voelkel's Lodge; Bert Lannier, High Drive Livery; Frank McGraw, McGraw's Ranch; Jack Eaton, Charles Livery; Cy Rumley and Chester Apgar at Beaver Point; Wiley Woods, Moraine Park Livery; and J. Frank Grubb and his son-in-law Don Kilton of Meadowdale Ranch and the big red barn across from the old post office, Grubb's Livery. And there was the unforgettable, Harry Lovern. Born in Oklahoma and an early day liveryman at Stead's and later the manager of the Elkhorn Stables, he was first a cowboy actor in some of the forerunners of Hollywood Westerns playing opposite such stars as Hoot Gibson and Tom Mix. Otis Whiteside, one of the surviving members of the Association, still sits tall in a saddle every summer while operating his stables with his very capable daughter Betty Whiteside. Otis named his stables Silver Lane Stables because the river near his original location, south of the Thompson river at the junction of Highway 36 with Elkhorn Avenue, he said "came rippling along and looked pretty silvery." He still recalls with affection and a husky bass chuckle his friend Harry Lovern long gone for more than twenty-six years. "Harry stuttered a lot, had false teeth and quite often smoked a pipe. Now then, when he started stuttering, those teeth --still clutching the pipe walked their way out. It sure was something to see. And there was another liveryman," Otis continued as his ribs shook with private mirth, " Don Adams, down in Glen Haven. He was the laziest man I ever knew with horses, but real good. Yes sir! You see, he was so good, but lazy, that he would only shoe a horse sitting down. None of that standing up business with Don. Maybe he was just conservative --wanting to be sure of his work, and I can understand that trait. *Not rushing into something* ran in my own family. One of my earlier relatives rode a horse from Kentucky to just west of Loveland **five** times before deciding to take up a homestead. Now **that's** being real careful, a real conservative."

The business of providing horses that were healthy, gentle yet energetic and trail smart to Lewiston's guests was as difficult as it was, and is, to predict the weather in the high country of Colorado. There were many grades of riders ranging from those completely unfamiliar with horseback riding to the bossy dudes who thought they knew more than the wranglers. Speaking of the variety of the clientele and the difficulty facing the wranglers, the late Jack Stirling, horseman, poet, artist, cartoonist, was above all a witty and talented fellow with loads of friends. While employed at the Silver Lane Stables he printed a number of postcards, containing his own verses and cartoons illustrating his personal experiences as a local resident and a wrangler, that he sold to tourists or more often gave away to his friends and local admirers. One humorously pictured two wranglers hoisting a large woman, cigarette holder clenched tightly, upon the back of a bewildered horse. Another characterized a group of many shaped dudes, their back sides facing the observing Stirling, leaning against the corral waiting for the wrangler to perform a near impossible task of selecting the proper mounts and a correct sized saddle for this diverse group. His words are worth repeating with an understanding smile. *Some's got big fannies, some's got small; but there never was a saddle maker that could fit them one and all.* Jack even carried his theme of wrangling, a life that I believe he most preferred to one as an oil painter hoped for by his artist father, into greetings he sent his friends including this whimsical poem included on an appropriately drawn card.

Santa's full of cowboy's blood,
Hear his spurs a-jangling;
Lookin for the reindeer eight,
He's goin out a-wrangling.
Soon he'll have them critters in,
And while the snow is swirling;
He'll hitch um up head and mouth,
MERRY CHRISTMAS from Jack Stirling.

The Lewiston Hotel appealed to the increasingly sophisticated traveler who had been lured west by the promotional efforts of this luxury hotel and its chief competitor, the Stanley. A favorite place for music and entertainment along more cultural and sedate lines was the Japanese Tea Room on the third floor of the Lewiston in full view of Long's Peak. There was a ball room and billiard room, manicure parlors and hair salons. Its brochure trumpeted something for everyone, even those who preferred just to "take in the air of the scenic splendor of the snowy range with its ever-changing colors and shadows viewed from the Lewiston verandas that brings forth involuntary exclamations of delight and approval." The luxurious dining room with its "absolutely best view of town" had drawing power equivalent to a circling rendezvous of trappers hungry for meat. It was very popular with "many big railroad men" who parked their engines down below and came up for the view, food and other offerings then in vogue. An attraction in the village gained broad attention through the midwestern and Rocky Mountain regions that made it a simile for the name, Estes Park. A blend of Coney Island, Las Vegas and Disney Land, all compacted into one exciting spectacle for young and old, was of course Riverside. Since this fun spot of near legend reputation no longer beckons with light and rhythm the modern day tourist, and inasmuch as those who spent their summers in the Estes Valley considered Riverside as important to them as fishing, horseback riding or even eating, I will break into my account of The Lewiston Hotel to recount a few of its credentials that gave rise to its memorable character.

First owned by Ted Jelsma and Cornelius Bond's son, Frank who became the Mayor of the Village, construction of Riverside Amusement Park commenced in October of 1922 with the excavation of a 40 x 80 foot outdoor swimming pool, suitable for all ages as the shallow end was only 18 inches deep and progressed to a depth of 7 feet. There were juxtaposed lockers and dressing rooms for the pool where many of the local people learned to swim in the only public pool in the Estes Valley. The pool had a water system described as "130,000 gallons of steam-heated, filtered, soft snow water that is continually changing in the tank to give place to fresh water, thus insuring a pleasant, clean and comfortable swim." The pool later was temporarily canvassed over and finally a permanent roof took its place to provide lengthened periods for recreational use and swimming lessons in cold and wet weather. But those refinements tended to obscure the great views of the Crags Hotel on Prospect Mountain and the more distant front range dominated by Long's

Peak. Riverside even offered to its patrons a sand beach right on the bank of the river where children created sand sculptures and the swimmers came over to sun themselves. It first opened its doors the end of May in 1923 with the lights turned on at the main entrance off of Elkhorn Avenue. You led your girl, or the whole family, down an intriguing alley way bordered by D. F. Godfrey's Clothing Store and Brinkley's Drug Store-Soda Fountain on the west side and Hayden Bros. Realty office to the east. If a boy really wanted to impress his girl friend, who more than likely waitressed at one of the lodges, he exchanged a quarter for a chance to swing the heavy mallet and ring the bell with the first powerful blow in the Arcade just before crossing over the bridge.

Riverside Park was located on the south side of Fall River but also accessible by an automobile entrance with parking provided on the east side of the property close to the Big Thompson River. There was a 106 x 60 foot recreation hall for dancing, an ice cream parlor, sandwich shop with rustic booths, a bowling alley and gaming devices were not far away up a set of stairs in one of the local brotherhood's lodge rooms. The dance floor could accommodate 200 people, but I am certain at those famous Fourth of July and Firemen's Ball dances others could always shoulder their way in to undulate to such rhythmic big bands as The Romancers, Sarge Farrell, Matt Betton, Johnny Neill, Lee Pickett's Screamers, Warren Durrett, Bob Swerer's Western Swing Band, Jack Wheaton's Dixieland Band and the ever popular Denver orchestra led by Dean Bushnell. This sounds like a true Nirvana right here in our little piece of the Rockies, and to many it truly **was** Estes Park. Despite a huge snowstorm that caved in the Quonset type roof of the dance hall one winter, citizens demanded that it be rebuilt. When it crashed down, old timers said they rushed from their beds thinking something had exploded or an earthquake had occurred. Riverside often was the highlight for so many during the summer, and printed tickets for one dance only cost ten cents. Ted Jelsma, successful in many business ventures in the Estes Valley including his own fish hatchery on Fish Creek, became the sole owner of Riverside in 1925.

Ted spent much time traveling in the wintertime to sign up his entertainment, particularly the bands, and I think the most popular band throughout the years at Riverside was the nine piece band composed of University of Nebraska students, and of course calling themselves The Nebraskans. They were the masters of syncopation who often gave impromptu concerts in Rocky Mountain National Park while frolicking in the snow drifts. One remembered the big dance on July 4th in 1927, pleased with the never to be forgotten evening. "The floor was so crowded, packed with people, that after paying my 10 cents for one dance I found I could not get off of the dance floor, so I danced the whole evening on that one ten cent ticket to the music played by a large band." Music was broadcast from the bandstand at Riverside by way of a loud speaker affixed to the main entrance opening on to Elkhorn Avenue. Associated with the music was a little singing and coaxing spiel by the leader of one of the bands, my old friend from Omaha, Lyle DeMoss, who sought to entice the strollers off the main street in Pied Piper fashion. The amusement park had everything, an arcade, swimming races, beauty pageants, Pan-Hellenic Dances for the visiting fraternity and sorority collegians, amusement games such as the shooting gallery, baseball, hoops and darts, Forsythe's Merry-Go-Round, Indian Pow Wow Dances, the popular Cowboy Dance and of course every Tuesday evening was square dance night. You name it, it was there, if not Ted would get it installed for next summer. It was an immense attraction for those who lived in Estes Park and certainly the thousands who spent their successive summers in the wonderful old lodges and hotels scattered about this quaint mountain resort.

The Dark Horse portion of Riverside, where libations sparked a wide assortment of jocularity, was built in 1933 after prohibition went the way of other unpopular examples of legislated personal conduct. The merry-go-round, that Mr. Jelsma had purchased from the owner at the close of the 1932 summer season, previously had operated on a concession lease at Riverside. It had been a sheer delight to the gaggle of giggling children who each adopted one of the wooden horses as their best buddy. But in 1933 it would no longer repeat its performance as Ted Jelsma was to discover. In his urge to get Riverside closed up as Labor Day of 1932 approached, he neglected to purchase the specially designed motor that made the circle of lights turn and the lively horses prance and its former owner had long departed the premises for unknown destinations. Being a good businessman he thought that the horses could be better used in his new Dark Horse, some times called the Dark Horse Tavern. After a good shiny coat of red and black paint was applied to cover the nicks and dents from aggressive young riders and appropriate names of real life race horses were inscribed on their necks and hind quarters, these colorful equines for years thereafter became partners with adults as bar stools for thousands of fun loving patrons in the Dark Horse. The big dance of every year was the Firemens' Ball at the end of the year, after the tourists had gone home. After the close of that final dance each season at Riverside, usually around Labor Day or shortly thereafter, the town closed up. George Peck, Sr., an early winter sports advocate and whose wife is a member of Sam Service's extended family, remembered. "They even had a Grand March, and everybody was there! It was absolutely wild on Labor Day! Everyone was at the dance. This town would jump for there was going to be a real blast at Riverside. Somers, across the street -- and they had a soda fountain inside and a water fountain outside -- had their restaurant going for people to come in after the dance. But when you'd get up the next morning and come down town, you would find the stores were boarded up, restaurants were closed down, and people were gone! Then we all set in for a long winter. They really moved out that quickly! They were just like the circus. They were gone!" Back in the 1920s through the 1950s, lodges and most businesses operating in tourist related vocations closed at a easily defined *end of the season*, with neither shoulder seasons nor winter holiday promotions to ring the last calendar dollar out of a lingering shopper. The sentiment of the community then was a reasoned approach to the fact that schools had reopened, workers returned to their desks and the air had taken on a decided chill with fewer people walking down Elkhorn Avenue. Locals said, "Back then the lodges were all just summer places, never meant to be winter places. That's where everyone lost his money trying to make them *all year*." And those who had businesses on Main Street always had problems with their water system. The water mains were wooden and often they would freeze and expand. When you had no water, and often no electricity for the electrical plant when it worked as it was often off line and down, it was best to close up your businesses.

Mr. Jelsma sold out to Messrs. Gillan and Sack from Nebraska in 1946. As swimming became less popular with the tourist, the pool was covered over to provide a floor for roller skating. But that recreation in turn fell out of favor with young Americans who had a decided interest in amusements that were much less structured and more individualistic though lacking clear definition. In the late fifties the old swimming hole-roller rink was restructured into the Dark Horse Theater with productions cast from 1958 until Riverside finally closed. Tourists were more mobile, not wanting to spend too much time in one place. An R. V. park for their home on wheels was sufficient, a hike on the trails, a sedate dinner in an upscale restaurant, now more suited their tastes. Even dancing fell out of favor at Riverside in its final years and the dance floor was converted to a large hall for pool and billiard tables as well as bell ringing gaming machines that induced idleness. The young people had their sooped up automobiles, the T. V. tube with its violent phantasmagoric soap operas and lots of money for an evening spent with ear wrenching rock stars who set the tone and direction for their entertainment. Who would be interested any longer in a 10 cent dance, square dancing, watching Gold Tony the horse go through his paces out on the dance floor or a pause to pick up a soda at Bert Brinkley's Drug Store?

Other uses were found for the valuable and centrally located tract of land, but without the buildings when Riverside was sold to the town for $160,000 in October, 1969. One final remembrance dance was sponsored by locals and many others who returned to an evening of nostalgic laughter and tears on January 31, 1970. After the final dance, and the music cases were closed for the last time, an era had come to an end. Then shortly thereafter old Riverside and the Dark Horse, part of our precious past, were torn down as too mundane, out of step with progress and much too cumbersome for modernity. They were replaced by parking lots and much later partially by a new Riverside Plaza at the confluence of the Big Thompson and Fall Rivers, hardly visionary substitutes for the worthiness of the magic that was Riverside. The locals were sad, as well as the thousands who had frequented the fun palace for so many years. It followed down the same road as did the old lodges in the National Park, as it, like they, was deemed unnecessary, unwanted and untimely. But you know, I can still hear the music and the voice of my old friend enticing in the young and old to a place that for only ten cents dreams were made and could never be forgotten. Riverside was the bright little spot by the river devoted to family recreation at a time when lives were less complicated. Now its name is primarily identified with the street sign down by the post office, a street that goes nowhere.

The Lewiston Hotel would meet its demise long before the amusement park, and those who see her gracefully posed upon the knoll overlooking the village have similar remembrances of this elegant lady. The summer season of 1941 had just closed and tourists were hurrying home to listen for the news that soon would plunge our country into another Great War that like its predecessor refused to end the hate, greed and malice of a world with a short memory for carnage. The final ball had ended for the season on the hotel's roof garden. The glow of the moon reflected off the guardian peaks and the aroma of wild flowers remaining on every table blended with the smell of pine and aspen trees wafting up on the breath of the rushing river below. On the morning of Thursday, September 4, 1941, when the village was quiet, preparations were underway for a concluding event for the year as it was not economical to remain open through the long winter. J. Russell McKelvey, its lessee, and his assistant managers Mr. and Mrs. John McMillan, were hard at work to prepare the hotel for a stylish banquet for executives and officers of the National Rotary Convention then in session in Denver. All of the fireplaces were blazing and every oven was in use baking the one hundred hams and thirty-seven turkeys required. The flues up in the attic were glowing bright red, obviously overloaded and beyond their capacity. Room clerk Bruce Cuthbertson by the afternoon smelled smoke in the attic, searched out the problem and alerted Mr. McKelvey. The wind, no stranger to the Estes Valley, that afternoon was estimated to be of more than gale-like intensity, probably gusting at 75 miles per hour in velocity. A little trail of smoke worked its way through the wooden shingles with a trace of red glow forming along the roof ridge line that created an illusion of a halo, yet suggesting horror. The Lewiston Hotel was burning!

All the lights on the switchboard simultaneously lit up as the smoldering fire slowly burned its way down to the basement where a recent delivery of six tons of coal awaited its chance to fuel the fury raging above. The hotel was built on a cliff that made difficult the access from all but the north side, and when the fire department arrived, alerted by a call from Wilma Glendening from her beauty shop window as she was trimming Mrs. Albert Hayden's hair, it was obvious that their task was going to be difficult if not impossible. People were removed from the upper stories, furniture, dishes, silver and whatever people thought to *save* were thrown out of the windows, and guests who were resting in their rooms, unaware of danger, were alerted by the staff and brought down the smokey stairwells. Fire fighting units from as far away as forty-five miles raced to assist the local Volunteer Fire Department but their cause was a hopeless one as the hotel contained too much tinder dry wood and other combustibles typical of older buildings. Mrs. Mabel Clatworthy, whose husband's photographic studio was on West Elkhorn Avenue said, "Out in front I could see the hotel gradually going, and tears came to my eyes." Pieter Hondius, Jr. remembered. "We heard some noise when we were in high school that afternoon. When school got out we scooted for football practice and looked up the hill to see the smoke. We piled in someone's pickup and went up there. By that time, everyone was at it and the thing was gone, of course, but someone salvaged five gallons of ice cream from the freezer. We sat there in our football suits eating ice cream and watched it go." Mrs. Hattie Myers who lived close to the hotel on the east side could still see the hotel burning when she gave this brief statement forty-two years later. "Well, the fact that the wind was blowing a hundred miles an hour and it was blowing the cinders down there so people had fire hoses or their garden hoses, I was out here on this side (i.e. west) with the hose all day because embers were blowing clear to the school."

The heat was intense as far away as several blocks as one resident retold. "I was living at the Riverside Hotel (i.e. formerly the Josephine) and as I looked from my front porch I could see the flames going clear up. You couldn't see the hotel, just the flames. The heat split windows down on Elkhorn Avenue near the old lumber yard. That was awful!" Otis Whiteside can see the beautiful structure burning in his mind even today. "Burning shingles were blowing all over town. They should have knocked a hole in the roof and let the heat out and the water in, but instead kept squirting water on the shingles and it just ran off on top of them. When they decided it was really going--," and he shook his head with some disdain at the rescuers' efforts, "they started throwing the furniture out the windows and it all broke to pieces!" Others, who were alerted when a man ran into the Legion Club on Elkhorn Avenue shouting "**The Lewiston is on fire!**", ran up to the red glowing inferno to witness confused people inside throwing the expensive piano off the front porch to certain destruction as well as the expensive china while others at the same moment were carefully carrying piles of linen tablecloths down the front stone steps in tragic-comic procession. It was a night no one will ever forget, of the blackening outline of the grand lady of the hotel industry silhouetted against the last rays of light in the western sky. Fire fighters concentrated their efforts to save the rest of the town from flying embers and extreme heat as it was evident that the hotel was lost as they were prevented from bringing their hoses close enough to the hotel positioned high upon the rock promontory over the river. With all of the coal in the cellar finally springing to life, the fire throbbed with belches of small explosions for days before finally extinguishing itself under deep piles of ash from the cremated treasures of A. D. and Anita Lewis. With the war years many of the citizens of Estes Park joined up to support their country's efforts and few tourists came to require additional hotel rooms. The expense to rebuild the Lewiston Hotel at a cost of $320,000 was prohibitive and the Lewis family sadly moved away. I don't think they ever fully recovered from that terrible day that forever closed the large green hotel register containing the names of the rich, powerful, prominent and influential men and women who thought The Lewiston Hotel **the** place to reside in the Estes Valley. Gus Lewis died on July 27, 1957 in Culver City, California.

If you are curious about the assemblage of stone ruins on the hill at the west end of Elkhorn Avenue, you are welcome to hike up to them. Climb the still impressive front stone steps and imagine entering the front lobby to be greeted by a uniformed attendant inquiring if he could assist you with your bags. If you listen quietly, the sound of music, tinkling dishes and the bustle of the little folks running past you to get to the children's room still fills the ghostly, charred surroundings. It is gone, but Mr. and Mrs. Lewis's efforts to build their beautiful Lewiston Hotel, in service for nearly thirty years, should be considered an important chapter in the book of lodging history of Estes Park that will never be closed.

Lewis Guest House, circa 1914 (Private)

Living Room In Lewis Guest House, circa 1915 (Private)

A.D. Lewis, 1923 (Town of Estes Park)

Lewiston Hotel, circa 1916 (EPHM)

Lewiston Hotel, 1920 (CHS)

Japanese Tea Room, Top Of Lewiston, circa 1920 (CHS)

Lewiston Offices & Cafe, Formerly Park Hotel, 1920 (CHS)

Josephine Hotel, Later The Riverside, circa 1920s (CHS)

Lewiston Chalet, Later Estes Park Chalet, circa 1920 (CHS)

Main Dining Room Of Lewiston Hotel, circa 1930 (CHS)

The Guests' Parlor Of Lewiston Hotel, circa 1930 (CHS)

Lewiston Hotel, by F.P. Clatworthy, 1937 (EPHM)

The Lewiston Burns, 9-4-1941 (EPHM)

THE CRAGS LODGE

I came to know of Enoch Josiah Mills, who preferred simply to be called Joe Mills, in 1978 when as a business investment through a partnership I purchased the historic Crags Lodge in Estes Park. Joe had died years before I became a resident of the village, yet his personality pervaded the atmosphere as I directed the restoration of his lodge gone dormant from succeeding owners' inappropriate use whose priorities of endeavors ranked lodge management and maintenance near the bottom. Old pictures in the lodge scrapbook and yellowing newspaper clippings of their work, joys and some sorrows testified to Joe's family's campaign to be a complete part of their community. Reading many of the letters and poems received from guests expressing complete satisfaction were clear evidence that the Mills family had given much of themselves to their beloved Crags Lodge. But let me back up a moment and examine in some detail how the Crags Lodge found itself upon the north slope of Prospect Mountain just south of the village, and why it was called *The House On The Hill*.

Joe Mills, named Enoch for his father's brother, was born in prairie country near Fort Scott, Kansas in 1880 to Enos and Ann Mills of whom I have written in my recollections of Long's Peak Inn. A worshiper of the open-air, Joe could spend hours watching a bird, study a fox creeping through the tall yellowing grass, or in fascination watch billowing clouds blow over his grassland hillside from the vast spaces in the West. In a study of his photographs he took over the years, I think his favorite subject matter were clouds, their intricate patterns he referred to as the *tracery of the heavens*. His mother and father had imparted to him many thrilling stories of their days on the gold prospecting trail in Colorado, such as when Indians tried to steal his mother's pot of stew and the huge snowy mountains filled with great horned creatures and clear streams teeming with fish. By the time he was ten years old he vowed that he would live in the West, and pestered his father about when he could leave. "Father put his foot down firmly, a sign that his patience was at an end," Joe emphasized in a book about his life, "so I postponed my adventure." In 1896, at the age of sixteen, his day finally came as he was given permission to spend the summer near Long's Peak. With but twenty dollars in his pocket, he strained out the train's window for the first hint of the Rockies while giving half an ear to mountain tales recounted by a miner seated next to him who was on his way to stake a claim near Grand Lake, Colorado. The rough trip over Bald Mountain Road from Loveland to Estes Park was not completed on the regular thrice weekly four-horse stage. The stage, costing three dollar that Joe judged reasonable, was rejected as not as interesting as hiking into his new mountain adventure. However since the single canvas bag was awkwardly heavy and the thirty miles of steep rutted roadway took some of the shine off his fantasy, he purchased a used bicycle for eight dollars and set off. After several headlong spills despite the small trees tied on behind for a brake and a near fatal encounter with an angry range cow with sharp horns, he was well on his way to, he later wrote, "the Mecca of my dreams."

His first glimpse into the Estes Valley elicited this mature, bard-like, response from one still in his teens. "Before me loomed the Rockies, strangely unreal in the moonlight and yet very like the mountains of my imagination. I gazed, spellbound. My dream was realized." By prior arrangement, his destination was Lamb's Ranch and Long's Peak House, nine miles south of the village of Estes Park. Reverend Elkanah Lamb, referred to by Joe as *The Parson*, was his mother's brother whom he admired and remembered respectfully. "The Parson was more than six feet tall, straight as a lodgepole pine physically --and even more so spiritually. He wore a long flowing beard, rose habitually and unprotestingly at four in the morning, and was a man of diverse talents and eccentricities." Joe was thrilled by his summer vacation, working part time and exploring whenever his duties permitted. Love for mountains and its wildlife was a part of his personality. In the Elkanah Valley he searched for broader methods of expression in copious reflections written in his pocket notebook of what he observed, and associated them with an abundance of photos, two activities that would occupy a great deal of his adult life. He returned the next summer intending to acquire his own homestead tract on the western slope of Twin Sisters Mountain, just below timberline in an area that appears on the maps as Cabin Rock, even though he was below the permitted age. It is not clear whether he acquired title in 1898, or only a leasehold, through his friendship with Dr. William S. Cooper who later became a Professor of Botany at the University of Minnesota. What we do know for certain is that he singlehandedly built his own little cabin with its unique outside fireplace chimney of troll-like appearance. He treasured his tiny cabin, referred to as *The Silent Place*, where for years thereafter, and as often as he could arrange a trip to the mountains, he sat before his fireplace reading intellectually stimulating literature and arraigned his photographs in albums with inspired visions to their future worth. Before the warm hearth the young man meditated upon the purpose for his life while codifying a superb code of ethics and conduct that would govern his later athletic, business and literary endeavors. Some local historians swear that the cabin was erected on a location once occupied by the famous scout Kit Carson, although Kit Carson was known to have frequented many areas up and down the Tahosa Valley. Sometime around 1968, long after Joe had died, two local boys accidentally burned the cabin to the ground with the only remnant now visible being that fireplace.

As the years went by he graduated from high school in Fort Scott and received a partial athletic scholarship to attend Colorado Agricultural College in Fort Collins where he earned honors as a triple letterman in football, baseball and track. Transferring to Denver University in 1903, he quarterbacked the football team, excelled as the shortstop on the baseball team, was the playing manager of the champion basketball team and still found time to coach the girl's basketball team. If that wasn't enough for an ordinary day of exertion, he joined the track team to set many records. From 1904 through 1906 Joe was hired by Fort Worth University in Texas as its football coach, and in 1906, as often was the case at small schools in the early years, served concurrently as coach, quarterback and captain at the age of 26 years. For his efforts on the field he was voted All-Southern Quarterback. His fancy footwork, and continuing interest in English literature, caught the attention of a campus resident. Ethel Steere, born in 1884 in Dallas, Texas and the youngest of twelve children, was literary editor of *The University Unit* published monthly by the school. Their friendship developed over the next few years as Joe was employed in 1907 as Physical Director for Polytechnic College in Fort Worth. Although small in stature, often being dubbed *the little man*, he possessed outstanding athletic and coaching abilities and strength with the result that many records in a wide spectrum of disciplines were achieved that stood for many years. His star took off on a bright path when in 1908 at the age of 28 he was named Coach and General Director of Athletics at Baylor University in Waco, Texas. His rapid rise in his profession of coaching and athletic administration was truly phenomenal and his praise was sung in the Baylor University newspaper, *The Lariat*, at the time of his appointment to its staff. "Enoch Mills is one of the best all around athletes that ever came to Texas and possesses the faculty of being able to impart his knowledge to others. He excels at all branches of indoor and outdoor sports. His services were in great demand for next year and Baylor is to be congratulated on securing the services of such an excellent instructor."

In May of 1909 after nearly two seasons at Baylor under his belt and some money in the bank, he married Ethel. Joe yearned to return to Colorado, at least for the summer season, and learned of the possibility of leasing an old stage coach stop in the Big Thompson Canyon called The Forks Hotel, twelve miles east of Estes Park and at an elevation of 6,200 feet. From 1909 to 1913, Joe and Ethel operated their summer tourist hotel, serving meals, renting rooms and where their first child, Eleanor *Peg* Mills Yeager, was born in 1911. During these years he became well known as a lecturer and an outdoorsman, especially adept in climbing where at The Forks he conducted a respected climbing school. During the school term, however, he returned to Baylor to coach and teach English. It was at Baylor and The Forks Hotel, during the evenings, that he strove to advance his emerging talent for writing. Submitting articles and short stories to many publishers of magazines, particularly those devoted to sports and business, an increasing number of those publications began accepting his works. Those publishers included, *Outdoor World & Recreation; The Canadian Countryman; The American Youth; The Round Robin Reader for Boys & Girls; The Business Man's Publishing Co.; Modern Methods Publishing; The Boys World;* and *The Housekeeper of Colliers.* He wrote on every conceivable subject concerning business and outdoor life. The price for the narratives accepted was not based so much upon the significance of the article but more on the length of the story, rewarded as the rate varied between one and four cents per word. The titles he ascribed to his stories were as unique as the story lines were diverse in content when he, as I do in this free spirited alliteration, frolicked to a farcical fascination with fictionalized fact culminating in sound and ethical conclusions. The following labels illustrate his wide span of subject matter: *Reversin' The Tables; Wanted, A Grouch; The Man With The Idea; Delivering The Goods; The Bundle Of Fur; Shadow; The Patent Churn; Banking The Middleman's Toll; The Spy; The Postponed Failure;* and *The Diary Of A Drinking Cup.*

In 1913 and 1914 he began referring to himself in his publications as Joe Mills instead of Enoch J. Mills and for the rest of his life was rarely referred to by his more formal and biblical sounding name. By 1910 his reputation as a coach and administrator, and his character as a fine human being had spread throughout Texas as well Colorado. In Baylor's newspaper that year was its own assessment of their coach. "Coach is a thorough gentleman, very quiet, does not have much to say, and never brags. He is a good spieler, a

241

clever schemer, and usually gets there. He is working hard for Baylor, and deserves the gratitude of the institution for his efforts toward giving to her a general system of sane athletics." In the Mills' early brochure printed for The Forks and in which his penchant for artistic expression in free verse was amply verified, it explained their method of operation that continued even after they had constructed the Crags Lodge, except for the cows and chickens. "We are at home to the world-weary traveler and delight to share our contentment with those who enjoy the natural life. Our furnishings are plain and simple, our rooms are clean and comfortable. Our meals are prepared by a woman who preserves the natural, homey flavor, and are served to you on clean, rustic tables, family style, --no menu and no excuse for tipping. Our source of foods is a thrifty garden which supplies a surprising variety of good things. Half a dozen cows supply clean milk and thick cream, and a large family of chickens add to the joy of living. In the yard a clear, cold spring overflows its generous supply of pure water. Climb the mountains and *get their good tidings*. There are wild flowers and birds, picnics among the silent places, and fishing, tennis, riding, croquet and exploring will call you outdoors. Now, as you see, we are well along toward solving the high cost of living, being producers as well as consumers. We charge you as little as we dare. All these good things are yours, in exchange, say, for ten or fourteen dollars a week."

Yet as much as they revered their first interlude with hoteling in the canyon of the Big Thompson, Joe and Ethel longed to be up within full view of the towering front range, high on a hill around Estes Park. By 1913 they had purchased more than forty acres on the north slope of Prospect Mountain and adjacent to the Big Thompson River. Around this period of time he accepted a position at the University of Colorado to coach the sports of golf, track and football as well as teach English. By 1918 he was named the university's Head Coach of Athletics for the depleted civilian manpower and military trainees housed on the campus. One of the outstanding members of his football teams was Byron *Whizzer* White who grew in legal talent as a lawyer to become an Associate Justice of the United States Supreme Court. Joe Mills was now home in Colorado, all year long. After designing the lodge, he named it The Crags for its sublime position "on the shoulder of the mountain that commands a wonderful view" that scrutinizes the village activities below. On this rocky prominence Joe and Ethel pitched a large tent, hired helpers, and set to work. Little did they know that the winter of 1913 would bring the deepest snows in the memory of the old settlers that complicated the attainment of their dream with an added formidable challenge. On June 20, 1914 the local newspaper reported, "It is expected that the beautiful Crags Hotel will be completed and ready for the accommodation of the public by July 1st. Enoch Mills, the proprietor, is doing all he can to arrange everything for the best interests of his guests." After much hard work they opened for dinner on July 4, 1914. Within a month, World War I began in Europe to later draw the United States into a firestorm that after its inadequate quenching would fuel from smoldering embers of hate and nationalistic revenge even greater conflagrations a few decades later.

The first year of business, two prominent persons visited the Crags. F. O. Stanley, a friend of Joe and Ethel and who had encouraged their efforts, "took Sunday dinner with his wife at the Crags," and from the dining room windows he could enjoy a distant view of his own hotel to the north that he was pleased to point out to his fellow diners. Former guests reported that "The Crags had a reputation for many years for excellent food." A number of the offerings that were offered to guests from Ethel's unwritten *Varying Menus*, only posted on the kitchen wall or appended to her cookbook, were "Fresh frog legs, Hashed lamb, Lobster wiggle, Mutton ragout, Planked lamb chops a la Tarbeaux, Salt codfish, Boiled calves tongues, Boned ham baked with sherry and frosted, Cottage meat pie, Crab flake timbales, Dunkirk meat pie, Spaghetti rarebit," and that ever favorite dish, "Burr Oak farm potatoes." As I had pointed out in my reference to the press's investigative technique to ferret out the important guests of the lodges, it was practiced on a truly famous customer of the Crags. In the news media that first summer, a reporter's coup revealed that "Clarence S. Darrow, the *prominent* Chicago lawyer and defender of the trade unions, is now a guest at the Crags." The next years would find the Mills' family, now increased to four at the birth of Mark Muir *Bud* Mills in 1917, busily hosting thousands of summer visitors. At the same time Joe was busy writing and teaching collegiate sports and of course occupying a seat on the faculty as Assistant Professor of English at the University of Colorado. The popularity of his nature talks, enlivened by personal observations of nature and photographic presentations of mountains, animals and the attributes required to both understand and survive the harsh and recalcitrant rules of the wild, were reaching beyond the State of Colorado. Thus he retained an agent to supervise his bookings, the A. K. Jones Agency of Chicago, as that metropolis in the 1920s provided a rich loam bed to germinate artistic seeds into budding circuit lecturers. The agent billed his lectures, *Adventuring In The Rockies by Joe Mills of Estes Park, Colorado.* The agency's promotional brochure for their new client advertised Joe as a multi-talented individual, as indeed he was. "He is unique among naturalist-lecturers, as he is an explorer, mountain-climber, guide, author and artist." He was a frequent participant on the rubber chicken circuit throughout the country from January 2nd of each year until May when the Crags Lodge was closed until the summer season. In nature sketches replete with a medley of wildlife associations, he was unassuming in manner yet fluently eloquent and captivating to all ages of spectators. Crafting his programs with tales of venturesome experiences in the wilds, he succeeded in explaining to his audience the importance of elk, beaver and other wild animals in the full complicated order of life. His goal was to enlist them in an alliance for the protection of those creatures and a reverence for the land in which they dwelt.

Joe Mills had much to do with the creation of Rocky Mountain National Park in ways similar to his brother Enos, yet at the same time with a different attitude that lacked neither political connotation nor the raw edge of vindictiveness to those that were in opposition. He promoted the National Park's importance through the news media, including early radio broadcasts and on the lecture platform through descriptions of the wondrous beauties of Rocky Mountain National Park highlighted by his own variety of colorful Autochrome photography. His opinions, written before 1915, embody his great love for this National Park and of its health-giving answers provided to lives too much wrapped up in the problems of modern day existence. A few of his views are worth repeating to generations who did not have the pleasure and privilege of hearing this unusual man.

"In this conventional age we are losing originality and individuality. These were the traits which made the pioneer men and women of a different mold. This is a ready made age. We try to buy health at a drug store, second hand. The air we breath is second hand. Most people are living such lives that they are afraid to go back to Nature. The fear of Nature, by process of evolution, has made us prejudiced against outdoors, hence a timid life is made more timid and materially shortened by being hidden from nature and the outdoors. Most everything is adulterated, even our lives. Outdoor life is our greatest friend, because it will make us do our best, make us independent. To one of Nature's children, there are few impossibilities. A Nature child is like the forest, full of possibilities, hospitable, hopeful, helpful. Without nature, man is as barren as the desert. Have you ever let a leaping brook sing you to sleep? The outdoor folk, the animals, have been basely gossiped about and slanderously misrepresented. In rambling the wilds I have never been in danger from attack of any wild thing. The mountains are Nature's great relief maps. By climbing them we enjoy strange, rare roof gardens and see inspiring sights that fill us to overflowing. In the outdoors you rely on yourself, self reliance, and that makes you strong.

"This region seems to be Mother Nature's favorite child. On it she has lavished her most precious and most miraculous gifts. Dashing torrents leap down its steep slopes, sparkling rivers wind through its lovely valleys. Everywhere are lakes, icy, emerald, spruce-fringed. Wild flowers color the landscape, blooming as the season progresses, first in the lower meadows, then gradually climbing the slopes til they scale the loftiest summits. In a short two hour ride from the village of Estes Park to Milner Pass, one may find the counterpart of climate, plants and animals one would find on a 1,500 mile journey northward to the Arctic Circle. Everywhere in this wonderland of the Rockies, open pretty little parks, some are merely openings among the great trees. Others cover miles of territory with green grass, carpeting flowers and scattered pines. Above all the mountains stand guard while the frequent summer showers sprinkle the valleys and dust the peaks with white. In this region, instead of an inverted divisor as the Grand Canyon might be called, the Rocky Mountain National Park will stand erect, high in the air. Because there is so much to this Park, in order to get it all in it was necessary that much of the material had to be stood on end as this Park has length, breadth and thickness too. Instead of curiosities predominating, this new Park possesses all the lovely and the wild, and visitors will return again and again who come under its spell. The Alps have long had their Alpine devotees. The Colorado Rockies, just as majestic, more inviting and offering more variety and just as many thrills, must have theirs too."

His life was not all so exciting as he and his family endured the long winters at the lodge in somewhat inadequate quarters as well as periods of separation when he was away teaching or lecturing. We must remember that at this time Joe and Ethel had two young children requiring regular parental attention, and the expenses for their large lodge investment, at a time when the world was at war and with few guests in residence, were substantial. Earnings from a short tourist season, meager lecture fees, a minimum of revenue from his writing, and his university position that paid little more than lip service and prestige, were well husbanded while the family lived conservatively. The family needed to conserve their assets as Pat Washburn, the granddaughter of Joe and Ethel, informed me. In the winters of 1914-1918, the family lived in the basement of the hotel to better economize on heating their rooms and because there was an employee kitchen located nearby that could serve them in several capacities. The water for the lodge was turned off in the cold weather thereby stipulating by necessity that Joe and Ethel haul buckets of precious water up the steep hill from the river. Early families, such as the Mills, had to depend upon their own abilities and muscles to cope with the discomforts associated with protracted winters in a village of 300 souls where public utilities were at subsistence levels. But they did have fun on their hill, two hundred feet above the rest of town, seated in front of their huge fireplace in the empty lodge and popped corn to string on their Christmas tree and feed the hungry and curiously unafraid deer and wild sheep who shared their knoll. The Colorado Mountain Club, of which the Mills were members, often came up to the lodge and used the driveway as a great run downhill for their toboggans.

Sports had always been a large part of the Mills's lives, especially golf in which both Joe and Ethel excelled. Joe posted a record setting 78 in the Northern Colorado Invitational Golf Championship of 1920 and won a number of trophies at the local golf course. Elected President of the Estes Park Golf and Country Club in 1921, the records during his term of office reflected numerous improvements including the construction of a new water storage reservoir building to provide a dependable supply of drinking water for golfers and their guests. This little rock structure is still to be seen near the club house, in need of attention, but perhaps forgotten by current board members of the governing Recreation District whose attention now is directed towards more sophisticated improvements to entice tournaments of non-residents with deep pockets. Ethel was not to be outdone as she was elected for a number of years the Captain of the Ladies Golf Association. Joe had a big heart for the children of his community and, since Crags property extended to the banks of the Big Thompson River, he excavated a fishing hole for small girls and boys that in 1993, after being filled in, is the site for a pizza restaurant. Over the years the well patronized *Joe Mills' Pond*, to which identification it was locally known, was regularly stocked with trout and freely available to all children 12 years and younger. Fishing derbies, including one called Huck Finn Days, regularly were held where older fisherman taught their sons, daughters and other small fry the special art of landing a big one. The Mills' family always welcomed to the Crags grounds students and their teachers, including Sunday School classes as Estes Park resident Ted Mathews informed me. "Our teacher was Cliff Higby, and often after our Sunday School lessons we all went on a picnic above the Crags Lodge where there was this wonderful spring." Ted, whose full name is Teddie R. Mathews and named for Theodore Roosevelt, apprised me of the fact that his father worked for Joe and Ethel at the time trenches were being dug for water line extensions at the Crags. It is not clear who were the culprits that early 4th of July morning, but I have my suspicions as does Ted when the town was awakened to exploding dynamite pirated from the Crags job as smoke was seen to arise on the hillside behind the Hupp Hotel.

A recreation building west of the main lodge was erected in 1920. On June 25th of that year, after a dinner speech to the Northern Colorado Rotarians in the lodge by Professor Charles Lory of the Agriculture School in Fort

Collins, all one hundred diners adjourned to dedicate in song and dance the new recreation hall, where over succeeding years splendid entertainment and square dancing would be provided for the guests. Over the succeeding years the lodge was enlarged substantially in girth, length and height as the Estes Park Trail revealed in 1923. "The Crags is rapidly growing in popularity and the contemplated improvements will enable Joe Mills to better care for those who wish to stop there. Some work will be done this spring, but much of it will necessarily be finished this fall. The dining room and lobby will be enlarged to accommodate 300 or more guests and probably 50 new guest rooms will be added. A number of cottages will be built at a cost of $50,000." Guests thoroughly enjoyed Joe and Ethel who were considered an excellent team. The animals likewise enjoyed the lodge illustrated by the fact that a family of chipmunks deemed it most hospitable of the owners to allow them to make their home in the piano over the winter of 1923-24. The twenty cabins erected along the winding road behind the main lodge, consisted of one, two and three room units. In addition to the two upper floors of the main lodge containing 40 guest rooms, there was constructed a fourteen room motel-like cottage, later reduced to seven modern units as dirt was pushed up against the first floor to leave only the second floor to look out upon the world in the 1950s. In 1924 the dining room was further widened on the north side and enclosed by a wall of windows as the newspaper reported when "Joe Mills and his cheery handshake bolted into the Trail's office." The view from those windows still is impressive as the twinkling lights of the town are revealed through the branches of those little trees now grown tall that the Mills planted long ago.

His speeches involving his early experiences when he first came to Colorado included one on October 21, 1921 before the Colorado Mountain Club in Denver from which he received lots of applause and an idea for a later book. After that presentation a reviewer acclaimed, "He delighted hundreds of people with his tales of experiences and camping in the Rockies and of the greater part of his life spent in the out-of-doors living intimately with nature." His energetic schedule of lectures, including one in Omaha, Nebraska on radio station W O W in 1924 and sponsored by the Burlington Railroad, kept him away for longer periods of the year leaving much of the work to his wife and their devoted friend Gus Schory. Gus settled in Estes Park around 1901 after functioning as a stage driver on one of those hard working 4-horse contraptions that were a Godsend to this and other communities. Those drivers wheeled in for years the three necessities of Estes Park, --mail, food and a dependable source of income, tourists. Gus made his home at the lodge from 1914 until his death, and over the winters in later years he was the only inhabitant of the Crags when the family resided in Boulder. A solitary man, who Joe said was "industrious, efficient, quiet and absolutely faithful and loyal," Gus possessed an endearing humor and was a man who mingled well with Crags' guests. He is remembered as a man who had "a host of furry and feathered friends" as scores of wild creatures patiently awaited Gus' appearance at the kitchen door with treats. His pet squirrel, however, received first choice of the offerings. To know him was to have a real friend, and when Joe wrote an epitaph when Gus died in April of 1925, he summarized a life in this poignant sentence. "He met the trials along life's trail with sturdy fortitude, and neither success nor illfortune made him waiver."

Picnic suppers every Wednesday evenings on lodge property were very well attended by lodge guests, especially after Joe and several of his friends had caught the trout the preceding day out of Lawn Lake and the other streams and lakes where Joe knew fish abounded. It was always a treat to see Joe cooking the fish and Ethel, attired in her Gypsy costume, filling the plates with as much as the guests could eat. In fact, after two or three helpings, guests hiked back, --thankfully downhill, to the lodge while singing western songs "just to wear off some of that great food so we could sleep as we were so full!" The lodge was the site for many conventions, social, business as well as political gatherings and was considered the *place to be seen* at gatherings of local organizations and special events. I firmly believe that Gus's final illness had something to do with Joe's decision to leave the university and spend more time at the lodge, for in 1924 he resigned from the University of Colorado where as football coach he had earned for himself the well deserved handle of *Battling Joe*. At the time of his departure he was basketball and track coach and his teams had won seven conference championships. He now intended to devote all of his time to the Crags, and his writing that was consuming much of his free time. Increasing his lecture schedule and continuing to write short stories for publications such as *Blue Book* and *Red Book*, headed by Karl Harriman who was a frequent guest, those accepted stories were considered wholesome and honest representations of the West. The *Estes Park Trail* commented upon his stories. "In today's stories of the West, most magazine readers associate the first mention of the West with some of the vast amount of blood and thunder stories with which most publications are filled these days. Many false ideas of the western portion of the United States have been created by these false stories. It has remained for Joe Mills to popularize a new type of western story. The blood and thunder are absent, but there is a decidedly wholesome interest from start to finish. The West can be thankful to Mr. Mills for his true picturization of it and can rejoice equally with him in his success, as many of Mr. Mills's stories have been excellent studies in an interesting and intelligent view of nature in the Rockies."

In 1926 and 1927 he wrote two books that received much acclaim and clearly established him as a quality writer. One was entitled *The Comeback*, about the love of a man and a dog for each other. The other one, more widely distributed and that gave him more notoriety, was entitled *A Mountain Boyhood*. Written for both adults and young people, this pervasive book chronicled Joe's life in the mountains and his friendly encounters with nature absent of unnecessary and unrealistic violence. I believe the appreciative remarks and the warmth of his audiences on his lecture circuit predestined that this charming story be published as it was in 1926 by the J. H. Sears Publishing Company. In token of his love and respect for his wife, he dedicated the book to her in these words, "To the one who made this boyhood possible, My Wife." I recommend them both to your libraries for their reflection of decency, sound ethics, high adventure and educational experiences of profound worth. One who spoke very highly of Joe and Ethel was Charles Eagle Plume, nationally known lecturer. It was to Joe and Ethel Mills that he owed his introduction as an entertainer as they were the first lodge owners in the early 1920s that gave him, and his associate Ray Silver Tongue, an opportunity to earn some extra money dancing, singing and lecturing. At the Crags Lodge he passed the hat after his first performance that initiated a long career. "In fact we passed it twice!" he later exclaimed. Joe and Ethel were always willing to help someone.

By 1929, Crags Lodge, after complete redecoration in 1925 and 1926 by the craftsman Charles Robbins, could accommodate 200. In an examination of his brochure for that year it is clear that he kept to his *modus operandi* originated twenty years earlier at The Forks but augmented with more balanced viands. "The Crags is not a dressy place. Most folks come for relaxation and a good time outdoors. Old clothes are fashionable here. We cater to wholesome, happy folks who enter into the spirit of the house and who want real rest and recreation. No snobs. The meals are served family style. The meals are scientifically planned and are balanced dietetically. There are no menus. Tipping is not necessary. Guests are served at tables seating six to ten. We try to select congenial folks in making up the seating lists. We do not have private or exclusive tables for small parties. We have tame chipmunks and do not want dogs. No grouches wanted. Located on a private road, there is no poison ivy, few flies and mosquitos, and no poisonous snakes. There are mountains to climb, trails and roads to ride, canyons and peaks to explore. Horseback trips are provided by Jud Carrel, guide. We have an on site tennis court and a swimming pool is available nearby at Riverside that also has a 10 piece dance band playing every night." The main lodge building in the 1930s consisted of three floors, with baths down the halls and a fourth floor for employee dormitories. Later private baths were added to each guest room as their numbers were reduced. A full basement contained the laundry, additional employee quarters and their own kitchen. The main floor, in addition to the huge dining room with that marvelous view overlooking the village, included large assembly rooms, screened-in porches, the office and an amply furnished kitchen. When I purchased the Crags I remember the kitchen still contained an elderly automated dishwasher in solid copper, still functional and manufactured by the Colt Arms Company. Many former employees over the years delighted in the fact that the old beauty, with which they labored through summer holidays, still survived to perform with some noisy, mechanical complaints deserving of its senior status. A large hitching rack and contrived corral lay immediately west of the main lodge where horses ordered by guests the previously evening would be waiting for them by 8 A. M. The recreation building later was divided to include a residence for succeeding owners to which was added a swimming pool.

Joe Mills loved being a host at his lodge, and wrote a small article about the attitude a lodge owner should have as he approached his job. He entitled his article, *The Way You Do It* and I will quote from it to illustrate his concern for his guests as well as his employees. I commend his wisdom to present day hotel and motel operators who could learn much from him.

"It's not so much what you do or say -but the way you do it, is a very old and a very truthful saying. And it is around this fact that we have built our business. A resort hotel offers many opportunities, though no more than the average business, for reaching its patrons in pleasurable and profitable ways. One of the chief amusements of a resort hotel is the indoor sport of eating three times a day. Through their stomachs you can reach them, but there are other ways. Anticipating the wants of anyone before they are aware of their desires themselves, is a sound way to quick popularity. It is the basis of ancient hospitality, and it is the spirit of modern times which will mark

any business as distinct whenever it is honestly employed. The lack of it puts a business into the chilly class known as cold-blooded business propositions. In our little resort hotel we have established our lives, we live in it, believe in it, take pleasure in it. Guests who come to us, we adopt into the family, and we share with them everything but the family skeleton, --which, of course, is kept where it belongs. The first consideration is to make a guest feel at home. It's not the big things that count most, but its the multitude of little ones that convince the guest that he or she is being appreciated. We go to great trouble and work to give campfire suppers in the woods, and no amount of pain is spared which will add to the enjoyment of these occasions. Together we enjoy the comradeship that comes from the frankness which we employ where we believe in our guests and they believe in us. Peanuts, hot from the oven, on rainy nights seem to fit in with the open fires and make the evenings complete. We are too busy practicing to preach, we do not theorize but act, and all doors are left unlocked. There are no rules as all are invited to join the spirit of the house. If they do not, they are out of place, and to be out of place is not a comfortable nor enduring feeling.

"Our success depends upon uniform service, not the sort commanded or bribed, but the kind that comes spontaneously from interested workers. These workers fit or they do not, and they go or stay. There is no scolding. Quality counts. We pay for it, and as hands are always plenty, we pay premiums for brains. It is our custom to tell the help the details of what we want to accomplish, suggest means to the end, accept suggestions and pay for them in rapid promotion. Several dishwashers have jumped to the front office, while cooks have been pensioned, and satisfaction is the spirit of the house. We believe in soap, as a clean and scrubbed floor with quaint rag rugs is more attractive at our house than dingy carpets. I don't suppose our beds are any better than our neighbors' but they are as clean and neat as an interested housekeeper can make them. The food we serve is the best and it is the pride of the house that this food is served tastily, and sent to the tables hot, not warm. Family style, no menu, is the way and there's no delay. One thing we do demand is promptness and folks must be on time. It is the habit of the house to be happy. That is the reason the shedder of gloom is unpopular, as No Grouches Wanted is a pointed paragraph in our little booklet, and we live up to every single section we advertise. If I had to give a single suggestion, or to name the thing most apparent in our success, I'd say, We Enjoy Our Business! Nothing, I believe, succeeds like genuine goods, no matter whether they be abstract or concrete. I believe our success has come from eagerly enjoying our guests, and in doing for them the simple, homelike things that make our place different from others. You see, it's the way you do it that counts."

Joe's lectures were much in demand in the early 1930s and his writings had caught the attention of such prominent publishers as the Saturday Evening Post. It was becoming apparent that his increasing manuscript approval throughout the country would crown his endeavors with financial success and colleagial recognition. At the end of the 1935 tourist season Joe and Ethel were living in an apartment in the Shirley-Savoy Hotel in Denver and their days never seemed brighter as letters arrived from convention managers, publishers and sundry organizations requesting his appearance for a program or annunciating his praise to his writing skills and simultaneously importuning him to favor their company with a publishing contract. However, a dark cloud began to eclipse his sunshine and his longevity for robustness demanded for his lifestyle became questionable. Unbeknown to most of his friends and business associates, he suffered from diabetes, and episodes of dizziness and other symptoms of the disease taxed his energy and endangered his life. The insidious malady struck him very hard on that fateful Friday evening of September 27, 1935. The entire state that had followed his career awoke the next morning to read in shock the headline in the *Rocky Mountain Denver News* Saturday morning edition, "JOE MILLS HURT IN CRASH." While driving home in his automobile on East Colfax Avenue at Pontiac Street in Denver after a lecture, he crashed headlong into a street railway car after falling into a diabetic coma. His skull was fractured and after lingering a few weeks, he died at the age of 55. The village of Estes Park closed down for his memorial service at which citizens from all walks of life recited poignant testimony to a life well lived that was dedicated to his town, and its citizens whom he greatly appreciated for their friendship and encouragement. The local newspaper printed the following tribute from Joe's Rotary Club that typified much of the sentiment of all of his friends. "The Estes Park Rotary Club and the citizens of the Estes Park region have suffered an irreparable loss in the passing of our outstanding citizen and friend, Joe Mills. We realize well the high esteem everyone in the region has held for Joe. It was a privilege to have known him, for it was he who uncovered the hidden beauties of our scenic wonderland. It was Joe, a man with a vision, who capitalized on our natural resources and was instrumental in the formation of the Rocky Mountain National Park. His untiring efforts and all his civic enterprises can never be fully appreciated. Now there remains an unquestioned responsibility for each of us to carry on in the locality that Joe loved."

A tree in the town park was dedicated to him on November 12, 1937 to stand as a continuing tribute to a life lived for others. The editor of the *Estes Park Trail* spoke of the tree and of Joe. "Only God Can Make A Tree. Many of us in Estes Park will think of that quotation as we watch the tree, which is being placed in the park this week in memory of Joe Mills, grow and develop with the community. It seems so fitting that a memorial that is bound to become an integral part of the community should be in memory of one of Estes Park's first citizens, a man who was always interested in the vital problems of the region. The tree will stand as a sentinel guarding the town, as Joe Mills always stood, willing and anxious to guard the best interests of the community. The tree will represent the spirit of Christmas each year as it is lighted and decorated during the Yule season. Christmas is the time of open-hearted, generous giving, and Joe Mills was open-hearted and generous, giving freely of his time and strength and worldly goods that the community he called home might prosper." Unfortunately after several years, the tree died and a grateful town turned their attention to other endeavors, forgetting their sentinel that was to have stood symbolically reassuring as the town's protector. This perhaps is a reflection of the attitude of so many towards those early lodges and their owners whose struggles to achieve recognition for a small village as **the** resort in the Rockies earned them little more than a few paragraphs in a history book that few wanted to read. Rocky Mountain National Park, through its Superintendent Dave Canfield, would not let Joe be forgotten. In 1948 he nominated him as a person who deserved recognition in a geographical feature -- more enduring that a tree -- and safe within the National Park. The paper work was forwarded to the United States Board of Geographic Names in Washington and several unnamed mountains in the National Park were suggested, one in the Mummy Range and the other south of Fern Lake and southeast of Lake Odessa. Inasmuch as Notchtop Mountain and the Odessa region were favorite photographic subjects for her husband, Ethel chose the latter. In 1949, that unnamed 11.078 foot peak would forever be officially designated in remembrance of this man's untiring efforts to create, preserve and honor this National Park. On the Fern Lake trail, take time to see Joe Mills Mountain. It will stand as a true sentinel to the ages, necessitating no maintenance by those who often are neglectful of their own.

Ethel and her manager Gilbert May continued the Mills tradition at the lodge and illustrated the lodge's brochures with snippits from the many rolls of Joe's 16mm films that had illustrated his lectures. Ethel de-emphasized her own importance, always deferring to the achievements of her late husband, to the extent that she was proud to refer to herself, not as Ethel Mills on the Crags' literature but simply *Mrs. Joe Mills*. Ethel resided in Denver for most of the year other than for several months when she shared her wealth of knowledge of the mountains and her warm, laughing personality with guests who returned year after year to the Crags. But it was not the same without Joe, and she knew it. In 1946 the lodge, with the main building's upper floors reconfigured into 34 guest rooms and suites and the cabins now steam heated, was sold to Ralph and Hazel Reed. They competently operated the lodge until 1950, now as *The Friendly House On The Hill,* as a valuable resource to Estes Park now grown to nearly 1,500 wintertime residents if one somewhat stretched the boundaries southerly and westerly. In 1950 the lodge was sold to the Reed's children, Duane and Dwight to continued on in its management until 1959 when Dwight continued as the solo operator. At his death in 1967, ownership reverted to Duane and Jo Theobald Reed who moved back from Sun City, California where they were managers of Del Webb's Kings Inn. The Duane Reeds successfully operated a Chuckwagon Dinner Playhouse at the lodge with only limited guest room accommodations open to the public, and subsequently the lodge was leased for summer time athletic exercises including a wrestling camp. Those years of alternate economic exploration, so alien to a domain attuned to a past reputation for quality summer lodging, exacted a heavy toll on the Crags appearance and urbane personality. After my partners and I restored it to a modicum of its previous rustic elegance, it passed through two brief ownerships until it became part of the inventory of resorts of an Arizona corporation. Although the main floor is still devoted to local events such as dancing, weddings, dining and small conventions, the former guest rooms have been converted into more modern and luxuriously appointed time share ownerships. All cabins have been moved off the upper premises, now under separate ownership, in preparation for division into individually owned home sites.

For many years Ethel sent out Christmas cards to friends and thousands of Crags Lodge guests with her personal poetry printed with beautiful companion pictures previous taken by Joe over his lifetime. One day I intend to publish a book with a selection of these photos associated with her poetry, his philosophy, and my own reflections. Ethel Mills experienced another tragedy in 1948 when her son, Dr. Mark M. Mills died. Mark, employed as the director of the radiation laboratory at the University of California, was killed in a helicopter accident in the South Pacific while participating in early hydrogen bomb tests for this country. Ethel died at the age of 85 in Denver on December 23 1969. Their daughter Peg, Mrs. Dorr Yeager, still resides in California with her husband who himself made significant contributions to Rocky Mountain National Park as a former Park Naturalist as well as authoring a number of excellent books on wildlife that are well worth reading. I am greatly indebted to Pat Mills Washburn of Estes Park, Peg's daughter, who has been of invaluable assistance in providing information and pictures about her grandparents. The Crags Lodge, Joe, Ethel and all of the Reeds deserve to be remembered as operating a quality mountain resort that brought much credit to themselves and to Estes Park. But when I think of the Crags I can't help reflecting upon Joe Mills. He was a man's man, a lover of people in the right sense of the word and of the great out of doors. He had two great interests, people and nature. In his two professions, operating a guest lodge and in writing stories about his special environment and ways to improve the lives and attitudes of people, his life, shortened though it was, was amply fulfilled. What he was, and I know still is up beyond those marvelous cloud formations that were his adorations, was best said in the memorial poem dedicated to him by his friend Edna Romig.

FOR JOE MILLS

He dreamed the Crags and builded it,
High and comfortable and beautiful.
More than a lodge, more than a home,
Rich in the lore of nature, and art,
An ingathering place of noted men,
A place where children played.
He was a mountain man.
He breathed this ozone as some drink champagne,
He loved the valleys and the swinging plain.
The peaks he followed, span, upon sunny span,
The canyons were his veins, The rocks his bones,
The winds his special speech, the varied tones,
Of weather, snow and rain.
Wild creatures were his joy,
He caught their secrets, trapped
By patient lens their shape and habitat,
With fervor of the scientist and boy.
His passion was to save the forest, all,
This empire of wild living things,
The noiseless foot, the colored wings,
The lake, the river, and the waterfall.
Gentle as wood things are,
In voice and hand he moved,
At home with hills.
Love at the core of it,
Quick to perceive and understand,
Beneath his understanding lay,
A flashing wit.

Joe Mills In His Cabin On Twin Sisters Mtn., 1901 (Mills)

Joe Mills & Scotch At His Cabin, circa 1902 (Mills)

Joe Mills At Long's Peak Inn, circa 1906 (Mills)

Ethel Steere Mills, circa 1908 (Mills)

Forks Hotel After Enlargement, circa 1913 (Mills)

Crags Lodge Begins Construction, 1913 (Mills)

View From Crags In 1914 (Mills)

First Phase Of Crags Lodge Nears Completion, 1914 (Mills)

Crags Lodge Grows In Size, circa 1920s (Mills)

Indiana Hickory Chairs Arrive, circa 1920 (Mills)

Sorority Convention At Crags, 1919 (Mills)

Horseshoe Match By A Crags' Cabin, circa 1924 (Mills)

The Staff, Gus Schory In Center, circa 1917 (Mills)

Stage Coach Rides From The Crags, circa 1923 (Mills)

The Joe Mills Family, 1921 (Mills)

Joe And Ethel Mills, circa 1932 (Mills)

A Cookout On The Hill At Crags Lodge, circa 1920s (Mills)

Joe Mills Challenges The Mountains, circa 1910 (Mills)

Crags Lodge In Winter Attire In Late 1920s (Mills)

Joe Mills & His Favorite Photo Subject, circa 1925 (Mills)

Why Crags Was Known As The House On The Hill, circa 1940s (Sanborn Souvenir Co.)

CHAPTER X - THE FIRST SHALL BE LAST

Sprague's Ranch - Sprague's Lodge
And Stead's Ranch

When I First Came Here,
There Weren't Any Mountains,
Just Little Hills,
And I Had To Come All The Way Out Here
And Help Build Them Up To The Way They Are Today.
Ours Is A Community Of Fine People,
Who Live Close To Nature,
And Recognize The Nearness Of God,
And The Soul-Cleansing Power Of Our Mountains.
So, Send Us Your Tired And Weary,
In Mind And Body,
Your Disillusioned Souls,
Our Highlands Will Provide A Cure,
And Make Them Whole.
Dave (Pye Eyed Pete) Stirling, 1960

The American genealogical line of the Sprague family commenced when the *Good Ship Ann,* from England, arrived in 1623 and Francis Sprague walked down the gangway to settle in upstate New York. In 1820 eight generations later, Thomas Sprague was born in Watertown, New York the eldest of nine children. After an unsuccessful time in farming the rocky soil that yielded a crop in miserly measure, he chose to became a sailor on the Great Lakes under the command of his uncle Hiram Sprague. When not working the ship on voyages out of the Port of Chicago, he learned of the availability of fertile land in Illinois and wondered if farming could again be possible. Then his brother Abner, for whom Estes Park's Abner E. Sprague was named, drowned in the Cleveland harbor while employed on a ship. Distraught and resolute, Thomas gave up the profession of navigation and in 1844 again became a farmer, this time in Illinois. Mary Wolaver, also born in New York state in 1831, moved with her family to Illinois where she met former Captain Thomas Sprague and to whom she was married in 1849. Thomas turned down the chance to buy lots in what was then a quagmire near Lake Michigan, electing to purchase 80 acres of fertile prairie land in McHenry County, Illinois near the Wisconsin line. That quagmire later became the City of Chicago.

Abner Erwin Sprague was born near Dundee, Kane County, Illinois in 1850, and described by neighbor women peering down upon this recent arrival as "a boy with a big head, skinny body, too white for a healthy baby, and a boy not long for this life." Their judgment and prognostication of longevity was in error for he lived to be 93. His sister, Areanna Sprague, called Arah by Abner and who later became the wife of another Estes pioneer Alson Chapman, was born in 1851. After five years of muddy roads, distant markets and inadequate prices for the labor expended, Thomas *looked west* even before the New York City newspaper publisher Horace Greeley had given the nations's youth his sage advice, "Go West Young Man!" Their first move was to Floyd County, Iowa, close to the Cedar River where trees, flowers, fish, birds and other wild life intrigued this young boy and developed in him through long walks with his mother and sister a life long love affair with the out-of-doors. It was here that Abner was toughened by pioneer experiences, especially the time in the winter of 1856 when he heard the cry of the timber wolf outside his cabin window that he said caused "his scalp to prickle for the rest of his life" whenever he heard a similar sound in the night. Into a new frame house the family moved where Thomas operated a grocery store in the front room and the family lived in the quarters curtained off in the rear. Here the third child, Fred Harmon Sprague, was born in 1858.

In 1864, Thomas and Mary Margaret Sprague brought their three children by covered wagon through Indian country to a new homestead claim east of Loveland, Colorado, then moved further up the Big Thompson River because it afforded the three children better schooling opportunities. That same year they enrolled the two older children in the first public school of the county, --a log structure with a sod roof presided over by their teacher Sarah Smith, and became members of the first class of eight students. Abner, a curious boy and one always in quest of knowledge, for the next four years made excursions into the surrounding hills and in 1868 first hiked up to a nearly empty Estes Valley. In May of 1874 Abner and his former schoolmate Clarence Chubbuck, the son of the County Superintendent of Schools, filed on two quarter section claims west of Estes Park. Flanked by thickly wooded hills, the land was bisected by a river flowing through in serpentine coils, hissing as it undulated the yellow-green willow boughs with a laggardly yet steady flow of life-giving glacier cold water. They named the wide meadow Willow Park. The two young men rode down to the territorial land office, filled out the necessary paper work, and with youthful enthusiasm returned to lay up a simple foundation. Rejoining their parents in their homes, they made plans to build their cabin the following month. Unfortunately Clarence was murdered a few weeks later at a cattle roundup by a man named John Phillips in a dispute over the ownership of a cow. Abner's father took up the young man's claim, later sold his own holdings in the Loveland area, and brought his family to their new home in Willow Park. Arah obtained her own claim but it remained separate under her married name of Chapman, and when Fred Sprague became old enough in 1878 he obtained his own 160 acre claim to increase the Sprague family presence in Willow Park to 640 acres.

The homesteads started out modestly as a cattle ranch, the first building only a fourteen by sixteen foot cabin with a nearly flat roof supported by a single large pine log. On the roof of closely fitted small pine poles was placed an eight inch layer of coarse meadow grass and swamp peat. It was discovered that the peat did not shed water as one would hope but sopped it up, sponge-like, with one beneficial effect however of producing dripping streams of pure, filtered drinking water. Abner and his mother occupied the cabin the first season with Father Sprague concluding business affairs in the valley below. Their claims, like those of all the settlers, were under threat by the Dunraven interests. But to the Spragues' great relief the Irishman's attempt to claim the whole Estes Valley from mountain to mountain did not include Willow Park or the Sprague claims. Although they would not have given up their claims without a protracted and vigorous fight, it was discovered that through a surveying and description error in the paper work submitted by Dunraven's agents, only the terminal moraine ridge hemming in the valley on the south was included in the portfolio of the Earl, not the rich meadow sheltered near the river. Into the homestead cabin were placed a dutch oven, an iron stove and a few sticks of furniture and shortly thereafter they were in business. The intent of the family was to continue in the agricultural business, garden crops and cattle. However, they quickly learned that this high valley was not receptive to the likes of farming, especially with the added impedimenta of rapaciously hungry and destructive wild life. The severity of rapidly changing weather coupled with the fact that the deer, elk, bear, lions, coyotes and beavers enjoyed the crops and their herds as much as the Spragues, their wheel of life was turned into a new road that headed them away from raising cattle into one that was exclusively devoted to shepherding and stabling satisfied tourists.

They never intended to get into the hotel business, far from it. People passing by on fishing trips, hunting, on a day's outing, or even those inquiring at the ranch for fresh provisions for their tents pitched nearby, made that decision for them. A party came one morning from Dunraven's Hotel to ride up Windy Gulch, and in passing by they asked Areanna and her mother if they could get dinner at the ranch on their way back. It was a chicken dinner they asked for and Mrs. Sprague agreed to prepare it. Therefore the first dinner served at Sprague's Ranch to tourists was chicken, biscuits and gravy, and raspberry jam and it was a culinary triumph. Mary Margaret Sprague's reputation for good food at reasonable prices quickly spread. More dinners were served to those who simultaneously requested a room for the night anticipating an equally appetizing breakfast. Sprague's Ranch esteem increased as their hospitality and wholesome food certainly was less costly than found in other hotels in the region. Finally tourists, and other settlers who had not as yet built their own house, asked to spend the whole summer, even the entire winter, at Sprague's and the lodging industry had added to its ranks a fully fledged new representative in Willow Park. "The hotel business was forced on us," wrote Abner in 1938, five years before his death. "We came here for small ranch operations, but guests and visitors became so numerous at first wanting to buy eggs, milk, and other provisions, then wanting lodging, and finally demanding full accommodations, that we had to go into the hotel business or go bankrupt from keeping free company. It never entered our minds when we settled in the Park that the region would attract others as it did us. Enjoying and loving the region as we did, we should have realized that other lovers of the out-of-doors would come to enjoy our streams, mountains, and forests, and soon our isolated lives would come to an end."

Soon the ranch was doing a thriving business as more cabins, a main log house with guest rooms, a dining room, kitchen and larger living quarters for the family were added on in 1878 using only simple tools such as double bitted axes, lot of logs, grit, sweat and determination. Before long the Spragues were in the accommodation business, known first as The Sprague House, then The Sprague Hotel, and by 1880 their little hotel business was serving thirty guests at one time. Then ten more sleeping rooms were added to the main building as the structure rose in the bright Colorado sky to a height of three stories. Mary Sprague and all of the family cut wood, milked the

Guernsey cows, tended the garden, and brought in pails of water. Brother Fred was away managing his new stage line that brought in hungry and tired travelers to be gently and graciously tended by the head of the enterprise, Grandma Sprague as Mary was to become known with admired affection. In Mrs. Sprague's milk house was a large flowing spring, the force of its flow sufficient to turn a wheel to churn butter, and where frequently could be seen swimming a large trout kept in readiness for the next dinner entree when unexpected guests came calling. Her large dairy herd produced milk products to serve her own resident guests and those campers in Willow Park she invited in who needed a real home-cooked meal once in a while. Back then it was a popular form of outdoor recreation to come up to the little valleys for a month at a time, pitch a tent near a ranch where you knew good food was prepared, and hope for an invitation from the rancher who might take pity *on a nice looking family out there camping in the rain.* Everyone loved Mary Sprague for what she was, --a lodge owner with class, well tempered, good humored with loving kindness and a darn good cook. Abner remembers his mother's cooking. "If one has never tasted the bread my mother baked in a tight dutch-oven, they have missed the best tasting bread that ever was baked, --and cake, and wild Huckleberry pie!" Of course an integral part of the operation was her husband who was proud of the effort expended by his family in their joint efforts to build a successful business high up in these often hostile mountains.

The Estes Park Hotel, appealing exclusively to the financially well off, was high priced and usually beyond the resources of the average family who really wanted more simple lodgings. Hence it was left to the MacGregors, the Fergusons, the Jameses and now to the Spragues to add a new term not then found in the tourists' lexicon of beds for rent. The Sprague's Ranch was not a true hotel, *check in, here's your room, smoking in the lounge and get your drink at the bar*, sort of place. It was different. It was an honest to goodness mountain pioneer guest ranch where the Sprague family considered their guests their friends and where the schedule of the ranch and its activities was in many ways dictated by the needs or desires of the guests. No glitter or pizzazz, nor bell hops with hands extended in pecuniary salute. No sir! They had given birth to a *lodge* that would never be cloned by others as each succeeding lodge had its own unique fingerprint. Sprague's printed 3 x 5 inch cards in 1880 explained their services.

SPRAGUE HOUSE, WILLOW PARK
T. E. Sprague & Son Proprietors
※※※※※※※※※※

Accommodations, second to none
in the Park. Free mail hack in
connection with the Stage Lines.
Good fishing & hunting close at
hand. Experienced guides furnished
for parties going to Long's Peak
or any part of the mountains.

Mary and Arah at the same time were running a little general store on Arah Chapman's ranch closer to the river and the main road on which son Fred freighted in both cargo and tourists. Charles F. Scott, Sr., a newspaper man from Iola, Kansas, purchased eight acres from Mary in 1898 on which Fred Sprague built for him a large log summer home he dubbed The Scottage. It still remains in the Scott family ownership, and his son, the late Ewing Scott remembered the appearance of the general store where his deed had been written. "The store had its end to the road a little east of the bridge across the Big Thompson River. On the opposite end was an addition, enough lower so that it could go under the roof of the original building. On the far end of the addition was another one, still lower, and so on until they ran into the ground, the last one being the wood shed." In 1879 Mary opened up in the back of the store the first post office for the west end of the Estes Valley. It was to be known as the Willow Park Post Office, but postal officials objected to the name as there were too many other post offices in other parts of America with a similar name. Abner came up with the name, Moraine Park Post Office, and henceforth their hollow between the two terminal moraines henceforth would be called Moraine Park. Arah Sprague Chapman and her sons Alson, Jr. and Charles also rented out rooms in a string of small cabins nearby wherein one of them the later famous editor from Emporia, Kansas, William Allen White, vacationed during the summer of 1889 in company with a group of University of Kansas students. It is amusing to read in Mr. White's memoirs of the rhapsody of youthful zest as this one little statement reveals. "We lived simply and gaily and had only two rules for our republic. Every man must clean his own fish, and no razor would be allowed in camp." With untroubled blue skies, abundant fish from the adjacent river, first rate food wolfed down in the dining room of Sprague's to hearty songs of *Go Jay Hawks* or a hermetic fraternity chant if Mary chose to admit such a bearded brotherhood of foot loose college men, it was a splendid summer with few human beings to block out a single ray of sunlight or a sliver of the full moon. Visitors then and now could be likened to the free running Big Thompson River as did W. T. Lee in his book *The Geologic Story Of The Rocky Mountain National Park*. "Like the tourist who leaves the humdrum existence of everyday life and enjoys a summer of unusual experiences in the mountains, this water in its eternal round of change through vapor, rain, snow, and stream, has visited the Park, has spent its vacation on the Snowy Range, and is now on its way back to less spectacular but more useful vocations." It was that way with many who came to Sprague's Hotel, throwing off cares and frazzled nerves from regulated living in exchange for a gentle horse that led them toward asylums of icy brooks, deep forests and flower mantled alpine tarns of true mental and physical refreshment.

Thomas Sprague's residency in the Park was not to be long lasting as he died in December 6, 1882 leaving to Mary, Abner, Fred and Arah the task of operating The Sprague House. The hotel was for a time operated under the name Sprague Brothers but most assuredly Mrs. Sprague was an important ingredient in the mix, the yeast that caused the recipe to rise into a marketable product. Abner's father did not encourage his sons to become farmers as he had been and as the result Abner was intrigued with mathematics and eventually learned a great deal, without any formal training, to become a fine civil engineer. Fred as well abjured from tilling soil, opting to enter the transportation trade, carpentry and achieved high marks as a premier trail maker and guide. Both Fred and Abner were superb guides, and of Abner those that knew him described him as "gentlemanly, patient, and very reasonable in his charges." Fred was a builder of structures as well as a network of trails, his most famous being the Flattop Mountain trail we use even today. Fred was a stage line owner, mail carrier, and mountain climber who guided others up Long's Peak more times than he could remember. He delivered the mail by contract from Loveland, later from Lyons, to the Moraine Post office daily in the summer and trice-weekly in the winter. As a guide for the Sprague Brothers enterprise, he was unsurpassed by few others, and to him Abner gave much of the credit for the early success of The Sprague House. Upon Fred's death, at the age of 65 on March 23, 1922, Abner wrote an epitaph to his brother's life, a portion of which is here repeated. "Fred was a pioneer guide to Long's Peak, to Specimen Mountain and Grand Lake. He enjoyed the work of a guide and his parties liked him as a conductor for he always saw the funny side of people, and could tell the stories around the campfires. He spent much time bettering trails on both sides of the Divide, and looking up new places of interest to show people, and how best to reach the beauty spots of the Estes Park region. He operated a stage line, carried and looked after the mail, failing to make the schedule but a few times and then on account of violent storms and deep snows. Regardless of rain, snow, or blizzard, the trip of from 8 to 12 hours had to be made, so that we in the Park might not be lost entirely to the outside world. Some may have accomplished more, but no one worked harder to make Estes Park what it is, than Fred H. Sprague."

Abner wrote this account about how he became a surveyor. "I decided to study when seventeen years of age along mathematical lines, surveying and subjects leading to civil engineering. I read everything I could get my hands on, good, bad and indifferent. I read up on navigation, geology, mineralogy, etc. I helped my father lay out a ditch with a common level and triangle, then later I borrowed a compass and a transit and did jobs for neighbors. I tried to get a job with engineering parties but at that time there were too many graduates from engineering colleges who would take any job for the experience. I ran for County Surveyor when I was old enough and was beaten by three votes. My father did not encourage me to follow farming as he knew I would starve out on a farm." During the 1870s and early 1880s every valley leading to a pass in Colorado had been staked in hopes of finding the proper grade for railroad trackage to pierce through the high Rockies. Such was the case with a railroad then called the Denver, Utah and Pacific. Through the efforts of T. J. Milner its Chief Engineer, the company determined that it was feasible for tracks to be laid up Forest Canyon and over the Continental Divide. This potential crossing at the elevation of 10,759 feet, still bears his name on Trail Ridge Road, Milner Pass. The Union Pacific Railroad had learned about that earlier survey and sent out its own crew in the summer of 1881 to confirm its alignment. The party of surveyors was housed in Sprague's original homestead cabin and took their meals at the ranch. Needing an assistant transit man to fill a vacancy caused by a recent resignation, and learning that Abner had knowledge of that job, the crew chief hired him as a member of the survey party for the next few months. Word of his abilities and conscientiousness was passed down the line amongst those needing a capable hand. The following spring found him employed for another railroad, this time on a narrow gauge line up Boulder Canyon. Then in 1884 his previous boss with the Union Pacific Railroad offered him a far better job, full time, back at Union Pacific headquarters in Omaha and from that time on he remained in the track surveying business, for the Union Pacific and Missouri Pacific Railroads until December of 1888. During his period of absence from Moraine Park, Mary and brother Fred worked very diligently to increase the size of the accommodations at the ranch until it could feed and house many more guests.

While surveying a line in Nebraska for the Missouri Pacific in 1887, Abner met Mr. W. L. Morrison, a prominent grain dealer from Hickman, Nebraska who served as the agent for the many farmers through whose fields men and surveying equipment needed to pass. When at the Morrison's home for Sunday dinner he met the two older girls, the two younger sons and the young 19 year old daughter, Mary Alberta Morrison. Born in Milan, Missouri and called Berta by her father and Bert by her friends, he fell in love immediately. As their courtship blossomed, he had doubts whether this young woman, eighteen years his junior, would, or should marry him. Was it right that she should become his lifetime partner in the high mountains of Colorado, leaving a sheltered life surrounded by a family of eight sisters, four brothers and adoring parents with financial security? "To ask a girl, many years younger than myself to leave a good home for a log house in pioneer Estes Park was something to think about seriously," he soliloquized while mustering up the boldness to ask her. "I did not think so much about the difference in ages as I still thought myself quite a kid. The final decision was up to her. I remember the answer her father gave me when I asked him for his daughter. His answer was, 'I think any man who writes his mother at least once a week, as busy as you are, will be good to a wife.' Some of those letter though were but a few lines like, *I'm fine, hope you are the same*." They were married the next year on December 20, 1888 and returned to Estes Park on Christmas Day. Mr. Sprague stood before the assembled group of friends who joined in their 50th Wedding Anniversary party in 1938, and recounted the arrival of his bride. "Mrs. M. Alberta arrived in Estes Park as a bride on Christmas Day from Loveland in the mail buckboard on a cloudy, foggy day, arriving in sight of the Park after dark, and at her future home in Moraine Park about 8 P. M. All her friends were strangers and she met them first as she took her place among them in those pioneer days in Estes Park. I presume some of the brides of today think they are leaving the world behind when they come to Estes Park. If they could only imagine what it was in 1888 --which they cannot, they would realize their luck in not being obliged to deny themselves some of the pleasures of life. Mrs. S. is thankful for the many friends she has made in Estes Park, in Colorado, and all over the world through her contact with people in the past 50 years."

After returning to work at the hotel for the summer of 1889 and part of 1890, he accepted a two year assignment again in eastern Nebraska for the Union Pacific to complete the main line between Omaha and Kansas City. Bert joined him except for periods in the summers when she assisted in the tourist business with the other members of the Sprague family. In 1892 he was through with engineering in Nebraska and joined in the full time management of the hotel. Fred then left the tourist hotel in 1893 to the capable responsibility of Abner and Alberta, and of course Mary, and the lodge would simply be known as Sprague's Hotel. He erected a saw mill propelled by water from Mill Creek that descended into Hallowell Park, and produced milled lumber with which he could construct new cabins and additions to the existing structures. Intrigued by Indian people, the result of friendly encounters with them while traversing the Nebraska plains in the 1860s, he gave to several of his cabins Indian names, such as the large cabin --still existing in another location around Estes Park, called Sagityhauk. To other cabins northwest of the main lodge structure, he dubbed with more pronounceable names such as Hayden, Columbine and one that sparkled with rustic welcome that inspired its name, Periwinkle. Abner named nothing for himself, that was to come later by others in recognition of his encouragement and contributions to the creation of Rocky Mountain National Park. But numerous mountains we observe today he memorialized for those he admired. Mount McHenry he named for a mathematics professor at Union Christian College in Indiana, B. F. McHenry. For a peak the Arapahoes referred to as The Bangs, denoting the place in 1870 where they killed a Pawnee with that hair style, he christened Mount Taylor in honor of the Albert Reynolds Taylor, the President of Kansas State Normal School, both of whom had been his hotel guests in the late 1890s and who had shared with him the exhilarating experience of mountaineering in the challenging peaks of the Front Range. For his brother-in-law, Edwin B. Andrews, who later was an employee of the National Park, Andrews Glacier would forever bear his name. There were few landmarks named for local people, mostly for visitors or even those such as Pike and Long who were never closer than 40 miles to their namesake. Other examples of this, although these names cannot be attributed to Abner Sprague, were Mount Otis, named for Dr. Edward Osgood Otis, a Boston physician and visitor and Mount Chapin for Frederick Chapin of Hartford, Connecticut. Those who nominated non-residents to endure as the place names for local landmarks had a difficult time acknowledging the importance of those neighbors living amongst them who better deserved these honors. Is it jealousy or an application of the failure to recognize a *prophet in your own home town* syndrome?

A lodge brochure around 1900 described Moraine Park and its association with Sprague's Hotel. "The Park is at the foot of the Continental divide on the Atlantic side, seventy miles north and west of Denver, reached via Lyons by 48 miles on the Burlington Ry. and 22 miles by stage over a fine mountain road, or via Loveland over Colorado & Southern Ry., thence by stage or mountain surrey up the Big Thompson River, one of the finest canyon drives in the world. To ride in a stage coach drawn by four or six horses from the Valley to the Park is a pleasure not to be missed and one that all tourists thoroughly enjoy. Moraine Park is the gem of the cluster of parks which have Estes Park for a center. Its situation is on the main stream west and south of Estes Park, and five miles from the snow peaks of the Continental Divide, the view of which from Sprague's include a semicircle of peaks covered with ever-lasting snow and ice fields. Due south is Long's Peak, rising on its immense base to an altitude of 14, 271 feet." (Ed. Note: The early pronouncements of this peak's height was often over stated, never under estimated, and this time by 16 feet.) There was even more to see that the brochure announced in poetic prose to break down any semblance of doubt that Sprague's was **the** place to stay, however a guest must not cough or wheeze to reveal a condition that was an anathema to lodge owners. "The sea breeze cannot enter in the same class with those that come over these peaks, down through forests of pine and fir, bringing their fresh odors to the travelers below. It is the desire and aim of the proprietors of Sprague's to conduct a home-like place, as far from hotel life and as home-like as possible. We do not take consumptives, for there are many better places in the state for their accommodation. Rates range from $8.00 to $15.00 per week according to accommodations desired, and livery rigs can be secured by the day or month."

Abner and Bert realized in 1902 that the business was getting too large for them, and for that reason took in some partners, Mr. and Mrs. James Stead from Chicago. James Stead, born in New York state, migrated at an early age with his parents to Carpentersville, Illinois where later he was fully engaged in the dairy business. Eudora May Wollaver Stead, Dora as she preferred to be known, was the daughter of a sister of Abner's mother. Like Abner, this cousin was born in Dundee, Kane County, Illinois nine years later, in 1859. Actually they were, as Abner's nephew told me, *double cousins* through a collateral family branch with common roots. Alberta fulfilled the requirements for the cook of the enterprise, Dora took charge of the laundry services, and the men folk were in command of construction, maintenance and the outside business endeavors necessary to a busy hostelry. It was expected that this might prove to be an amicable and productive relationship and though the cousins were friendly enough, the arrangement rapidly soured. By 1904, though the business was thriving, it became evident that the partnership was a loser as it provoked much ill feeling between the two wives. As an old neighbor gently put it, "The ladies did not see eye to eye." Another was more blunt in his finger pointing. "Mrs. Stead was very opinionated and overbearing." Abner gentlemanly assessed the partnership formation in his memoirs. "This proved to be a mistake. The partnership was not satisfactory, and to avoid working under disagreeable conditions we sold our interests at a sacrifice," the price later discovered to be $20,000. The Spragues would have bought out the Steads, however at the time Mr. Stead was in command of more ready cash and thus prevailed. In 1904 the name was promptly changed to Stead's Ranch to remain by that signature through its remaining years of service to the vacationing public.

As another point of information concerning structures within Moraine Park, the four cabins that the Chapman brothers had built near their parents store on their ranch, to which I have made an earlier reference, were at this same time becoming decrepit, sagging, and the roofs leaked. To the south of the Big Thompson River and up against the moraine, building lots had been surveyed for summer cottages, and by 1904 several had been spoken for by families living in the hot and humid agricultural basins of Kansas, Nebraska and Missouri. Several of these old cabins were purchased by those lot owners for $25 a piece and Reverend Albin Griffith, no longer in the active ministry but working in the lumbering business, skidded them over to the lots where they became the overture for several new summer homes. Most are still in service, have stood the test of time, and continue to provide enjoyment and places of cool refuge for succeeding generations of their builders' progeny. Immediately in front of these new summer homes, in the southeast portion of Moraine Park, was planted a nourishing fields of oats. It served as a welcoming pasture to tired horses that had labored to conquer the strenuous grade from Lyons with cargo and guests for the resort and cabins in this park. There the stage coaches drivers bedded down their horses until the next day when the whole routine would be repeated eastward. The west end of Moraine Park was planted in Timothy grass for Sprague's cattle, then for Steads, and later for the Brinwood Lodge herd that would occupy the lush meadows in a few years. Throughout the history of Sprague's-Stead's Ranch, the owners possessed excellent water rights appropriated from the Big Thompson River out of which at least three irrigation ditches were dug and maintained to nourish the thirsty grass needed for the cattle and the hundreds of horses grazing the Moraine Park basin. Closer to the main ranch buildings, James Stead attempted to raise potatoes, turnips and other garden crops for his tables, but in a few years the deer devastated the crops with their insatiable appetite for such delectable ruffage. That dictated more foodstuffs must be freighted in from Lyons on Fred Sprague's stage and those of increasing numbers of competitors.

A 1913 advertisement described Stead's Ranch that bore a similarity to earlier copy composed by Abner. "Of the cluster of parks which have Estes Park for a center, Moraine Park is said to be the gem. Due north from Long's Peak, and commanding a magnificent view of a semi-circle of snow covered mountains, it lies in a protected valley at the foot of an extended ridge, or moraine, from which is taken the name. The effects of extinct glaciers can be studied in Moraine Park and the adjacent mountains by any who are interested in this great geological subject. Lateral and terminal moraines, great deposits left to mark the location of these great ice rivers, are revealed on every hand, and this probably accounts for the great fascination possessed by Moraine Park for lovers of nature. The largest hotel in this region is conducted by J. D. Stead and wife. It consists of a large rustic hotel building surrounded by cottages that will accommodate a great number of tourists. It is the expressed aim of Mr. Stead to conduct a place as far from hotel-like and as home-like as possible. The table is supplied with hearty, nourishing food, designed for the appetites of mountain climbers and automobile parties. Not only hotel accommodations but also entertainment is provided by the management at the most reasonable rates. Easily accessible are such sports as fishing, mountain climbing, tramping, horseback riding, driving, picnicing, camping trips, and also impromptu entertainments and hops, for which purpose a spacious building called *the bungalow* is provided."

Walter Baldridge came to Estes Park to work at the ranch in 1915 as an employee of a Denver electrical contractor. His assignment was to electrify the ranch buildings and guest facilities for the first time. After his job was completed and receiving an excellent recommendation from Mr. Stead, he was hired by F. O. Stanley as his chief electrician as well as manager of Stanley's hydroelectric plant on Fall River. By 1920, Stead's Ranch consisted of general lodge buildings, barns, employee housing and at least twenty-seven well constructed cottages. The newer cabins, in different sizes from one room to as many as fifteen, were constructed through the physical labor of J. D., who locally was considered a man of many talents, including carpentry. It is historically significant to note that in excavating on the ranch for ditches and structure foundations, there were found under a foot of soil early Indian artifacts such as grinding stones and implements to evidence the fact that an early people deemed Moraine Park a worthy location for primitive agriculture. Milk was produced in commercial quantities on the ranch, as well as some vegetables survived to reach the kitchen before wildlife and the cold weather nipped their growth before harvest. The domestic water was provided by that same wonderful spring still flowing with exuberance for the guests whose room rates remained reasonable at $17.50 to $24.50 per week per person, including three meals. J. D., an entrepreneur of the dairy trade before moving to Colorado, continued with a fine string of thirty Guernsey milk cows that he penned up in the lower level of a large barn south of the main lodge during inclement weather of the winter and when they needed milking. Since his spring produced more water than was necessary for the domestic needs of the ranch, the excess was allowed to flow by means of a four inch diametered pipe into a two by six foot cistern in the barn in which the cans of fresh milk and cream were kept chilled. His herd grazed as far west up the Thompson drainage as Cub Canyon on self seeding Timothy grass and a high altitude variety of clover. As a further point of information, the Stead's **S** brand theme was hand painted onto the white china used at the ranch in a green colored, rope-like, letter *S* especially kiln fired for Stead's at the New Castle, Pennsylvania pottery works.

A vigorous business of selling milk and butter produced at Stead's was conducted during the ownership of J.D. by the ranch managers William J. Heubner, and later Lyman Green. Jane Heubner Blair, a present resident of Estes Park, recalls her father, and mother Margaret Downing Heubner who was raised on a Montana ranch, left the employment of the local Y.M.C.A. in 1916 to work for Mr. Stead. She remembered how her father attended to the stock for $75 a month while her mother worked in the ranch laundry to carry out the orders of the efficient Head Housekeeper, Mrs. Hostetler, who demanded that the cabin linens be impeccable. Both of Jane's parents guided parties of guests on horseback rides high into the surrounding mountains for unforgettable alpine experiences so foreign to those dwellers of the large cities that claimed their permanent residency. From 1916 and well into the 1920s Mr. Heubner sold large quantities of milk and butter to many of the surrounding lodge owners, hotels in Estes Park and to many of the prominent families of the village with recognizable names as Freeburg, Anderson, Schwartz, Peltz, Baldridge, Wiest, MacDonald, Francis, Service, Byerly, Church, Reed, Lindley and Bond. In Mr. Heubner's account book there appear the names of the best producers of milk that supplied the tables of Estes Park's finest in 1918. There were Roany, Milky, Low Belly and a beast somewhat reluctant to yield her production, Red The Kicker. Horses were rented out by Messrs. Huebner and Green to produce a steady and reliable supplemental income for Stead's and steady employment for employees quartered at the ranch throughout the year. The horses also had colorful names reflecting their size, color or disposition such as Goldie, Big Bird, Cricket, Quick Silver, Jumbo and Pet.

Stead's Ranch, in recognition of its increased size and resources necessary to a complete resort experience, amended its title to read Stead's Ranch and Hotel and extended its season to commence on May 25th through the 20th of September. Cottages with more than one room, such as the large fifteen room unit, were restructured so that each room was capable of separate rental with a door to the outside porch or set of steps. The rates in the late 1920s were edging up slightly to range between $18.00 and $26 per week and the activities remained the same except there were square dances offered to guests at social halls not too distant from the ranch. At the ranch itself, guests and those invited from the public at large enthusiastically took to a new recreational pursuit called The Cowboy Dance. The setting for the dance often was moved from one lodge to another each year, but in 1925, with it enlarged dance hall, Stead's Ranch became a more regular venue for the high spirited gathering. The news item of August 27, 1927, published the day after the occasion, captured the mood and atmosphere of the revelry. "Scores of cowboys and cowgirls invaded the village with their shouts and screams. We soon discovered these were the Stead's people, all dressed up in full regalia and pepped up for the big Cowboy Dance which is an annual affair at Stead's Ranch. The dining room reminded one of the old barroom and country store with its hams, flour sacks, etc. hanging around the wall and piled in the corners. The waiters and waitresses carried this idea out both in dress and actions. An orchestra furnished music during the meal. From noon until the wee small hours, everything done carried on back to the days of the wild west. The dance in the evening was a huge success and was attended by people from miles around. Prizes were given for best costume." In later years it would be reclassified from an amusement of dance and good food to one of drunkenness and physical combat when its respectable profile mutated into a form characterized as a noisy bacchanal onslaught of frenzy and fracture. When regular cowboys and vacationing hot bloods in big hats -- fueled from the effects of high altitude mixed liberally with alcohol -- came hurtling through windows, National Park officials put an end to this inappropriate conduct and future dances.

Not only could a guest rent a horse, livery rigs also were available for a romantic turn up a curving mountain road. Autos for hire was another convenience at the ranch, and if you brought your own vehicle, garages were provided for a small charge. Beginning in 1908, Mr. and Mrs. Prouty operated a store and lunch room called The Pine Cone Inn, and when he died Julia Prouty continued on until her death in 1924. Julia's little store, adjacent to the original homestead cabin and where everything was sold from knitting needles to fishing lures, was remodeled in 1925 into a combination soda fountain and tea room. About the same year the Steads enlarged their dining room so that it could seat 250 guests at one time. The augmented dance hall became the site for embryonic forms of square dances increasing in popularity as *alaman left* and *swing your little lady* commands now echoed off the surrounding mountains for thousands of happy lodge guests and their friends. Square dancing at Stead's was not to reach the high degree of prominence and sophistication until its last owner increased the size of the recreation bungalow into an excellent dancing facility remembered with affection by those who today walk down the nearly invisible trail to that fun palace long ago removed. Mr. Stead, *J. D.* to his friends, played a commanding role in most everything important to a growing Estes Valley such as a founding director and President of the village's only bank. Considered "a great guy and loved by many," he never shirked from community responsibility, "nor was he a man to ever say a cross word to any one." Dora, while J. D. was alive, kept to the background and no longer commanded the laundry duties as in earlier days nor assumed the kitchen assignment. However, she was a thoroughly competent taskmistress and left no question about who was in charge of the maids and other household staff. J. D. Stead competently attended to the finances and entertainment of the guests and, not neglectful of his wife, constructed for her an elegant residence known as the Rock House high on a hill just east of the assemblage of ranch buildings. Rounded rocks used in its architectural enhancements were laboriously carted up from the Big Thompson River.

264

Tennis courts did not make their appearance at the ranch until the 1950s and were located immediately to the north of this fine home for the use of the owner's family and lodge guests. A workman well remembers when the courts were built. Upon waking from a previous evening's watermelon bust whereby the fruit's natural juices had been doctored liberally with vodka, he recollected years later, "The cement trucks arrived to commence pouring at the ungodly hour of 6 A. M.! What a day that was!" J. D.'s busy life had brought on an inordinate amount of pressure but, proving up to the multitude of challenges, was reluctant to deny himself a further opportunity to improve his resort or to render service to his adopted community. While stressed with preparations for another tourist season, James Stead died on May 16, 1931 of a stroke and William C. Lewis and his wife Myra from Illinois joined in to assist Dora reopen the guest ranch to its 1931 season.

Will, to which shortened name Mr. Lewis preferred to respond, obliged for the next five years as the ranch and hotel manager for Dora. Myra Wollaver Lewis was the sister of Dora and thus another cousin of Abner Sprague, and, upon Dora's demise in 1936 without any children surviving, Myra Lewis inherited the ranch facility and all of the real property. Will was an accountant in Illinois and as such applied his professional talents to continue the ranch on a sound financial foundation. Myra had been a grade school teacher before her marriage. She was quiet, laid back, well liked, and local folks claimed "She was as different from her sister Dora as day is from night, always smiled, and never had anything bad to say about anyone." Will and Myra Lewis, considered in the community as *lovely people*, ran a fine operation in keeping with the well earned reputation of the Sprague and Stead families. Even though they did not construct any new buildings on the ranch, they continued in its improvement resulting in the ranch's increasing popularity as a sought out destination of travelers. Will Lewis grazed no dairy cattle on the ranch as before but was proud of his champion herd of 60 white faced Herefords that continued to wear the Stead's brand.

The primary access into the National Park in the 1930s was gained by crossing a bridge close to the present Dunraven Restaurant on the road to the YMCA. You can still walk across it but vehicular traffic has been diverted to the Beaver Meadows and Fall River entrance stations to the north. That original Park road ascended a steep grade on the south side of Eaton Hill, named for the family whose lovely two-story home caught the travelers' attention as Moraine Park came into sight. At the top of the hill the Park visitor gaped in excitement at the grandest view of Moraine Park with its western ruffle of snowy mountains within which the mighty Big Thompson River sprang into full throated thunder from a chorus of many singing brooks and springs. Summer cabins then were seen nestled into the trees on both sides of the river and on Eagle Cliff to the right, and the road continued west to pass by the remnants of a vanishing Moraine Lodge. Then in full view, over the radiator cap insignia with the temperature gauge encased in glass registering *hot*, was Stead's Ranch, artistically situated on the south shoulder of the northerly slope of the valley. Descending into Moraine Park, a spring house was partially hidden amongst a darkly beautiful grove of aspen and blue spruce trees that former lodge owner Imogene MacPherson had used as a water supply for her guests and neighbors. Cars drove close to the river near the present bridge just west of the main highway where the Chapmans ranch, store and in earlier

265

days the Moraine Park Post Office stood ready to provide supplies and news of the day. To reach Stead's, one continued northwesterly to pass to the south of the Rock House where the Lewises resided. Next, on the left side of the entrance road was Prouty's converted store, Abner's homestead cabin and other small structures. Then you stopped in front of the east facing Stead's Ranch hotel and were surrounded by a clutch of cabins and other major guest facilities. To the south of the main hotel building, but respectfully down wind, was the horse barn, stable and corrals. In these and other structures slept the dining room help and, as local resident and former educator Sam Gates remembered in his frequent visits to the ranch to court one of the waitresses, Kittie Parker, "The help slept along with the bats which created periodic waitress hysteria by cruising through the open shuttered windows from dark to dawn on a seemingly regular schedule."

Menus during the mid 1930s for Stead's *Cowboy Dinners* were descriptive to the absurd, which buffoonery delighted all and brought a smile to even the most city hardened businessphile. The food was excellent to the palate regardless of the outlandish titles, and each meal never was an ordinary affair but an anticipated and entertaining event. Children adored the menus shaped like a saddle, and more often than not a menu wound up as a souvenir in a young, or older person's scrapbook. Have you ever tried selections off of the *Heigh Ho* or the *Feed Bag* version of the menu? Well! For starters was the Whoopee Cup, Backache salad or Slum Gum Soup. The *awntrays* were Coyote's Fancy Dish, Maverick Slabs, Cowboy's Buckaroo, 4 O'Clock Bugler with Slopgolly, American Standby Buttered Buck Shot, and that ever faddish food Dogie Slats with *sogum* sauce. One might find items to perk up saddle weary bodies such as Fodder Salad, Adam's Downfall, Smothered Toothbuster Pie, Tenderfoot Dream, Glacier Goo with Trimmins, and an all time favorite Throat Gargles of Mississippi Mud washed down with a generous cold dash of Elk Milk. It certainly was a fare that would have baffled, yet delighted even the staid and proper Amy Vanderbilt. There was a sense of belonging for the guests that Mr. Gates recalled. "Ranch guests frequently stayed for the entire summer season and became *family*. They came to know F. O. Stanley, Joe Mills and other village notables on a first name basis, while receiving their mail addressed simply *Stead's Ranch, Estes Park, Colorado,* and occupied cabins with titillating names such as Shingle Side, The Home Cottage, Liberty Lodge or The Dew Drop Inn."

By 1947 the ranch operated on nearly 1,000 acres after adjacent meadows and timbered tracts were acquired. Its lengthened list of activities offered made it extremely difficult not to choose Stead's during that brief period of regained world peace before hostilities once again broke out in Korea, a country that as children we called Chosen and where most could not locate on a map. The advertisement in 1947 announced "We have good saddle horses, endless trails and wide open spaces, good fishing, golf, picnics and dancing. If a perfect rest is desired, with wonderful mountain scenery and good things to eat, we have the ideal spot for a real vacation." Robert H. *Bob* Cheney, a resident of Estes Park when he and Lois are not off galavanting to Alaska and other still challenging recesses of America, has been a horseman it seems for ever. Originally hiring on with Harry Langston's Hupp Livery and then to handle the dude horses at H Bar G Ranch, an opportunity arose to be associated with Stead's. He signed on as a summer wrangler in 1949 for Mr. Pearl

Miller, who owned and personally managed the horses at Stead's and where Bob would remain a valuable adjunct to the ranch until nearly the end of its existence. Julia Prouty's former store on the ranch, managed by Pearl's wife who answered to an equally gem-like name of Coral, had an assortment of new missions and purposes. In addition to functioning as a traditional store with curios, food, clothing and vacation bric-a-brac important to tourists, it was the Miller's residence until 1950. Also, the back room of the structure filled in as a dining room for Pearl's wranglers and as a small recreation hall with pin ball and soft drink machines for both employees and guests. By the fall of 1950, the resort was capable of accommodating 180 guests per night and soon the store would take on a completely different look as we shall later see. But for a moment, let's pause in this narrative about Stead's for a look back at what became of the Abner Spragues after they sold their interest in their hotel.

Abner and Alberta Sprague moved down to Loveland, Colorado in 1904 where he opened an office as a civil engineer and surveyor. Active in laying out many of the valley towns such as Loveland, he was nominated for the office of County Surveyor and elected to serve three terms. The bulk of his business had none of earlier thrills associated with trail blazing new pathways over mountains and through grain fields as the direction of the railroads had dictated. The problems to solve now related to irrigation ditches, lot line surveying and others projects identified with an industry he had sought to avoid, --farming. During the next four years his heart and soul were wrenched back up to his mountains where he determined one way or another he must return. He was homesick for the high reaches of nature that had been so much of his very fiber for nearly forty years. Wearing a suit and tie, residing in a neat but ordinary city house around which prowled domestic animals and an occasional squirrel, began to bore him. Where were the deer and elk that formerly met his gaze with curiosity, the sound of the coyote's doleful moan to the Manitou of the forest, the wind rushing through the tall pines and the open Moraine Park where he felt clean and free? Yes, he was hopelessly ill with homesickness and was determined to cure himself. Securing a lease in 1908 from the federal Department of Agriculture in one of its Forest Reserves, now a part of Rocky Mountain National Park, it became his intention to forsake the openness of eastern Larimer County at least in the summers. He confided to his journal his degree of melancholia that led to his decision. "I sought to prevent my homesickness for Estes Park and the mountains from becoming chronic. Loveland was too tame and too flat for a hill billie," he added.

Abner had previously homesteaded land further west, encompassing the regions we know as Mills Lake and Loch Vale, and though proven to be much too high and inaccessible for permanent residence he acquired title to the land. Bert's sister Mabel and her husband John Stopher, also living in Loveland, agreed to join with the Spragues in building a cabin that later became the first part of a resort eight miles southwest of the Village of Estes Park at an elevation of 8,700 feet. The site selected where both families had camped together over the years, was on the south bank of the plunging, glacier fed torrent locally called South Fork as it was the south branch of the Big Thompson River. We know it now as Glacier Creek, a prime source for the water supply of the Town of Estes Park. The two couples planned upon sharing the cabin for their summer vacations, thereby escaping the heat from the hot country in the flat valley more than three thousand feet below. Unfortunately this truly happy partnership lasted for only a short time, but for a vastly different reason. John Stopher had not been well and he left Colorado to enter into the ranching business in Idaho with the hope of a changed climate and lower altitude might restore his former robustness. When his health further deteriorated, he returned to his Loveland home, and on August 22, 1909 at the age of 32 years he died. The death was tragic in itself, but his passing was made more grievous for it occurred just six weeks before the birth of their second child, Edgar Morrison Stopher. Another child, Alberta Stopher and the namesake of Mrs. Sprague, had been born eighteen months previously.

Both families continued to improve the cabin in the summertime, and over the years an idea of re-entering the lodging business crossed the Spragues' minds with increasing frequency as they remarked to friends and strangers stopping by that there was more room by their cabin for additional buildings. But then as it is with so many who dislike having to abandon a perfect vacation hideaway for the angst associated with returning to a job that had lost its zest and purpose, Bert and Abner realized in 1914 they no longer desired to live any part of their lives in a flatland community. Like so many of us who live out of sight of the snowy mountains, unable to breathe in the freshness that permeates the high forests after the sunshine draws up the evening dew back into a great puffy cloud, they came to a decision to reside permanently in their mountains. There they knew they could regain the peace and tranquility in metaphysical alliance with the water, wild animals, tall trees and dwarfing mountains that from 1888 to 1904 had given them solace and shelter. Now peace was ever more important to them as their nation in 1914 was rushing headlong into a world war that was senseless, xenophobic, and possessed of little redemptive value even for its perpetrators. The Spragues had no children born to them although Mabel's two children, Ed and Alberta, were as close to them as their own children would have been. Of these children, Abner recorded his thoughts in his senior years. "Having no children of our own, that girl and boy of Mrs. Sprague's sister, Mrs. Mabel Stopher, made up for that loss. I took the place of a father they never knew, and I think just as much of their womanhood and manhood as though I were their father." They never adopted the children out of respect they had for John Stopher. He would always be the children's father, even in death, but for all intents and purposes the children were treated by Abner with all the love and consideration expected of a father. To Ed and Alberta Stopher, Abner was not their father but they considered him "like a father," and over the next seventeen years Mabel and the children lived with the Spragues and worked as one family in Glacier Basin to improve the mountain property.

Permission was granted by the Forest Reserve officials on April 14, 1914 authorizing the Spragues, and Mabel Stopher as a silent financial partner, to 'conduct a place of entertainment for tourists,' and their previous lease was amended to increase the leasehold from sixty to ninety-five acres with a proportional rise in the annual fee from $35 per year to $50. Immediately Abner launched into an accelerated construction project since a very short building season at nearly 9,000 feet did not bode well for a more protracted program. Sprague's Lodge thereupon was spawned on the south bank of Glacier Creek to mature from a small fry summer cabin into a family lodge whose name began appearing on agency lists as another mountain destination available to their traveling clients. The main lodge building enveloped the original cabin that became physically incorporated to function as a lounge alcove where guests could congregate in good fellowship before the fireplace. The entire roof line was raised to a two-story aspect through the efforts of Abner, young Ed, Edwin Andrews and a few other craftsmen. The records are confusing, but it is safe to say that a small lodge was open for limited business by 1916, possibly a year sooner. Bert again returned to her cooking duties after a twelve year absence from the ranch in Moraine Park, young Ed served as the chore boy, nine year old Alberta tended to the front desk and Abner and Mabel took charge of the customers' other needs. Abner particularly enjoyed entertaining and enlightening his guests with detailed and illuminating stories of nature, mountain climbs and Indians. During the winter, when the entry road into the lodge was impassable, often clogged with nearly four feet of snow as late as the middle of April, they all dwelt in Estes Park in a small home that still greets the morning sunshine on Big Horn Drive. Later they moved to a larger home Abner constructed next door.

Over the next couple of years additions were made to the lodge and open porches, later enclosed, afforded their guests a better opportunity to enjoy the serene splendor of the near primeval setting. In 1917 a large two-story log cottage, called The Stopher Cottage, was built in which Mabel and the two children occupied the first floor during the summers. Mabel, in addition to her variety of duties around the lodge, made candy at her cottage for sale to guests. Her confectionery craft was certainly appreciated by the fishermen whose soiled and tattered fishing vests always included small bags of their favorite sweets they called their *energy rejuvenaters*. A stairway, attached to the northwest side of the cottage, afforded access to the second floor rooms rented out to summer guests. During the winter of 1917-1918 workers including Abner, Ed Andrews and a man named Burgess, lived in the Stopher Cottage while the main building was enlarged to its full three storied height. The dining room at the same time was enlarged on the northeast end of the lodge with a penultimate addition made to the now enclosed porch. Only one of the lodge's sleeping rooms had its own private bathroom, Number 16 over the kitchen, and that *rustic luxury* was the summer living quarters for Abner and Bert. All of the bathrooms for guests were located *down the hall*. But in 1932 the third floor rooms, that previously contained only open storage space, were remodeled into more private managers' quarters including another bathroom, and Number 16 became a higher priced rental unit.

I should pause here to bring in a new element that would forever effect Sprague's Lodge, the new Rocky Mountain National Park created in early 1915. Abner felt that the government officials at the inception of the Park had not been fair to him. "By the Forest Service lease we were granted ninety-five acres, but by the lease from the National Park Service we were granted only twenty acres," he explained years later. "The bill creating the Park protected all claims and rights secured before the passage of the bill. My lease from the Forest Service was ignored, and I was given one for only the smaller acreage, but I was told they would protect my fishing rights as far as possible." He determined then and there that he must try to secure fee title to his leased ground before other government decrees might make it impossible to recoup his life savings and Mabel's inheritance invested in the lodge.

Abner's other land in part comprised fee title to 80 acres including a high lake, Loch Vale, to which we now enjoy hiking and preserving its pristine qualities in photographs. Abner first labeled the beauty spot *Lock's Vale* for one of his friends from Kansas City, a banker by the name of Lock who had enjoyed the area greatly before his death in 1909. Awaking to the fact that this lake was the prime reason for hikers to venture into this back country climax of the Creator's cosmos, and that *Loch* sounded more appropriate than *Lock* for a serene pool of ice blue water sheltered beneath craggy turrets of gray-green stone, he gave it the present name hoping his deceased compatriot would understand. The name he attributed to one of the pinnacles in the Mummy Range, Mount Chiquita also known as Mount Chipeta in honor of the wife of Ute Indian Chief Ouray, never changed perhaps in recognition of a woman's wrath that might haunt him from the great beyond.

Mr. Sprague also owned an interest in the land encompassing Mills Lake. His plan had always been to prevent any private development on either parcel in those high, scenic portions of the wild gardens of nature, and further meant to have them eventually included as a component of the National Park. There was a question about the title to the Mills Lake property, -- whether Abner owned all, part or nothing inasmuch as another person, the same Mr. Frank G. Bartholf whose name was associated with Glacier Basin, questioned the wisdom of this philanthropic approach to land investment. Mr. Bartholf, whose name has been given by geologists to the glacier that scoured out Glacier Basin, died before the issue that clouded the title was resolved. His heir, Judge Greeley Whitford of Denver, thought the better approach was for him to be paid for his putative claim to inherited wealth and agreed to sell his legacy to the Spragues. Abner informed the National Park officials, that if he could scrape up the $6,000 necessary to quiet title to himself, he would deed to the National Park Service his Mills-Loch Vale 200 acres **if**, and only if it in turn would deed him the 160 acres surrounding his lodge.

Then the waffling started with government officials postulating 'Why Mills Lake and Loch Vale ground is not worth as much as the Glacier Basin ground.' Negotiations ceased after the National Park Service talked only of granting a twenty year lease while at the same hoping that Abner would donate the high ground to the public when Superintendent Roger Toll praised Abner for his *valued friendship and assistance rendered* in the establishment of the National Park. Abner did not succumb to the blandishments, however sincere they may have been, but tried a different approach when he offered to exchange just the Loch Vale property of 80 acres for only 40 acres around his lodge. All negotiations broke down, even though Superintendent Toll went to bat for Abner when he wrote his assessment of the individual with whom Washington was engaged in bureaucratic arm wrestling. "Sprague has been one of the most loyal and helpful friends of the Park and entitled to all the liberality that could clearly be given." Mr. Toll genuinely wanted the Mills and Loch Vale properties and advised his superiors of his opinion as well as pointing out that property lines for Sprague's lodge property could be drawn to prevent it being observed from the scenic byway of Bear Lake Road. His efforts, and Abner's generosity and pioneer honed persistence in and out of Washington, paid off as the news item of March 20, 1925, though incorrect in some details, reported. "Congress passed a bill authorizing the granting of a patent for the 160 acres upon which the Sprague Hotel is situated in exchange

270

for a deed to 200 acres of land owned by Abner E. Sprague which includes Loch Vale. He had been occupying the hotel property on a year to year lease from the National Park. The Park was glad to own the beautiful Loch. A previous bill was filibustered last year and not passed."

To back up for a moment, after John Stopher's estate was settled in 1910 Mabel became a silent financial partner to Abner and Bert. She provided them additional capital in order to make the needed improvements at the emerging resort that I have discussed including funds to establish two lakes. The Sprague, Morrison and Stopher families were closely knit, loved and trusted one another, and worked together in a viable collaborative partnership to earn Sprague's Lodge high marks with the tourists throughout its entire life-span of fifty years. During the winters of 1925 to 1927, workers lived in the Stopher Cottage again while two adjoining cottages were framed up and roughly finished to blend into the trees just west of the main building. The one closest to the Stopher Cottage was called simply the Middle Cabin, while the other was designated the Perry Cabin for Lee Perry, an avid fisherman from Chicago and a close friend of Abner and Ed Andrews and who was a wealthy owner of the Vesta Battery Company. Lee Perry became the first occupant of this cabin where he remained entrenched for successive summers and fished every day for rapaciously hungry trout. These two cabins --each containing four sleeping rooms, three baths, and a central sitting room for the common enjoyment of all of the cabin's guests -- cost $12,000 to build and rented for between $6.45 to $7.50 per day per person, including meals, and from $32.50 to $42.25 per week. Until 1932 while Abner was in charge, he housed 40 guests on an average from Memorial Day through Labor Day. Six Guernsey cows lived in the barn where the present day livery operations are located, and fresh milk, cream and butter were regularly supplied to the guests. Stabling no horses, Abner knew his guests preferred to hike and fish, although he regularly secured the services of a local wrangler in Moraine Park to bring in horses for those guests who wanted another recreational diversion.

Like his brother, Abner was a competent mountain climber and guide for his guests. He registered his first ascent of Long's Peak in 1874 and fifty years later climbed it on July 18, 1924 at the age of 74 years accompanied by the son of his first hiking companion, his nephew Alson Chapman, Jr. He was a talented, caring and resourceful man for all seasons whose life could serve as an example to today's youth seeking direction, leadership and ethical principles. Bert kept nutritious food in abundant quantities on the tables of her guests being remembered as "a great cook and organizer." Ed Stopher greatly loved his *Aunty Bert* and firmly believed that she was one of the very best of those pioneering women we revere. She took charge of the cooking, the laundry, the cleaning and had time to sit with guests and listen to their needs and recount her tales as a pioneer lodge owner. Abner, although he had many duties himself about the premises, was the entertainer and raconteur to the guests but he always gave full credit to any success he achieved to his *Mrs. S*. In his 90th year he was more in love with his Bert than ever, and attributed his long life primarily to her. He also had thought a great deal of Bert's father and was grateful that Mr. Morrison had found him worthy to marry his daughter. He joshed with his wife at a large gathering of friends but publicly acknowledged to Bert, "You were not my first love." Bert shot playfully stern glances at her hubby, guessing that his statement was not completed. A smile slowly crossed his handsome face as he took her hand on his 90th birthday party in 1941. "You see, I first fell in love with your father even before I did you." As a lasting tribute to Alberta, Abner bestowed her name upon the gracefully photogenic and beautiful plunge of water near the trail leading up from Glacier Gorge parking lot. Its fine qualities, like her own, will bring a smile and some mist to your face as you stand admiring Alberta Falls with all nature framing it in a picturesque perspective.

To summarize the appearance of Sprague's when fully developed, I must ask you today to turn off the Bear Lake Road at the Sprague Lake exit and wind across Glacier Creek. As you enter the circular drive, pause for a moment. There was no road to the right when the lodge was in operation, just the road to the left. In the center of the grassy area, now occupied by a large restroom building, was the approximate location of the dining room with the rest of the lodge extending to the south and west. The smaller privy, now for winter use at the west end of the circular drive, was the location of the three cabins previously described. The present livery stable is not the original stock building that after 1932 came under the capable direction of the livery-men Shorty Greenlee, John Casey Kemp, Les Piatt and finally Art Card. The log cabin near the stables is the Perry Cabin, moved to its present site by the National Park Service for use by wranglers in the present day concessioned livery operation. It alone survives as the last trace of Sprague's Lodge. The dimensions of the main lodge of carefully fitted logs in 1927 measured 70 feet by 42 feet. In the lodge, after the final additions were completed, were dining facilities, a comfortable lounge with a stone fireplace, the kitchen, butler's pantry, bathrooms, laundry and store rooms. There were seven guest rooms on the main floor with another ten upstairs, some of which served as employees' quarters in former years. The thoroughly enjoyable screened-in porch, later enclosed, provided guests and visitors awaiting dinner a fine view of the horses patiently escorting laughing guests back from a ride to Dream Lake or beyond. The roar of Glacier Creek nearby was a soothing tonic, often sleep inducing, to the gentlemen and ladies found dozing after a full day of hiking, horseback riding or angling for those big Brookies with a Rio Grande King dry fly or other concocted lure secreted away in a canvas vest pocket.

Sprague's was famous for its trout dinners with the entrees having been swimming in Abner's lakes only an hour before. In the summer of 1914, Boulder Brook was dammed up to form two lakes, afterwards the effervescent tumble of water flowed to the northeast to join forces with its larger relative, Glacier Creek. The smaller of the two bodies of water Abner simply identified as Lower Lake. It often was referred to as Cabin Lake as early on in the history of the lodge the Spragues had leased a building site near Lower Lake to their friend Carl Buckingham, a banker from Boulder, Colorado, on which he erected a fine cabin. The small pool, just west of the present lake and adjacent to the existing circular drive, was created by the further damming of the same little brook through the good services of the late lumberman John Griffith to enhance the guests' first impression of the perfect setting of the lodge and be clearly visible from the front porch as well. Both lakes were stocked annually by Abner with thousands of Eastern Brook and Rainbow trout fingerlings purchased from a hatchery on the western slope. The local weekly reported on March 5, 1926, "Abner Sprague's Hotel will receive a shipment of 50,000 eastern brook trout for his private lakes about May 1st, for trout dinners are a specialty at Sprague's and they are home grown." Ed Stopher remembers that one of his favorite duties as the general chore boy, after he was through cutting wood and milking the cows, was to regularly net out large numbers of trout from the big lakes, transfer them to live holding boxes in the nearby pond, and clean them when the big fish dinners were scheduled for the guests and invited outsiders. "We had all kinds of fish dinners!" he recounted with a twinge of nostalgia that unintentionally was imparted to me. "We had good fishing in the lakes that were restricted to the use of the family and the guests, --and a selected few friends, with boats provided for no charge." The two lakes totaled 20 acres in combined size with Upper Lake, being the larger, encompassing nearly fifteen acres with a depth of nine feet. It is now generally referred to as Sprague Lake. Idyllically situated, Lower Lake after its acquisition by the National Park Service, was torn out years later after maintenance of its dirt levees had been deferred for too long. On Sprague Lake, now grown smaller and more shallow the result of silt, Abner provided steel boats free for his guests. It now continues to provide free opportunities for all, including the handicapped on a paved trail around the lake. I hope, as the present day anglers reel in a fat *Brookie* or Rainbow, he or she will give a silent thank you for the hard work of Abner Sprague. Their catches probably represent the descendents of his annual efforts, since now the lake is no longer stocked in accordance with governmental regulations that many suggest "tampers too much with recreational opportunities in the Park."

Early into the operation of Sprague's Lodge the drinking water came to the resort from Boulder Brook through a two inch pipe high up on the north facing slope immediately south of the main lodge. Electricity was provided to all of the buildings from a hydro electric plant on the north side of Glacier Creek just west of the lodge buildings. Later, when Ed Stopher took over, he constructed a backup power plant powered by a Ford V-8 motor that was started up at supper time when greater demand for electrical current was expected. Of course another creature, that was thoroughly admired by Abner for its workaholic capacity yet so successful that his buildings often were in jeopardy, had to be taken to task otherwise his resort would have been centered in a vast pond. The beavers chewed most anything on which they could grip their incisors, and annually at least ten of the most persistent of these nocturnal engineers required transplantation. It was not an easy task as their homes often were positioned amidst deep, muddy pools entangled in the most impenetrable of willow swamps. Over succeeding years, the hydro plant's impeller wheel frequently became clogged and shut down. More often than not the culprit to such misdeeds was a migrating beaver whose fur, teeth and whole carcass often were picked out of the apparatus in pieces by a frozen hand of an employee called out in the night as his wet flashlight's yellow glow discovered the source of the problem. Bob Cheney well remembers his travails with the impudent Beaver family. "I got so tired of those beavers and having to break out their dams! So one night I took a light with a flashing beam that came on and off and put it by the ditch that brought the water to the power plant hoping the light would scare them away. But the next day, there was the light still blinking away, --and a new dam constructed. I guess the critter used the light to better see to build his new structure for the light

273

certainly had not bothered him in the least."

Another woodland resident, which had lost much of its fear of humans, kept all lodge operators on their toes. Lack of fear of the bear to man and vice-versa was due largely to efforts of vacationing mothers and fathers to feed the bears and other wild creatures. Parent's failure to distinguish for their children the difference between an untamed creature from the more humanized variety found in fairy tales with cuddly talking bears as the chief characters, was always a tragedy ready to happen. Abner and the other men about the lodge worked constantly warning the guests not to familiarize with the bruins while they at the same time repaired damage from marauding black bears that thought it good sport to invade the store rooms where feed and other supplies were stockpiled. One night, as the story was reported to me, a mother bear became overly protective of two cubs she was chaperoning about lodge grounds while teaching the young ones the fine art of scavenging. Management became alarmed for the guests safety who apparently had thrown good sense to the winds as they stood in front of the lodge, pajama clad, probing the darkness with their flashlights hoping for a photo opportunity. The incident appeared comical as this disheveled band of blanket wrapped city dwellers laughed and shouted in a scene fraught with unrecognized danger. Two *experts* were brought in the next day who vowed to solve the problem. They would simply trap out the mother and the cubs would follow to where their mother was removed. "Quite simple," one rationalized with an air of superiority, pulling down smartly the brim of a weathered western Stetson. After several abortive attempts to capture the intruder during successive nights, at last the bear specialists claimed victory. The trap had been sprung and the local National Park ranger was called to assess the situation and determine the bear's new home. While guests scrutinized the quasi-military maneuvers from the security of the front porch and the trappers stood by in puffed up pride of accomplishment, the Ranger peered closely and ever so carefully into the cage where the beast growled ominously. Turning slowly to those who expected praise, the Ranger slowly exclaimed with rolling deep eloquence that possessed a biting quality, "That ain't no mommy bear! I think you got the old man!" Eventually the situation was solved when daddy, mom and the kids voluntarily took their permanent leave for more friendly and less hectic hunting grounds. One of the guests, learning the result of the deflated trappers' efforts, put in the final blade of sarcasm with a twist when he shouted, "How are you fellas at catching some bass out of that trout pond?"

Abner had always been good with words, both in print and spoken with studied authority on many subjects. Until his death he was considered the unofficial historian of Estes Park with that reputation anchored with dozens of articles authored since 1910 until his death. His subjects were legion, on the National Park, beavers, wind, glaciers, his fellow citizens, roads, mining, mountain climbing, camping, -- you name it. His gripping account of journeying across the midsection of the United States in the 1860s, self published and titled *Reminiscences Of A Pioneer*, was detailed and illustrative of that period of time. It was replete with Indian lore, hardships, adventure and examples of high ethical conduct. It should be on the shelves of every library and available to the eyes of children who need a better idol for conduct than currently available on the sports fields or film screens of America. Abner Sprague lectured at his lodge on the need of tourists to know this mountainous basin in which they now occupied space. An example of his wit and wisdom was in the summer of 1931. "I told the audience at the Lodge there are three good examples of these wonderful forces of nature, the glaciers and the resultant moraines, to be seen in this region. They are Horseshoe Park, Moraine Park and Glacier Basin. Ages ago ice must have filled the Glacier Basin at Sprague's to the depth of at least 1,000 feet. I wish more of our visitors understood and took more interest in this ancient history of these mountains and valleys." He paused to conceal a smile, and continued. "A good story along these lines fits in here. A bus driver who felt obliged to explain what a moraine was to a woman tourist said, 'It was brought down from the high mountains by a glacier.' She asked 'Where is the glacier?' The bus driver gave the answer, nearer correct than he realized. He said, 'it has gone back for more rocks.' If history repeats itself his answer was correct."

In the spring of 1927 more private baths were installed to which improvements their advertisement confidently proclaimed, "A new water system was laid that will provide the purest water in ample quantities for any emergency." Further modern conveniences were added such as "the Alamo lighting system and a new heating plant." Also the dining room was further increased in size and capacity as those fish dinners were in constant demand. But the conveniences of the big city really arrived when the lodge proudly reported, "New furnishings are being bought in Denver!" Colorado was the place to be, the Spragues maintained as they urged on potential guests in advertisements, "*California or Florida, If you are old, COLORADO If You Wish To Keep Young,*" and thousands responded. In the early 1930s a wood frame ski jump on the south side of Upper Lake was erected at the same time ice skating was permitted by the Spragues on the lake as local people were always welcomed to Sprague's Lake as their destination for crisp winter sports and family enjoyment.

History was to repeat itself in 1931, but not in a geologic way, as further trouble was moving up Glacier Basin from Washington D. C. as surely as the ice had moved relentlessly forward millions of years before. Abner was 81 years old and tiring and the effects of the depression hung on with fewer tourists with dollars to spend. The National Park Service was eager to acquire the Sprague's holdings, and thus the family reexamined their alternatives. That year the lodge still could accommodate fifty guests per day, if they could be lured up to spend $6.00 per day or $30.00 per week including bath. Now, however, the meals were charged separately at an additional $1.00 per plate except for trout that cost $1.50 but the lodge still produced a reasonable income though with a lot more effort and advertising expense. Abner was not going to give up without a fight and agreed to listen to what the National Park had to offer with the result that the lodge was purchased in 1932 by the National Park Service for $35,140. Abner was granted a 20 year period in which to operate it under lease and the family continued to improve their resort to the extent that even steam heat was added to all of the buildings by 1938. In 1940, determining to protect Ed who essentially was his partner and realizing that his own length of life was drawing to a close, Abner requested and received permission from National Park officials to transfer the lease into the name of Edgar Morrison Stopher. Ed's sister's future was settled when in July of 1933 Alberta Stopher was married in the lodge to Robert Miller of Chicago as Ed stood by proudly as a substitute best man for their father.

While the Spragues lived at the lodge during the summer tourist seasons after 1932, Ed and his bride, Dorothy Eleanor Hansen whom he married in October of 1940, were fully in charge beginning with the 1941 season. They paid Abner each year an agreed upon sum of money equivalent to the value of the lease transferred. The Spragues previously erected last home in Estes Park in 1932, now in 1993 functions as a bed and breakfast guest house.

Ed, at the time he entered the tourist industry with his uncle, became very active in local community affairs and especially in his own industry, and in 1938 was elected President of the National Park Service Operators' Association whose other officers at that time were Jack Woods, Roland Reed and Jim Bishop. The Stophers lived in Denver during the winter time where Ed sold real estate and, like most lodge operators mandated a second career to supplement the short twelve to fourteen week tourist season. By 1941 over 150,000 guests had stayed at the lodge including many famous persons. As an example, Judge Harlan F. Stone, while vacationing at the lodge that year was sworn into the office of Chief Justice of the United States Supreme Court by U. S. Commissioner Hackett as Abner stood by as the witness. As World War II drew the United States into another protracted conflict of monstrous proportions and Ed joined up with the Armed Forces, Dorothy carried on running the lodge with the assistance of Bert, Abner and Mabel and a competent staff of young summer employees. Also, in the winters, Dorothy was in charge of another resort property -- Monte Vista Ranch in Wickenburg, Arizona --they had purchased. On May 8, 1942, Abner, unable to serve in any previous war effort for his country, tried to register at the local Town Hall for the military draft despite the fact that he was 92 years of age. The following October, joining in the scrap drive to get metal for the war cause, he donated his historically valuable double bitted ax used to cut logs for his first cabin and later his hotel. He was not only a pioneer, but a staunch patriot. Abner died at the Brown Palace Hotel in Denver, Colorado of a bleeding ulcer on December 27, 1943 at the age of 93 after moving from Estes Park only eight days before. Bert followed her man to glory, the result of a heart attack, on February 22, 1948. As he neared the end of his life in 1942, Abner responded to a question about what the next seventy-five years would bring to these environs of his happiness. "Would there be as much change in the Park?" he was asked. Reflecting over the years since he first walked upon the raw prairie of the upper Big Thompson River valley as a youth so long before, he offered a realistic opinion. "I'd like to be here to see it! I made many minor decisions, which have changed the course of my life and the lives of others. Even a hermit cannot live the life of the isolationist. Two people have shared their cares and troubles for 54 years are approaching the end of life much more happy than was hoped for many times through the years. As for me, I feel I was born 90 years too soon."

His historically significant articles included his own assessment of the lodging industry that speaks eloquently of his guests, and others even now more numerous who rush about without pausing long enough to reflect upon this National Park. "In the entertainment of tourists, I prefer to call tourists *guests*, still there are those you can call nothing but *tourists*. Those that go tearing from coast to coast and back again on their vacations are tourists. When they reach home from their travels, they are not certain where they saw this or that. Unless they brand their pictures or buy post cards, they will not be able to tell which is Mt. Hood, Mt. Baker, Mt. Ranier, or Long's Peak from Pike's Peak, or what state they are in. They will have their road map as a record of their travels, showing what cities they visited, but will have to keep a careful diary to tell what they saw here and there, whether in Chicago, Cheyenne, Denver, or any other towns visited. There is no better place than Estes Park to differentiate between a tourist and a guest. The *tourist* comes in from the east or west, tired from travel. He wants to know at once the best way to see Estes Park, --the next day, or in time go to Denver or some point west of the Divide. The only and best answer we could give to that would be --that we had lived in the Park for more than sixty years and had not seen all that was of interest to see in the region. The *guest* comes to stay every minute of his vacation he can spare. If he fails to see every nook and corner of the place on one visit, he comes year after year. There are parties and families that have been coming to Sprague's and other places of entertainment in Estes Park for fifteen years or more that still anticipate seeing places visited many times on former trips. They know by experience that they get new thrills every time they travel the same old trails, the view changes with the light and shadows. The artist finds he must finish his picture at one sitting, for it will never look the same again. Our guests never get tired, the same old urge to visit spots seen more than once brings them back on their next vacation. They go home rested." The same thing could be said about Abner. Once you had seen him, and shook his hand, you wanted to see him again. To know him was an exciting learning experience and I for one would have opted to be a member of the Guest category shunning any identification with the infamous Tourist class.

Ed returned to full management of the lodge in 1946 and Sprague's Lodge was again welcoming in new and former guests, but this time with some sadness because of the absence of Abner and those who had fallen in battle after giving their full measure of patriotism to a cause that those who now follow should never forget. Abner was climbing more exalted new trails yet his presence was always apparent about the lodge. How could it be otherwise with such devotion to a land that bore so much of his personality? In 1947 Sprague's promoted these recreational activities in its promotional tract. "We are located in Glacier Basin, in Rocky Mountain National Park, the ideal vacation place. Horseback riding, fishing, tennis, boating and golf. Transient meals are served upon reservation, and we are operated under government supervision." A laundry building was erected, new quarters for the help constructed to free up seven additional rooms in the main lodge for guests, and four Quonset houses were moved in from the completed Lake Estes project of the Bureau of Reclamation. These utilitarian buildings were remodeled and positioned behind the Stopher Cottage for additional guest space. As with most of the earlier lodges, Ed followed suit and placed within the trees four tent houses thereby increasing his lodging capacity to eighty-five in 1950. At one time the lodge was so popular that some of the employees were moved into Abner' former chicken house, converted to human nesting quarters, thereby providing more area for paying guests. The resort now consisted of eleven substantial buildings, mostly of log frame on masonry foundations, not including the tent houses and previous egg laying factory. The staff was boosted to twenty seasonal employees plus the family during a regular summer season. Ed could see the end coming for Sprague's Lodge now that the initial lease term had less than five years to run and embarked upon a prudent course of action. Learning of the possibility of purchasing Stead's from the Lewises, after Will's diminished vigor following a fall from a horse that restricted him to his winter residence in the Brown Palace Hotel in Denver, Ed and Dorothy sold their ranch in Arizona in 1948 to commence negotiations for Stead's purchase. Stead's Ranch returned to more closely related Sprague family control when Will and Myra sold their entire interest in Stead's Ranch to Ed Stopher in October of 1950 for the sum of $90,000. The assets sold included 100 head of registered Hereford cattle. The S brand burned into the hides was altered into a *lazy* E bar S pattern. Will died eight years later and Myra followed in 1961 thus terminating all Stead family identification with the historic ranch.

While Park officials were examining the direction for the Park with respect to extensions of concessionaire contracts, they permitted the Sprague's Lodge lease to be extended through 1958, and literally the old lodge had a new lease on its life, albeit a brief one. One of the officials of the old transportation company was the same Claude Verry, formerly of the Lewiston Hotel, who in the mid-1940s was in a mercantile business in the village. His son, Dalton, had married Willa Jean Wolford of Lincoln Nebraska and in the early 1940s they operated the Sky Ranch, a rustic dude ranch thirty-six miles west of Fort Collins, Colorado and fourteen miles south of the Poudre Canyon near Comanche Peak. The business had not been as successful as they had hoped and they sold the ranch in 1946 and returned to Estes Park in search of a better opportunity for financial security. While living at the Estes Park Chalet during the winters of 1947 and 1948, a job was offered to them by Ed who knew Dalton and his father. Since Stead's Ranch was taking so much of Ed's and Dorothy's time, they were hired to manage Sprague's commencing with the 1950 summer season. They opened up the road into the lodge the middle of May and set to the tasks of making ready the lodge for its Memorial Day opening. Willa Jean, now the wife of a respected former member of the Estes Park Board of Directors, Byron *Barney* Graves whose father was a long time Mayor of this community, described the appearance of the lodge that first year of her six seasons at Sprague's. "Sprague's was rustic, with every room having a hang down light fixture. There were no lamps in the rooms and only two guest rooms in the lodge had private bathroom facilities. The rest of the guests' rooms had community facilities, down the hall. The floors were wooden and partially covered with small throw rugs, and the walls were paper thin. A popular area was the enclosed porch with the big fireplace, and there was another enclosed room with Navajo Indian rugs on the walls and floor that was usually crowded when Charles Eagle Plume regularly danced and lectured once a week. But people were on vacation and accepted a lot less in creature comforts." She paused to pick up a picture torn from an old magazine that featured Sprague's, and smiled at the horseback riders waving in front of the lodge. "They knew it wasn't a modern motel and didn't want it any other way!" she asserted with a smile and obvious pride for the way it was, but would never be again.

Guests in the 1950s had as their prime recreational activity hiking as well as horseback riding, especially for the children, under the competent wrangling of Les Piatt who had worked for the Stophers at their ranch in Arizona, then Art Card who also had taken over the horse operations in 1953 at

278

Stead's. Dalton handled the outside work including signing up guests for horseback rides to the extent that Art Card knew how many dudes needed horses, how many were adults and kids, what kind of riders they were, and what destination they sought to reach. Guests were not interested in breakfast rides made popular at other lodges as Sprague's residents preferred to sleep in after a very active itinerary out on the mountain trails. Many foreign guests were found at Sprague's who were very fond of walking with their alpenstock tapping out a regular cadence into the high vistas accessed by Flattop Mountain trail and Storm Pass. A week at Sprague's in the 1950s was still very reasonable at the adult rate of $125 per week, including three meals. Sometimes the guests preferred to remain out all day and thus requested a sack lunch by placing their names on a sign-up sheet the night before. The usual luncheon fare at the lodge was a full smorgasbord of culinary delights offered by Chef Art Persons. Willa Jean scratched her head as she remembered the spartan lunch often ordered by many of the foreign guests. "Remember, they were paying for three meals, but many of them wanted only some raisins, a few apples and a little jug of water!"

In 1951 Chef Persons transferred to Stead's Ranch where he could confound its more luxury demanding clientele with his culinary capabilities and concoctions. Stead's Ranch guests, as Ed Stopher described them, "were more of the horsey type, upscale, and not as much of the outdoors type as the guests were at Sprague's." Chef Persons at Stead's originated the first buffet in this region where exceptional food was spread out in long rows before the guests on flower decorated tables graced by intricate ice carvings. Although Mr. Persons had moved on to greater triumphs surrounded by adulating men and women clad in the latest fashions adapted to the saddle of a horse, the deck of the swimming pool or poised professionally on the tennis court, Sprague's did not lack for quality food and it was appreciated for its quantity, wholesomeness and lack of pretence in its presentation. Located only seven and one-half miles west of the village it seemed lost to the *outside* world of strain and struggle, but still offered its own special variety of laid back living as its terminal year's advertisement announced. "We have a smorgasbord every Wednesday for regular guests and transient visitors, wiener roasts and supervised trips for children. We have modern comfort in the lodge or in cottage accommodations, and fishing, boating and *swimming* in Sprague's private lake." Can anyone now imagine leaping into the lake where the temperature never reached more than 50 degrees, even on a rare hot day? But Ed Stopher did say that "these were outdoor people," and so they were, and as the result each of his resort properties fulfilled a distinctly different purpose for the traveling public.

The dining room, in the northeast corner of the lodge, was staffed only by waitresses as the male help were assigned other tasks out of doors or in the kitchen washing the dishes, pots and pans. The dining room was a large, friendly room wherein all of those seated at the square wooden tables had a superb view through the many-paned windows. Willa Jean described to me one feature of the dining facility. "It had a *wave* to it, because there were little dips in the floor where new sections were added to the old part that created a wavy look to it as one entered the door." Sprague's Lodge catered to families, usually consisting of father, mother and the two kids, who stayed weeks or often a month at a time. Dining tables were assigned to a guest family upon its arrival and over the years returning guests expected to be seated at *their* table. Those intending to stay at Sprague's during the most popular month for tourists, August, sent in their reservation deposit early hoping for a cabin where they would be closer to nature. Now in the 1990s the most popular month in the National Park is July as the inauguration of earlier school terms in late August have revised tourist patterns for holidays. Willa Jean, whose chief responsibility lay in the office as the receptionist and official greeter, commenced her typical day by assuring that breakfast items were ready and on the tables by 7:30 until 9 A. M. Lunch was served between noon and 1:30 P. M. and dinner, open to the public if there were space, was served from 6 P. M. through 7:30. by surprisingly qualified young women whose youthful appearance belied their expertise. The young men and women I suppose considered Willa Jean, young herself, as a combination of house mother, teacher, supervisor and friend. Notwithstanding her senior status in authority, she did not judge it her responsibility to discipline the staff under her control. "The girls and boys I put on the honor system, and as they had no automobiles they hitch hiked into town for entertainment although they had a lot of fun around the lodge. Their greatest dream as soon as they arrived was to climb Long's Peak. After their dream was realized, they were not worth a darn for the next two days as their muscles ached and they moved slowly through their chores, all fatigued."

Many of the guests were picked up in town for the reason that groups of them arrived at valley towns by Union Pacific Railroad tours then continued up to the Estes Valley by motor coaches. The large midwestern cities, especially Chicago, accounted for immense numbers of guests who longed for a wilderness experience away from the discordant sounds associated with crowds, trams and the regularity of a disordered and mind numbing urban existence. Willa Jean said, "People at Sprague's **had** to enjoy nature when they came for there was no television, no liquor served in the lodge, no telephones in their rooms and the only news we and they heard came from newspapers or was brought in by the tales of an arriving guest." The main difference between Sprague's and Stead's Ranch was that guests at Stead's expected a more upscale resort experience whereby they wanted to be pampered and looked after through the office of the Ranch Hostess. On the other hand, Sprague's people demanded a less structured habitat where they provided their own entertainment shared with night creatures, silence and solitude spotlighted only by a shaving of the new moon. Mr. Stopher said, "Sprague's was a place where people hiked and were very busy, --tired at night, so that there wasn't a lot of evening entertainment." Both groups of guests were always invited to partake of recreational opportunities at both of the resorts, with Stead's guests enjoying the fishing in the Sprague's lakes and Sprague's guests heaping their plates full at those wonderful Sunday buffets, possibly swimming in the much warmer pool or promenading about the colorfully crowded square dance floor to the whine of a fancy fiddle. Two evenings a week, Wednesday and Sunday, were devoted to square dancing for guests of Stead's and others who sought out this now nearly forgotten brand of fun. Once a week dancers swirled around the smaller recreational facility at Sprague's, all to musically staccato directions of professional callers such as Frank Lane whose wizardry managed to keep most all of the promenaders free of collision. Most all of the lodges in the Park sponsored a night or two of square dancing and, if dance devotees could only manage but one week's stay in the National Park, the *doe-ze-doers* could find many a square forming up each evening at a different lodge as well as at Riverside or Grover Voelkel's recreation hall east of the Y.M.C.A. Who needed television, video or rock music back then, and think of what that prancing did for the figure as it shed calories accumulated from ample portions of lodge cuisine. But by the way, who counted calories before the 1970s anyway?

The summer of 1957 found another young lady attending to the front desk after Willa Jean had departed for new endeavors. Lois Warfield, also from Lincoln, Nebraska, had been employed at the Remuda Ranch in Wickenburg, Arizona which ranch was owned by Dana Burden. She and Dana were invited by Ed Stopher to manage Sprague's though they had no idea that this year would be the last one for the lodge. "I handled the front desk, was the greeter, and was impressed with Sprague's as the kind of lodge that one would imagine a mountain lodge to be. It was very popular." She remembered her room at the lodge quite vividly as it was located in a building that hung over the torrent of Glacier Creek. But her most important remembrance of Sprague's is meeting its maintenance superintendent, Bob Cheney of whom I have earlier written and to whom she has been happily married for well over three decades. As the end of Sprague's lease extension was approaching next year in 1958, Ed Stopher was fully occupied with improving Stead's Ranch, a resort from which he derived the lions share of his tourist dollars. He ascertained that it might be best to end the Sprague lease at the end of the 1957 season when guests would remember it as a lovely rustic spa, viable and still capable of thrilling the most obdurate of spirit with a true mountain experience. It must end in its prime, not in a dying posture which would have been the situation during the last season scheduled for 1958. After the last year of lodge operation, certain items of the furnishings, special to the Sprague and Stopher families, were removed to Stead's. The doors were closed for the last time after Labor Day and all of the buildings, except Perry Cabin, were demolished by 1960. Mercifully, Abner was not in this life to witness the destruction of his beloved lodge, nor was Mabel Stopher around to see the bulldozer push over her cottage as she had died in 1958 at the age of 82.

Why did people choose Sprague's? All with whom I have discussed this subject said it was the view and the surroundings that told the whole story. It had everything necessary for a happy vacation. There were the beckoning mountains looking down on the lodge from the west, the trout stocked lakes to the east and the musical brooks on both sides of the lodge and cabins. It had remoteness from traffic, absolute stillness of the night and a forest of giant, sweet smelling trees where guests' pleasure was graced by an awareness that they shared their good times with animals of the forest not too timid to prevent a close association in this intimate surrounding. What was special about Sprague's to Willa Jean Graves after it was all gone? "I remember the lovely people who came back every year, --to see the children return as they were growing up and to listen to their trials and tribulations. People wanted the lodge, cabins and everything to be the way it was! They came back every year, wanted the same accommodations and always asked if a friend or family was back. This was one time of the year when these families all got together and they planned it that way. If one family was missing, there was a distinct void." Haven't we heard that same perceptive comment

281

before as we reflect back upon the other lodge stories in this book? What was the purpose of hideaways like Sprague's? There was a congeniality, a personality, about the whole lodge that decanted a wine of warm welcome to strangers who eagerly quaffed it to become new friends that over time and distance would ever be revered. Sprague's became their second home. Could the lodges, the way they were thirty or forty years ago, still attract guests in the 1990s to old buildings with the *bathrooms down the hall?* Is a tumbling brook, a fish fry, a square dance or a time of solitude in the darkness of the night listening to the night creatures reason enough to draw modern travelers away from their favorite television show, discos or a room filled with wing-ding gadgetry? Willa Jean doesn't think so. "It's so different now that the lodges are gone, but people probably wouldn't accept those old structures in their rustic conditions as people are too spoiled." Reluctantly I must agree, though I yearn for an opportunity to prove that judgment of the modern character is faulty.

Ranger Bill Grove, after leaving National Park duties, with his beloved wife and partner of more than half a century, Joyce, were owners of numerous successful business enterprises like Grove's Toggery in Estes Park. He obliquely reflected on the same question I had proffered to Willa Jean. "The caliber of the visitor to Estes Park and the National Park has dropped considerably since they eliminated the lodges," he said shaking his head sadly after more than forty-six years in residence in this valley. "Now they only have motels. When people stayed in the lodges they could stay right in the Park, do the things out of doors that were important. They didn't need to be entertained for their entertainment was all about them. The lodge visitors had the town to visit, but they didn't need it as the Park was what they came for. Now the Park visitors are holed up in some in-town motel and they are a different bunch. Estes Park should work for the quality of the experience for its guests, not just the numbers of people who come to town." Lois Cheney looked me straight in the eye when I asked her about the loss of Sprague's and later Stead's. "The fact that there are no more such places in the Park is a shame because people now don't have the same opportunity. Guests of the lodges took good care of the National Park because they were not just day users. It was their second home since they had been coming here year after year. I could tell by what guests were registered what month it was or even the day of the month since they always came back to their mountain home about the same time. When I returned in early 1958, thinking I would again be at Sprague's front desk and each morning before the guests were up going over to Stead's to pick up hot breakfast rolls as I did in 1957, I found there was no more Sprague's and it was a great disappointment!" Dorothy Stopher took the demise of Sprague's especially hard, as Bob Cheney put it, "Sprague's was her baby. I can well remember my last day with Dorothy when I was working at Stead's in May of 1958. She had fixed supper for us working on the ranch, and when I got in from work, she was gone, --died." The cause of her death at the age of 41 I was informed was related to a heart condition, and perhaps that is so. But as such physical maladies are closely related to emotions and stress, a secondary cause could have been a broken heart. She truly loved that artistically synthesized old pile of logs that had been Abner's and Bert's, and her own, hidden treasure and place of refuge shared with their guests who became their life long friends.

In 1959, all that was left in the National Park that represented an industry that indirectly gave it birth and nurture was Stead's Ranch, Abner's original homestead. But its days too were numbered to a precious few as winter's westerly winds of change were again blowing, this time out of the east that had effectively blown away Sprague's Lodge. At Stead's, the many cabins averaging fourteen feet square in dimensions and erected by J. D., contained no private bathrooms, and thus the first two years of Ed's ownership saw a year around crew of six spending thousands of hours remodeling them, --including the ten tent cabins that Dorothy mildly resented being referred to as *the tents*. She changed their identification to numbered cabins and they were modernized to remove any resemblance of their rudimentary canvas hut origins. An ever increasingly sophisticated flock of loyal guests returned from previous visits to be joined by new customers who were attracted by the efforts of the Stophers traveling to distant cities to unfold before new prospects a vision of their new dude ranch. Guests came to expect *luxuriously sophisticated rustic hard times* where they could dress up like ordinary cow pokes with scuffed high topped boots and wide brimmed hats, yet bed down in well appointed cabins with hot baths and at least two thick blankets over crisp sheets of white linen. The name of the ranch would remain **Stead's** for Mr. Stopher admired J. D. a great deal. "He really established it and I wanted his name identified with it for he really had made it go," Ed commented when asked why it was not now Stopher's Ranch. Their friendship went way back in years, even to the time when Ed's bull wandered away from Sprague's Lodge over the moraine to Stead's in the early 1920s and in its retrieval young Ed and the father figure of J. D. enjoyed great times together leading the animal back home. Letting the pages of his life reopen in his private survey of the past, especially the fun he had with J. D., his eyes took on a clouded expression, distant, in his remembrance. "Yes, J. D. was a great guy and I loved him," he quietly added and you knew he meant it.

The dance hall was enlarged, and a large swimming pool, gunnite lined, was hacked out of the native sod and which still remains today lost from view under fresh soil. Adjacent to the pool was spotted a volley ball court that was very popular. The water and sewer system was radically improved when water lines were extended from the main spring's large cistern and pumped up the hill in a 4 inch pipe to the north into a reservoir from which it was allowed to flow by gravity to all of the buildings as usage demanded. Although there were ample water rights derived out of the Big Thompson River, only spring water was used for human consumption as it was absolutely pure and fine tasting. It never ran dry and, despite efforts by later day Park personnel to plug it, the enduring spring with a strong heart still chugs away to sustain a flourishing array of wild flowers that welcome the warm sunlight to a silent meadow in which Abner first built his cabin. Later an additional spring was accidentally revealed at the time the swimming pool was excavated -- some say even a better one than the first -- and both were tied together to provide a greater abundance of fresh, cold water for the flourishing number of guests now being attracted by increased advertising efforts of the Colorado Dude Ranch Association. Ed had been very active in this organization since 1932 and subsequently served as its President. The water from this second spring in the 1990s is now piped up the hill to the north of the ranch site and is a source of water for the present day Moraine Park

Campground as the efforts of the National Park employees to dig wells higher up on the moraine resulted in nearly dry holes. Before the Stopher's made their year around residence at the ranch, the Stead and Lewis families lived away in the winter because the water lines were too shallow for sustained cold temperatures associated with Moraine Park in the wintertime. In the early 1950s a well was dug south of the Rock House and water was piped up the hill to the house in a deep trench. This, and the fact that the entrance road into the ranch that drifted badly over the years was now regularly plowed by Park employee George Swift, enabled Ed and Dorothy to move out from Abner's former home they owned in Estes Park.

Mrs. Prouty's little store, enlarged over the years as ownership in the ranch changed, took on a different posture, one that I am not certain Julia, who was related to Mrs. Stead, would have approved. Showers and restrooms were added downstairs and on the second floor was the bar and lounge that became a very popular gathering point for swimmers, horseback riders, golfers, and about anyone else who drove into the ranch to check it out for potential reservations. It was located immediately west of, and attached to, the swimming pool, and in 1957 was given a new name, Homestead Room and Coffee Shop. For the next five years it was a busy scene for late evening dinners, cocktails, pool parties and private entertaining, with good viands, sociable people, and superb views of bathing beauties as well as the surrounding mountains and flowing river. Throughout its long history, Stead's had the reputation as a "comfortable, relaxed, low key kind of place," a former guest informed me.

In its heyday Stead's staff consisted of maids, laundry people, wranglers, office staff, recreational supervisors and dining and kitchen staff that totalled nearly sixty men and women of all ages. The wranglers hung out over the large barn in quarters that, although somewhat spartan, were warm and adequate while the other male employees were housed in a dormitory converted above the tool shed, shop building and garage. The female workers stayed in more style in upscale rooms within the main lodge. Over the years there were no major problems with the help, other than an occasional bit of homesickness, for the crew was well fed, treated fairly and became comrades in a well oiled working machine who knew they were associated with the premier dude ranch of the Rocky Mountains. Of course there were the usual romances, one of which was remembered by Bob Cheney. "There was this 19 year old cabin maid who became smitten with a kitchen worker who was nearly 35. Well, after a spell they ran off together, and when her parents came out to see how she was getting along, she couldn't be found. Well!, we all did quite a bit of explaining but what could anyone do? Another romance had blossomed, but her folks sure were unhappy." After Bob married Lois, she joined the ranch staff to work in the office beginning in 1958. The couple lived in a caretaker's house, called the Homestead Cabin between the main lodge and the pool, until 1961 but during the prime summer months they were required to move to less opulent quarters that was reduced to its lowliest definition by Lois as "a little old cabin without a bathroom." The caretaker's cottage was well suited for more richly endowed guests who 'wanted a little cabin down in the meadow with trees.' Ed said Abner's Homestead cabin "was a good cabin to rent," and so it was on a regular basis. The Cheneys were frequently observed in the main lodge building, not just for socializing with the guests but for the fact it was equipped with the nearest location for their lavatory requirements.

It took a lot of effort to maintain and manage a lodge in the high mountains of Colorado, and Stead's was no exception. The effects of winter wind and intense sunlight with desiccating effects of fading and cracking, required constant roofing and painting of the plethora of lumber sided structures scattered about the ranch. It appeared that outside touching up was always in progress to the extent that each building effectively was repainted at least every five years. There were no major problems at Stead's over all of its years of catering to the public that in itself is a tribute to craftsmanship and capable management. There was one fire in the chimney flue of the main lodge building that was quickly extinguished so that the old lodge would not become a casualty to flame like Cascade Lodge and the Lewiston Hotel. The main lodge building always held the first priority for maintenance, remodeling, repair and frequent polishing of the floors and furnishings. It sheltered in its south side the dining room and kitchen that were as busy as a train depot on a 4th of July holiday morning in our grandparents' times. In other areas of the main lodge were several guest lounges with welcoming fireplaces, the game room that included a pool table, and a front desk that was loaded with western decor and wild flowers behind which stood several smiling faces ready to point you to your desired destination about the premises. On the upper floors were more than a dozen rooms, often used by single men and women guests who preferred to be closer to where the action was taking place. In the rear of the lodge was the employees' dining room adjacent to the spring house. A regular practice before dinner was for the employees on a hot day to go into the spring house and use the big dipper for a cool drink. That old tin implement was such a valued part of the old ranch, hanging on the hook by the bubbling spring for longer than anyone could remember, that when the ranch was finally closed one of the long time employees received that beloved and battered tin dipper as his souvenir. If you examine the grounds where Stead's once stood and see the spring rewarding with its cold elixir the flower bestrewn meadow of showy colors, you will know that you are standing in the employees' dining area. You must cup your hands for a drink of cold water as the old dipper now dangles from another's wall of memories.

The story of Stead's would be incomplete without revealing the tale of Swill Hill. And you might be asking yourself, what in the dickens is he talking about? In the early days, and for that matter through most of the life of Stead's, the disposal of the accumulation of kitchen detritus, garbage if you please, was always a constant headache as it was for all of the lodge operators. In Stead's case the problem was solved by utilizing a location cut off from the intrusion of man, and by the ownership of a hungry bunch of hogs. As the Big Thompson River meanders through Moraine Park several channels are cut creating high ground here and there, the approaches to which in the summer time are marshy, swamp-like, and unfriendly to the average tourist. Out of one of such dry spots projects a hill topped off with rocks, trees and grass. That is Swill Hill, named for the fact that Stead's hungry hogs made this their home and to them was delivered the kitchen and dining room residue and tasty scraps. It was a satisfactory arrangement, at the time environmentally acceptable, and the hogs porcine proportions prospered. I knew that bears roamed the ranch then as they do now, but certainly in much larger numbers forty years ago, and so I asked Bob Cheney if any hogs were lost to the wild creatures. "Heck no," he exclaimed with a laugh. "Those large hogs could really hold their own. There were fights between the hogs and bears over the food scraps we brought out to the hill, but we never lost a hog for there was plenty of garbage for them all." In fact the hogs, who were not confined to the hill by any fences, were so daring and unafraid in their fit condition that they rummaged through the willows all the way up to Brinwood Lodge in hopes of locating a variation in their diet. Park employees routinely collected garbage from the lodges under government supervision, such as Sprague's after 1932, and it was scuttlebutt that either the progeny of Swill Hill's brood had widely migrated even as far away as Endovalley Campground, or maybe other private lodges or summer cabin owners raised their own porkers. That undocumented rumor hatched a story that certain Park employees had no trouble emptying their trucks as the scattered swine told no tales nor questioned the source of their sustenance.

Over the years, since the excess spring water was not needed for cooling milk cans, it was allowed to flow down into a new lake that Ed constructed south of the large horse barn and which he stocked with Rainbow trout for the pleasure of his guests. The basin of the lake is still visible just east of the road that winds westward towards Fern Lake parking lot. After the ranch was purchased by the National Park, the lake was drained and the remaining trout were netted and given to Andy Anderson who operated Trout Haven in downtown Estes Park. The 1957 ranch advertisement projected the image of Stead's Ranch over the years that it had a lot to offer to a particular species of patrons. "Stead's is a resort hotel of distinction and historical background, yet offering every convenience and service to please today's discriminating guest." About everything was available to the guests since Ed Stopher nearly guaranteed that the recreation bill of fare would be complex, complete and all encompassing to the degree that no guest could possibly fail to find an activity to match his or her requirement for pleasure. Hostesses were employed under the supervision of the Senior Hostess, usually a woman with considerable experience in recreation. Hostesses were hired because of their personality, recreational skills, and ability to make friends with all the guests. To gain a guest's confidence and respect, and keep it was a talent of Senior Hostess Toni Robb, a teacher from Illinois. She was the last professional recreational coordinator at Stead's before its closure and about whom Ed Stopher had these kind words. "We took good care of the people if they wanted to be taken care of, and Toni was a great woman especially in this department. She did everything from picking child counselors, to leading the kids on wienie roasts, to organizing the square dancing and card games to handing out the ribbons at the horse shows at the ranch. She was great!"

I asked a former employee what was a typical day at Stead's. Without hesitation he summarized it all in three words, "It was wild!" And so it was with horseback riders coming and going, the antics around the pool, steak fries, breakfast rides, square dancing, golf, hiking, fishing, tennis, badminton, shuffleboard, star gazing, employee arm wrestling, moonlight serenading, parade floats down Elkhorn Avenue, lectures, Indian dances, conferences, motion pictures and little britches horse shows that alternated each Sunday between Stead's and Elkhorn Lodge where every child won a ribbon. Yes it was wild, and wonderful, with the two hundred guests in residence on an average day finding little if anything to complain about and showing their praise for a job well done by returning year after year. The record for consecutive summers at Stead's was held by three guests. The first was the former chairman of the Caterpillar Company of Peoria, Illinois who logged in 50 straight years culminating his last year with he and his wife celebrating their 50th wedding anniversary. That record must be shared by the Gable sisters from Des Moines, Iowa who also experienced 50 straight seasons at Stead's. To dwarf any other guest' claim to equestrian excellence, the Gable sisters rode their horses **every** day for those fifty years! Though the U. S. Board of Geographical Names might hold a contrary opinion, I really believe that the mountain peak west of the ranch, Gable Top, was named for them, or should be, for who could top that record. The *infamous* Cowboy Dance had been outlawed by Park officials, and for that matter Ed Stopher never participated in it after he took over the ranch. Instead he invented a new device that more elegantly channeled the enthusiasm of his guests into a mirthful fantasy known as the Lord Dunraven Ball. One of the last events of the year, it is so signatured for *His Lordship* of whom I have devoted probably too many pages to his episodic capers. Ed's mother and Alberta Sprague were members of a large Nebraska family consisting of nine girls and four boys. Over the years the extended family had accumulated a large array of 19th and early 20th Century, *fancy clothes* as Ed called them, that had found their way into two large trunks of his Aunty Bert and long stored at Stead's. "So we had a costume party, a band and a dance with prizes for the best costumes," Ed explained, "and it was held in the recreation building during the last part of each August." It was so popular that few guests failed to attend, often picking out a costume from one of the trunks or creating one of their own special concoction of plumes, padding, baggy trousers and whiskers. Outsiders contrived someway to wangle an invitation to this bohemian extravaganza that might have looked out of place. But it was real in its comic relief to those participants who waited for Ed and some contrived *dignitary* to lead the decorous throng to the recreation hall when he piloted a polished Model T Ford that announced their presence with several stentorian blasts of the horn.

As the years went on, the string of nearly 100 horses was sold to Art Card in 1953 who continued to stable them at Stead's. Ed went after the convention business as the enlarged recreation building could seat more than 250 persons. Every year, as an officer of the Colorado Dude Ranch Association, he joined other dude ranch owners in travels to distant large cities such as Saint Louis, New York City and Chicago to put on shows to attract new customers out to their respective enterprises in Colorado. Johnny Holzwarth, the owner of the former Never Summer Ranch near Grand Lake, and Ed Stopher were two of the organizers of that Association. Those promotional campaigns were so successful for Ed, and others I must presume, that by the time he returned from the annual winter trip half of his next summer bookings were filled and the remaining spaces allotted to returning guests from previous seasons. But despite the overabundance of activities available at the ranch, those convention planners demanded for their members access to a *dignified* sport that was devouring huge mouthfuls of cheaper landscape and farms throughout America. Thus all the cattle were sold and the grassy meadow down by the river was reconfigured into a 3,500 yard, nine hole golf course with grass greens that opened in August of 1960. If a ball headed into the river or willows, --forget it. The small round *object was* now the property of large Rainbow and German Brown trout beauties which filled the beaver dammed pools and white foamed eddies to thwart searching probes with an old wooden mashie. Long after the course was returned to it previous meadow condition -- in fact as late as 1990 reported the late Betty Hedlund who devoted so much of her life to the Estes Park Area Museum, people were still finding golf balls hidden in the willows of Moraine Park. Betty told me, "There must have been some wild shots out there!" As we reminisced about Stead's, her *no question about it* positive attitude on history of Estes Park and her observances of human character took on a subdued tone as she smiled in remembrance. "You know, that spring out there at Stead's .... was the most beautiful spring I have ever seen!"

Bill and Fannye Robinson, after Fall River Lodge was sold to the National Park Service and closed in 1959, purchased the string of 120 horses from Art Card and supplemented it by their own herd of 40 horses that for many years had carried the guests of Fall River Lodge up the trails to Lawn Lake and beyond. With material furnished by Stopher, Bill Robinson, who now was fully in charge of the horse concession at Stead's and would remain so until the ranch was sold, erected a huge barn capable of stabling up to 110 head at one time. Bill's expertise was so well established from nearly twenty years at Fall River Lodge, that when he took over the horses at Stead's his talents and his mounts were in constant demand by many in the Estes Valley including guests at the local Y.M.C.A. complex south of Stead's. Bill's arrangement with Ed Stopher, was about the same as was the practice of most liverymen who owned the horses at the lodges. The business of hiring the horses out to the guests was strictly in the control of the liveryman who paid ten percent of his gross receipts to the lodge owner. The liverymen bought his feed, supplies and tack and also purchased his meals and those of his employees from the lodge owner. The grass also was not free, but much effort was expended at Stead's by the wranglers and ranch employees to keep the irrigation ditches open and flowing. Horse management was a tough and demanding business, with overhead, problems, long hours and stress yet mentally and financially rewarding. The liverymen of the Estes Valley, operating under their own association rules of good business ethics and high safety standards, were a valuable resource to the lodge owners as were Pearl Miller, Les Piatt, Art Card and Bill Robinson certainly were to Stead's.

Up to and including its last year of operation, Stead's was always filled, and with a long waiting list. Although the length of stay had dwindled from a month or more to between four days and a week, it remained an important aspect of tourism within the National Park and a haven for large numbers of children who were never more in heaven than when they rode the horse with stirrups on the highest notch. Notwithstanding what lodge naysayers have suggested, "lack of interest by the traveling public in the Park's inholders' lodges" as further justification for the removal of the lodges from the Park, if Ed had built even more cabins they too promptly would have been occupied. It was an immensely popular and successful guest ranch in the finest traditions of the Old West, and everyone, even its detractors, knew it. If all was well at the ranch with business success never in question, why was the ranch sold? Ed reported that in 1958, after his new sewage plant was in operation, the State of Colorado was constantly urging him to put in a larger and even more expensive sanitation system despite the fact it would be in use for only four months of the year. Pressure from the National Park Service's 1932 policy to return the Park to pre-development years, were causing Ed Stopher to reconsider his plans of further expansion and modernization of the utility infrastructure. On August 10, 1962, the lead article in the *Estes Park Trail* announced in bold headlines, **"THEN---, NOW, AND SOON TO BE A MEMORY"**, the sale of Stead's Ranch. The original ranch, that had been put together over nearly 100 years of Sprague's-Stead's-Lewis-Stopher ownership in eight different parcels, still had intact in 1962, in one parcel, approximately 600 acres. Albeit that the ranch during its final season still hosted more than 185 guests daily, "the eventual acquisition seemed inevitable," rationalized Ed Stopher as he remembered the difficulties he had experienced from government authorities that preferred Moraine Park finally rid of the intrusion of man's and woman's development, much of which private property ownership predated the National Park's genesis. He chose his words carefully in 1962, not wanting to offend anyone although he much would have preferred to remain a dude ranch owner. "It seemed wise to conclude the Agreement of sale now rather than to continue with further expansion and improvement," he explained after Superintendent Allyn Hanks purchased the ranch for $750,000. Disposing of the furniture and fixtures, and while Bob Cheney and other loyal employees partially dismantled the buildings, the sod on the nine golf greens was rolled up and trucked to The Old Baldy Club near Saratoga, Wyoming and the big front doors were closed for the last time. In a visit Ed and I had in my home in the summer of 1993, he recapped the reasons that led to his withdrawal from Moraine Park. "It was 1958. I didn't want to sell but the government kept bugging me, and my wife had died and I had two children to look after. A former Superintendent of the Park, who believed in lodges within the Park, had told me that year 'It is going to be rough to continue in business within the Park.' I just couldn't keep up my enthusiasm. I was sad to have to sell. I'm still sad! I was not angry, just sad, for I would miss the hotel business. I loved it! Those were the best days of my life."

Lodging in Rocky Mountain National Park now would only be a cherished memory to all those who had once signed all of the colorful registration books. The newspaper's editor in 1962 printed an editorial that reflected the majority view of the citizens of the community as I imagine of others who had been guests of the ranch as well as other lodges removed from the landscape only a few years before. "The community will be poorer without Stead's, impoverished spiritually if not actually. No man ever lived who could afford to lose a single friend." The National Park Service justified its actions once again by setting forth its goal, now sounding hollow, hackneyed and mentally threadbare to the old timers who had reluctantly stood by since 1932 to witness the absolute and now total destruction of so much of their past happiness that had been associated in great measure with the lodges. "We seek to restore the area to its natural state," the Superintendent read from his prepared text. Many old timers queried scarcastically, but perhaps with a perceived anxiety for their own future existence, if they too would be removed as well, replaced by the Utes and Arapahoes who government officials might rationalize to be more natural to the Park setting. Bob Cheney said recently, "Stead's was my home for many years, and at the time it closed still had more than 125 horses in use. I didn't want to see the buildings go down in 1963.

Some of the cabins were removed to several locations around town including The Annex that stands over by the church north of town. The recreation building is now the main building at the Highlander Cottages on the road to the Y.M.C.A. Other than those buildings, everything else was destroyed. The main lodge and the Rock House were dozed down and burnt. I did not want to see them destroy anything out there so I stayed away." There still remains a living memory of Stead's presence in the form of the old dapple grey horse named Cowboy. He is the last survivor of years of dedicated service to Stead's guests and at the age of 43 years lives with Bill and Fannye Robinson, content with a bag of oats, a rub behind the ears and remembered affection of so many who appreciated his stout heart and gentleness. Somewhat naive to the consequences but cognizant of a resurgent demand by tourists for a closer identification with the Park, Moraine Park Campground as it was named was sculpted out of the terminal moraine north and west of Stead's. The site, previously unsullied by harsh human intrusion, is now capable of processing many hundreds of camping vehicles, some as large as small versions of freight cars. That action engendered the wrath, justified or not, of local residents who deemed the impact upon an area previously untouched "a poor trade off for old Stead's Ranch."

After Stead's was sold to the National Park Service, Ed did continue to be a vital participant in the hotel business, leaving the Estes Valley to occupy important positions with Del Webb's organization, the Sheraton Hotel Corporation, as well as managing the Red Stone Lodge in Red Stone, Colorado. He brought back to life the nearly moribund resort in French Lick, Indiana and for two years returned as the general manager of The Stanley Hotel. He now divides his time between his two places of residence, Steamboat Springs, Colorado and Tucson, Oracle Valley, Arizona. I asked him how import were the lodges and dude ranches to the Park. "The value of Stead's as far as I am concerned was that people coming out now don't know the Park like I think they should. They come in and stay a couple of days and are on their way. The guests who stayed with us stayed right in the Park, and we took care of them! Our guests were our friends, for over the winter Dorothy and I traveled the country visiting our summer guests. Through the ownership of a lodge we acquired an extended family. When the lodges were gone, something was taken away, an awareness of the National Park and an identification with the past. People now who visit the Park don't understand as much about it as when they lived intimately within the Park as a member of our Sprague's and Stead's, - -and Stopher's large family. Our guests **lived** the Park, now visitors just pass through. We took them fishing, hiked with them, and we really got them out into the woods and they so enjoyed it!"

I am not certain if Abner would have approved of all of the changes. As the conservationist Sigurd Olson once said, "Man lives in a jet age, the industrial age, the space age, an age of automation, growing technology, urbanization. The result was a hunger in people to escape for a little while and return to the natural, primitive scene where they could feast their souls on scenery and to catch this elusive something called primitive." Yes, the mountains remain, graced by trees, waterfalls and herds of awe inspiring wild creatures. But Stead's Ranch has long gone the way of the bull dozer and wrecking ball to be replaced artificially in function by parking places for recreational vehicles, a trade off dictated by the crush of millions of vacationers, perhaps seeking a primitive scene but who would not fit into log cabins absent of flush commodes and television sets filled with adventure stories from the Good Ship Enterprise. Today, you have to possess a lucid imaginativeness of the mind coupled with a pull on the old emotions in order to glimpse a mental picture of those free spirited days when Stead's and all of its predecessors were king, vital to an early Estes Park economy as well as a significant resource for visitors' comprehension of the ecology and ethos of this National Park. May you be at home with your recollections as you reconstruct in your mind's-eye those great times that made for bright and enduring experiences for both former guests as well as those *devil may care, first time away from home, we are having a ball* constituency of dude ranch crews who *made our day*, or the whole summer, the greatest of the greatest. I wouldn't mind having another slice of Smothered Toothbuster Pie just for old times sake. How about you?

Sprague Homestead Cabin, 1875, Photo Of 1916 (Jane Blair)

Sprague's Hotel, circa 1880s (EPHM)

Guests At Sprague's Hotel, 1892 (EPPL)

Interior Of Sprague's Hotel, 1890s (EPPL)

Abner & Alberta Sprague, Late 1890s (EPPL)

Stead's Ranch, 1910 (F. P. Clatworthy)

First Auto At Stead's, Enos & Joe Mills In Back Seat, circa 1908 (Mills)

Stead's Touring Sedan, James Stead On Right, circa 1915 (RMNP)

The Guest Lounge At Stead's Ranch, 1910 (RMNP

Horseback Riding At Stead's Before Twin Sisters Mt., 1916 (Jane Blair)

Julia Prouty, On Left, At Her Store, circa 1917 (Jane Blair)

Front Desk In Stead's Main Lodge, 1911 (RMNP)

Dining Room At Stead's, 1910 (EPPL)

Waitresses At Stead's, 1919 (Jane Blair)

Mrs. Stead, Top, With Part Of Her Crew, circa 1919 (Jane Blair)

Laundry Staff, Margaret Heubner Second On Left, 1917 (Jane Heubner Blair)

Chapman Ranch In Moraine Park, 1880 (RMNP)

Libby Chapman At Her Post Office, circa 1905 (RMNP)

Chapman's Cabins In Moraine Park, circa 1880s (RMNP)

The Spring House At Stead's, 1910 (EPPL)

Rock House At Stead's, circa 1920s (RMNP)

Eaton & Patterson Homes, On Road Leading To Moraine Park, circa 1920s (RMNP)

Will and Myra Lewis, 1930 (EPPL)

Dining Room At Stead's, 1930 (EPHM)

Sprague's First Cabin Near Glacier Creek, 1908 (RMNP)

Interior Of Sprague's Cabin, 1908 (RMNP)

Expanded Cabin And Visitors, circa 1912 (RMNP)

Sprague's Lodge, 1923 (RMNP)

Stopher Cottage, 1924 (RMNP)

Middle & Perry Guest Cabins, 1924 (RMNP)

Interior Of Enclosed Porch, Sprague's Lodge, circa 1920s (RMNP)

Visitors At Loch Vale, circa 1930s (EPHM)

Sprague's Lodge In Winter Of 1940 (RMNP)

Upper Sprague's Lake, circa 1940s (Clatworthy, Colorvues)

A Final Ride At Sprague's Before Closing, circa 1950s (Willa Jean Graves)

Stead's Entrance Sign In Moraine Park, 1950-1962 (RMNP)

Ed And Dorothy Stopher, circa 1950s (Private)

Abner Sprague's Historic Hotel As It Appeared In 1960 (RMNP)

The Art Cards, The Bill Robinsons, Chef Art Persons, 1954 (Robinson)

Those Steaks At A Cookout Were Wonderful, 1960 (Robinson)

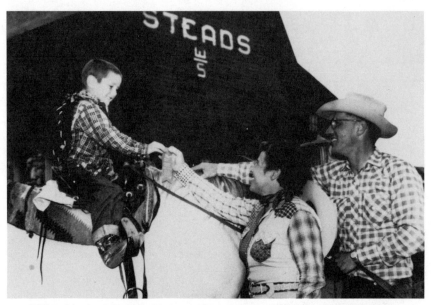

Bill Robinson & Toni Robb Award Young Ross A Ribbon, 1961 (Robinson)

The Wranglers In 1959 (Robinson)

Fannye Robinson Leads Off From Stead's To Mill Creek, 1960 (Robinson)

Swimming Pool Next To Homestead Room, circa 1950s (Robinson)

Standard Guest Cabins, 1961 (RMNP)

Luxury Guest Cabins, 1961 (RMNP)

Lobby & Guest Lounge At Stead's, circa 1950s (Private)

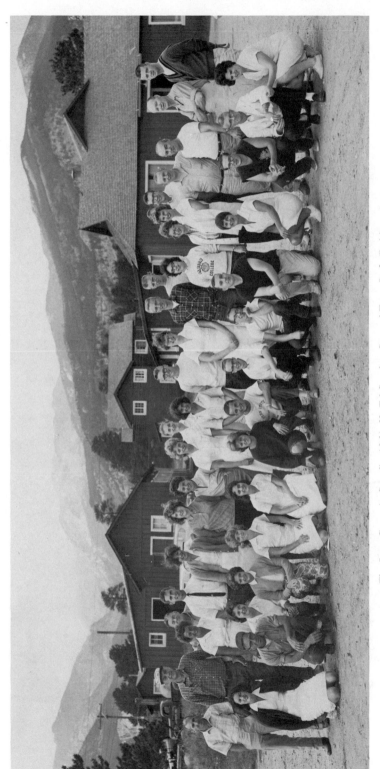

The Last Crew At Stead's, 1961-62. Ed Stopher Second From Left (Robinson)

Cowboy, Age 43, Remembers Stead's Glorious Past, 1993 (Private)

Stead's Ranch Before Its Demolition In 1963 (Flatiron Post Card Co.)

A Final Farewell To Long's & Meeker With A Promise To Return, circa 1920-30 (Private)

A FINAL THOUGHT

The lodges were built, like the *Field of Dreams*, and the people came. The fields alone remain but not the hostelries that **were** this National Park to the untold thousands who could never separate their particular lodge from the image of a National Park. To most they were one and the same, just one large package of pleasure. To separate a mountain lodge from the concept of a National Park is comparable to removing James Hilton's Shangri-la from its place in his novel *Lost Horizon,* or as inconceivable as asserting that sunlight has no place in a rainbow. Lodge and Park just went together as did joy and laughter, for from both a visitor derived inspiration, solitude, knowledge, friendship, exercise, fun and refreshment from stressful daily routines temporarily sent packing on sabbatical. It mattered not whether the provider of vacation happiness wore an official badge and green uniform or but a flannel shirt with a lodge logo stitched onto a pocket. Could possibly the National Park Service's Mission 66 program, vaunted with great promise to bring about better access to National Parks and enlarged opportunities for citizens to enjoy them, have gone awry with an unintended reversal of Park policy? With the resultant construction of miles of roads and thousands of parking pads in previously undisturbed glens and groves for oversized recreational vehicles, have nature's pristine qualities been compromised and diminished by such planned reactions to intensified public and political pressures? There are thousands now hunkered down, not in a second home provided by lodge hosts and hostesses with rules of the house expected to be followed, but in an extension of their cluttered urban existence complete with television sets that tune out the beauty of silence in an environment that once inspired poets, painters and castle-builders to contemplative creation and achievement.

Only time will tell if modern planners' objectives were myopic. But if we could miraculously, serendipitously, rebuild all of the lodges within this and other National Parks and sod over the scars left by excessive use of the land that was mandated to be conserved and protected, --would we? If so, what then? Would men and women still consider drafty old lodges, with paper thin walls, bathrooms down the hall and rooms heated by wood stoves, worthy as a destination in which to spend their hard earned dollars, jilting more glamourous digs equipped with all the contrivances of a well stocked catalogue of wishes? Or have we over these past thirty years since the last lodge vanished from the proscenium of this mountain amphitheater grown into a new set of values that no longer mesh modern gears with older drive systems that gained pleasure from an evening gathered in front of a blazing fireplace in denim clad togs listening to a guitar strumming cowboy wailing a lonesome version of *Home On The Range*? Did you ever sit on the comfortable swing out behind the dining room waiting with gustatory anticipation your freshly caught trout being prepared by the lodge chef? How about that flush of exhilaration, the sense of confidence one experienced after a brisk horseback ride across the moraine knowing that you had finally conquered the contrariness of that saddle. And wasn't it ego building to bring in a whole creel of big fish knowing that your fellow guests would reward your prowess with praise. Is modern America so satiated with all the gadgetry invented to make lives more simple, yet complicated them more than we care to admit, that it cannot find joy without speed, noise, violent sports and *Quick Pick* lotto cards? Is it incapable of achieving mental and physical refreshment from the demands and dangers of a crazy mixed up globe of horror and bizarre codes of selfish ethics to assume the relaxed posture of silence as did those who once resided at a mountain lodge with no radio, no T. V., no telephone and no pressure from whatever lay out beyond the shadow of the mountain?

Have some purists among us become so infallible by practicing sophistry even upon themselves to believe that the history of human involvement in this National Park should not be included in the prologue to the preservation of this magnificence that today only costs the small price of a one day admission fee? Should the prescriptions of pioneering people of the Estes Valley, to inoculate unconcerned elected officials with a germ of infectious pride for a small segment of the Rocky Mountains, deserve the rubbish bin of neglected honesty? Did those pioneering lodge owners play a part in posterity or were their dreams only for fools? Abner Sprague was asked whether, after more than eighty-seven years, he had anything more of which to dream. "*When one becomes too old to dream*, is all right as a title for a song, but the implication that one can become too old to dream is all wrong! What of dreams of castles in the air, dreams beyond the hope of ever coming true? Even if some of those dreams have proved to be disappointing, and failed to come true, we dream of the days when we dreamed those dreams. No, not to dream is not to think, not to think is death. When that time comes it will be too late to dream, --but not until then."

Is there still time to go back to a slower cadence, even without the lodges, perhaps only existing in the recesses of distant memories, or would we want to if we could? The lodges were a guest's private paradise, a slow moving vehicle on which they could buy a ticket for an opportunity to intimately share in a special parcel of God's own wilderness that deserved appreciation on its own terms. Lodges were sanctuaries, recreational sanitariums in a good climate and a landscape of unparalleled reassuring beauty from which jaded lives departed more refreshed and happier in mind, body and soul and as permanent friends and protectors of *their* National Park. Yes, they were pampered with great horses, square dancing, good grub and wagon loads of new friendships that would last a lifetime. Can a numbered campground bereft of pioneer personification reach that same degree of loyalty and pride? Perhaps it can, if the patron understands his or her place in the National Park. At a lodge, immediately outside the door, was a rock of a not too unusual shape, size or composition. But it was **your** rock when you shared space with it. You sat on it, carefully examined the moss and lichen growing on its sides, and that giant, three hundred year old reddish brown Ponderosa pine tree outside your cabin window, nothing different than the hundred others within your view. But it was **yours** to touch, smell, protect and stand in the coolness of its shade, and you would defend it with your life. What about the flowers growing close by in a patch of sunlight, of blues, reds and unclassified yellows? They were everywhere, but these were special to you because **you** could enjoy them every day, and *fee fie foo* on anyone who tramped upon them or much worse plucked them to deny you and others their beauty of fragrance and pigment. What I'm struggling to convey is that the lodges and their owners served many purposes not the least of which was to identify their guests individually, personally, emotionally with their surroundings and to educate them to appreciate wherein they were fortunate to be, -- in a National Park. Their unwritten creed was *love it, live it or leave it*. Ed Stopher said, remember, "Our guests lived the Park, and we really got them out into the woods." Nowadays, Park visitors have to work very hard to live, love and understand the Park without abusing it intentionally or otherwise. There is less federal money available for programed interpretive opportunities by a decreasing number of overworked Park staff so we all must strive very hard to learn as much about it as possible on our own, from well authored books, stimulating lectures, asking questions and perceiving history in its totality absent of our own personal bias. Those lodge owners, and their own gang of ninety day wonders temporarily on recess from their school books, served this purpose when the National Park staff was depleted by war service and budget constraints.

I know the feeling voiced back in 1964 after the last lodge was finally gone when a former National Park official said, "No more adulteration by man! My God! --now this Park is something special!" I agree with that opinion to the extent of the speciality of Rocky Mountain National Park, and, yes, it would be difficult to improve upon it. Yet I still yearn for that sign pointing the way to an old log lodge, and though they have been reduced to sawdust and ash they did provide an atmosphere where dreams came true. There are those who yearn to touch once more the stone fireplace laid up by nearly forgotten stonemasons. It exuded a warmth of individual personality, fueled in great measure by burdens well borne by strong and determined hotel men and women who loved a National Park so much that they themselves were eventually consumed in a firestorm of aggressive National Park Service policy that considered them unnecessary impendimenta to their own dreams for absolute naturalness. I will not forget those men and women, for to do so is as difficult to imagine that there never was a sunrise on Long's Peak or a sunset behind Hallett's sharp pinnacle. Certainly the lodges were once here, and even more importantly they **were** an essential ingredient to the mix for the potter's wheel, without which the moist clay of public support to create and protect an everlasting object of beauty, this National Park, might have hardened into a shapeless lump of apathy. Many men and women needed a decent place to sleep, dream and to compose their thoughts about why this mountainous land should be given a protective status. The early lodge filled this need and was the kettle in which the public juices of opinion were distilled into a heady brew of resolution sufficient to stimulate the nation's leaders to create and financially support Rocky Mountain National Park. Those lodges provided humans with an opportunity to experience a closeness with wilderness yet in a more comfortable venue. One early day visitor of 1875 made this assessment of Moraine Park, then called Willow Park, when she stopped off at Sprague's Hotel. "In Willow Park, after galloping over on our horses from MacGregors, we were invited into a spring house for a drink of milk, and of water from a fine spring that was harnessed to do the churning by means of wheel and shaft. On one side stood a freezer of ice cream, most tempting to warm and tired scenic enthusiasts. There was a scrupulous neatness in every pan and board, and from this friendliness we became aware of all that surrounded us."

The catalyst for creation of the Rocky Mountain National Park came not from Washington D. C. nor from those of short sighted vision once called "nattering nabobs of negativism." The impetus came from lodge people, such as Mills, Stanley, MacPherson, Reed, Workman and Sprague and others, those who already loved this area and were willing to welcome others to share their blessed retreat they considered the very best of God's creations and accomplishments. To acknowledge the small lodge owner's existence, their pioneer vitality and historical importance, does in no way denigrate the honor and admiration we extend to Rocky Mountain National Park as a special shrine to naturalness. The words *Lodge* and *Park* must be associated together as partners as the memory of the former and the present awareness of the latter march on together towards the Twenty-First Century. The two are like the mask of Janus, the one side --lodges -- now faces the glorious past as a provider of resting places for those whom the government at that time had no comparable facilities and bequeathed a legacy of hospitality to strangers seeking comfort associated with nature. The other face, Rocky Mountain National Park, remembered by its struggle to be born and greater challenge to gain public acceptance of its maturing purpose as a precious gem in the diadem of the National Park Service, looks to the future. It strives for citizens' identification with, and understanding of, nature on its own terms. While we are mindful of the valued contributions of the lodge owners and the dedicated services they rendered, the Park has succeeded beyond all expectations to simultaneously produce an appreciation for, and education about, this unique investment in which we all own equal shares. Our dividend is pure enjoyment of an asset that can only be devalued by our own lack of interest. I stand in awe of both of these partners.

I will look forward to meeting all of those pioneers now in the great beyond, explorers, wagon masters, trail builders, government servants, and all the private citizens who were the joint exponents of all that was good and wholesome and decent that shaped and massaged this once harsh and inhospitable land of snow and wind into our Estes Valley and our National Park of which we are very proud. We therefore should, every day, rededicate ourselves to love, live, but never leave these mountains where our dreams and those of the millions of new visitors each year can come true. These Snowy Mountains, skirted in rushing rivers and green valleys, offer great promise to all who truly care about the present and the future without being neglectful of the true significance of a glorious past. The final curtain has descended on Those Castles Of Wood, and we applaud not only the play but the performance of all of the actors and actresses who scripted and produced an entertaining and unforgettable 100 years of pure pleasure. My parents first bled into my veins a love for animals, trees, mountains, streams, --and pioneer people whose grasp upon my soul have attracted me like a strange magnetism to an affinity for subjects that perhaps are relegated to past generations that may become lost in time with the onslaught of computer generated scientific fascination. I will end this story with a poem, that could be a summary of the sentiments of all those who occupied a cabin or a room of a bygone lodge. It was composed by my late father, Henry F. Pedersen, Sr., who though not a fisherman, mountain climber nor avid horseback rider, found time from his busy law practice in Omaha to grasp an appreciation from these mountains that to him were a special tonic for restored vigor.

These were his impressions set forth in poetic verse. I wish to share them with you.

THE SNOWY RANGE

Up on top of the Rockies in the lofty Snowy Range,
Where sky and mountains seem to touch,
And the atmosphere's wild and strange.
Where the snow dappled peak and valley,
Merge in a symphony,
Of the beauty of boundless nature,
And the human soul seems free.
Where hearts beat a little faster,
And troubles seem far away,
Where worries roll off like water,
And you're happy the livelong day.

Up on top of the mountains,
In the National Park reserve,
Where there's silver lakes and sparkling streams,
And there's Pines and the Alpine Fir.
Where moon and stars in Heaven,
Seem close enough to touch,
And you realize you are lucky,
To be privileged so much.
To be in this primeval grandeur,
Unspoiled by this modern day,
Midst the handiwork of the Master,
In His own mysterious way.

So give me a home in the Rockies,
Up high in the Snowy Range,
Where the peaks are tipped with silver,
And the atmosphere's wild and strange.
Where friendship made is lasting,
Hospitality real and true,
Where when they say -'glad to meet you,'
They mean it through and through.
So if travels should take you,
Near mountains and the sage,
Do yourself and your family a favor,
Spend some time in the Snowy Range.

THE END

ABOUT THE AUTHOR

Henry F. Pedersen, Jr. has written numerous stories on various subjects. After a career as a lawyer and legislator in the State of Nebraska, he brought his family consisting of two children, Scott and Lisa, and his best friend -- his beloved wife Sara --west to Estes Park, Colorado in 1973. He has a great love for the out-of-doors, and living adjacent to Rocky Mountain National Park has been just the place to observe and write about history, and the individuals of the mountains who are his neighbors. He has published several books about the Estes Valley, one entitled *ROUGH IT WITH EASE, The Story of the McGraw Ranch*, in which he describes with fact and emotion the birth and demise of an historic guest ranch in the Estes Valley. The second book, entitled *JOY, The Life Of Charles Eagle Plume*, recounts the life and philosophy of his late friend who operated an historic trading post and who became a legend to thousands of residents, customers and school children throughout the United States. This current book about the lodges of the Estes Valley continues in this series of historic vignettes about those people, places and events that had much to do with creating, shaping and caring for this special place of beauty, this Estes Park and of its neighbor, Rocky Mountain National Park.

* * * * * * * * * *